D0866195

Innovation in Mass Education

CONTRIBUTORS

ROBERTA ASH, *Assistant Professor, Department of Sociology, Barnard College*

CHRISTOPHER T. HUSBANDS, *Graduate Student, Department of Sociology, University of Chicago*

MORRIS JANOWITZ, *Professor, Department of Sociology, University of Chicago*

TIMOTHY LEGGATT, *Lecturer, School of Social Studies, University of Sussex, England*

MARTIN MAYER, *Free-lance writer living in New York City*

RAPHAEL O. NYSTRAND, *Assistant Professor, College of Education, Ohio State University*

ROBERT J. PARELIUS, *Assistant Professor, Department of Sociology, Douglass College of Rutgers University*

MARY A. QUEELEY, *Research Associate, Research Division, Bank Street College of Education*

BRYAN R. ROBERTS, *Lecturer, Department of Social Anthropology and Sociology, University of Manchester*

ROSEMARY C. SARRI, *Professor, School of Social Work, University of Michigan*

THOMAS S. SMITH, *Assistant Professor, Department of Sociology, University of Michigan*

ROBERT D. VINTER, *Associate Dean, School of Social Work, University of Michigan*

Innovation in
Mass Education

EDITED BY
David Street

WILEY-INTERSCIENCE

JOHN WILEY & SONS   NEW YORK · LONDON · SYDNEY · TORONTO

Library of Congress Catalog Card Number: 69-19100
SBN 471 83325 8

Printed in the United States of America

Acknowledgments

Except when otherwise indicated, the researches reported in this book were supported by the Russell Sage Foundation, directly through a grant for the study of the organization of large-city school systems and indirectly by its aid to the Center for Social Organization Studies of the University of Chicago. I am deeply indebted both to this foundation and to Morris Janowitz, who has continually provided extremely stimulating collaboration in the effort to understand the schools.

I am also grateful to the U.S. Public Health Service for the aid it provided through a training grant, 5 Ti MH 8933-03, awarded to the Department of Sociology, University of Chicago; to various staff members of the Chicago public schools, especially Jerome H. Gilbert (now of the Berkeley, California, schools) and Curtis C. Melnick, for their cooperation with some of the original research; and to Judith Kidd for her editorial assistance. Finally, I appreciate the several benefits that have come from my relationships with the volume's contributors, many of them once my students, but all fine colleagues now.

DAVID STREET

Contents

Innovation in Mass Education

Educational Change in the Mass Society

David Street

The term "mass society" has two somewhat contrary denotations: the first, of massive size and scale and of the atomization and standardization of persons and of constituent units;[1] the second, of the full incorporation into a society of those of its members who have been living at its bottom reaches or periphery.[2] Yet the problem of change in education in American society shows both of these features in sharp contour. On the one hand, change is sought in a public educational system which is gigantic and is broken into literally thousands of units, but which despite extreme fragmentation shows a substantial uniformity. On the other hand, the changes pursued reflect a great social urge to bring in the people at the bottom or on the edges of society—the poor, especially the Negroes, who, along with Appalachian whites, Puerto Ricans, and others, have largely existed at the margins of the educational and social systems.

The effort toward incorporation does not primarily reflect a new altruism, although changes in the social conscience are relevant. The American public school system has always been unique in its stress on incorporation, expressed historically through the victory of the common school over the Latin Grammar School and later in the partial incorporation of Dewey's ideas about education and democracy and in the development of the comprehensive high school to serve all academic styles and social classes. The basic transformation is in consciousness. Among many changes, three developments since midcentury can be listed as crucial in producing a heightened awareness of the educational system as a basic integrative element of the society. First, changes in the technology and values of the society have put a new premium on educational

---

[1] William Kornhauser, *The Politics of Mass Society* (New York: Free Press, 1959).

[2] Edward Shils, "Mass Society and Its Culture," in Norman Jacobs, ed., *Culture for the Millions?* (Princeton, N.J.: Van Nostrand, 1959).

1

attainment as the criterion for entry into the labor force and for assessing
social worth, so that in the last decade the schoolmen have come to
recognize that there is no place into which the bottom educational groupings can be sorted. Second, the concentration of Negroes in the cities
and the rise of racial protest and Negro expectations and demands have
thrown the schools into crisis and have led to a popular recognition
of the inadequacies of urban schooling. Third, the national reaction
to Sputnik has produced a new concern with quality and curriculum
in higher education, leading in turn to a new interest in innovation
in secondary and elementary education.

These changes partially merge with and are partially discordant with
the major continuing thrusts of American education: great growth in
size and moderate movement toward centralization. Education shows
the obvious trends to more and more, to steady decreases (toward some
limit) in the numbers of functional illiterates and high school dropouts,
and to the dramatic expansion of higher education. To a substantial
degree, this growth proceeds in the way it generally has historically:
essentially through a replication of old units (colleges, universities, and
schools) in new or modernized facilities. Thereby continues the paradox
that American elementary and secondary education, so decentralized
when compared with European systems, continues in practice to show
little variance beyond that which the socioeconomic characteristics of
affluent communities can be expected to impose on their school facilities,
teacher salaries, and the like. The common acceptance of the high school
"units" required for college entrance and thus as the curriculum elements
of programs at lower levels, the rise of accreditation associations for
public schools and for institutions that train teachers, and the growth
of a national textbook and curriculum-materials industry have helped
to standardize the system. Furthermore, although American education
is much more differentiated at the higher levels, expansion here (especially among junior and community colleges) is also largely taking the
form of extending the standardized academic curriculum to larger
numbers.

It is in the difficulties of extending the American public educational
format to all groups, expressed often in a concern that some persons
do not "fit" or lack "proper motivation or skills" and seen in the failure
of the various programs for the "deprived" to show immediate positive
results, that a new crisis in education can be seen. And behind it is
a crisis in incorporation. The movement toward greater centralization
of the educational system partakes heavily of a recognition of these
crises. Inadequacies in financing education in many localities have led
to a heightened dependence on state and, increasingly, federal levels.

Moreover, among several sources of a "nationalizing tendency" in education,[3] recognition at the federal level of weaknesses of the present schools in educating lower-class and minority groups has played a major role, especially in creating special programs, facilities, and curriculum materials for these groups.

Herein lie the critical contemporary problems of education in a mass society. It is clear in the first instance that there is a series of standard but important educational questions which still have no clear answer. For example, what educational programs can best "reach" the groups peripheral to the system? What curriculum materials are appropriate, and how shall better teachers and educational leaders be trained? It is also clear that a series of broader, more macrosociological problems are at least as important. We must ask, for example, what changes in the organizational format of the schools are necessary to make educational improvements more likely. We need to ask whether specialized programs of compensatory education tend to heighten the separateness rather than the incorporation of those they aim to help. And we must raise the question of whether or not criteria broader than academic performance need to be used to evaluate the impact of the school on the peripheral groups. Racial integration has been used as one such indicator, but with segregation progressing so fast in the cities this measure becomes, for the time being at least, increasingly irrelevant. In the mass society opportunity to have self-respect must be offered to all. Yet in its ordinary workings the school does much to teach the student to generalize his academic failures. Given the difficulties in finding educational innovations that easily raise achievement levels, new educational programs oriented wholly to producing immediate gains on standardized tests may only depress levels of self-respect, and thus incorporation, even further.

THE STUDY OF EDUCATIONAL INNOVATION

The chapters of this book collectively begin to answer such broad questions about mass education as those just raised, and they begin to demonstrate some of the potential gains that can come from educational innovation when it is conceived of in a macrosociological manner. In so doing, papers presented here also imply quite a bit about the characteristic weaknesses of most studies of educational change made available to date, weaknesses that have helped to engender a new sense

[3] Roald F. Campbell and Robert A. Bunnell, eds., *Nationalizing Influences on Secondary Education* (Chicago: Midwest Administration Center, University of Chicago, 1963).

of despair about effective educational change for the unincorporated segments of the population.

One critical source of the general weakness of research on educational change can be found in the fact that in recent years such studies have continued to come forward largely as research on "educational innovation," a field that for decades percolated along principally as a study of the slowness of educational change and of the tendency to adopt small-scale curriculum and administrative innovations in the more affluent and education-valuing suburbs (the "adaptability tradition" of the students of Paul Mort).[4] The study of educational innovation flowered after 1950 under the impact of the sudden great upsurge of concern with innovations for national defense and for the "culturally deprived" in the great cities.[5] Although some researchers have introduced interesting leadership recruitment and institutional elements into the analysis of innovation (such as Richard O. Carlson's finding that school systems are more likely to adopt modern mathematics if their superintendents have high prestige and social visibility in the profession[6] and Ronald Lippitt's data on the resistances teachers have to communicating their innovations to their colleagues[7]), this tradition has been unable to add much in the way of theoretical elaboration of the standard "diffusion of innovation" models used in studying innovations in several fields.[8] Another result has been the underdevelopment of theoretical and research models relevant to the field experiment situation that has been offered by the great numbers of inner-city innovations of the 1950's and 1960's. In the cities, innovation has been seen not just as a prestige-producing activity for the superintendent and the system but also as a crucial effort to save the disadvantaged from educational failure and possible life-long dependency.

It is probable that this underdevelopment of ideas about educational change has helped to induce the pessimistic reaction toward innovation

[4] Paul R. Mort, "Studies in Educational Innovation from the Institute of Administrative Research: An Overview," in Matthew B. Miles, ed., *Innovation in Education* (New York: Bureau of Publications, Teachers College, Columbia University, 1964), pp. 317–328.

[5] See the collection by Miles, *ibid.*, passim, and also that edited by A. Harry Passow, *Education in Depressed Areas* (New York: Teachers College Press, Columbia University, 1963).

[6] Richard O. Carlson, "School Superintendents and Adoption of Modern Math: A Social Structure Profile," in Miles, *op. cit.*, pp. 329–341.

[7] Ronald Lippitt, "The Youth Culture, the School System, and the Socialization Community," in Albert J. Reiss, Jr., ed., *Schools in a Changing Society* (New York: Free Press, 1965), pp. 99–120.

[8] Everett M. Rogers, *Diffusion of Innovations* (New York: Free Press, 1962).

that is setting in now within the urban schools. Great numbers of innovations have been tried, but most have been only piecemeal and many have been unstudied. Moreover, of those that have received study, project after project has been shown to produce only minimal or transitory academic benefits[9] or positive outcomes that could not be sustained when the experiment was diffused to additional schools.[10] What was a social movement of urban educational innovation may now be hardening into a cult of pessimism as negative results and apparently irreversible racial changes in the city schools are seen as consistent with the *Equality of Educational Opportunity* findings[11] which imply that what the school does is of minor importance compared to its socioeconomic and racial characteristics. That the conclusions of the report by Coleman et al. derive from a summing up of a large sample of ordinary public schools (thus showing little variance in what the school does compared to what it could do under experimental conditions), and that the report may statistically reify the notion that socioeconomic status variables are supreme,[12] are facts which are largely ignored.

It is not to be denied that the study of educational innovation as diffusion has produced some important findings and ideas. To the extent that this field has focused on diffusion and contagion processes, however, it has simultaneously avoided an analysis of larger social processes and structures. The dominant mode of analysis leads to a focus on the individual adopter or on sets of adopters. This process makes sense in view of the decentralized nature of the public school system, but it loses validity in the light of the centralizing tendencies in the system, the knowledge we have of the interpenetration of the schools and other community units, and, especially, the fact that the true problematic issue for top school system management is not the question of whether

---

[9] For a summary of the negative results of various experiments in compensatory education in New York City, St. Louis, Philadelphia, and elsewhere, see the report of the U.S. Commission on Civil Rights, *Racial Isolation in the Public Schools* (Washington: The Commission, 1967), Vol. I, pp. 120–140. On the recent major project in New York City, see David J. Fox, *Expansion of the More Effective School Program: Evaluation of New York City Title I Educational Projects, 1966–67* (New York: Center for Urban Education, 1967).

[10] This is what happened with New York's Higher Horizons Program; see the U.S. Commission on Civil Rights, *op. cit.*, pp. 122–126. Regarding resistances to innovation in large-city schools, see David Street, "Public Education and Social Welfare in the Metropolis," in Mayer N. Zald, ed., *Organizing for Community Welfare* (Chicago: Quadrangle Books, 1967), pp. 62–105.

[11] James S. Coleman et al., *Equality of Educational Opportunity*, Washington: Office of Education, 1966).

[12] See Henry M. Levin, "What Difference Do Schools Make?" *Saturday Review*, January 20, 1968, pp. 57–58, 66–67.

or not to adopt but of how to implement. Furthermore, the tradition has tended to encourage a gratuitous selection of the dependent variables of innovation, taken operationally to be either any acquisition of new curriculum elements, facilities, or personnel types that can be measured over time, or—as in most big-city studies—narrowly restricted to quantitatively measured academic achievement. In studies of educational experiments, this indiscriminacy in selecting the dependent variables has often been coupled with a total inattention to measuring independent experimental variables other than "exposure to the program." With the question unanswered of whether or not any real change in staff behavior is induced by the existence of "the program," the no-difference results of many evaluative studies tell us very little.

Thus the study of educational change has had too narrow and microsociological a focus. With a broader theoretical perspective, it could have looked more comprehensively at organizational and social structures and processes and at a larger range of variables bearing on the macrosociological issues of mass education. To stress the need for development of a macrosociological view of educational change is not to deny the need for study of individual change or for further work on the microsociology of educational systems. Yet many of the key foci of attention, not only in the innovation studies but in the sociology of education in general, might have benefited greatly if they had been more often linked to outside social structures or if teacher decisions to adopt an innovation had been more frequently related to the changing nature of the profession.

THE MACROSOCIOLOGY OF EDUCATIONAL CHANGE: RESEARCH ISSUES

Proceeding programmatically, I shall identify five key areas of the macrosociology of educational change in need of substantial probing.

1. Revision in Organizational Format

Despite all the educational innovation, there has been little change of organizational format in the public schools. The crucial question is whether or not the organization's capacities to handle the problems of mass education can be substantially improved. The problems are present in school systems large and small, but are most apparent in the inner-city schools. These systems are tied to inflexibility (and, in New York City, to bureaucratic indolence), not only by virtue of their weak resources (this is not the case in New York City) but also by a number of built-in structural constraints. These include (a) a heavily institutionalized set of universalistic standards, the inheritance of an earlier age of fighting off corruption and political influence; (*b*) a great in-grownness in the selection of administrative staff; (*c*) a weakness of organizational procedures of socialization and control—seen, for example, in the token quality of most in-service training; (*d*) the overcentralization of curriculum construction and managerial decision making; (*e*) rigidities in the division of labor, which mitigate against the full use of subprofessionals, paid and volunteer, to solve the great problem of insufficient financial and human resources to staff the schools; (*f*) a defensive stance toward outsiders, which minimizes the opportunities for fruitful collaboration with external agencies and preserves marked social distance between the schools and lower-class parents; (*g*) rigid practices of grouping and dividing students into grade levels, which formally assume that all children learn at the same rate; and (*h*) internal structural inertia and external cross pressures, which make effective, entrepeneurial top leadership difficult.

Inquiry needs to be directed at the conditions and consequences of attempts to alter any and all of these dimensions and at the question of what combination of changes would be necessary to cross a "threshold" barrier. In all studies of innovation in organizational format it is useful to consider the changes undertaken in light of the distinction between specialists and generalists. Innovative efforts differ in the extent to which they are dependent upon easing the role of the practitioner by reducing it, through relieving him of specialized tasks, as against seeking to enhance his general capacities. If there is any master trend in the relatively ephemeral attempts at general organizational reform which have been popular in recent years, it is toward reduction of the role through specialization—a trend slowed mainly by the militant financial demands of the teachers' unions, which make it difficult to find resources for anyone but standard classroom teachers. Under this trend, however, the teachers are likely to find their role to be more residual than specialized, a development hypothetically inimical to their authority and their sense of autonomy and competence.

Of special significance for studying attempts to change organizational format are experiments in radical decentralization, which are going to emerge through the creation of educational parks and "experimental school districts" in the inner city. Previous attempts at decentralization in the large-city systems have been essentially token, providing district superintendents with little discretion about "administrative decisions" that underlie almost all educational decisions and with little in the way of resources or staff aid. Presumably, experimental districts will be given some substantial freedom of action; and unless they then become embroiled in local political controversy or pressures that lead to a stalemate between laymen and educators, the experimental districts may provide a critical opportunity to find out what can be done, with relief from many of the constraints of the larger system, to develop a more flexible style of organization. Political constraints should be less threatening to educational parks, which presumably will have a quite diffused constituency. Given freedom, it may be enlightening to see whether more specialized or generalized formats emerge.

All but one of the chapters in this book take the question of organizational structure as a point of departure. The exception is quite interesting: in their research, Rosemary C. Sarri and Robert D. Vinter started out to assess the impact of the introduction of a particular innovation, the use of a social work technique, group work, for handling pupils' behavior difficulties. After seeing the limits of this innovation, however, they conclude—and with some data—that reform in organizational structure is a first necessity. The paper illustrates well the point that piecemeal innovations are usually inadequate without prior revisions in organizational format.

That organizational reform can have substantial potentialities, as well as limits, is shown clearly in five other chapters. First, Roberta Ash's study of an experimental summer school for underachieving youths documents many of the gains, at least temporary ones, that the project could achieve. In addition, it gives an indication of the cultural strains such a project may induce and provides a model for innovation utilizing a division of labor with innovative nonprofessionals working side by side with more traditional teachers. Second, Mary A. Queeley's paper on the introduction of nongrading in an urban slum school provides a careful and comprehensive analysis of the character, intermediate steps, and consequences of this organizational innovation. That it could have as much impact as it did, operating within severe administrative limits and essentially as a "subterranean" innovation (later to suffer "death by incorporation" as it was quickly phased out to the entire urban school system), suggests that the nongraded format may have a very substantial potential for the schools of the slum. The paper also makes clear the need to be specific about what is and is not "nongrading," a term often used quite loosely by educators. Third, Bryan R. Roberts provides a study of the creation and impact of a new teachers college specifically designed to prepare teachers oriented to urban teaching. Comparing this school with two others, Roberts finds evidence of some positive changes, but also uncovers ways in which the subject matter biases of the faculty recruited to the new college limited its capacity to achieve its innovative ends.

The fourth paper dealing with revision in organizational format is a research report by Thomas C. Smith, C. T. Husbands, and myself, documenting the depressing effects of interschool mobility on pupil IQ scores. The authors conclude that revisions in bureaucratic attendance procedures could make a substantial difference. The final paper dealing with organizational reform is the book's concluding statement, "Institution Building in Urban Education," by Morris Janowitz. This is a comprehensive policy discussion of organizational change in large-city schools that frames a whole host of questions around the author's development of the distinction between specialists and generalists or, as Janowitz elaborates it, between the *specialization* and *aggregation* models of organizational change.

2. The Teaching Profession

Here the most immediate research issue involves assessing the short- and long-run character and consequences of the teachers' style of white-collar unionism. In recent years, America's big-city teachers, essentially solo practitioners with little time for on-the-job colleagueship and limited opportunity for professionally relevant contact in off-hours social life, have responded to militant unions as an alineated mass. The reaction of these teachers is understandable, for the lack of professional attachments and stimulation, the bureaucratic treatment received from the school system, and the irrelevance of most pre- and in-service training received in schools of education to the realities of urban teaching take their toll.

The trends here are uncertain. It is clear that the immediate consequences of continued teacher militance are greater pressure for universalism in school operations and thus further reductions in organizational flexibility as teachers press their claims not only for higher pay, which takes finances that otherwise could be used for special purposes, but also for standardized working conditions. As the unionized teachers make substantial income gains and find that reduced class size is no nirvana, however, they may become willing to negotiate substantial exceptions to their universalistic demands in the name of professional values and educational crisis, as the New York City teachers have done with the More Effective Schools Program. In addition, the gradual changeover toward predominantly urban-rooted Negro teaching staffs in the cities may eventually lead to a rejection of the gradual schools of education as the appropriate training sites for urban educators and a willingness to accept in-service training and/or separate institutions run by the school system or at least constituted in and of the inner city as the appropriate place to train for the realities of inner-city education. An al-

ternative is the adaptation of present graduate schools to greater cooperation with the public schools. Whether or not the growth of separate
inner-city training institutions could contribute to the development of
increased professional capacity is unclear. Furthermore, there is the substantial danger that stronger teacher unionism and greater separatism
will widen the schism between teachers and administrators and thus
make positive organizational change involving enhancement of the role
of the generalist in education even more difficult.

The longer-run professional questions also bear on professional capacities, not only for teachers but for principals, middle-level administrators,
and superintendents. Again the dominant trend appears to be toward
specialization and fragmentation of the administrator's role, rather than
a heightened integration of social science and subject matter components
with administrative skills.

Of the papers in this volume, only one, that by Roberts on the experimental college for urban teacher education, deals primarily with the
larger questions of the teaching profession. Roberts finds that teacher
trainees generally become less and less enthusiastic about inner-city
teaching as their college careers unfold, but he also, more hopefully,
discovers strong indications that the social backgrounds of the trainees
do not make them unmalleable in the process of professional socialization.
The paper by Ash and one by Timothy Leggatt, on the use of nonprofessionals in large-city school systems, also bear on significant issues of
the profession as they speak on new divisions of labor involving subprac-
titioners. Properly introduced, the subprofessionals could raise both the
status and the capacities of the teachers.

3. *The Political-Support Base for Education*

The large-city schools exist in a situation of political and racial stalemate over what is to be done for, or with, their unincorporated groups.
No big-city school system has been able to develop a substantial program
of stable integration or even a small but model program of managed
integration having racial quotas explicit and certain enough that the
more-than-immediate effects of stable integrated schooling can be adequately assessed. Variation among cities comes principally through the
symbolic acquiescence to civil rights demands,[13] the grace with which
racial change is adapted to, and the genuineness of efforts to preserve
the comprehensive school in the face of pessimism about racial change.

---

[13] See Robert L. Crain and David Street, "School Desegregation and School Decision-
Making, "*Urban Affairs Quarterly*, Vol. 2 (September, 1966), pp. 64–82. The senior
author does not believe that the acquiescence is principally only symbolic.

This situation of stalemate, together with the need for greater financial resources in most cities, defines a continuing political crisis for the schools.

In this setting three major issues arise over the fate of the political-support base of the large-city schools. The first is the question of the acquisition of needed monies. It can be expected that, however unevenly, state and federal financing will eventually pick up much of the slack. (Political practicalities make any attempt to create metropolitan school districts as a way of mobilizing resources out of the question.) It also can be expected that federal monies will be allocated in such a way as to promote specific innovative programs, which means that these funds will be dispensed with an eye to the likelihood of change in the proposed recipient unit. As a result, federal intervention is likely to introduce, at least in the short run, substantial variations in the ways that large-city school systems are run. Just what form these changes may take is uncertain, although if Office of Education officials continue to play a major role in dispensing funds, variations in traditional educational criteria like class size, along with the new federal concern with integration, can be expected to receive the greatest emphasis.

The second issue involves the relationships the schools develop with external agencies in the urban community, as these might yield not only innovative collaboration but new bases of professional and interest-group support. In general, the schools have avoided such contacts because they define them as "political" or disruptive and because the contacts threaten the schools with taking on additional social responsibilities beyond those with which the schoolmen already feel overburdened. A good case in point is the resistance to collaboration with outside agencies shown by the schools which helped to break down or weaken the various President's Juvenile Delinquency Projects in the early 1960's.

If the demands and proposals for changed education put forward by various outside agencies and groups in the community continue to be ignored, however, the support base for public education may be further eroded. Social workers, social planners, and other groups may opt for community support and federal monies to run educationally relevant projects outside the schools, not only such projects as Head Start but also day-time programs for older youths. Such programs might be useful for the children participating and in the long-run might serve as a competitive stimulus to school reform. However, they might simply undercut the support base for the public schools further and leave those who remain in the system even more disadvantaged. Under this circumstance and with the assumption of a continued increase in the use of parochial and other private schools by middle-class residents, public stipends for poor persons who want to buy private schooling for their children might become necessary social policy.[14]

The third issue is that of the workability administrative decentralization coupled with a high degree of local political autonomy, bringing the schools "back to the people." As embodied in the reactions to the Bundy report on New York City[15] and in the operations of three new experimental districts there, the strategy demonstrates what high aspirations for reforming the schools can be mobilized in ghetto areas. Clearly the available structure of large-city schools is overcentralized not only administratively but also as measured by the inapproachability of school officials to the lower classes. However, the reaction to these plans also indicates what dangers of local tyranny, in the name of Black Nationalism, can be aroused, and what great fears and action can develop among the professionals.

We can expect that demands for political decentralization will continue to increase in all the large cities, that often these demands will contain nationalistic elements, and that, until assurances can be developed that some kind of balanced state will obtain between professionals and laymen, the professionals will feel threatened by these proposals to the point where they will strongly oppose them, often with militant union action as in New York City. There is certainly the risk that some neighborhoods do not have (or have not yet had the opportunity to develop) stable and responsible leadership groups for the proposed autonomous districts, and that the breaking up of large-city school systems may destroy existing procedures for allocating teachers and programs on a relatively equilitarian basis. Finally, the urge to Black Nationalism or Black Power as a criterion for operating the schools may only heighten the feeling of separation without providing a compensatory sense of heightened self-image. Here then is a profound dilemma, of participation versus incorporation.

The chapters by Leggatt, Raphael O. Nystrand, Martin Mayer, and Robert J. Parelius all bear on the relationship of the schools to the community and on their political bases as well as questions of organizational format. The reader will find substantial parallels between Nystrand's paper on the relationship between community action councils and school systems in three medium-sized cities and Leggatt's paper on the use of nonprofessionals in five large cities. In both cases the

---

[14] A la Milton Friedman, *Capitalism and Freedom* (Chicago: University of Chicago Press, 1962), pp. 85–107.

[15] Mayor's Advisory Panel on Decentralization of the New York City Schools, *Reconnection for Learning: A Community School System for New York City* (New York: The Panel, 1967).

outcome appeared to be substantially dependent upon the character of top leadership in the school system and of the type of relationship—defensive, accommodative, co-opting, or controlling—that the leadership developed with outside groups.

The paper by Mayer, a first-hand account of the realities of bureaucracy and of its impermeability and inflexibility in the face of local community needs in New York City, documents as perhaps nothing else could the need for some kind of decentralized reform in that city's school system, but at the same time indicates the complexity of reform. The final paper in this group, that by Parelius, is a study of social structure and school politics in a low-income all-Negro suburb. It raises the question of the wisdom of decentralizing control over school matters to a population so disorganized and deprived by the larger social structure as the group he studied.

Issues of school-community relations are also touched upon in the Smith-Husbands-Street paper, which suggests that greater flexibility in administering the neighborhood school may lead, paradoxically, to a strengthening of the "community school" concept.

4. The Rise of Meritocracy

Although written as a negative utopia about Britain, Michael Young's *Meritocracy*[16] highlights many of the problems of mass education in America. For the United States it raises the spectre of movement toward an educational system that is highly stratified, if only by presumed merit, and that operates so as to provide those low in the system with no explanation of their position except that they in fact *do* lack merit. The movement would be abetted by extensions in the use of and real and imagined improvements in the predictability of standardized testing. It would be expressed in greater differentiation among universities, colleges, and schools, among suburbs, and between suburbs and cities, in the weakening of the comprehensive school, and in the further reification of self-fulfilling track systems. In this country presently the spectre is raised most dramatically in proposals for suburban boarding schools for bright students from urban ghetto areas and most concretely in the development of master plans for higher education that would distinguish among students and institutions with great detail and rigidity.

Patterns of resegregation and educational inadequacy in the inner city, coupled with the national search for talent, make this an especially plausible hypothesis for the metropolitan scene. Importantly, the movement toward meritocracy may be more harsh in its consequences for

[16] Michael Young, *The Rise of the Meritocracy* (London: Thames and Hudson, 1958).

the Negro population than for the white. The central issue here, however, is not to test the meritocracy hypothesis but to discover its limits. Such limits are implicit in the relatively spontaneous reactions against the use of testing data that occur from time to time (e.g., in the New York City schools, where rising fears of the reified use of IQ scores led to their abandonment as part of individual pupil's records). And these limits are explicit in strategies for minimizing the degree of segregation by track and for enhancing movement between tracks and in setting up educational parks as a means to preserve the comprehensive school. (Of course, if the emphasis in educational parks is on elite, specialized "magnet" curricula located in separate buildings on the campus, the park can have a meritocratic effect too.)

Several of the papers in this volume touch on the issues of the social functions of education suggested by the image of meritocracy. Especially relevant is the chapter by Queeley, whose research deals with an innovation which consciously seeks to remind teachers that there is variegated timing of growth among students and that the propensity to permanency in tracking should be avoided. Very pertinent too is the paper by Sarri and Vinter. Their conclusions directly address the problems of tracking in the high school, and their research efforts subsequently led officials in the schools they studied to attempt to abolish or soften the line between the academic and "general" tracks. Issues of meritocracy are also prominent, although mostly implicit, in the policy paper by Janowitz.

5. The Social Functions of Education

All of the articles bear at least in part on the social functions and goals of education. The image of the all-Negro inner-city school system, run on a minimalistic basis like a public assistance agency and losing its best pupils as they are selected for better settings, stands as the negative utopia of meritocracy in America. A school in this system would probably be basically custodial, coupling rigid controls with exhortation along the lines developing in many ghetto high schools today. Or, as it became adapted with social science "sophistication" to the "cooling-out process" for those who are going nowhere,[17] it might come to stress counseling and in this very limited sense become humanistic.

Clearly the school must become a more human institution. But it is too simple to say that the schools must broaden their goals. They must also limit their aspirations. In large part, the issue is whether or not the schoolmen are to retain the notion that they must assume nearly total responsibility for socialization to achievement in this society. Under this mission the schools have little motivation to collaborate with

---

[17] Burton R. Clark, *The Open Door College* (New York: McGraw-Hill, 1960).

other agencies or to think of the industrial order, the larger community, or the military establishment as providing collaborative "second chance" opportunities for those who do poorly academically. Moreover, under the weight of this responsibility (and no other institution but the schools would have the audacity to have accepted for years the presumption that they could "solve the Negro problem") and with limited resources, the schools have had little choice but to put all their stress on the achievement system.

If the schools are truly to address the problems of mass education, they must give up this presumption of a monopoly of responsibility. The educational institution must continue to emphasize achievement, but with realism and within the context of other social values and true cooperation with other institutions. It must allow for self-respect among its students, even those who under the present technology never will achieve satisfactorily, and also among its faculty. If the system is to function as a meaningful incorporative institution, it must balance academic and humanistic concerns. The papers in this volume suggest that research on the macrosociology of educational innovation can make some contribution to achieving this balance.

An Educational Experiment in the Inner City: a Participant-Observer's Report

Roberta Ash

Once an object of study for the anthropologist, the problem of culture contact now has serious implications for the metropolitan school system. Diverse programs and projects have been developed to introduce youthful bearers of the lower-class Negro subculture to representatives of the dominant middle-class white culture. The attempt that is described in this record of observations will illustrate two striking ramifications of such contact. First, we will see that some of the white project staff members were perhaps more profoundly changed by their introduction to the ghetto culture than were the Negro teen-agers by their contact with middle-class values. Second, we will find that the greatest accomplishments of the program (but also its greatest problems) stemmed from the fact that the achievement-oriented middle-class culture was actually represented by two distinct and sometimes antagonistic subcultures—that of a cosmopolitan university, known for political and social nonconformity, and that of the public school.

This paper will describe a summer project established on the campus of a university located in a large American city in order to stimulate the academic interests of a group of boys from an inner-city public high school. The project was held in the summer of 1965. Initially, the boys were all to be underachievers from low-income ghetto backgrounds, but in order to achieve racial integration and to include students who could serve as role models, a somewhat more heterogenous group of twenty-nine boys were selected. Their common characteristics were teachers' perceptions of them as underachievers, a minimal willingness to participate in the program, and at least average intelligence.

The research for this article was supported by The Center for Social Organization Studies of the University of Chicago; during the same period the author was supported by a National Science Foundation Fellowship.

They were primarily drawn from the nonremedial upper three of the high school's five ability tracks.

For eight weeks, six hours a day, they were to be exposed to the teaching of five public high school teachers and to the educational efforts of eight university students. The project had a dual aim: in the words of the principal the boys were to "get excited about learning"; they were also to be led to the realization that they could use the school system for educational and occupational advancement. Initially, some members of the program staff assumed that many of the boys were potential college students, but during the course of the summer the theme of college attendance was fully developed with only some of the boys, although it was perhaps useful as a stimulus to the others.

In the following pages, the author will analyze how the project succeeded in increasing the boys' interest in learning and in improving their attitudes toward the staffs of educational institutions. Much of the project's success stemmed from its ability to function as an alternative to the gang, a powerful force against learning in the boys' lives. The short duration of the project impeded a complete development in this direction.

The key factor in the success of the project was the role of the junior staff of college students. They were able to establish close relationships with the boys and thus to provide the interpersonal rewards that the boys had previously not obtained from school personnel. But at the same time, the college students experienced dramatic changes in their initially favorable attitudes toward lower-class Negro culture.

The author was an observer in this project, and this document is a report of her observations. Classes were observed (most intensively in the first and last two weeks), as well as activities, special events (field trips and speakers), and school ceremonies. The author also attended less formal phases of the project—lunch hour in a university cafeteria, informal meetings of the junior staff, and two parties (one of them kept secret from the senior staff). Observations were made of interviews with parents, the admissions session of the staff early in the summer, the first two planning sessions of the staff, and all staff meetings during the eight weeks of school and the week of evaluation, including one meeting closed to the senior staff of teachers and another closed to the junior staff of college students. A log was kept that included verbatim accounts of many conversations with and among the boys and the staff. The author was introduced to the boys as someone interested in new ideas in education and as a university student.

In addition to collecting information as a participant observer, the author had access to some other data: the boys' high school grade records, their high school disciplinary records, their IQ scores from the previous year and the end of the summer (California Test of Mental Maturity and Otis), a number of achievement test scores, "Draw a Picture" projective tests, and protocols of their interviews with a university psychologist.

THE PROGRAM AND THE STUDENTS

The Formal Structure

The Selection and Organization of the Students. Most of the students were selected from the local high school, which served two distinct areas: a middle-class integrated community and a predominantly working- and lower-class Negro community. The student body of the school was 94 per cent Negro, reflecting the age structure of the Negro community and the tendency of white residents in the area to prefer private schools. The high school was overcrowded.

To select the students for the project, one of the high school guidance counselors asked teachers to submit names of boys in their classes who were perceived as working below potential, with a few comments about them. A list of about 100 boys was made, and each received a form to take to his parents and a request that he and they come to an interview. Forty of the boys responded. They were interviewed by one of the five teachers or the principal, who then in a joint session eliminated 8 of the 40 as unsuitable (not bright enough, in most cases). Of the 32 boys selected, 4 decided not to enter the program and 1 did not return after the first day. However, 1 boy joined on his own initiative on the second day of the summer, and another was invited to do so in the third week. Thus during most of the summer there were 29 boys in the program.

The boys attended classes, tutorials, and activity sessions. For classroom work, they were split into four groups, at first randomly; later they were regrouped twice in an attempt to keep the groups as heterogenous as possible in ability, age, race, and personality.

The boys were asked to observe a minimal number of regulations, including some in regard to clothing and a no-smoking rule that was later modified to permit smoking at lunchtime with parents' written approval. In general, the teachers favored a continuation of school discipline, while the college student assistants were concerned only with infractions that interfered with learning. Thus the assistants were concerned with absences and tardiness, but not with smoking, standards of dress, or "playing the dozens." The assistants' view prevailed in many situations and gained strength during the course of the summer.

The students were formally organized only by the division into four smaller groups of carefully planned heterogeneity. Informally, differences of class, race, intelligence, personality characteristics, and age formed the basis of a number of cliques.

The Formal Organization of the Staff. The organization of the staff was somewhat more elaborate than that of the students. The sixteen staff members fell into four groups: two observers, five public high school teachers, eight university students who acted as teaching assistants, and a principal.

The observers were Mr. A., the assistant principal of a Negro high school in a nearby city, and the author, then a graduate student in sociology. They were described as the school administration observer and the sociological observer, respectively. Differences between the observers in age, sex, occupational role, and race produced differences in their interactions with the boys and the staff. These pre-existing characteristics were of greater importance in determining their roles than the formal descriptions of their position on the staff. They took no part in the planning or execution of the curriculum. The principal of the program exercised some control over their behavior, but they were not included in the authority system of the school. Henceforth, the term "staff" does not include the observers.

The public school teachers had been chosen for their excellence in teaching. Four of them were in the local public school system (two of them at the local high school) and had been selected on the basis of recommendations of their superiors and observations of the program principal. The fifth taught in another city but had become connected with the university on a fellowship. Formally, the teachers had the role of planning the curriculum and teaching the material in their respective subject areas—English, social studies, physical sciences, humanities, and physical education.

The eight college students (known as assistant teachers or teaching assistants—TAs for brevity) were selected by the principal from about twenty-five applicants. Their roles were not defined clearly at any point in the program; as we shall see, this lack of a clear role definition proved to be both a central problem and an asset of the program. An exposition of their formal duties or position on the staff is difficult precisely because their role was so ambiguous.

The teachers were paid $2000 for the eight weeks of the summer school and the week of evaluation. The TAs received $50 a week.

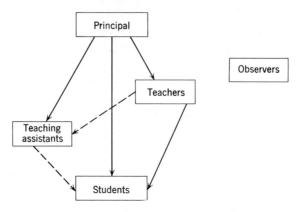

Figure 1   The authority structure of the program.

The principal was the source of authority for the staff, the disciplinarian for the students, the arbiter of funds, and the representative of the project to other organizations and the public. The internal structure of the project is shown in Figure 1. The solid lines indicate clear and unquestionably legitimate channels of authority. The dotted lines, on the other hand, represent channels of authority that were frequently either not exercised or not accepted as legitimate by the parties involved. We note, however, that the principal provides a second-order link of firmly established legitimate authority among all major groups in the organization. In other words, he frequently had to act as a mediator between the two pairs of ambiguously related groups—the TAs and students, and the TAs and teachers. The diagram also indicates that the principal provided the only clear relation of authority for the TAs.

The Curriculum. Initial scheduling was rigid, with four academic subjects (English, science, art and humanities, and social studies), physical education, and weekly field trip. In the second week an added activity period offered a newspaper, urban politics, two foreign languages, instruments and music appreciation, and oriental culture as topics. Some boys chose to have tutorials instead. In the middle of the summer the tutorials were extended, the boys were given a limited choice of what classes they wanted to take, and a program of prominent speakers from the university and the community was added.

Four of the TAs both worked with the classroom teachers and conducted activities and tutorials, while four confined themselves to the latter tasks. In the fourth week the students were asked to complete self-evaluation forms that they then discussed with the teachers and TAs. In the fifth week, interviews were held with the parents, of whom all but two came.

The Staff

The teachers were more diverse than the TAs in their social backgrounds and educational and occupational experiences.

The science teacher, B., was the oldest member of the staff. He had received his training at a major private university and taught in a predominantly white working- and lower-middle-class high school. His age, heaviness and slow deliberate speech at first appeared to make him unsuited for the program's student body, but he became the best liked and most respected teacher among both TAs and students.

C., the physical education instructor, was one of two Negro teachers on the staff. He had gone to a teachers college and taught at the local high school. He was stern and highly concerned with character building and good sportsmanship in competitive activities.

D., the English teacher, was an attractive young Negro woman, educated at a state normal university; she had had two years of teaching experience and taught at a high school in a middle-class Negro neighborhood.

E., the social studies teacher, had received a B.A. and an M.A. from a large urban university. He was in his middle thirties and had had about twelve years of teaching experience; he was teaching at the local high school.

F., the art and humanities instructor, claimed to have grown up in the roughest sections of a major U.S. city during the depression, to have served in the Civilian Conservation Corps, and to have been kicked out of three colleges before he settled down. He perceived the boys as repeating the problems and mistakes of his own youth.

C., D., and E. seemed bland and conventional in appearance and speech. On the other hand, B. with his grandfatherly air and F. with his goatee, short temper, and rough tongue seemed more capable of capturing the boys' imagination.

The TAs were markedly different from the program's student body in their high school training. They had variously attended the university high school, a Catholic girls' school, a local city public high school with a substantially Jewish student body, a metropolitan music and art high school, two suburban schools, a selective inner-city high school of another major city, and a Latin American institution. All eight were students of either the humanities or the social sciences, and they showed a certain amount of hostility toward the natural sciences. For instance, they complained that, if the project were continued, it would be impossible to find students in the natural sciences to work as TAs because they could all secure higher-paying summer jobs; this remark was made in a tone of resentment. During a presentation by a scientist, two TAs in the back of the room muttered to each other about the disparate amount of funds invested in the sciences. At least four of the TAs had had experience as tutors in a tutoring project for Negro high school students.

The principal had attended a local teachers college but had received graduate degrees from a major university. Despite his youthful appearance, he had had a large amount of experience as a teacher in the public schools and as a principal. At the time of the project, he was principal of the university laboratory high school. Thus he belonged to both of the spheres from which the staff was drawn—the academic environment of the university and the environment of public secondary school education.

The Students

The boys came from rather diverse backgrounds. But with a few exceptions they shared a number of characteristics: a distrust of intellectual endeavor, an instrumental attitude toward learning, a lack of communication with their parents, and few sources of stimulation beyond the mass media and the interpersonal rewards of association with their peers.

Background. We can establish a number of broad categories of social background. Table 1 presents data on class and race. For this table, the author defines the Negro lower-class group as boys supported by

Table 1   *Class and Race*

Category	Race and Class	Number of Boys
I	White professional	3
II	White business	3
III	White working class	3
IV	Negro middle class	5
V	Negro working class	7
VI	Negro lower class	2
V or VI	Negro, unclear whether working or lower class	6

Table 2 *Family Composition*

Family Composition[a]	Category[b]					
	I	II	III	IV	V and VI	Total
Stable nuclear family with biological father present	2	1	0	5	4	12
Mother remarried	1	1	2	0	1	5
Mother head of household	0	0	1	0	7	8
Other	0	1 (adopted)	0	0	2 (grandparents, aunts, and uncles)	3

[a] One unknown.
[b] As in Table 1.

Aid to Dependent Children payments. Of the Negro working-class parents, not all necessarily hold secure jobs. Occupations represented in this group are beautician, postal clerk, drugstore clerk, and truck driver. The Negro working- and lower-class boys were in many ways similar; for example, they both lived in the Negro ghetto, and they both were actual or potential gang members. The middle-class Negro boys lived in the integrated area of the school district.

The white boys differed markedly from the Negro boys in their scholastic skills (which were greater) and in their impression management (they seemed more immediately at ease with a staff of predominantly white adults).

The boys ranged in age from thirteen to seventeen. Most were freshmen or sophomores, some for the second or third time because of failing grades.

Data on family composition are shown in Table 2. More than half of the boys, including two-thirds of the white boys and about two-thirds of the non-middle-class Negro boys, lived in households that did not include their biological fathers; almost a third of the boys (nine) lived in households lacking permanent adult males (although the mother's brother may have had an important role in a boy's life). However, the situation in even some of the stable households with a biological father present may have encouraged patterns of rebelliousness or scholastic indifference. Thus, for instance, in the family of G.H. (Negro middle class), mother and son independently confirmed that the boy had not spoken at all to his mother for a full year. The family of H.I. (white business), with three pampered sons, had already been forced to send one to a military school because of his record of failure. The father of I.J. (white professional) held a graduate degree and a professional job, although he had finished neither high school nor college, and I.J.'s oldest brother had reinforced this pattern by dropping out of high school but then attending a local college. J.K.'s (white professional) older brother had been forced to take a year's leave from an Eastern university. K.L.'s (Negro middle class) mother had communicated her fear of cars, trains, planes, and water to her son, virtually incapacitating him for urban life. L.M. (Negro middle class) was his ambitious and successful father's last hope, for the older son had flunked out of college. M.N. (Negro working class) still slept with his mother.

The author is suggesting not that the family patterns of the students were direct causes of their poor scholastic performance, but rather that subtle relationships may have been present.

The Influence of the Gang. Many of the boys were members of a peer group whose standards they observed with the characteristic rigidity of teen-agers. The most powerful of such peer groups are the gangs that exercise control over adolescent boys in the Negro slum. The gangs strongly affected the behavior and, above all, the scholastic performance of the working- and lower-class Negro boys in the program.

The program included the whole range of gang leaders, gang members, and marginal members. Between 12 and 15 of the Negro boys in the program belonged to a gang; of these, all belonged to the same large, local gang. They claimed to engage in gun battles with their rival gang, although the author is inclined to doubt some of their stories, which may have been told to impress the TAs. The TAs encouraged the boys to discuss the activities of the gangs, and the boys showed no hesitation in doing so.

The gang can exert a considerable amount of influence, since it has at its disposal the sanction of violence, not available to the typical adolescent peer group. Violence is used chiefly to penalize those who attempt to evade gang membership. Because he refused to join the gang, one boy in the program was beaten up so badly that he had to stay home for several days. Another boy had maintained his membership in the rival gang after moving into the major gang's territory; the members showed their displeasure by beating him with a bicycle chain. He spent the first two weeks of the summer pressing his hands to his throbbing head and bloodshot eyes, but the other boys were satisfied that "— —'s more friendly with everyone now."

Another factor in the power of the gang is its territorial organization. Unlike the school-centered middle-class adolescent group, the gang has as its locus the block and the neighborhood. Therefore it can exert influence after school hours and during the summer. A third factor in the gang's influence may be the lack of alternative models of masculinity, courage and independence.[1]

The gang depressed the scholastic performance of the boys. Gang leaders were especially subject to sanctions for answering in class or doing homework. N.O., a gang leader, complained, "In school I know the answers, but there're always guys sitting in my classes who wouldn't like it if I talked or raised my hand or showed I know the answers."

The gang valued strength and used it as a prerequisite for leadership. Strength could be shown both in physical fitness and in illegal possession and use of weapons. Thus N.O. worked out in a neighborhood gym; his followers periodically came to see him box, that is, to check whether he still had the skill and prowess that qualified him for leadership. He described this display of strength as a test of leadership alternative to possessing a gun.

Cognitive Style. That most of the boys were good readers was evident from the speed, vocabulary recognition, and comprehension of their classroom reading. Several of them read for pleasure, generally adventure, detective, and sports stories. Some of the white boys liked to talk about TV programs, but the Negro boys only rarely mentioned them. Perhaps the reason was that their own gang was more immediate and exciting or that the world of TV shows was too distant from their own. Sports competed with mass media consumption. The non-middle-class Negro boys were most involved in out-of-school boxing and baseball and in high school football and basketball.

Among many of the boys there was an enmity toward learning. It was characterized not by a distrust of the intellectual, but rather by surprise that an activity as tedious as reading and writing could be carried out largely for its own sake, that the process of searching for answers was as important in many respects as the usefulness of the answers. The intellectual was not a threat to an established order, but rather an enigma. For example, upon being given a book of essays on politics, O.P. expressed surprise that anyone would write such essays, since there was not much money in a book of this type. Nor did these boys want to accept the idea of research and abstraction for its own sake. For instance, William Whyte's *Street Corner Society* (of which

[1] See Allison Davis and H. Dollard, *Children of Bondage: Personality Development of Negro Youth in the Urban South* (Magnolia, Mass.: Peter Smith Publisher).

they read parts) remained very mysterious. P.Q., who had been arrested and placed in a juvenile detention home on a car theft charge earlier in the summer, said, "Whyte must have written this book to warn young guys not to join a gang." Several claimed that Whyte had made up all of his data because he thought a book on gangs would be exciting and would sell well. The boys did not fear the intellectual as a person undermining religion, the nation, or the natural order (the Communist professor or mad scientist versions of anti-intellectualism), but viewed him as merely eccentric, a man unmotivated by gain.

But the boys thought of gain in only very short-run terms. Thus a boy made an enormous wooden giraffe in art class and immediately sold it for two dollars. Many of the Negro boys were half asleep by noon because they worked late hours at a variety of menial jobs. (It had mistakenly been hoped that the payment of a weekly four-dollar allowance would prevent them from seeking jobs and free their time for learning.) This attitude was not found among the white boys.

Insofar as knowledge was acceptable, it had to be presented in small, concrete, and preferably tangible units. The science teacher, B., was a favorite not only because he had a grandfatherly air but also because his subject matter was more easily broken into small units and could be seen and touched. The topics of the English and social science curricula were not as measurable or concrete. The social studies teacher had originally planned a map project, but the TAs bullied him out of it and made him work on politics and *Street Corner Society* instead. In retrospect it seems that the map project might have been more compatible with the boys' cognitive style. A number of boys could not see any similarity between the situation described by Whyte and their own lives. The dissimilarities of race, age, and style of gang life (a greater recourse to violence and a rhetoric of democracy in their own gang) obscured the similarities, the common attempt to impose norms on the behavior of young men in a slum. They refused to think of Doc's boys as a gang, and this refusal hindered all further attempts to relate the book to their own lives. The mother of a middle-class Negro boy who supported her son in his complaint that in the program teachers and TAs merely raised questions and led discussions but never provided answers represented another example of dissatisfaction with knowledge that was not presented in a simple way and in definite units.

Another revealing remark about teaching methods was made by a working-class Negro boy in a conversation about high school football teams. O.P. complained about the poor performance of his school's team: "Well, it must be the coaching. (Pause) Yea, it is the coaching. Now you take Vocational. They win all the time. Their coach is rough on them. He cusses them out all the time. I was watching practice there and a guy fumbled a pass and the coach hit him." "You think that's a good way to train a team?" "Yeah, that coach, he's always cussing at them. They got a good team."

CHANGES AND IMPACT

The Emerging Structure of the Staff

Encroachment and Resistance. The principal source of the project's vitality and of its difficulties was the role and activities of the TAs. As suggested earlier, the role of the TAs could not be clearly defined, and the scope of their authority vis-à-vis students and teachers remained problematic. As early as the end of the first week, the TAs' subordination to the teachers existed in name only. Their role as assistants, that is, subordinates, changed in two directions: three of the teachers resisted any attempts by the TAs to encroach on teaching activities and, in doing so, made very little use of the TAs as assistants; and two teachers allowed their own positions to be filled by the TAs.

During the first week each of the four groups of students was accompanied to all classes by the TAs assigned to it; the TAs dismissed this task as "being a nursemaid." In addition to being dissatisfied with their assigned duties, they were dismayed by the classroom styles of most of the teachers. They pressed for a change in role and were appeased by the principal, who gave them the opportunity to work with the teachers rather than with the student groups. Only four of the eight, however, decided to work with a teacher.

The teachers differed in their ability to use their new assistants. They had not been prepared for this innovation, which took place in the second week of the program, and each developed a separate solution in his interaction with the TAs who volunteered to work with him. Some of the teachers were unable to maintain control over their new staff and allowed the TAs to usurp their role as classroom leaders and curriculum planners. Others resisted the attempted encroachment of the TAs.

The most extreme example of resistance was set by F., the art instructor. The TAs had immediately taken issue with teaching style, a vigorous and domineering one in which he cursed at the students, repeatedly demonstrated his authority over them, and spoke of them (sometimes in their presence) as "lazy bums who won't get off their asses." He intended to introduce them to "real music," as opposed to Negro pop music. All these forms of behavior were highly distasteful to the TAs.

who entered the program with a warm regard for Negro culture, a great deal of sympathy for the students' dislike of the school system, and a desire to be friends with the students rather than superiors. F. did not want to have anything to do with the TAs; he made very obvious his unchangeably different pedagogical ideas and his intention to use the TAs as nothing more than tour guides on field trips. Only one TA, very reluctantly, offered to work with him, but F. paid no attention to him whatsoever. F. was keenly aware of the TAs' attempts to assume teaching roles, and angrily but proudly announced to the author in the sixth week, "They're getting in everyone's way, except mine—I didn't let them." During the staff meetings the TAs often showed hostility toward him by snide remarks among themselves, to which he reciprocated in kind rather more openly. Toward the end of the program, however, after a frank discussion with a number of the TAs he praised them very highly, told them they were responsible for the success of the venture, and was rewarded by the TAs' quiet acceptance of his style of behavior, manifested by a decrease in hostile remarks about him and eventually by respect and some measure of agreement.

B., the science teacher, and C., the physical education teacher, represented more subtle cases of resistance. They were both protected by the disinterest of the TAs in their subject matter and by their own self-confidence and experience. Only one TA volunteered to work with B., since most felt they were unqualified; this TA had explicitly stated that she felt she did not want to teach and thus constituted no threat to B.'s role. C. received occasional help from the male TAs, but none of them was interested enough to concern himself with teaching physical education.

E., the social studies teacher, and D., the English teacher, were the two displaced teachers. The usurpation was carried out by three male TAs and was manifested in a takeover of classroom teaching, curriculum planning, and choice of teaching materials. The successful encroachment took place because the TAs had definite ideas about how to teach these two subjects, because they were, perhaps, better acquainted with the recent literature in the fields than the teachers, because they had advantages of social class and, vis-à-vis D., of race and sex (such advantages increased their confidence), because they were more articulate, because they were numerically stronger, and because they were not stopped but rather were supported by the principal. All these factors contributed to the TAs' success.

E.'s case is simpler to analyze than D.'s, because in the view of the TAs his position was weak from the start of the program, so that no dramatic changes took place in his relationship with them. Despite his educational background and experience, his teaching style was seen by them as dull and slow, characterized by his running out of things to say (i.e., early dismissal of class), frequent quizzes, and occasional small factual errors. In addition to his lack of magnetism and energy, E. had weakened his position by selecting the map work, which bored the TAs, as his major subject. All the TAs complained about him from the very first day, and in the second week three volunteered to work with him, a relationship that the TAs described as "helping him." Thus, as mentioned previously, they talked him out of most of the map work and substituted Whyte's book and a number of discussions of city politics, urban problems, and gang structure. One male TA (Charles) conducted all of the class sessions of the three-week unit on Whyte. E., however, conducted tutorial sessions with the boys. Therefore the TAs functioned as teachers, while E. accepted the tutoring role initially planned for the TAs. E. was generally popular with the boys; his partial abdication of a teaching role increased his popularity, since he did not have to assign homework or impose sanctions in the classroom, and hence was perceived as "easygoing," a favorable evaluation.

The case of D. involved marked changes in her relationship with the TAs. It was further complicated by her ascriptive characteristics as a Negro and a young woman, which at first made her attractive to the TAs but in the long run weakened her ability to maintain authority over them. Although during the first week the TAs expressed a few doubts about her "talking down" to the students, that is, oversimplifying the material, and her decision to teach Shakespeare, she was their most popular teacher. She invited, rather than merely accepted, assistance from the TAs and tried to offer them roles in writing and oral instruction. Three TAs eagerly volunteered to work with her, perhaps attracted by the opportunity to develop a close but subordinate relationship with a Negro. During the course of the summer, however, they became disenchanted with what they believed to be a weak command of modern literature and limited knowledge, evidence perhaps of her normal college training. There appears to have been less of a conscious effort to take over D.'s duties than existed in E.'s case, but usurpation occurred, nevertheless. Unlike E., D. reacted more openly and less resignedly to the encroachments of the TAs, which took the form of decision making about topics and materials and the assumption of teaching duties. By the last weeks of the summer she occasionally described herself as depressed or sick of her work; her dissatisfaction with the project as a whole was overtly displaced onto her involvement in the management of the newspaper-writing activity, which required increasing amounts of her time and presented technical failures less personally wounding than her teaching difficulties. She did not complain to the TAs directly or in the staff meetings about their usurpation of her teaching duties, but rather complained to other teachers that the TAs "got in her way." The TAs did not perceive her dissatisfaction until the last few days of the program, if at all. D. lacked the popularity with the boys that in part had compensated E. for the loss of his teaching functions.

Thus within the broad categories of encroachment and resistance there were four levels of teacher response: violent opposition and refusal to accept any interaction with the TAs, limited acceptance of TAs in minor nonteaching roles, resignation to encroachment, and distress at encroachment. I had already suggested that social characteristics, personality, and the nature of the subject matter interacted to make the individual teacher more or less vulnerable to the encroachment of the TAs. It is important to bear in mind that only three male TAs participated in this process, since the others confined themselves to tutorials, activities, and other nonteaching tasks.

The boys gave no indication that they observed this process, nor do their sociometric choices of teachers reflect it in any systematic manner.

Interaction within the Staff. The key to the TAs' frequent success in imposing their views on the staff as a whole lies not only in their personal characteristics but also in their informal organization. Diana, Arthur, Bill, David, and Amy formed the nucleus of a group to which Beatrice and Charles were somewhat marginally attached. Beatrice was never fully integrated into the dominant TA clique, perhaps because her lower-middle-class Catholic background (and, to a lesser extent, her freshman status) set her apart from her fellow TAs; however, they shared with the boys respect for her friendliness and her great personal involvement in the project. Charles remained somewhat marginal because he failed to follow the example of the other TAs in trying to diminish the social distance between himself and the boys. Carol appeared to be a true isolate, exceedingly quiet, shy, and retiring with the boys and fellow staff members alike. The clique formation of the TAs was manifested chiefly in after-school meetings, mutual support in staff meetings, convergent views, and an overlap of outside contacts with other university students.

To a great extent, David acted as the spokesman for the TAs. Charles was also a frequent speaker in staff meetings, but he was not as well integrated as David into the dominant clique of TAs; therefore his comments more often reflected his personal opinions than the opinions of the TAs as a group. Bill was third among the TAs in volume of speech at staff meetings. These three male TAs were the ones who had assumed teaching duties. Most of their remarks were directed to the problems discussed at the meetings, but occasionally they made hostile whispered comments about the teachers or the boys.

Three female TAs—Amy, Beatrice, and Diane—also took a very active part in discussions at the biweekly staff meetings and in informal conversations.

Arthur and Carol scarcely spoke at all during staff meetings, although the former occasionally grumbled to himself. For instance, during a discussion of different homogeneous groupings among the boys (gang boys, younger boys, etc.), he muttered, "This is a lot of shit." Through his silence and his whispered comments in staff meetings he appeared to indicate that his primary allegiance was to the boys.

The TAs were stronger numerically, more vocal in staff meetings, and more unified in their views than the teachers. These factors gave them the upper hand not only in their interaction with individual teachers but also in the staff meetings, where policy decisions were made and everyday operating procedures determined. The teachers did not form any enduring subgroups.

The Role of the Principal. As the organization of the staff lost its initially simple structure, the principal became increasingly important, since he was the only person with a clear position of authority. The bases of his dominance were both personal (his ability as an administrator and his vast enthusiasm) and situational (his stake in both the academic community and secondary education, and the problematic nature of other staff relationships).

His role within the staff can be divided into two components: a role as a decision-maker and a role as a mediator. His decision-making role was chiefly exercised during staff meetings when TAs and teachers were deadlocked on a number of issues. Several situations can be cited in which the principal, with a smile and the comment, "It is time for an administrative decision," resolved a dispute: should students be allowed to smoke? (yes, in the cafeteria, with their parents' permission); should absence notes be required? (no, the matter would be handled personally by the principal); should staff or fellow students select the graduation speaker? (staff); etc. Fairly frequently the principal made an administrative decision in order to force the more venturesome views of the TAs on the teachers without directly exposing the latter to the embarrassment of having to acquiesce to their inferiors in age and occupational status. Thus the decision making of the principal operated as a face-saving device.

In addition, the decision making of the principal gave structure to the staff meetings and hence to the program as a whole. He drew up the agenda and led the discussion. The total chaos of the single staff meeting that he did not attend is evidence of the importance of this function. Although a small task had been agreed on in advance, the meeting broke up after 20 minutes of aimless paper shuffling amid exclamations that the task at hand was overwhelmingly huge and could not be done.

The principal assumed the role of mediator with decreasing frequency during the course of the summer. The most decisive assumption of this rule occurred on Monday of the second week, when the TAs met with him for a meeting which they anticipated would be "revolutionary," a word that appeared repeatedly in the vocabulary of at least one TA. In it they heatedly attacked teaching styles, sometimes for contradictory reasons (too dull and uninvolved—too wild and emotional; too much concerned with subject matter rather than students—not providing competence in basic skills, etc.), and demanded an end to their nursemaid role.

Operating as a go-between, the principal assuaged the doubts of the TAs, offered them a closer association with the teachers, and in gentler language presented their demands to the teachers at a closed session on the following day. After the principal's skillful handling of the TAs' complaints in the Monday meeting, one of them exclaimed, "He's amazing!" These words were frequently repeated during the summer in appreciation of his ingenuity in maintaining harmony in a staff of very disparate individuals.

Immediately after the end of the summer session an unfavorable reaction set in among the TAs, who now interpreted the principal's skill in organizing the staff as hypocritical manipulation, his attitudes on discipline as prudishness, and his leadership of the project as a professional prestige-seeking device. This extreme shift in attitudes in part represented a surfeit of involvement in the program and a crude conscious and subconscious attempt to detach themselves from it. In time their resentment ebbed away so that during the course of the year all but one of the TAs abandoned their antagonism and were able to evaluate the principal with sober respect.

In addition to his role within the staff, the principal functioned as a representative of the program to other organizations (the high school, the university, foundations, and the community), as arbiter of funds, and as disciplinarian. He was able to maintain his popularity with the boys, despite his role as disciplinarian.

The simplest way to summarize the preceding observations is to present a second version (Figure 2) of the organizational chart. Earlier the structure of the staff at the beginning of the term was shown; here Figure 2 suggests some of the relationships extant in the seventh or early eighth week. Although at first the teachers were given some authority over all the TAs, at the end of the program channels of authority existed only between four of the TAs and three of the teachers. Furthermore, four of these five channels were reversed from their initial direction, that is, the TAs determined the contents of the course and the teachers acted in facilitating roles. On the other hand, Carol, Arthur,

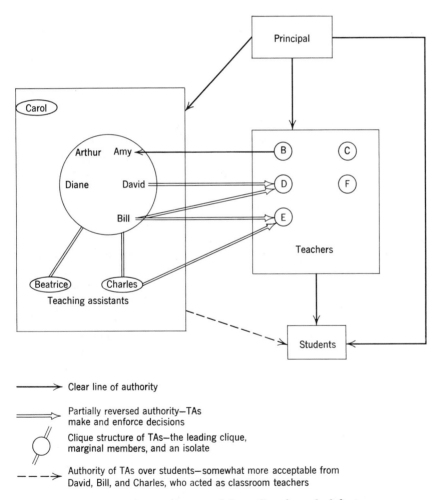

Figure 2   The organization of the staff at the end of the term.

Beatrice, and Diane conducted tutorials and activities in which they interacted little with the teachers, and hence were not involved in authority relationships with the teachers.

As classroom teachers, Bill, Charles, and David established more authority over the students than did the other TAs, since they assigned homework and imposed class participation. However, the students did not perceive the TAs' authority as quite as legitimate as that of the teachers, and on one occasion they described David as "power-hungry."

The principal in the eighth week was still the source of all legitimate authority and the connecting link among the various groups in the program.

Figure 2 also indicates the clique of TAs. Handsome, self-confident, and highly articulate, David not only was central to the TA clique but also represented it to the rest of the staff; his views came to be identified as those of the TAs in general.

The Staff and the Boys

Initial Attitudes of the Staff. Because the staff's behavior was self-conscious, planned, and sensitive to feedback from the boys, it fluctuated frequently and changed its course from one staff meeting to the next. Here only the major trends in the staff's beliefs and behavior will be specified.

Different staff members entered the program committed to different beliefs about underachievers, particularly Negro ones, and trained to express these beliefs in different rhetorics.

1. Attitudes of the teachers. The teachers had generally unfavorable ideas about the students they were to teach. First, the students had been selected for their truculence and apathy as well as for their scholastic potential. But the teachers' unfavorable beliefs were based on more than their observation of the boys in the admissions interview; they also drew on their teaching experience in slum schools and on generally held beliefs about the performance of students at such schools. Thus, B., the science teacher, predicted that the police would frequently appear in the project to inquire about the boys (actually, only one boy had any difficulty with the police during the summer). A less exciting but perhaps equally unfavorable image of the boys was held by E. and F., who thought of them as lazy; F. in particular often referred to them as "lazy bums—they won't get anywhere unless you give them a good kick." E. spoke of the characteristics of the underachieving or lower-class Negro students that he had had in his classes.

More interesting than the rather predictable content of the teachers' ideas about the boys was the language in which these ideas were expressed. The dominant rhetoric was that of the guidance office, a tone set by Mrs. Y. of the local high school, who carried out the task of identifying candidates. Based on a psychology too watered down to be traced to any distinct theoretical tradition, it reduced adolescents' problems to matters of family structure, identity formation, and unconscious motives; yet it did not express these relationships very precisely or consistently, but generally couched them in popular phrases: "His mother has a lot to do with it—she's a nut"; "He's been rejected by his mother"; "His parents push him too hard." The boys' family backgrounds encouraged a psychologically based explanation. Guidance office rhetoric, however, often obscured reality by substituting an explanatory phrase for a concrete observation. This rhetoric disappeared very early in the summer for at least two reasons: the close contact with twenty-nine individuals made it obviously inadequate, and the principal very decisively discouraged it.

A second distinct rhetoric was that of C., the physical education teacher, who used the language of pre-Freudian morality. Thus he spoke of "playing the dozens" (formulas of insult) as "morally reprehensible"—"We should tell the boys that we find this repugnant"—and described one of the boys as "depraved." These forms of expression often made the TAs wince; they seemed too embarrassed to take issue with him.

Because the teachers had such low expectations of the students' academic potential and behavior, they found the boys' interest and responsiveness very surprising and rewarding. Toward the end of the program they took pride in describing the achievements of individual students to outsiders, especially to those who had known the boys as failures in high school. In addition to their heightened expectations of the students, the teachers became more willing to instruct the boys as individuals, that is, to draw them out in class, to spend time with them, and to be friendly and patient with them. They agreed that the most important lesson they had learned as teachers was to concentrate more on the apathetic student.

2. *Attitudes of the TAs.* The TAs represent an altogether different case. They entered the project both more confused about their role and more vocal about their beliefs than the teachers. In many ways, their attitudes and beliefs changed much more radically than those of the teachers. They had better-formulated categories for describing boys like the students in the program and a more ideological stance, and therefore less flexibility in adjusting their verbal behavior to their new-

found observations and beliefs. By the fourth week in many respects their opinions converged with the teachers' views of the boys as crude and hard to teach, but they continued to speak about the students in the same manner as before.

Their initial beliefs were centered on three premises: (a) that they were to be friends of the boys, although they were uncertain as to how to carry out the expected role of friend; (b) that the boys were justified in rebelling against the school system; and (c) that there are valuable elements in lower-class Negro culture.

A few examples will support the claim that these three premises were very important to the TAs. The uncertainty about roles, as well as the preference for a buddy relationship is revealed by the first two questions asked by the TAs at a preterm planning session: "Can they call us by our first names? Are we to be their buddies?" Although the principal answered both questions negatively, the TAs insisted that they should be called by their first names, and the boys adopted this practice on the third day of the term. The TAs believed that the use of first names was a symbol of an egalitarian relationship that might become a friendship.

The TAs showed their belief in the second premise (that the boys were justified in opposing what the TAs called the System) in a number of ways. First, they very forcefully opposed any attempts to impose the typical regulations of the school system on the boys. They favored only the attendance regulations that were directly necessary to ensure exposure to instruction. They led the staff to decide to handle absences by personal investigation by the principal rather than by requiring a note. Even this decision was a compromise, for initially the TAs favored letting the boys come and go as they felt motivated. The TAs opposed the smoking regulations and succeeded in having them eased after the third week. Since they conceived of the program as demonstrating ways of learning alternative to those of the school system, they refused to consider the difficulties the boys might have in readjusting themselves in the fall to the regulations of the school.

Second, they encouraged the boys to disparage their high schools, that is, to describe the defects of the staff (especially the administration) and the discontent of the student body. The TAs tried to introduce the students to the concept of "alienation," which they described to them as a sense of "not belonging." The TAs did not seem to sense that they were contributing to a crystallization of the boys' hostility toward school.

Finally, they often showed that they were unconcerned about the boys' return to school. In the words of one TA, David: "It might be better if this kid dropped out and bummed around the country, if it helps him become a better writer. It is more important to adjust to yourself than to the system." A main purpose of the summer program was to indicate techniques of study that were not encouraged by the school and to prepare the individual for intellectual interests that he could pursue even if he did not continue his formal education. The more moderate example of the TAs' belief in these goals was the encouragement given the boys to read for pleasure. The more extreme example, which was frequently voiced by some of the TAs in staff meetings, was the opinion that the public school had essentially no new skills to offer its students and that it had even blunted and distorted their existing skills and sensibilities.

The third premise (the positive aspects of lower-class Negro culture) appeared early in the summer in the remarks of the TAs. The preterm meeting was the scene of a fierce debate between F. (with the principal's support) and David on the relative merits of teaching classical music and Negro music. At this meeting some of the TAs voiced the feeling that learning should be related to the boys' own interests. The TAs soon discovered, however, that many of their preconceptions of the boys' interests were invalid; they rapidly adjusted to this situation and spent the first two or three weeks questioning the boys about their world. The information the TAs obtained forced them to revise their initially favorable belief that lower-class Negro culture fostered spontaniety and was at least potentially conducive to widespread artistic creativity.

The TAs expressed their concept of the boys' lives in two rhetorics, a psychological and a sociological one. In general, the TAs used psychological terminology to describe the white boys and a combination of psychological and sociological terminology to describe the Negro boys. Their psychological rhetoric in many ways paralleled the guidance office rhetoric, but substituted "adjustment to the self" for "adjustment to the System" as a goal. The sociological rhetoric centered on the concept of alienation; a number of the TAs viewed the boys as an alienated group, alienated as students in an impersonal school system and as Negroes in American society. They encouraged the boys to think of themselves in these terms and to draw parallels between a sense of nonbelonging as the cause of a riot that had occurred in their school during the spring and as a cause of the Watts riots. In these endeavors they were really only successful with two highly race-conscious boys, one of whom said, "In social studies in this project, the most important thing I learned is that I am a member of a powerless minority."

The Disillusionment of the TAs. The TAs were not recruited from the most ideological groups on campus, but four of them were connected

with a college student tutoring project and shared the belief in egali-
tarianism, opposition to the school system, and interest in Negro culture
that characterized the tutoring project's leadership. Furthermore, they
were more ideologically oriented than the teachers because their humanistic education and (in some cases) superior intelligence disposed
them to construct a more structured view of the world. Although they
espoused no particular ideology, they organized their beliefs about lower-
class Negroes and about the aims of the program into more carefully
formulated and consciously developed categories than did the teachers.
Therefore, although the views of the TAs changed during the summer,
their commitment to a set of beliefs and a rhetoric of alienation and
adjustment inhibited a change in verbal behavior. Their change of views
was manifested in their conduct, but not in the categories and assumptions that they used in describing the boys and the aims of the program.
That is, their behavior in the classrooms and their opinions about individual boys showed a departure from their three initial premises, but
they never abandoned them entirely and especially continued to support
them vis-à-vis the teachers in staff meetings. Their greater propensity
for ideological thought reduced the flexibility of their language. The
teachers, on the other hand, were able to abandon the guidance office
rhetoric and to express fully their surprise at the unexpected performance
of the boys.

The change in the TAs' views is one of the key aspects of the program.
Each premise underwent different modifications.

   1. The premise that learning can take place more easily outside
   of the conventional school classroom and that the project was hence
   to point the way to alternatives to the school system was not
   abandoned or even modified. The TAs, however, acquired a better
   understanding of the problems that confront the inner-city school
   teacher.
   2. The premise of friendship was modified but essentially maintained.
   3. The premise of the value of lower-class Negro culture was
   completely abandoned.

The experience of teaching and the growing knowledge of gang life
led to these revisions of attitudes. In the face of the boys' attitudes
toward learning and the evidence of the dullness and brutality of the
gang world, the TAs took a more rigid stand toward the boys' in-school
behavior than they had at the preterm session, and they lost their romantic ideas about the slum.

The impact of teaching experience was greatest on the three TAs who went beyond activities and tutorials to actual classroom teaching, but all of the TAs felt it since they all conducted some form of instruction. Teaching brought the shock of reality, the recognition that their methods were no more effective than those of the teachers in producing interest and participation among the boys. During the course of the summer, classroom participation did increase, but sometimes only in the form of a rise in sullen opposition to the choice or contents of the topic. The TAs assigned more homework than the teachers and found that it was rarely done. They therefore developed the same antagonism toward the laziness of the boys that the teachers had from the start. Thus, for example, the TAs were more eager than most of the teachers to start "getting tough" in the middle of the summer. Insofar as they were teachers, the TAs had to relinquish the buddy role. Furthermore, they resented the boys' persistent antagonism toward learning, particularly noninstrumental learning of the literature and social studies courses designed by them. They perceived this non- and even anti-intellectual attitude as growing out of the boys' environment, which they therefore came to evaluate less positively.

The TAs changed their beliefs about the world of the ghetto as they learned more about it directly from the boys. They discovered that it was violent, yet also dull and petty. First, the TA who had so enthusiastically supported "Negro music" before the term started conducted a music session in which he tried to interest the boys in jazz; he found to his disgust that they would have no more to do with jazz than with classical music.

Second, the TAs found that the boys were extremely concerned with money, especially the most petty sums. Their concern with gain was not focused on the choice of lucrative careers but on short-run considerations. They worked at menial jobs for trifling remuneration instead of doing schoolwork. They schemed to make or save small amounts. For instance, one boy tried to fool the summer program newspaper into paying for developing several rolls of his family's snapshots. These attitudes toward money were related to the boys' instrumental attitudes toward learning, which the TAs found disturbing. Not only did the TAs find these attitudes foreign to their own values, but they were also greatly dismayed to discover them in a group they had believed to be generous and spontaneous, untouched by parsimony and greed. (On the grounds of deploring the boys' instrumental orientation, the TAs opposed the weekly allowance paid to the students.)

Third, the TAs found that the important role of violence in the working- and lower-class Negro boys' lives was alien to their own background and distasteful. The presence in the program of two boys who had been beaten up brought the TAs nearer to the consequences of violence than did their reading or their talks with the boys. In the students' presence the TAs showed fascination rather than repugnance for the details of gang life, but from more private interaction it was evident that they had not expected the slum community to be as violent or suspicion-ridden as the boys described it to be. Since the local gangs were atomistic, gang members were not even able to trust each other.

Fourth, the TAs had not expected the active hostility of the gang toward the scholastic efforts of its members, especially of its leaders, of whom there was at least one in the project. They were frustrated by being forced to compete for the boys' involvement with an organization that had such powerful sanctions at its disposal.

The teachers took these aspects of the boys' lives more for granted. The physical education teacher passed moral judgment on them, but he and the other teachers—unlike the TAs—did not seem surprised or disillusioned, for they had not shared the initial premise that lower-class Negro culture has many favorable aspects.

The Staff's Interaction with the Boys. To a large extent the TAs continued to follow their premise about the value of a "buddy" role. But at the same time such a role was to some degree untenable in the face of the barriers of age, race, sex, position in the project, and the teaching role assumed by some of the TAs. Depending on their characteristics, the TAs were more or less successful in being buddies with the different students.

The term "buddies" refers to a diffuse, individualized, affective, altruistic, and egalitarian relationship. The TAs tried to conform to all components of this definition. The teachers treated the boys altruistically and individually, but interacted with them only in the specific teaching context and never as equals. Their affective involvement with individual boys was less than that of the TAs, although they felt as great a commitment to the goals of the program.

The major exception to the generalization that the TAs behaved in accordance with this definition was that the individualized approach of some TAs to the boys was in many ways superficial, since their behavior was based largely on their feelings and beliefs about lower-class Negroes as a group. The most extreme example was Diane, who conducted an activity session on urban politics in which she stressed alienation and race consciousness. During evaluation week she admitted that the boys' race interfered with her ability to treat them simply as persons. Other variations in the friendship role were introduced by the personalities and role of the TAs, for some were perceived by the boys as colder, stricter, and less easygoing than others; the easygoing were the popular ones.

The friendship role of the TAs had two dysfunctional consequences. The first was difficulty in enforcing discipline, and the second was aimlessness in schoolwork. The TAs grudgingly agreed to enforce the project's rules, for although they disagreed with a number of them, they saw the need for consistent behavior on the part of the staff. But by diminishing the social distance between themselves and the boys, the TAs greatly weakened their position as disciplinarians and as assigners of schoolwork. The boys occasionally refused to accept the TAs' authority as legitimate, since they perceived attempts to exercise it as betrayals by friends. One consequence of the decrease in social distance was the frustrated attempt at sexual involvement by one student toward two of the TAs and a friend of theirs in the week after the end of the program. In part, this attempt was a testing of the limits of what the boy perceived as white liberalism (it is perhaps not coincidental that he was one of the two race-conscious boys). In part, it reflects the boys' belief that friendship with a girl must include a sexual element.

Aimlessness resulted from the TAs' commitment to an egalitarian relationship and to democratic procedures. Some of the discussions in the TA-conducted classes and activity sessions drifted interminably, resulting in no increment of knowledge and perhaps in a lowered rather than a heightened opinion of democratic procedures. Some discussions not only failed to lead to the precise answers that some boys wanted, but also did not even offer a true exercise in speaking or debating skills. The boys were allowed to argue about the value of studying a given topic. They frequently issued opinions based on no information; because of the difficulty in assigning homework, some discussions were based on very sparse funds of knowledge. For example, the urban politics activity often consisted only in a repetition of personal sentiments about race by the more vocal boys and vain encouragements to read more by the TAs.

Of course, the TAs varied greatly in this respect; for instance, David, aggressive and powerful, after usurping the English class from the regular teacher, directed it decisively, yet without sacrificing discussion to lecture.

Differentiation and Clique Formation. Differences in personality and background within the student body led to differences in association within it and to differences in interaction with the staff.

Within the student body four major cliques appeared; a white clique centered on a working-class boy and a professional-class boy, but peripherally involving many of the white boys; a younger white clique centered on business-class boys and loosely linked to the older white boys' clique; a gang clique of the older Negro boys, rather hostile to the older white clique; and a rather loosely articulated younger Negro group, including both middle- and working-class boys. There were a number of pairs, some of them isolated from the cliques and others linked into the cliques. One of these pairs was notable because it consisted of a lower-class Negro boy and a professional-class white boy; it seemed to exist chiefly during school hours (both had out-of-school ties to boys of their own social backgrounds) and to function so that the white boy could assume the role of a staff member toward the Negro boy. The former was overheard remarking, "I was picked as a pace setter and am having a lot of fun helping the other boys." Three Negro boys were isolates.

The TAs and teachers perceived this structure of the student body and provided nicknames for the different subgroups. The older Negro gang group they referred to by the name of the local dominant gang; the younger Negro group they called the "Nice Boys"; the two white business-class boys at the center of their clique the staff called the "Gefüllte Fish Twins"; and all of the younger boys, regardless of race or clique membership, the staff designated together as the "Crib." Several staff meetings were devoted to reshuffling the four staff-created sections of boys to break up the Crib and the gang clique, since the members of these informal groupings tended to disrupt classes if they were allowed to stay together. One staff member twice suggested homogeneous grouping, that is, a sectioning according to perceived subgroups, but the others opposed it on the grounds that some of the resulting groups would be too difficult to handle and that it would remind the boys of the high school ability track system.

Friendships between the TAs and the students were more easily formed with the older boys. The best-developed ties were between David and the two leaders of the older white boys' clique, Beatrice and three of the gang boys, Diane and one of the more isolated older Negro boys, Arthur and a number of Negro boys involved in his music activity, and Amy and a white working-class boy.

The boys responded differently to different staff members. The boys' sociometric choices of the staff were revealed in an informal popularity poll in the project newspaper and in a short interview with a psychologist. In both settings a majority of the boys selected B., the science teacher, as their favorite teacher; Beatrice and Arthur were their favorite female and male TAs because they were "easygoing." The quality of easygoingness, "not getting on your back all the time," also won E., the social studies teacher, a substantial number of votes. The psychologist also obtained their choices for the least liked. Opinion was most divided on F., the individualistic art teacher. The lower-class Negro boys generally disliked him and focused their complaints on his roughness and cursing; "unfit for a teacher" was their judgment. More flexible in their expectations of proper performance of the teacher role, the white boys tended to select F. as their favorite teacher. On the other hand, the white boys more than the Negro boys disliked C., the physical education teacher, for his stern moralism. D., the English teacher, was the least frequently chosen as best liked and most frequently chosen as least liked. From the boys' remarks to the psychologist one cannot deduce the basis of their likes and dislikes, and in D.'s case the negative choices may have been based on a dislike of English as a subject as well as on her personal characteristics. D. was visibly hurt when the psychologist discussed the boys' preferences at a staff meeting during the week of evaluation; they augmented her sense of failure.

The positive choices of TAs by students centered on Beatrice and Arthur, but negative ones were more dispersed. Charles was believed to be too distant and too much of a disciplinarian. With David, as with F., the strength of his personality and the forceful individuality of his style produced strong likes and dislikes among the boys.

Of some interest is the manner in which the boys paired off the TAs into "good couples." Arthur and Beatrice were grouped together because "they're nice and easygoing, so friendly." Charles and Amy formed a couple because "they're concerned with discipline, not so friendly." David and Diane were paired as "bossy, like to lead the discussion." Bill and Carol were grouped together because they "were left over." To the author, Bill seemed to belong in the same aggressive category as David and Diane, while Carol was quiet and isolated—hence the mismatched fourth couple. The boys' pairings indicate insight into the personalities and attitudes of the TAs.

Effects: Changes in the Boys

The major change in the boys' behavior occurred in their behavior toward the staff of the program, both in relatively formal situations such as the classroom and in informal conversations and encounters.

In the Classroom. One very important aspect of the project is that the boys' classroom participation increased greatly. At the beginning of the summer most of the boys were content to sit quietly, sometimes with such a vacant expression on their faces as to make clear that they were not even trying to pay attention; a small number of boys—all but two of them white—dominated the class discussions. During the course of the summer, however, most but not all of the boys took part in class work, voluntarily giving answers and offering suggestions. Early in the summer a number of the boys would mumble the correct answer to the teacher's question, but at so low a volume as to be inaudible to all but the student himself and the observer sitting nearby. This secretive form of answering gave way by the third or fourth week to open volunteering and audible presentation.

The methods used to achieve this improvement were varied but were made possible largely by the small class size (about seven students) and the large number of staff members. Students were at first forced to participate by being called on to read or to answer simple questions, thus establishing confidence in their ability. The small class size and flexible schedule allowed a student to be heard frequently and to take as much time as he wanted in formulating an answer. TAs sitting in the back of the room were able to hear the mumbled secret answers and encouraged these students to share their correct responses with the rest of the class. Some of the material presented touched on the interests of the reticent boys but was remote from those of the vocal boys, thus occasionally reversing the usual distribution of contributions to the discussion (such a reversal occurred when the students read *Street Corner Society*).

The boys themselves realized that their class participation had greatly improved; many commented on it in a self-evaluation form in the third week. A number mentioned that they now were no longer so afraid of being laughed at; perhaps at their own high schools they had been ridiculed for their difficulties in answering, or perhaps ridicule was a sanction of the peer group against those who tried to participate in school work.

In Interpersonal Behavior. A second set of changes in the boys involved their informal interpersonal behavior. At first shy, they rapidly accepted the diffuseness of the relationships offered by the TAs and, to a lesser extent, the teachers. They began to adapt their behavior to the staff members as individuals, meaning that they ceased to treat all with grudging deference, a deference that in its taciturnity and undifferentiatedness implied hostility rather than respect. Early in the program, they were quiet in face-to-face contact with the staff, whispered and laughed among themselves, and were reluctant to initiate a conversation with a staff member. (About five or six boys—white professional and working class and Negro working class—were exceptions to this generalization and were eager to talk with the staff, to sit with staff members at lunch, and to have the staff as an audience for their opinions.) Later the students began to distinguish characteristics of the staff, to react differently to them, and to present themselves as individuals as well. A number of them developed close sibling-like relationships with staff members of a category with which they previously had had little contact. They seemed to develop a greater sense of their own worth, for they were generally treated as something more than lazy students, recalcitrant children, or members of a lowly valued minority group. They found that white adults took their wishes and their future seriously. They manifested their newly found self-confidence by being able to carry on relatively lengthy conversations where previously they had confined themselves to a few grudging monosyllables. They revealed a number of their ambitions and problems in greater detail than they previously would have cared to to do. Most soon spoke rather freely to the TAs, although they remained cordial but guarded with the teachers; the principal also gained their trust in personal matters.

To a large extent, the greater articulateness· and the partial mastery of guidance office rhetoric of the white boys allowed them to speak more freely of their personal problems to the TAs. Some of the Negro boys talked very freely about gang life, and two voiced racial antagonism. Conversations centering on these topics took place during lunch hours, activity sessions, tutorials, and the long bus rides on field trips. The boys' increased self-confidence made possible their talking to the strangers who were occasionally introduced to the group—guest speakers, spouses and friends of staff members, visitors at a graduation ceremony, etc. Rates of progress in these directions were rather different for different boys and did not adhere closely to race or class lines. The staff's evaluation of the white boys in purely psychological terms led to a perception of these boys' problems as essentially beyond the scope of the project, that is, as being too individual and too deep-seated to be handled by persons untrained in psychotherapy. The Negro boys, on the other hand, seemed more responsive to the essentially symptom-oriented techniques of the project.

Another manifestation of increased confidence and individualized responses to interpersonal stimuli was the disappearance of the sartorial props of the boys' underachiever role. When the students first came to the program, may affected a type of uniform that invited an undifferentiated treatment of them as underachievers or troublemakers. Two always wore sunglasses, even indoors; several wore hats, also indoors; one sported a leather wristband and an exaggeratedly masculine swagger; several had unconventional hair style—extremely long, unkempt Beatle cuts, ducktails, processed hair à la Sugar Ray Robinson, etc. One of the sunglass wearers also turned up his shirt collar, and a number of the boys were "gousters," a group currently in vogue at the local high school and characterized by sloppy clothes and very baggy pants. (One of the boys came to the project wearing shabby green janitor pants with one leg rolled up halfway to his knee, so that at first the author thought him poverty stricken, although actually his father was a well-to-do doctor and landlord.) These various affectations, consciously adopted symbols of being underachievers and inviting treatment as such, disappeared during the program and for the most part did not reappear at fall meetings in October and December. The significance of these changes in dress is great, for all the boys were drawn from an age group in which clothes are the measure of the man, and many came from classes in which a relatively large proportion of funds is spent on appearance.

Additional Observations. A brief summary of various data of varying degrees of reliability that support the author's observations of changes in the boys' behavior may be of value.

1. Statements made by the boys and their parents. A source of information about the program's effects are the statements of the boys during the summer and at a fall meeting. Encouraging to the staff was the interest that all but two or three of the boys indicated in a continuation of the program in the following summer. This enthusiasm contrasts with their attitude early in the summer, when many of the boys tried to present a challenge to the staff that its members thought could not be met; on the first day, one said, "No one will show up at all by the second week." Yet the boys not only continued to attend but even were interested in spending a second summer in a similar way.

During the course of the summer the boys all became attached to the program. One boy spoke of it as being like a family: "You feel like you belong to it, and you know everyone." Despite the racial antagonism that occasionally was openly expressed, there was also an *esprit de corps* among all the boys in the program. Negro and white boys stood around outside the school and joked and talked together; they developed few close friendships, but their shared experience in the program gave them the same basis for amicable casual interaction.

This sense of belonging was felt in relation to the staff as well as to fellow students. The boys contrasted the program to their high school, where no one ever saw the administrators; they were encouraged to think in these categories of belonging and alienation by a number of the TAs. Early in the summer their main complaint about high school was that it was boring, but later in the program they began to evaluate it by the quantity and quality of contracts between the students and the staff. They were openly appreciative of the warm personal relationships with the staff that developed in the summer project.

But about half of the boys did not go beyond approval for the interpersonal aspects of the program and did not admit to feeling any excitement or pleasure in learning. They expressed some interest in the work done in class, but they did not develop out-of-school intellectual pursuits or show curiosity in further studying the topics that could be presented only briefly in the limited time available in the summer. The TAs seemed to be more disappointed than the teachers in the continued absence of overt scholastic interests among a sizable number of the white business-class and Negro working- and lower-class boys.

At a fall meeting (attended by sixteen of the boys about six weeks after the beginning of school), three or four said that they now thought more about learning and less about grades (an almost meaningless statement in light of their grades of the previous year), reflecting the "adjustment to self, not the System" rhetoric of some of the TAs. One or two boys cynically remarked that the program had made them realize the necessity of brown-nosing and grubbing for grades. A third group, the largest, piously claimed that they now wanted both knowledge and good grades.

At this meeting the boys also gave more concrete evidence of improvements in their relationship with the school, in particular of improved contact with the high school faculty. They mentioned that the teachers and guidance staff were giving them more formal and informal attention, and that arrangements were even being made to place them in more challenging, higher-track courses.

The favorable statements made by the boys were corroborated by their parents, who were interviewed in the fourth week of the summer and seen again at "graduation" on the last day of the term. The parents of only two boys failed to come to the interview, and of those who came only two reported that their sons were dissatisfied with the program (one because he continued to be bored, and the other because he disliked the other boys—opinions in which the boys appeared to be supported tacitly by their parents). The parents expressed their enthusiasm most concretely by remarking that they and their sons hoped the program would be repeated during the following summer. No further summer project has been held.

2. *Attendance.* The attendance record for the program was exceptionally good. The tardiness rate was 11 per cent and absenteeism only 4 per cent, although most of the boys had truancy problems at high school. One boy had attended only thirty days in the whole year, and another had been present only two days of the second semester. These

were exceptional cases, but about half of the boys had had very poor attendance records at high school. Despite the excellent attendance during the summer, the principal's first question at the fall meeting: "What's happening to you fellows over at X—— High School this Year?" was met by six or seven shouts of "exclusions" (suspensions for absenteeism), indicating a return to habits of truancy.

3. *School performance in the year that followed.* Twenty-one of the 29 boys in the program completed the 1965–1966 school year. Two boys who were old enough to drop out of school and had planned to do so before the summer changed their minds and decided to return; both were non-middle-class Negroes. One working-class Negro boy joined the Marines, a deliberate decision in his case, since it was a means of escape from the gang leadership that had already brought him into serious difficulty with the police and that could not be evaded as long as he remained in the environment. Two white boys dropped out of school in the fall (although one of them was attending night school); both represented the seriously disturbed students that the program could not successfully treat in the symptomatic fashion that appears to have been effective with the non-middle-class Negroes. The other boys were for the most part too young to be confronted with this decision.

For the 21 boys who completed the 1965–1966 academic year, a general tendency to improved grades could be seen. For this group, the mean grade average as of June, 1965, just before the project started, was 0.868 (on a four-point scale, with failure equaling 0); by June of 1966 the mean grade average had risen to 1.296. This gain can be expressed also in the fact that the 21 had failed a total of 28 courses in the year preceding the project; in the year that followed they failed a total of 14 courses. Twelve of the 21 boys showed all the improvement, having a collective grade average rise from 0.625 to 1.548, and a reduction in numbers of courses failed from 22 to 5. Five boys essentially had the same grades as before. Four had worse grades, with a fall-off from a 1.19 average to 0.67 and an increase in flunked courses from 3 to 7. No control group was defined, although project personnel computed grade averages on a group of 13 boys who had been selected for the project but declined to participate, and found this group to be doing much more poorly by June, 1966.

Despite the net improvement in grades, it is apparent that a very rudimentary follow-up program that was held was insufficient to conserve and consolidate the gains of the summer. Although there was a net improvement in the grades of the boys who stayed in school, these grades did not rise far above the very low level of the preceding year; only one boy succeeded in attaining more than a D average.

The follow-up program consisted essentially in meeting with a school guidance counselor once a week. Some of the boys felt that after the project they received more attention and encouragement from their teachers than before. Also, there were four project events: two rather structured meetings in October and April, one unstructured meeting that both the staff and the boys found unsatisfactory in December, and a well-attended party in May.

Dramatic success was achieved by a white working-class boy whose grade average rose from 0.5 (i.e., D— or F+) to 3.25 (B+). An ex-Science Fair winner—sloppy and blimp-shaped, fascinated by the Skid Row derelicts and hillbillies among whom he searches for his vanished father—Y.Z. is not yet working at his full potential, but his progress is encouraging to the staff and observers of the summer school.

Disheartening, however, is the withdrawal from school of the two most intelligent and articulate Negro boys. Efforts to contact them have failed; sullen and embittered, they have disappeared into the ghetto that they resented and have perhaps made a fuller commitment to gang activities.

Some observations on variation among the boys in their performance during 1965–1966 may be taken as suggestive but not conclusive. Those who had shown the greatest changes in manifest behavior toward the staff—the working- and lower-class Negro boys—were also the ones whose 1965–1966 school record is least satisfactory. The whites and middle-class Negroes whose problems were more often defined as psychological by the staff and whose manner of speech and behavior changed relatively little appear to have completed the school year more successfully. The explanation of this apparent paradox lies primarily in the low level of the lower-class Negro boys' social skills; their ability and desire to converse with middle-class whites were so lacking that any improvement during the course of the summer was noticeable, often dramatic, and generally heartening to the staff. Most of the white and the middle-class Negro boys were more able and willing to interact with adults—that is, to respond in class and to make suitable small talk. Therefore improvement in this respect was less noticeable among them than among the lower-status boys. The process of establishing personal relationships with the higher-status boys resembled that of making friends with middle-class peers, a familiar experience to the staff; the corresponding process of gaining the trust of the lower-status boys contained novel and hence more memorable elements—a reduction of sullenness, the gradual dissipation of blank looks, and sizable increases in the volume of interaction.

Nevertheless, although the changes among the lower-status boys were the ones most easily observed by the staff, they took place in boys who had been cut off too long from contact with middle-class adults; the boys found too much difficulty in generalizing and transferring their new relationships to non-staff members—in particular to high school teachers in the following school year. Scholastic encouragement came at too late a stage and for too short a period to combat the influence of the gang. (Unfortunately for the project, in 1965–1966 the gangs of the area grew much stronger and gained many new—and often coerced—recruits; doubtless this unforeseen efflorescence of gangs diminished the successful impact of the project.) Of course, the very fact that there was any improvement *at all* (and in some cases, no change for the worse) for many of these boys may be taken as somewhat encouraging, for the usual trend in school performance for ghettoized Negro youths is a steady decline with increasing age. However, in the case of the lower-status boys the project was attempting to undo a lifetime of discouraging experiences and hence could achieve only particularistic trust and temporary friendships. For the other boys it was primarily trying to combat adolescent stubbornness and dejection—short-lived conditions that in part gave way to the staff's techniques.

SUMMARY

The changes that took place in both the staff and the students during the course of the summer have implications for organizations that have as their goal the resocialization of clients. The students were exposed to two types of instruction: that of a group with ideas and loyalties radically different from those of the typical secondary school (the TAs) and that of a group which could integrate the new experience of learning with the requirements and regulations of the school to which the students were to return (the teachers). The presence of an idealistic and self-confident group in the staff, the TAs, enabled the program to diverge from the boys' experience of school and hence to present a new view of learning to the students. The strong teachers, F. and B., and the principal reinforced the impression that the TAs made. While the TAs tried to communicate an enthusiasm for knowledge in a fairly close relationship, the teachers and the principal interacted with the boys in a context more nearly like that of the public school and thus helped the boys to translate what they learned from the TAs into the more conventional setting of the classroom. The weaker teachers were less able to integrate the innovations of teaching assistants, small class size, individualized instruction, and flexible scheduling with the more conventional format to which they were accustomed. As the boys were drawn into an educational enterprise, the TAs were forced to revise certain attitudes toward both the school system and the boys' culture.

The strength of this project, as well as its function as a model for other experiments, lies in its having two differing staff groups. Perhaps any resocialization program should contain both members who innovate dramatically and subject the clients to new experiences and others who function to reintroduce the clients to the society to which they must return by integrating the new experiences with the realities of the old society. Another implication is that the very innovative staff members may have to be replaced frequently as contact with the realities of the clients' culture and environment dulls their enthusiasm. This problem probably is heightened among nonprofessional workers.

Postscript: February, 1969

In the light of the spread of the Black Power movement and the rebellions in various cities, the author now questions the possibility of success for any project such as the one described here, namely, one carried out largely by a white middle-class staff and aimed at individual mobility through the school system. The refusal to return and accommodate to school—in short, the alienation—of the two brightest and most race-conscious ghetto youths in the project is given a broad and disturbing meaning by these recent events.

Nongrading in an Urban Slum School

Mary A. Queeley

My concern is the applicability of a specific organizational innovation in education, nongrading school children in depressed urban areas. More specifically, I shall be concerned with, first, examining the nongraded elementary school as an educational innovation having special relevance for the problems of mass education in the inner city, where a large portion of children are educationally handicapped in terms of the requisite skills and knowledge; second, analyzing the results of a study of an urban slum school in which a program based on the philosophy of nongrading was implemented; and third, discussing the implications of nongrading in the mass education environment of big-city school systems.

NONGRADING AS AN INNOVATION

"Nongrading" as well as "grading" refers to the instructional organization of the school. The two terms denote systems of organizing curriculum materials for the purpose of developing a body of knowledge and skills among pupils over the entirety or part of their formal educational career. A brief historical overview of the organizational nature of the public elementary school will serve to bring the contrasting organizational formats of grading and nongrading into sharper focus.

The organizational nature of the school springs from its attempt to implement its socially specified goals and functions, which include the transmission of social values and the teaching of academic skills. When a limited number of subjects were taught and only a small fraction of the population attended school, the one-room schoolhouse with teacher and pupils of varying ages sufficed. However, with an increase in the school population and a more complex and broader curriculum, an administrative apparatus had to be added to the teacher-pupil duo and a more elaborate technology evolved to respond to the increasing complexity of the school's functional task. The graded structure was one of the organizational responses to this situation. The addition of an administrative superstructure and a greater division of labor are two hallmarks of increasing bureaucratization, a process that usually occurs when an organization's major tasks become more complex and the number of people who use its services increases sharply. The graded structure was an example of the greater division of labor. Pupils were divided into manageable groups to facilitate teaching and learning.[1]

It seemed most efficient to put pupils of the same age together for instruction. Curriculum materials were divided in such a way that each grade had a course of study judged appropriate to the levels of physical and mental maturity of the children in that grade. The basic assumptions of such a structure were that there was relative uniformity in learning rates among pupils of a given age and that a given pupil of a certain age would show a uniformity in learning in various subject areas. The child moved through a succession of grades, learning the material designated for each grade level, until he completed the set. Successful completion of the material in one grade was rewarded by promotion to the next higher level. Failure to meet this criterion was punished by nonpromotion, a practice seen as providing a motivation for self-improvement.

Soon after the graded structure appeared in urban areas and before its introduction into rural areas, reservations were expressed about its efficacy.[2] This early discontent culminated in serious questioning of its value during the first part of the twentieth century. Criticism revolved around the high percentage of pupil retentions that grading produced and the lack of concern with the individual pupil it appeared to encourage. A growing body of literature at that time and since indicated several undesirable consequences of failure for the child emotionally, behaviorally, and academically. This research also indicated that the alleged function of failure—that it would act as a stimulant to motivation—was hardly fulfilled. These factors, coupled with developments in the philosophy of education and changes in views on child development, provided the major sources of disenchantment with the graded structure. The dissatisfaction generated in educational circles eventually resulted in rejection of the graded structure and experimentation with nongrading by some administrators.

[1] Charles E. Bidwell, "The School as a Formal Organization," in James G. March, ed., *Handbook of Organizations* (Chicago: Rand McNally, 1964), pp. 972–1022.
[2] John I. Goodlad and Robert H. Anderson, *The Nongraded Elementary School*, 2nd ed. rev. (New York: Harcourt, Brace and World, 1963), p. 49.

The Philosophy and Implementation of the Nongraded Structure

The first experimental nongraded structure appeared during the 1930's. Several modifications that had been made in the graded plan since its inception in 1848 contributed to the overall design of this structure.[3]

The nongraded structure and its various modified forms[4] pertain to the vertical organization of the school, focusing on the progress of a child through a body of knowledge. Such a structure is based on the principle of continuous development (or discontinuous development, as it similarly and even more appropriately might be known). Each child is allowed to progress through various subject areas at his own speed, as opposed to the lock-step orientation of the graded school, under which he is required to absorb a given body of knowledge within a specific period of time or suffer the penalty of failure. The underlying assumption of nongrading is that unequal and uneven intellectual as well as social and psychological development occurs among children and within any one child. Consequently, among children of a given age there will be much variety collectively and individually. Nongrading recognizes differential development, and as such it is a response to the inadequacy of the graded structure to do so. The graded structure's mortality rate, in the form of nonpromotion, has been of great concern because it has inflicted considerable harm on the students who have not met its requirements. By allowing the child to progress at his own rate without being subject to the rigid time schedule of the graded structure, the nongraded school holds promise of promoting better social and emotional health among its students and in so doing of stimulating better academic achievement.[5]

In practice, the nongraded school usually has involved (*a*) the removal of grade level designations;[6] (*b*) the grouping of children along some dimension, for example, reading ability, with regrouping for other subject areas as individual needs required; and (*c*) acceptance of the theory

[3] *Ibid.,* pp. 49–53.

[4] Several names have been used to designate plans based on the theory of continuous development and characterized by the absence of nonpromotion. I prefer the terms "nongraded structure" and "nongrading," because the former is the one used by Goodlad and Anderson, currently the major exponents of this form of organization. Their works serve as guidelines in the establishment of programs based on the theory of continuous development.

[5] Goodlad and Anderson, *op. cit.,* pp. 217–218.

[6] However, some plans that have incorporated the philosophy of nongrading have made other modifications, such as grouping several grades or ages in one classroom on the basis of pupils' levels of ability. The nongraded structure that I studied used this method.

of continuous development. Nonpromotion is no longer an applicable concept because of the absence of the time requirement in the learning process. Beyond these broad characteristics, the model of the nongraded structure is still not well defined, a fact that is substantiated by its variability in practice across the country.[7] Some plans that accept the philosophy of continuous development do not even go under the name of "nongrading." The nongraded structure is as variable as its many manifestations. Because of this fact, it is impossible to describe this type of structure or plan per se outside of the broad philosophical and organizational contours mentioned above.

An examination of the implementation of the nongraded structure that I observed in three large cities attested to this variability. The schools visited all subscribed to the general philosophy of nongrading; however, the names used to designate the plan, as well as the detail of implementation, varied not only from city to city but also within one city from school to school. The programs observed retained many of the organizational characteristics of the graded system. Levels, which represented smaller units than grades, usually replaced grades. In two cities, the traditional grade level designations were removed and the pupils were permitted to proceed as fast as they could through assigned curriculum materials. However, their progress usually was limited to the classroom to which they had been originally assigned. There was little evidence of flexibility in these schools.[8] Although lip service was continually given to the philosophy of continuous development, flexible measures to maximize and implement this philosophy were sorely lacking. In the third city, Chicago, where I did the study discussed later in this article, greater flexibility was seen.

Available Studies of Effects of Nongrading

Several handbooks, bulletins, and articles describing the nongraded plan in operation[9] have been written and distributed by schools and their staff members. In addition, some writers have conducted surveys among schools known to have implemented this plan. One such study, conducted by Goodlad and Anderson in 1960, indicated that schools reported higher achievement and fewer disciplinary problems among

---

[7] Goodlad and Anderson, *op. cit.*, pp. 217–218.

[8] For further discussion of the problem see Stuart E. Dean, "The Future of Nongraded Schools," in David W. Beggs III and Edward W. Buffie, eds., *Nongraded Schools in Action: Bold New Venture* (Bloomington, Ind.: Indiana University Press, 1967), pp. 11–119.

[9] See the bibliography titled "Nongraded School Organization," in Goodlad and Anderson, *op. cit.*, pp. 238–244.

the pupils as well as greater involvement and cooperation on the part of teachers since the institution of nongrading.[10]

Turning to relatively systematic researches involving control groups, we find rather inconclusive results. Some findings have been negative. Carbone compared two groups consisting of pupils in the fourth, fifth, or sixth grade. One group had attended a nongraded elementary school during the primary years, and the other group had attended graded schools during the same period. The groups were matched for age, sex, and IQ. In all areas of achievement, the graded pupils fared significantly better than the nongraded ones.[11] Other studies show little or no difference. Cocklin, comparing the achievement test results of children leaving an ungraded primary unit,[12] with a previous cohort from a graded structure, found little contrast between the two groups.[13] More recently Hopkins, Williamson, and Oldridge, in a research project in Los Angeles County, compared students completing their primary education in nongraded schools with those doing so in graded schools. No significant differences in reading achievement and attendance were found between the groups.[4]

More often, however, the results have been fairly supportive. In a Milwaukee study, children in graded and nongraded schools were compared in terms of achievement and personality adjustment. The results slightly favored the nongraded school.[15] In a study similar to Cocklin's, Bockrath found an "appreciable" improvement in the reading scores of the ungraded cohort.[16] Buffie's comparison of two groups of pupils in the third year of the primary grades, one from a school system employing the traditional graded organization and the other from a school

[10] Robert H. Anderson and John I. Goodlad, "Self-Appraisal in Nongraded Schools: A Study of Findings and Perceptions," *Elementary School Journal*, Vol. LXIII (February, 1962), pp. 261–269.

[11] R. F. Carbone, "Achievement, Mental Health and Instruction in Graded and Ungraded Elementary Schools," unpublished Ph.D. dissertation, Department of Education, University of Chicago, 1961.

[12] "Ungraded" is often used interchangeably with the term "nongraded."

[13] W. H. Cocklin, "A Study of an Ungraded Primary School," unpublished Ph.D. dissertation, University of Pennsylvania, 1950.

[14] Kenneth D. Hopkins, Malcolm L. Williamson, and O. A. Oldridge, "An Empirical Study of the Comparative Reading Achievement and Sociometric Status of Pupils in Ungraded and Graded Schools," paper presented at the AERA and IRA Convention, Chicago, 1963.

[15] "A Study of Primary School Organization and Regular Class Organization at Primary 6 and 3A in Eight Schools," Milwaukee Public Schools, 1952 (mimeographed).

[16] Sister M. Bernarda Bockrath, "An Evaluation of the Ungraded Primary as an Organizational Device for Improving Learning in St. Louis Archdiocesan Schools," unpublished Ph.D. dissertation, St. Louis University, 1958.

using the nongraded structure, favored the nongraded group in academic achievement and mental health, although not in a radically conclusive fashion.[17] Finally, in a three-year study by Hillson in Pennsylvania, kindergarten children in a school were randomly assigned to graded and nongraded classrooms, as were the teachers. In a "half-mark" evaluation the children in the nongraded classrooms showed significantly higher grade placement in reading and fewer "below-grade-level" reading scores than children in the graded classroom.[18]

Theoretically, the nongraded structure should allow a more realistic recognition of the special deficiencies in ability and the unevenness of learning of inner-city children.[19] Moreover, it should discourage the cumulative retardation, apathy, and alienation that so often result from the repeated experience of failure and nonpromotion. By allowing the child more time to learn basic academic skills thoroughly without the threat of nonpromotion, nongrading seems likely to deter many of the emotional barriers and undue pressures that inhibit learning. In so doing, it seems likely to stimulate better academic achievement in the intermediate grades, by which time many children in the inner city are hopelessly retarded and have resigned from active learning.

Teachers in inner-city schools are to be admired for some of their efforts. However, many of the teachers, like the pupils, have "given up." A sense of hopelessness, apathy, and alienation is characteristic of many. Stereotypic images of their pupils inhibit recognition of individual differences and deter teachers from capitalizing on the strong points of different children. The proponents of the nongraded structure have suggested that it encourages concern with the individual pupil and discourages evaluation of him solely in terms of grade level expectancy. This structure, allowing the pupil to progress as fast or as slowly as he needs to, demands flexible procedures to accommodate different rates of learning. If such procedures truly were implemented, the teacher would need to be sensitive to and knowledgeable about her pupils. Finally, the need for such sensitivity and knowledge on the part of the teacher in the nongraded structure might serve as an inroad into the negative stereotypes of pupils so prevalent among inner-city

---

[17] E. G. Buffie, "A Comparison of Mental Health and Academic Achievement: The Nongraded vs. the Graded School," unpublished Ph.D. dissertation, School of Education, Indiana University, 1962.

[18] Maurie Hillson et al., "A Controlled Experiment Evaluating the Effect of a Nongraded Organization on Pupil Achievement," January 11, 1963 (mimeographed).

[19] See the following for further discussion on this topic: Edward G. Buffie, "A Historical Perspective," pp. 21–23, and Stuart E. Dean, "The Future of Nongraded Schools," pp. 120–121, in Beggs and Buffie, op. cit.

teachers. Sensitivity and knowledge should enhance a teacher's understanding of the pupils and encourage an evaluation of them, not on
the basis of gross characteristics allegedly common to children in the
inner city but on the basis of individual need.

The foregoing comments serve only to highlight some of the ways
in which the implementation of the nongraded structure in inner-city
schools might alleviate some of their current problems. I am cognizant
of the great disparity that often exists between the ideally expected
and the actual result. Some of the problems of implementation from
which this disparity may spring will be discussed in the final section
of this paper.

A Study of Nongrading in the Slums

It is possible to make a preliminary assessment of the potential of
nongrading for the inner-city school through an examination of the results of an exploratory study that I made of two public elementary
schools in a depressed area of Chicago. I was able to gain access to
a school, which I will call School X, in which the principal, acting on
his own initiative, had led his staff in developing a nongraded program
for the primary grades. In addition, I was able to collect information
in a nearby school, School Y, which had the traditional graded structure
from which X had changed about two years before the study. Data
were collected from grades one to three in each school. The major dimensions along which the schools were compared were (a) achievement,
behavior, and attitudes of pupils; (b) instructional grouping and flexibility; (c) attitudes and behavior of teachers vis-à-vis pupils as well as
their participation in school activities; and (d) the principals' administrative style and the teachers' perceptions of the principals. The major
sources of data were (a) pupils' cumulative records; (b) questionnaires
completed by each teacher; (c) ratings scales of teachers' behaviors
and attitudes completed by the principals and the researcher; and (d)
extended observation of each principal and teacher by the researcher.

Problems of reliability and bias should be mentioned. The exploratory
nature of the research and the crudeness of some of the measures used
cause many of the findings to be couched in qualifications. However,
as much precaution against eliciting easy results was taken as the research context would permit. Both the principal and the researcher independently rated teachers, and before the analysis of field notes and
judgmental descriptions of teachers by their principals two independent
coders were used. In instances where disagreement existed and could
not be resolved, the data were not used.

Characteristics of the Community and Pupils

The Community. Both School X and School Y were located in the same community area, Woodlawn, on the South Side of Chicago, although in noncontiguous census tracts.[20] The community in which the two schools were located had experienced the traditional white-Negro transition about a decade before and had gone through some of the characteristic succeeding phases, such as extensive physical deterioration, high degree of social disorganization, and planning for urban renewal. The 1960 census reported that 89 per cent of the population was Negro.[21] The remaining 11 per cent was composed primarily of persons related to the University of Chicago, who lived in the northernmost tip of the area.

An overall view of the socioeconomic characteristics of the community is seen in Table 1, which compares them to those of the whole city. The figures in the table are self-explanatory. However, some additional facts bring the character of the community into sharper focus. If we look specifically at the eastern part of the community area, the section in which both of the research schools were located, the picture is even worse.[22] In 1960 30 per cent of the housing units in the eastern area were 70 or more years old and only 1.5 per cent of the housing had been built during the previous 20 years. Most of the structures were multiple-dwelling units, and 48 per cent contained 'ten or more living units. There were some single-family houses interspersed among the kitchenette and apartment buildings, rooming houses, and apartment hotels. A large proportion of the houses were in a dilapidated condition and were characterized by an overuse of families and comparatively high rentals for the condition of the buildings.[23]

Although the educational level of the residents of the community compared favorably with others in the Chicago area (20 per cent of the nonwhite adults, 25 years and older, had completed 4 years of high

[20] School X's attendance line boundaries were coextensive with those of the census tract in which it was located with the exception of one block on the north end of the tract. School Y's boundaries were wholly coextensive with those of the census tract in which it was located.
[21] Evelyn M. Kitagawa and Karl E. Taeuber (eds.), *Local Community Fact Book: Chicago Metropolitan Area, 1960* (Chicago: Chicago Community Inventory, University of Chicago, 1963), p. 98.
[22] Irving Spergel, "Selected Social Facts about Woodlawn," School of Social Service Administration, University of Chicago, November, 1962 (mimeographed.) This report is concerned only with the eastern part of the community area, in which both of the schools studied were located.
[23] *Ibid.*, p. 4.

Table 1   *Social and Economic Characteristics of Woodlawn and the City of Chicago as a Whole*

Characteristic	Woodlawn	City of Chicago
Housing		
Houses owner-occupied	8.8%	32.7%
Houses in substandard condition	30.0%	14.0%
Education		
Median number of years of school completed	9.9	10.0
Income		
Median family income in 1959	$4797	$6738
Unemployment		
Unemployment beneficiaries per 100 persons in the labor force	4.2	1.7
Occupation		
Professionals, technical workers, managers, officials	8.5%	18.4%
Clerical and sales workers	14.8	18.7
Craftsmen, foremen	11.2	21.3
Operatives	29.5	24.3
Private household workers⎫ Service workers ⎬ Laborers ⎭	36.0	17.3

Source: Evelyn M. Kitagawa and Karl E. Taeuber, eds., *Local Community Fact Book: Chicago Metropolitan Area, 1960* (Chicago: Chicago Community Inventory, University of Chicago, 1963).

school, which was not very different from the figure for all whites in Chicago),[24] the income levels showed a great disparity. Forty per cent of the nonwhite residents in the eastern section of the community area had median annual incomes of less than $4000, and almost one-third had incomes of less than $3000. The proportion of nonwhite men unemployed was 12.2 per cent. More than 22 per cent of all persons in this section were recipients of public welfare in May, 1962, in comparison to 7.7 per cent for the city of Chicago as a whole.[25]

[24] *Ibid.*, p. 2.
[25] Kitagawa and Taeuber, *op. cit.*, Table VI-6, p. 329.

Further indicators of social disorganization include the facts that separation and divorce were four times higher than for white adults in Chicago and almost one-third of the babies were born out of wedlock (1961).[26] The rate of delinquency (per 100 boys 12 to 16 years old) was approximately 25.0 per cent, as opposed to slightly more than 10.0 per cent for all of Chicago.[27] According to a report by Irving Spergel, the public and private social and welfare agencies were wholly inadequate for the population and problems of the area. Schools were overcrowded, although this problem has been considerably lessened as a result of the expanded school building program in the area. Recreational facilities lacked sufficient funds and were woefully understaffed.[28]

The composite picture of the community area, especially the eastern portion of it, that emerges is that of an inner-city slum teeming with a socioeconomically impoverished population whose environment is characterized by the most of the serious forms of social disorganization.

The Pupils. Table 2 presents a summary of the pupils' social background characteristics for which data were available in the school. It is apparent that the total school population on which the research was conducted was (*a*) one in which a substantial degree of migration had occurred, especially from the South; (*b*) one whose members' social class would primarily be designated as lower-lower;[29] (*c*) one in which a high degree of residential transiency had occurred; and (*d*) one in which there was a high percentage of school mobility.

The populations from the two schools are almost identical except in regard to socioeconomic status. School X's pupils are somewhat better

---

[26] Spergel, *op. cit.*, pp. 2–3.

[27] Kitagawa and Taeuber, *op. cit.*, Table VI-6, p. 329.

[28] Spergel, *op. cit.*, pp. 5–6.

[29] The information provided included the address and/or the name of the parents' place of business, the type of work the parent did, or the family's source of income if it came from a nonwork source, for example, Aid to Dependent Children (ADC), pension, or unemployment compensation. This information was missing, incomplete, or inadequate. In order to maximize use of the available data in spite of this situation a two-part code was devised. It consisted of what was called determinate and indeterminate information. "Determinate" information was that which allowed one to code the source of family income or the occupational status of the parent with a high degree of assurance. This type of data made possible a definite statement of the parent's occupation or a specific notation of "ADC," "veteran's pension," etc. The "indeterminate" code afforded the opportunity to make educated guesses about the source of family income. For instance, the name of the parent's place of employment was often given, and on the basis of our general knowledge of the type of business and of the type of jobs people in the neighborhood usually held, the probable occupation was inferred.

Table 2　*Social Characteristics of the Pupils*

Characteristic	School X	School Y	Total
1. Birthplace	$N = 381$	$N = 489$	$N = 870$
Chicago	76%	76%	76%
The South and border states	18	19	19
Elsewhere	7	4	5
2. Residential transiency (number of home			
addresses)	$N = 377$	$N = 484$	$N = 861$
1	46%	48%	47%
2	29	28	28
3	11	13	12
4 or more	14	12	13
3. School mobility (number of schools			
attended)	$N = 378$	$N = 485$	$N = 863$
Current school only	39%	49%	45%
1 other	34	19	26
2 others	13	18	16
3 others	8	8	8
4 or more others	7	5	6
4. Occupational status of parents	$N = 233$	$N = 364$	$N = 597$
Professional	4%	2%	3%
White collar, sales, civil service	14	7	10
Skilled	5	3	4
Semiskilled	10	10	10
Unskilled	36	30	33
Unemployed, pension	5	6	5
ADC	25	43	36

off socioeconomically than School Y's, a fact that threatens to confound our analysis. If the difference were of real importance to this analysis, however, we would expect to find correlated differences in intelligence test scores, because IQ scores usually have a significant relationship to social class level. As a result, School X's children should have an intelligence advantage. As we shall see, however, this was not the case.

The academic background and performance of the pupils are what might be expected on the basis of previous research and commentaries on children in depressed urban areas. Attendance in kindergarten occurs among the majority of the children, but, as Table 3 indicates, a rather substantial minority do not attend kindergarten. An examination of IQ scores, especially the summary measures of the mean and median, indicates that the largest portion of the research group falls within the normal range, although in the lower half of it, with much dispersion about the mean. It should be noted, however, that 70 per cent of the IQ scores on which these statistics were based were given at ages five and six. As the children became older, there were increasing proportions in the below 90 category.

Reading readiness tests are given at the end of kindergarten or during the first grade in order to determine whether or not a child is ready to begin the formal reading program. These tests assess the child's knowledge and awareness of written symbols and his discriminatory skills. Item 3 of Table 3 shows what data we were able to obtain from fragmentary evidence on readiness scores. If "average" is considered the cutoff point for deciding whether or not the child should start reading, we see that 50 per cent of the children were adjudged not ready to read at the time this test of basic skills was given.

Again the two populations are almost identical except on one charac-

Table 3 *Academic Background Characteristics of the Pupils*

Characteristic	School X	School Y	Total Group
1. Kindergarten	N = 337	N = 451	N = 788
Attended kindergarten	86%	89%	87%
Did not attend kindergarten	14	11	13
2. IQ[a]	N = 315	N = 416	N = 731
Less than 90	31%	19%	24%
Between 90 and 110	59	70	65
Over 110	10	11	10
Mean	95	98	96
Median	96	98	97
Standard deviation	16	9	14
3. Reading readiness[b]	N = 166	N = 323	N = 489
Average or above	49%	49%	49%
Below average	51	51	51

[a] Only Kuhlmann-Anderson test scores are used. The score on the most recent test was used for each pupil, regardless of the chronological age at which the test was taken. Source: F. Kuhlman and Rose G. Anderson, *Kuhlmann-Anderson Intelligence Tests*, 6th ed. (Princeton: Personnel Press, 1952).

[b] The reading readiness test used by School Y was *Metropolitan Readiness Tests*, by Gertrude A. Hildreth and Nellie L. Griffiths (Chicago: World Book Co., 1949). School X used *Lee-Clark Reading Readiness Tests*, by J. Murray Lee and Willis W. Clark (Los Angeles: California Test Bureau, 1951).

teristic. Here we see that School X, which seems to have a higher socio-economic background, strangely enough appears to have a somewhat lower IQ distribution than does School Y. This can be seen in the percentages with scores below 90—31 per cent at X against 19 per cent at Y.

The pupil populations can also be characterized by data on achievement and retentions. Tables 4 through 6 present this information for the merged populations of both schools only, as I will report the be-

Table 4 *Reading and Arithmetic Achievement as Rated by Teachers*

	Below Level	On Level	Above Level	N
Reading				
Total	68%	22	10	850[a]
Grade level				
1	56%	37	7	240
2	65%	21	14	319
3	80%	12	8	263
Arithmetic				
Total	36%	53	11	758[a]
Grade level				
1	32%	49	19	237
2	37%	59	4	250
3	38%	52	10	240

[a] Totals include a small number of fourth graders in the research group who are not included in the enumeration below the totals.

tween-school differences in these respects later as part of the comparative evaluation of the effects of nongrading.

Achievement in reading and arithmetic is indicated by proportion of pupils working "below," "on," or "above" their grade levels in the respective subject areas, according to teachers' ratings of each of their pupils. Table 4 shows, first, a very large amount of underachievement among the research group, with one-third working below level in arithmetic and two-thirds doing so in reading. Second, there is a definite increase in underachievement in reading as the children go on to higher grades. There is no such consistent pattern with regard to arithmetic, where roughly the majority seem to be working on level regardless of the grade.

Table 5 presents achievement test results for reading. The same pattern obtains as in Table 4. There is a decrease in the percentage of pupils performing at their grade level equivalent as the grade level placement increases.

The data on retentions (Table 6) indicate a substantial rate of failure. Slightly more than one in every four pupils had been retained at some time during their school career. Most of the retentions (78 per cent)

Table 5 *Performance on Standardized Reading Achievement Tests[a] (N = 685)*

Grade Level at Which Test Was Taken	Grade Level Equivalent of Performance[b]			
	1 (1.0–1.9)	2 (2.0–2.9)	3 (3.0–3.9)	4 (4.0)
1	88%	10	2	—
2	37%	47	12	4
3	14%	49	35	2

[a] Both schools used a variety of tests. The last test administered was the one used regardless of its name. The tests used included the following: Harold Bixler et al., *Metropolitan Achievement Tests*, Primary Batteries I and II (Chicago: World Book Co., 1959); Willis E. Pratt, Robert Young, and Miriam E. Wilt, *American School Achievement Tests* (Bloomington: Public School Publishing Co., 1955); Ernest W. Tiegs and Willis W. Clark, *California Achievement Tests: Upper Primary* (Los Angeles: California Test Bureau, 1957); and Truman Kelley et al., *Stanford Achievement Tests: Primary Battery* (Chicago: World Book Co., 1953).

[b] Grade level performance was interpreted in whole years; that is, if a child was in the second grade, as long as he performed somewhere between 2.0 and 2.9, he was considered to have obtained his grade level equivalent on the test.

had occurred at the beginning or the end of first grade. The majority of these children had been retained because they were judged not competent to deal with first-grade work. Information on attendance also indicates educational problems. Eighteen per cent of the pupils were missing school more than an average of one day a week.

Altogether, the data on the research populations attest to their low socioeconomic status and exposure to such unfavorable conditions as high degrees of residential transiency and school mobility, both of which are likely to be detrimental to academic performance. Such effects are seen in their performance on standardized tests of reading readiness and achievement, as well as in the levels at which they were actually reading. Overall, the data suggest that the two schools were relatively comparable. The substantial difference in occupational levels was not reflected in the pupils' intelligence scores.

Table 6   *Percentage Distribution of Retentions and Grade Levels of Retention Occurrence (N = 823; Pupils in Grades 1 to 3)*

	Percentage
Retention category	
Never retained	70%
1 retention	22
2 retentions	5
3 or more retentions	2
Grade level at which retention occurred	
Kindergarten or 1C[a]	54%
Grade 1	24
Grade 2	17
Grade 3	6

[a] Included in this category are pupils who went from kindergarten to 1C or who were placed in 1C upon their entry into school. 1C is a kind of extension of kindergarten into which the child is placed when, on the basis of testing or teacher judgment, he is not ready for the formal reading program of beginning first grade.

The Schools

In searching for a control school to compare with X, we found School Y to be a good choice because (*a*) it was in the same community area as X; (*b*) it was also a kindergarten-through-sixth-grade school; (*c*) impressionistically, it seemed to have a similar pupil population; (*d*) it had no experimental program in progress at the time; (*e*) it was not so large or complex as to be unwieldy to study; and (*f*) its administrator seemed receptive to our research.

The schools, however, presented contrasts with regard to several characteristics. School Y was much older and somewhat larger. This school was 57 years old, whereas School X was built and opened a little less than 3 years before the research was conducted. The older school had approximately one and one-half times as many teachers and pupils as the younger one. Specifically, School X had about 780 pupils and School Y about 1200. Furthermore, the teaching faculty at School Y had more professional experience. Slightly more than 60 per cent of its faculty had taught for more than 5 years, whereas only about 40 per cent of School X's teachers had more than 5 years' experience. Moreover, 56 per cent of School X's teachers had taught only in School X during their careers, while 21 per cent of School Y's teachers had taught only in their present school. Class size was on the average larger in School X than in School Y (38 and 34, respectively). Mr. Smith, principal at School Y, had been at his post for 4 years, and Mr. Jones, principal at School X, had been his school's administrator since it had opened 3 years previously.

Thus, the two schools presented strong contrasts in some important organizational characteristics, for example, size. In addition, they differed along such dimensions as teacher tenure and class size. On balance, the odds seem to have been weighted against School X. The effect of such differences is not known: however, their existence should be kept in mind in considering the findings.

The Nongraded Structure at School X

In view of the variability in the meaning of "nongrading," it is important to clarify just what the nongraded structure at School X was. The program at this school was referred to as the "multigraded developmental plan," and also occasionally as the "continuous development plan." It represented a modification of the nongraded structure in that grade level designations were maintained to some extent. However, it may be considered as a part of the tradition of nongrading in that the principal employed the assumptions and principles of the nongraded structure within the limits of the already existing graded structure of the larger school system.

The nongraded orientation was reflected in the threefold stated purpose of the multigraded development plan: (1) to provide continuity in skill areas; (2) to permit children to progress through skill areas at rates commensurate with their current levels of maturity, readiness, and achievement; and (3) to eliminate the need to retain children. The term "multigrading" was, for the most part, descriptive of the ostensible organization of the classrooms. In the multigraded structure there was usually more than one grade level in a given classroom (ordinarily two or three), for example, 1A, 2B, 2A, 3B. Within a classroom the children might be classified for instruction on as many as three different levels not necessarily analogous to their grade level designations in the graded structure.

Briefly, the implementation of this structure involved, first, classifying the children by their years of school experience and by reading achievement. Within these groupings children were grouped further on the basis of mental ability. They would be regrouped, if necessary, for arithmetic. If within a given classroom there was not a group appropriate to the child's level of achievement in some skill area, the child would be sent to another room for instruction in that area. Curriculum content in the areas of reading, arithmetic, and language arts was divided into a series of sequential units. A given child could proceed through the sequences at his own rate of speed. Frequent evaluation and high sensitivity to each child on the part of the teacher were sought. More frequent assessment of the pupil was built into the multigraded structure through regularly scheduled pupil evaluation meetings, at which teachers could request the transfer of a pupil into a more compatible grouping in another classroom. Nonpromotion was eliminated because it was no longer insisted that the child learn a given amount of information in a given period of time or be failed.

The major characteristics of this multigraded structure can be summarized as follows:

1. Flexibility in movement through curriculum sequences within the boundaries of a given classroom, as well as outside of the classroom if there was no intellectually compatible group in some subject area in the room to which the child was assigned.

2. Pupil evaluation sessions at regularly scheduled intervals.

3. Absence of nonpromotion in the traditional sense of requiring repetition of already learned as well as unlearned materials.

THE FINDINGS

An underlying assumption of the research was that the nongraded structure would have its effects on pupils mainly as it affected the teachers, principal, and instructional organization of the school. In assessing the effects of any innovation in an organization, we must be cognizant not only of its consequence for the organization's product—here, the pupil—but also for changes in the components of the organizational structure itself. The implementation of innovation involves change directly or indirectly in many parts of an organization other than those to which it is directed. For example, the innovation of nongrading was directed toward curriculum organization. However, the effects might extend far beyond this limited sphere and onto other prescribed and expected behaviors, attitudes, perceptions, relationships among personnel, linkages with other systems or agencies, etc.

The Teachers

For the child, the teacher is the personification of school. The administrative structure is reflected through her, and its directives are translated by her. Her attitudes, behavior, and skills are of paramount importance to the school's successful attainment of its social goals in any form of organization, graded or nongraded.

The cursory references to teachers in the research on nongrading suggest the existence of possible changes in these staff members with the implementation of this structure. Our expectations regarding differences between teachers in the graded and the nongraded structures stemmed from these references as well as our analysis of the nongraded format.

By providing the opportunity to make regularly scheduled adjustments in academic groupings and requiring frequent judgments about the progress of each pupil, the nongraded format at School X seemed likely to enhance the teacher's general level of knowledge about and sensitivity to her pupils. As a consequence, we also expected greater understanding and more positive perceptions and attitudes about her pupils in general. We expected this positive orientation on the part of the teacher to lead to more favorable treatment of her pupils and to encourage higher levels of teaching skills and knowledge about educational practices that would make for more appropriate academic grouping of pupils. Finally, the provision for more flexible interclassroom groupings and movement to enhance learning was likely to enlarge the teacher's general participation in what went on outside her classroom. In this respect, we hypothesized increased participation in meetings, greater willingness to share her classroom domain with others, and a better orientation to matters concerning pupils in informal conversations at lunch, before school, and at other times.

The sources of data included the observations made in the individual classrooms and around the school in general, short-answer questionnaires filled out by the teachers, and judgments of teacher behavior made by the principals and the observer. With respect to some dimensions, we had to rely on ratings that the principals gave their teachers.

Attitudes and Perceptions. There was little indication of differences between the two schools on ratings having to do with teachers' general attitudes and perception of their pupils. The results of the principals' descriptions and of rating scales that they checked were essentially identical for both schools. On a large list of items concerning teacher perceptions of pupils there were a few and relatively inconsistent differences between the schools. School X's teachers more often saw their pupils as coming from both middle-class homes and those receiving Aid to Dependent Children (ADC) and more frequently regarded them as "teachable," while School Y's teachers more often tended to see their pupils as having average IQ's and coming from education-oriented homes.

Knowledge about and Sensitivity to Pupils. Four measures were used to assess the knowledge about and sensitivity to their pupils on the part of the teachers in the two schools (Table 7). These measures were based on descriptions teachers gave of ten pupils selected randomly in each classroom, principals' ratings on the sensitivity of the teacher to her pupils, and observations made in classrooms and during conversa-

Table 7 *Teachers' Knowledge of and Sensitivity to Their Pupils*

	School X	School Y
Highly specific, intimate, concrete knowledge about particular pupils		
Percentage of teachers with such knowledge as indicated by descriptions given to interviewer about ten pupils selected randomly	53%	46%
Percentage of teachers with such knowledge as observed during day in classrooms and in conversation[a]	75	21
Sensitivity to individual differences among pupils		
Percentage with high sensitivity as rated by the principal[b]	50	50
Percentage with high sensitivity as observed during day in classroom[c]	100	79

[a] The observer attempted to transcribe notes on everything relevant that went on in the classroom or in conversations with the teacher. The field note protocols were coded by the observer and by an independent coder on various rating scales. In cases where differences in ratings between coders could not easily be reconciled, data on the particular classroom were excluded from the analysis. Here, the percentage refers to those with 3 or 4 on a four-point scale.

[b] The principal was asked to comment on each teacher's "sensitivity to her pupils, i.e., understanding their social, psychological, and academic problems, knowing the reasons for them, and her awareness of differences among her pupils." The percentage refers to those with 3 on a three-point scale.

[c] Coded as in footnote a, the percentage also being 3 or 4 on a four-point scale.

tions with teachers. In the case of the principals' ratings on sensitivity, the percentage of teachers rated high was the same in both schools, whereas for the teachers' descriptions of ten pupils the differences were in the expected direction but small. The remaining two measures were in accord with expectations. Substantially higher proportions of School X's teachers were considered to have specific, intimate, or concrete knowledge about particular pupils and to be highly sensitive to individual differences.

Treatment Accorded Pupils. Data on this dimension were derived from rating scales of teachers' characteristics completed by the principal and the observer. The attributes on which the teachers were rated appear in Table 8. Substantial differences between the two schools (using a criterion of 10 per cent) appear on three of the scales. The principals' ratings on the autocratic-democratic and the aloof-responsive scales strongly favor School Y, whereas the observer's ratings on the restricted-

Table 8   *Ratings of Treatment Teachers Accord Their Pupils*

Characteristic	Percentage with More Positive Rating[a]	
	School X	School Y
1. Autocratic-democratic		
Principal's rating	40%	60%
Observer's rating	44	53
2. Aloof-responsive		
Principal's rating	50	67
Observer's rating	56	53
3. Restricted-understanding		
Principal's rating	67	60
Observer's rating	78	53
4. Harsh-kindly		
Principal's rating	60	53
Observer's rating	78	53
5. Unhelpful-helpful		
Principal's rating	60	67
Observer's rating	78	73

[a] On the above characteristics teachers were rated on a scale from 1 (most negative) to 7 (most positive). The number shown is the percentage with ratings of 5 or higher.

understanding and harsh-kindly scales favor School X (although the differences are not substantial; the principal's ratings on these last two scales are in the same direction as the observer's).

Teaching Style and Skill. Both principals rated each teacher in his school on scales dealing with her teaching style—whether evading or responsible, erratic or steady, and uncertain or confident. In addition, the principals were asked to comment on each teacher's knowledge of educational practices and teaching materials. Field note protocols were examined for indications of an ostensible dependence on curriculum guides while teaching and the extent to which a teacher's academic subgrouping for instruction seemed appropriate in that the groups formed appeared to be relatively homogeneous. The results are shown in Table 9. On four of the six items there are substantial differences between the schools. Larger percentages of School X's teachers are seen

Table 9   *Ratings of Teaching Style and Skill*

Characteristic	Percentage with More Positive Ratings[a]	
	School X	School Y
1. Evading-responsible		
Principal's rating	70%	57%
Observer's rating	78	67
2. Erratic-steady		
Principal's rating	60	67
Observer's rating	78	64
3. Uncertain-confident		
Principal's rating	70	71
Observer's rating	78	64
4. Knowledge of educational practices and teaching materials		
(Principal's rating)	70	47
5. Independence of teaching guides (no ostensible dependence on guide while teaching)		
(Observer's judgment)	100	67
6. Appropriacy of academic groupings		
(Observer's judgment)	100	55

[a] On characteristics 1 to 3, the numbers are the percentages rated 5 to 7 on a seven-point scale; on characteristics 4 to 6, the numbers are the percentages having 3 on a three-point scale.

as being responsible, having a good knowledge of educational practices, grouping their pupils well, and being relatively independent of the curriculum guide while teaching. The findings on the other two dimensions are difficult to interpret because of the differences in direction between the observer's ratings and those of the principals. The observer's ratings both favor School X's teachers. Overall, the findings on teaching style and skill are in keeping with our expectations.

Relationships to Others. Principals rated teachers on their levels of participation in school meetings and on their general attitudes toward "sharing the classroom domain." In addition, the observer noted the extent to which the teachers utilized their informal contacts with their colleagues to talk about pupil-related topics rather than other items of conversation. Data are in Table 10. On the first scale, participation

Table 10   *Teachers' Relations to Others in the School*

Measure	Percentage with High Rating	
	School X	School Y
Participation in school meetings (Principal's rating)	60%	53%
Attitude toward sharing the classroom domain (Principal's rating)	70	53
Content of informal conversations (uses conversations to discuss pupils) (Observer's judgment)	64	55

in meetings, the difference is small but in the expected direction. On the second, regarding attitudes about sharing the classroom domain, more of School X's teachers (70 per cent) than those at School Y (53 per cent) were rated as willing to share. On the third measure, the content of informal conversation, it was found that the teachers talked primarily about pupils; this was true in 64 per cent of the conversations heard at School X, while the percentage at School Y was 55 per cent. Although the differences in two of the three items were less than 10 per cent, the findings were all in the expected direction.

The Principals

Data on the principals were limited. The major sources were a list of attributes on the teachers' questionnaire from which each respondent was to choose those descriptive of her principal, and field note protocols. The findings presented pertain to only two individuals. However, they are of some value in that they suggest some of the possible antecedents, concomitants, and consequences of the nongraded structure.

The responses to the questionnaire item regarding the principals indicated that the teachers at School Y more often saw their principal, Mr. Smith, as being (a) friendly, (b) fair, (c) relaxed, and (d) considerate of the opinions of others. Mr. Jones at School X was more often seen as (a) conscientious, (b) authoritarian, (c) helpful, (d) supportive, (e) familiar with curriculum materials, (f) overconcerned with administrative details, (g) placing an overemphasis on his own ideas, and (h) having ideas and a philosophy too far removed from the practical situation of the school.

Observations of both principals by the researcher lend support to the teachers' characterizations. Mr. Jones at School X consciously tried to implement the prescribed rules of administrative behavior in his daily interaction with his teachers. Moreover, he always made reference to the philosophical, psychological, and social ramifications of a given situation in an attempt to lift his teachers above the mundane problems and activities of their individual classrooms and to broaden their perspective. At times this concern with the philosophical was dysfunctional because its guidelines were not so easily translated to a real situation. In his role as innovator of the nongraded structure Mr. Jones was involved at every level of the educational process with regard to both curricular materials and teaching practices. He made conscious attempts to get each teacher to adopt and implement the program and its underlying philosophy. Moreover, his role as innovator required a critical orientation, and he carried on continual evaluation and assessment of the school's activities in light of the principles of nongrading. He was more critical of his teachers but also more sensitive to them as individuals. Rather than describing a given teacher as "good" or "bad," he usually called attention to her strong and weak points. Mr. Smith at School Y was more casual and spontaneous. His administrative style was more *laissez-faire* in that he relied to a greater extent upon the teacher's sense of professionalism than upon his direct intervention as a source of control over her actions. This was partially demonstrated by the oft-repeated positive comment by School Y's teachers that Mr. Smith "leaves you alone."

The fact that Mr. Jones was seen as more supportive, helpful, and familiar with curricular materials implies the existence of greater cooperation between the principal and teachers at School X on pupil matters. However, the teachers' perceptions of him as being authoritarian, overconcerned with administrative details, overemphasizing his own ideas, and having ideas and a philosophy too far removed from the practical situation of the school suggest some of the possible consequences of innovation in terms of the negative perceptions that teachers may have of an innovative administrator. Obviously, Mr. Jones's characteristics cannot be said to have resulted from nongrading. Instead they are probably antecedent variables and may, in some cases, be interpreted as characteristics important to an innovator.

Instructional Organization

The major proponents of the nongraded structure have continually stressed that such a plan refers to the vertical organization of the school (the movement of children from one grade to a higher one) and not to the horizontal organization, which focuses on subgrouping among children in a given grade. However, because of the stress on individualizing instruction and continuity in the learning process, we also expected greater flexibility in handling pupils horizontally in the nongraded school.

Data were collected on the number of subgroupings in reading and arithmetic that each teacher had within her class. Table 11 presents a summary of the findings in this respect. In teaching reading, no teacher in either school broke the classroom group into fewer than three sub-

Table 11   *Subgrouping Practices*

	Number of Teachers	
Number of Subgroups	School X	School Y
Reading[a]		
3	2	4
4	4	5
5	3	1
6	1	0
Arithmetic		
None	0	7
2	10	6
3	0	1

[a] Figures on School Y exclude third graders because School Y pupils at this level are grouped by classroom for reading instruction.

groups. Four of 10 teachers at School Y had no more than three groups, however, while only 2 of 10 at School X had this few. In contrast, only 1 of School Y's teachers had subgrouped to as many as five groups, whereas at School X 3 teachers had five groups and one had six. Findings on subgrouping for arithmetic are parallel. Half of the 14 teachers at School Y had no subgroups, while all 10 teachers at School X had two subgroups.

To measure flexibility, data were secured on the number of permanent interclassroom transfers and the number of interclass exchanges made for daily instruction during the semester. The findings derived from Table 12 meet with our expectations that the nongraded structure as implemented in School X was more flexible and responsive to individual differences among its pupils. Not only is there indication that a greater attempt was made in School X to place students in appropriate subgroups, even if doing so involved crossing the boundaries of the individual classroom, but also the involvement of a larger number of teachers in School X is indicated.

Table 12 *Flexibility: Number of Changes Made for More Compatible Academic Grouping[a]*

	School X	School Y
Number of permanent interclass transfers during the semester	27 (4 of 7 teachers involved)	17 (3 of 12 teachers involved)
Number of interclass exchanges for daily instruction	16 (7 of 10 teachers involved)	5 (5 of 12 teachers involved)

[a] Numbers of teachers vary according to whether the teachers returned the fact sheets and whether alternative sources of information were available. For the third graders in School Y, only exchanges for other than reading were considered because pupils at this level were all sent to homogeneously organized classrooms for reading.

Summary of Findings on Staff and Organization

The findings on the differences between the graded and the nongraded structures with regard to the teachers, principals, and instructional organization are, on the whole, in keeping with our expectations. On most measures the results of comparisons between the two schools were in the expected directions, although in some cases the differences were small. The smallness of the differences may possibly be explained by the fact that at the time of the study the nongraded plan had not had its full impact because of the shortness of the period in which it had been in operation.

The data suggest that the teachers at School X were more knowledgeable about and sensitive to their pupils. In addition, they seemed to talk more about their pupils in informal conversation, to participate to a greater extent in meetings, and to be more amenable to sharing their classroom domain with other members of the school staff. The differences with respect to the first two findings were in the expected direction but not greater than 10 per cent. On the various measures of teaching style and skill, larger percentages of X's teachers had more positive ratings. Little differences existed between the schools with regard to attitudes and perception of the teachers with respect to their pupils. The findings on treatment accorded pupils are uncertain. Teachers at School Y had higher ratings on the autocratic-democratic and the aloof-responsive scales that did not meet with our expectations. On one (unhelpful-helpful) of the three remaining scales, the observer's ratings favored School X and the principals' ratings School Y, and on the other two (restricted-understanding and harsh-kindly) both the observer's and the principals' ratings favored School X as expected.

As expected, there appeared to be more academic subgroupings for instruction at School X and greater flexibility in its instructional organization. The fragmentary findings on the teachers' perceptions of their principal imply somewhat more cooperation, although perhaps abrasively so, between teachers and administrator on pupil-related matters in School X.

Findings on Pupils

Comparisons between the pupils in the two schools deal not only with academic performance but also with behavior and attitudes. The latter two dimensions were included because of the stress laid on the potentiality of the nongraded structure in improving the social and emotional health of children. It has been suggested that this format, as such, may not directly affect the performance of children, but rather it may facilitate the attainment of conditions that are conducive to maximizing their academic potentialities.[30] From surveys conducted among schools implementing the nongraded plan and from miscellaneous comments distributed throughout the literature, the impression created is that the

[30] George Henderson, "Nongraded Education: A Practical Solution," *Negro Digest,* Vol. XV, No. 7 (May, 1966), pp. 17–23.

nongraded structure can reduce tension, anxiety, and other undesirable emotional symptoms among children, as well as behavioral and discipline problems.

Data on pupil classroom behavior and attitudes were gleaned from field note protocols based on classroom observation. An attempt was made to code these protocols, using ratings from negative to positive. The speci-

Table 13   *Pupils' Grades*

	Percentage Distribution of Grades	
Grade Category[a]	School X	School Y
Good	45%	43%
Fair	38	46
Poor	17	11
N	(325)	(480)

[a] In both schools pupils were given periodic evaluations for various subject areas in the form of letter grades on a report card. These letter grades were as follows: E, indicating excellent performance; G, good performance; F, fair performance; and U, unsatisfactory performance.

In addition to a grade for each subject, an overall scholarship grade was given that represented a summary grade or evaluation of the pupil's performance. For the purpose of analysis grades were divided into three categories: good, fair, and poor. Grades of E or G were considered "good," F, "fair," and U, "poor." In cases where an overall scholarship grade was not given, the grades for arithmetic and reading were used. Any combination of E and G for these two subject areas was considered as "good" and placed in that category; a combination of G and F in the "fair" category; and one of F and U in the "poor" category. Combinations of E and F were placed in the "good" category, and of G and U in the "fair" category.

fic dimensions included in the analysis were motivation, response to the teacher, work habits, and general classroom behavior. The findings were not in keeping with our expectations. There was little difference between the schools.

Academic performance was the major area of concern. A variety of measures was employed—scholarship grades, reading and arithmetic levels, and performance on standardized achievement tests. The measurement of this dimension was fraught with many difficulties stemming from a lack of uniformity as to the type of tests and the timing of their administration, as well as from the fact that the data on what levels of reading and arithmetic achievement the pupils had reached had to be collected at the end of the second semester of one academic year in School X, and at the end of the first semester of the following year in School Y. These limitations imposed by the research context must be borne in mind in an examination of the findings regarding academic performance.

Grades. Table 13 indicates that substantial differences in the grades given by the teachers to the pupils did not exist between the two schools.

Reading. One of the ways in which reading achievement was measured was by comparing the level of the book in which the child was reading with his grade placement in school. In this way, we could determine whether a child was working below, on, or above the level expected of one of his grade placement in the school. Table 14 presents a distribution for the pupils of both schools in terms of their levels of reading performance. The most significant finding is the patterns of change within each school, especially with respect to the first and second grades. Looking at these levels, one sees a reduction in the percentage below level in School X, contrasting with an increase in those below level in School Y. Among the third graders at School X there is a sharp increase in the below-level proportion. This negative trend at School X among the third graders might be attributable to their shorter and delayed exposure to the benefits of the nongraded structure. That is, they had been in the program for a shorter period and not from the first grade. The pattern observed in the first and second grades in the

Table 14 *Reading Levels (Percentage Distribution of Pupils Reading below, on, and above Grade Level Expectancy)*

	School X			School Y		
Performance	1	2	3	1	2	3
Below level	75%	66%	84%	41%	64%	77%
On level	21	24	16	50	19	9
Above level	5	10	0	9	17	14
N	(107)	(140)	(110)	(133)	(179)	(153)

two schools implies greater success in arresting and reversing retardation in the nongraded structure.

Arithmetic. Table 15 summarizes the findings on arithmetic performance, also ascertained by asking every teacher whether each of her pupils was working "below," "on," or "above" his grade level expectancy. Arithmetic achievement does not seem to be affected in any consistent fashion by nongrading.

Table 15 *Arithmetic Levels (Percentage Distribution of Pupils Working below, on, and above Grade Level Expectancy)*

	School X			School Y		
Grades	1	2	3	1	2	3
Below level	7%	20%	45%	52%	51%	30%
On level	63	79	50	38	43	54
Above level	31	1	4	10	6	5
N	(107)	(110)	(115)	(130)	(140)	(125)

Performance on Standardized Tests. Here we had great operational difficulties. The best set of comparable tests existed for 3A pupils, for throughout the city all schools were required to give tests at a specific point during the 3A semester. However, at the time the research was done all schools were not required to use the same test—and X employed the Stanford Achievement Test whereas Y preferred the Metropolitan battery.[31] Furthermore, as we have seen, third-grade measures are not the most appropriate because School X's pupils at this level had come into nongrading belatedly.

In any case, results on these tests can be compared, and they show (Table 16) somewhat less retardation at X than Y. The percentage below level is 61 at Y and 52 at X. Thus we see some advantage for the nongraded school.

Another analysis can be made using data from achievement tests taken by second and third graders in grade 2A. The complications that resulted from the facts that all pupils had not been tested and that all those tested had not taken the same test were ignored in an attempt to obtain

---

[31] The tests used were as follows: Truman L. Kelley et. al., *Stanford Achievement Tests: Elementary Battery* (Chicago: World Book Co., 1953) and Harold Bixler et al., *Metropolitan Achievement Tests: Elementary Battery* (Chicago: World Book Co., 1959).

some additional comparative measure. Findings are given in Table 17. These data also show the nongraded school in a better light, with a smaller percentage below level at X (27) than at Y (42).

Summary. The findings on the pupils do not provide a consistent picture that would indicate a superiority or lack of it for the nongraded

Table 16   *Results of 3A Achievement*
            Tests in Reading

Grade Level Score	School X	School Y
2.9 or below	52%	61%
3.0–3.4	30	21
3.5 or above	18	17
N	(71)	(70)

format. The assumption that classroom behavior and attitudes are important intervening variables between the nongraded structure and academic performance did not seem to be substantiated. However, in the comparison of both schools in terms of achievement, School X, the nongraded school, had a slight edge.

Table 17   *Reading Score Results on*
            All   Achievement   Tests
            Given to Second and Third
            Graders While They Were
            in 2A

Grade Level Score	School X	School Y
1.0–1.9	27%	42%
2.0–2.9	57	41
3.0 and above	15	18
N	(124)	(142)

The exploratory study does lend a degree of support to the hypothesis that the nongraded structure may have important relevance to the problems faced by schools in depressed urban areas. The findings indicated measurable gains resulting from the implementation of nongrading. The school with this structure (School X) seemed to show greater teacher knowledge and skills, wider participation in school activities on the part of the teachers, more flexible and differentiated instructional organization, and, tentatively, higher levels of pupil achievement than did the graded school (School Y). Little difference was found with respect to pupils' attitudes toward school and teachers' attitudes toward and perceptions of their pupils. The findings with regard to treatment accorded pupils were inconsistent and difficult to interpret.

In many instances differences between the schools, although in the expected direction, were small. However, it would seem unlikely that the innovation of nongrading would produce "revolutionary" changes because of the short time in which School X was exposed to this type of structure, the modest nature of the innovation, and the limitations imposed on its implementation by the larger school system. Further study of the potentials of nongrading in the slum school clearly is in order.

BROADER IMPLICATIONS

Beyond the findings which have been presented, the research implies some possible consequences and important considerations regarding the performance of the teacher's role in inner-city schools and the operation of nongrading in big-city school systems. Several problems inhibiting the implementation of nongrading may also be noted.

The discussion of the implications must be carried on in light of the changing nature of the population currently in public schools. In American society as a whole, there is increasing diversity among the children attending school, especially in terms of socioeconomic status and ability. This has resulted from changes that have taken place in the populations of central cities, in promotional policies, and in school-leaving requirements, as well as from a decrease in availability of jobs for youngsters who are not academically inclined. Although the school population has become more diverse, the schools in the inner city have grown increasingly homogeneous socioeconomically and racially. As poorer nonwhites and whites have crowded into these schools, the results have included a decline in academic performance, lower staff morale, and, currently, the search to use private and public monies for enrichment and compensatory education programs in such a way as to upgrade the academic performance of the pupils.

The graded structure, with its assumption of uniformity in learning rates, seems impractical for many middle-class pupils, let alone for lower-class pupils with insufficient preschool experience to satisfy the academic and some of the behavioral demands placed upon them in school. The undesirable consequences of the graded structure for nonwhite pupils, especially in depressed urban areas,[32] demand change.

Nongrading would seem to have special importance for the teacher-pupil relationship in the inner city. Because of some of the consequences of the social stratification system of the larger society, the attitudes, and their effects on teaching have been mentioned by several researchers and observed on more than one occasion during the present study. The enforced change in the behavior of some teachers necessitated by nongrading may eventuate in changed attitudes. Perhaps, then, the non-graded structure has even more important implications for the inner-city school than it might have for the middle-class one, in that it is one device whereby some of the unfavorable attitudes and consequent behavior of teachers may be eliminated or at least lessened as a result of the requirements of its format.

Analysis of the teacher's role along with my observations suggest some additional consequences for the task of teaching. The classroom teacher is subject to two systems of control with respect to her role performance, the bureaucratic and the professional. These systems conflict at points, a situation abetted by the nature of the teaching task—working alone in a classroom with students and free of interference with much autonomy on how subject matter is to be presented and taught. Lortie refers to this characteristic of one teaching task as the "autonomy-equality pattern."[33] This pattern is somewhat antithetical to the nature of the bureaucracy of which the teacher is also a part. Vagueness and disagreement regarding the goals of education and difficulty in developing adequate and workable criteria for evaluating teaching performance further complicate the operationalization of both systems of control.

Keeping in mind these problem areas in the teacher's role, let us return to the dual systems of control to which she is subject. As a member of a bureaucratic system, the teacher is required to perform certain tasks regardless of her job commitment or personal attitudes. Moreover, she may be subject to some surveillance to ensure adherence to these requirements. As a professional, the teacher is a member of a group with values and normative prescriptions, however rudimentary, that provide guidelines for the performance of her professional duties

[32] See, for example, the following: Alan Wilson, "Residential Segregation of Social Classes and Aspirations of High School Boys," *American Sociological Review,* Vol XXIV, pp. 836–845; and Robert J. Havighurst and Bernice L. Neugarten, *Education and Income,* 2nd ed. (Boston: Allyn & Bacon, 1962), pp. 154–155; Stuart E. Denn, "The Future of Nongraded Schools," in Beggs and Buffie, *op. cit.,* p. 121.

[33] Dan C. Lortie, "Craftsmen and Colleagueship: A Frame for the Investigation of Work Values among Public School Teachers," unpublished paper delivered at the annual meeting of the American Sociological Association, August, 1961.

and criteria (despite vagueness and confusion) for evaluating performance. She will subscribe to these norms and values with varying levels
of commitment. The autonomy-equality pattern discussed by Lortie may
be considered an aspect of the professional system of which the teacher
is a part. However, as he mentions, such a pattern is a two-edged
sword—rather than inducing commitment, it may encourage a loss of
dedication.[34] It gives the teacher the freedom to adapt to individual
learning situations and to perform her task as she thinks best. However,
it also frees her from outside pressures and allows her to fall short
of professional expectations with little fear for being discovered.

In an actual situation, the administrator may choose consciously or
unconsciously whether the bureaucratic or professional system of control
will predominate. School X and School Y present contrasts in this respect.
In School X the principal's involvement on the various levels of organizational activity from curricular materials to teaching practices had implications for the total amount of control that could be exercised over
the teaching staff and the amount of uniformity in role performance
that could be attained. The absence of many formal requirements and
Mr. Smith's *laissez-faire* administrative style at School Y caused heavier
reliance on the professional system of control. Less involvement on his
part in the various details of the teaching-learning transaction resulted
in less bureaucratic control over the uniformity in performance but
increased the possibility of creative solutions to problems on the part
of individual teachers. However, the poor and inexperienced teachers
with weak or underdeveloped professional controls were left alone to
do a less than adequate job.

The foregoing comments provide the background for my conclusion
that the two systems of social control to which the teacher is subject
need not be antagonistic but can be complementary. When the nongraded structure becomes a formal part of the bureaucratic structure
of a school, it enhances the performance of professional duties on the
part of the teacher. This structure has the potential for providing certain
controls at the bureaucratic level that in an alternative form of organization (the graded structure) might be considered within the scope of
professional controls. Moreover, nongrading as a part of the bureaucratic
system of control may even enhance or strengthen the professional system. In my study, the findings and my general observations showed
that the nongraded structure engendered less a change in the basic
practices of the school than a requirement and inducement to the teachers to live up to professional standards in being sensitive to their pupils'

---

[34] *Ibid.,* p. 20.

differences and progress. The requirement of the format and the operation of the nongraded structure served as stimuli to better professional
performance. Perhaps the nongraded structure is not likely to improve
the good teacher very much, although the flexibility it provides in the
larger school organization may ease pressures on her. However, it is
likely to encourage the mediocre teacher to do a substantially better
job.

Brown, in his discussion of the nongraded high school, feels that nongrading also entails changes in the function of the teacher in terms
of enlarging her skills, knowledge, and techniques.[35] Perhaps a more
correct way of indicating what Brown refers to as "function" would
be to say that nongraded structure can encourage professional development in terms of willingness to explore new teaching strategies for slow
and bright pupils, and to incorporate new areas of knowledge in the
traditional curriculum, especially for the bright child. As Brown puts
it, "Teachers must throw out the old knit bag."

A final consideration in the area of the teachers's role has to do with
communication among colleagues. Both Street[36] and Lortie[37] call attention to the problem of communication among teachers that occurs because they are solo practitioners and because their professional organizations are relatively passive compared with those in other fields.[38] Street
mentions that there is "little-on-the-job lateral communication and few
peer supports."[39] Nongrading at School X required more formal communication among teachers on pupil-related matters, and it also appeared to lead to greater informal communication on the same topics.
Such increase in communication would undoubtedly increase in-service
socialization among teachers, which is sorely lacking, as well as staff
morale and, possibly, professional commitment.[40]

Important practically in assessing any innovation is cost. Rogers has
concluded from the education diffusion studies that the best single predictor of innovativeness among schools is the educational cost per
pupil.[41] This need not continue to be the case. The development of

---

[35] Frank Brown, "The Nongraded High School," in John A. Dahl et al., (eds.),
Student, School and Society: Crosscurrents in Secondary Education (San Francisco:
Chandler Publishing Co., 1964), p. 156.
[36] David Street, "Public Education and Social Welfare," in Mayer N. Zald (ed.),
Organizing for Community Welfare (Chicago: Quadrangle Books, 1967).
[37] Lortie, *op. cit.*
[38] *Ibid.*, p. 2.
[39] Street, *op. cit.*, p. 81.
[40] *Ibid.*
[41] Everett M. Rogers, *Diffusion of Innovations* (New York: The Free Press, 1962),
p. 40

nongrading in School X required no additional expenditures. Similarly, Brown, describing his nongrading program at Melbourne High School, states, "Sweeping changes do take place in a nongraded school, and without an increase in budget."[42] The time of large grants from government and private organizations may pass, especially if resistance to sound evaluation continues. The serious problems of financing education in the inner city will continue.

PROBLEM AREAS

Finally, some of the important problem areas in the successful implementation of nongrading, particularly in the inner city, can be noted.

The Need for Explicit Formulation of the Nongraded Structure on the Operating Level of the Local School and the Larger School System

Mention has already been made of the fact that, aside from a few guidelines, the nongraded structure appears to be quite variable in practice. It would be wise if the major writers on the philosophy and general architecture of nongrading would suggest explicit operating procedures that would specify plans for implementing and maintaining it and would also suggest concrete ways to avoid the danger of merely cloaking the graded structure with new terminology. Several individual schools have prepared handbooks, written articles, etc., describing their particular nongraded plans. Perhaps what we need, however, is a series of major conferences among academic educators and local school practitioners to formulate explicit guidelines and to thrash out the problems that inevitably accompany the implementation and maintenance of nongrading.

Some school systems, including those in Chicago and St. Louis, have developed handbooks to facilitate the implementation of the nongraded structure. Even though this may appear to be a step in the right direction, "death by incorporation," as Street calls it, "may also result. . . . [New practices] . . . are so successful that they are 'phased out' to other schools or to the whole system, where they may operate without the special resources or careful understanding involved in the original effort or may become 'standard operating procedures' embodied in aging memoranda."[43] After what was considered the successful experience at School X, the Chicago system decided to implement nongrading very quickly

---

[42] Brown, *op. cit.*, p. 24.
[43] Street, *op. cit.*, p. 70.

all over the city, but has achieved very uneven results. A full and careful understanding of what was involved in the original effort seems to be called for if nongrading is to be implemented in more than a superficial way and is to overcome the tremendous attractiveness and administrative convenience of the graded structure and the strong habituation to it.

I have seen in both Chicago and St. Louis that rapid adoption on a system-wide basis has many unfortunate consequences that deter an adequate test or assessment of the possible relevance of the nongraded structure. The tendency is merely to superimpose the innovation on the existing structure without changing or discarding the latter and then implementing the former. In St. Louis, new terminology and some reorganization of graded structure were called nongrading. However, these represented a mere glamourizing of the traditional format with some of the concepts and strategies of the innovation. The rigidity and inflexibility in philosophy and practice of the traditional format remained to a large extent. In the case of Chicago, inadequate preparation of teachers and administrators make regression to traditional ways of thinking and acting very easy.

Rapid expansion of the nongraded structure results in uneven development and only superficial adoption of the requirements for the successful implementation of the plan.[44] Goodlad and Anderson, the major exponents of the nongraded structure, caution about such rapid adoption and about the dangers of lack of careful planning and implementation. Time is quite an important factor in the successful implementation of any program—time to understand, examine, plan, and then implement carefully and cautiously. The time lag required for adoption[45] is due not simply to the reluctance of people to try something new but also to the fact that the relative advantages of a given innovation must be carefully explained by a knowledgeable person to those who must implement the program, perceived as "better" and understood by those who will implement it, and given adequate time to displace its forerunner gradually and successfully. Moreover, the complexity of the innovation is all too often overlooked when it is implemented on a large scale. An attempt to simplify the innovation to facilitate adoption often dilutes it beyond recognition and increases the likelihood that it will not seem very different from its predecessor. The frequent reaction of teachers, "We've been doing this all the time," is indication of this problem.

[44] Robert J. Havighurst, *The Public Schools of Chicago* (Chicago: Board of Education of the City of Chicago, 1964), pp. 178 ff.
[45] Rogers, *op. cit.*, pp. 40–41.

The Importance of the Local School Administrator

I see the principal as being very crucial to successful implementation of any innovation. The teacher looks to him for day-to-day help, guidance, and knowledge in implementating an innovation on the classroom level. Beyond his knowledge of the central office handbooks and memoranda on the implementation and maintenance of the nongraded structure, the individual school principal must be well versed in the details of the new format. He must also be committed to at least giving it a fair test, whether or not he agrees with its basic assumptions and principles. If he is not so committed, chaos will result or the status quo will go undisturbed. In one of the Chicago schools that adopted the nongraded format in the flower of its popularity in the year after the research, teachers were confused about several details of its implementation as well as its principles, but the principal was unable to answer their questions. Such a situation hardly could be expected to contribute to the successful implementation of the program. By contrast, the principal at School X, the nongraded school studied, was thoroughly versed in the assumptions, principles, and details of the nongraded format. Although his teachers may have been dissatisfied with some aspects of the program, they nonetheless had a knowledgeable person on whom to rely.

Another consideration with respect to the principal deserves mention. He, as well as the other staff members in the school and the larger system, has to learn to withstand disruptions in the early days of implementation and to increase his tolerance for criticism. The principal must learn not only to withstand criticism from others but also to be self-critical. The principal at School X was continually assessing the program as instituted. His self-critical attitude was one of his salient characteristics, and one which the writer believes is very important to an innovator. His role, which is likely to entail interference with the traditional autonomy of the classroom teacher, may threaten the teachers. However, in developing an enlarged capacity for criticism the principal must realize that costs almost inevitably accompany gains.[46]

Individualization in Overcrowded Classrooms

The nongraded structure demands individualization in the learning process. In order to accomplish this, the teacher must have more than

---

[46] For further discussion of the importance of the principal see David W. Beggs III, "The Nongraded High School," pp. 67–70, and Roy A. Larmee, "A Strategy for the Development of Nongraded Schools," pp. 80–81, 88–89, in Beggs and Buffie, op. cit.

a superficial knowledge of her pupils. Extensive familiarity with each pupil is hardly possible now in many inner-city classrooms, where the pupil populations range from 35 to 40 children. It is incumbent on school adminstrators to do something about lowering the teacher-pupil ratio. Lowering this ratio should not be viewed as an end in itself, however, as was the case during my study in Chicago, where the top administrator indicated that this would solve all of the schools' problems. Such a step is only one of the many that must be taken in giving the nongraded plan a fair test.

The teacher-pupil ratio is tied to the supply of teachers, which currently is short. In this situation we must look for other devices requiring organizational flexibility. The traditional classroom organization may need to be questioned, especially in the primary school. Might it not be wise to consider the ratio of subject area to number of pupils, rather than teacher to number of pupils? What I am suggesting is that the number of pupils being instructed at any one time be dependent on the subject area taught, rather than determining across the board how many pupils one teacher has in all subject areas. The principal at School X used extra-service teachers to tutor slow pupils and to relieve teachers for in-service meetings, rather than assigning them to self-contained classrooms. Brown, in his discussion of the nongraded high school in Florida, mentions that an examination of the traditional classroom organization led to the realization that some subjects, such as typing, could be taught to larger classes than prevailed under the traditional organization, thereby freeing some teachers for subject areas that required smaller classes than the older format permitted.[47]

Residential Mobility of Inner-City Children

The study reported here, as well as many reports and publications, call attention to the high rate of transiency of children in schools in slum areas. Such mobility discourages continuity in the learning process and severely inhibits many efforts at motivation by a teacher. Often, as soon as the teacher gets to know a pupil and develops strategies for overcoming his learning difficulties, he bids her good-bye and is off to another school where some other teacher must start the process all over again. This problem is a source of frustration among many teachers in depressed urban areas.

Again, we need to look for creative solutions that require organizational flexibility. One possibility suggested by the experience of such large cities as New York and Chicago is that we have more flexible

[47] Brown, *op. cit.*, p. 150.

attendance boundaries. Often, although the moves of an inner-city pupil are only short ones, the new residence is outside the boundaries of the school he was attending.[48] Exceptions could be made. If the residential move was not too far from the original school, the pupil would be permitted to continue to attend it. Another possibility is a more highly developed central record-keeping system of pupils in a given school district. Records that include more than cold statistics on grades, performance on standardized achievement tests, date of birth, etc., would be necessary. A running summary of teachers' comments about the pupil with respect to special learning problems, teaching techniques that proved useful, etc., would be included, as well as a careful record of the child's working level in each subject. If this were done, the new teacher would have somewhere to start with the child. She would still have to wrestle with the problem of rapport, but even this might be facilitated by her knowledge of the records.

Need for Multiple and Simultaneous Actions

The vertical organization of his school is only one small segment in the total life-space of the child in the slum area. Any one innovation cannot be viewed as a panacea to problems stemming from several sources. Changes must also be made in areas other than the school's format to combat underachievement and retardation. The introduction of preschool nurseries may lessen some of the gaps in knowledge and skills so that the school can give greater attention to the not-so-basic skills. Still the need will remain to provide for differential rates of development, as is also the case in predominantly middle-class schools.

[48] See "Pupil Mobility and IQ Scores in the Urban Slum: A Policy Perspective," pp. 256–272 of this book.

Group Work for the Control of Behavior Problems in Secondary Schools

Rosemary C. Sarri and Robert D. Vinter

The public school presently confronts serious problems in the requirement that it educate all youth without regard to ability, interest, or prior preparation. Often it must do so with fewer resources than are believed essential for such an ambitious task. In the present ferment about public education the school is expected to perform new roles. There is general agreement that the school's primary goal is to prepare individuals to meet the knowledge and skill requirements for adult occupational roles. The public school is also expected to further its pupils' character development and preparation for responsible citizenship, and it is increasingly held responsible for aiding those who have been educationally disadvantaged by cultural, family, or community conditions. The emphasis on enhancing educational opportunities for all pupils has brought into greater focus certain problems within elementary and secondary schools. These include underachievement and academic failure among those believed to be intellectually capable, pupil misconduct that disrupts classroom procedures and school discipline, and the tendency of youths to drop out before high school graduation.

A variety of approaches are being developed and tested to resolve these problems. This paper will report our experience with one such approach—the use of group service methods, tested as a means of reducing malperforming behavior among junior and senior high school pupils.

Principal support for the project reported here was provided by a curriculum development grant from the Office of Juvenile Delinquency and Youth Development, U.S. Department of Health, Education, and Welfare in cooperation with the President's Committee on Juvenile Delinquency and Youth Development, and by a research grant from the National Institute of Mental Health, U.S. Public Health Service. The authors gratefully acknowledge the contributions of their faculty colleagues in this project: Maeda Galinsky, Frank Maple, and Walter Schafer.

The initial objectives of the project were (a) to modify pupil behavior that curtailed effective learning and/or was disruptive of classroom procedures; (b) to strengthen pupils' commitments to educational objectives and finishing school; and (c) to change or to propose modifications in school practices that hampered effective education for malperforming pupils. As the project progressed over a three-year period, it became apparent that school organization, curricular design, and staff behavior were even more important factors in malperformance than we had initially expected. As we shall note subsequently, these findings led to some modifications in our intervention approach.

THE PROBLEM IN PERSPECTIVE

The school must develop specialized procedures for pupils who are not adequately prepared, are insufficiently motivated, or are unresponsive to classroom behavior standards. Within limits the school seeks to increase pupils' motivation to achieve academically, to ameliorate personal and social stresses that circumscribe student learning, and to cope with behavior that jeopardizes classroom processes. Some of these efforts center on improvement of curriculum or teaching procedures; others include special services for pupils with particular problems, needs, or disabilities. Much available evidence suggests, of course, that there are still many defects within the educational system for which adequate solutions have not been devised. As a consequence some pupils, particularly lower-class youth, are especially handicapped by prevailing educational conditions and practices. Evidence also suggests that the school, because of its strategic role in the lives of youth, plays a less than optimal part in helping these youth to move into legitimate adult roles.

Increased demands upon public schools have produced crises in many school systems, particularly in the large cities. Problems include poor physical plants, pressures toward standardization, overcrowding, racial segregation, the lack of special or compensatory education for those most in need, and stable or decreasing economic resources in a period of increasing demand.[1] Students as well as parents are exerting pressures on the schools to provide improved educational opportunities and also to allow participation in decision making about curriculum, personnel, and practices. Demonstrations, boycotts, and other forms of protest, which have existed for several years at the college level, are increasingly

[1] Glen H. Elder, Jr., in "The Schooling of Outsiders," *Sociology of Education,* Vol. 39 (Fall, 1966), pp. 324–343, presents data from a study of a "continuation school" on the West Coast that is particularly relevant for this demonstration effort. He points to the importance of the public reputation of the school and the degree of articulation between it and meaningful adult vocational roles.

prevalent in junior and senior high schools. Responses by boards of education and school personnel have often been piecemeal and inadequate.

The changes required are substantial if the new demands are to be met even at a minimal level. In view of past stalemates and the lack of change, innovation strategies must pay attention to interrelated component parts and must include plans for phasing each of those parts into the on-going operations of the school. To achieve lasting and successful change it is probable that the strategy of "phasing in" may be as important as the substantive content of the change. In this particular demonstration-research project we attempted to consider both of these aspects of change.

CONCEPTIONS OF MALPERFORMANCE

Standards for academic achievement and for desirable conduct vary among schools and, to some extent, even within the same school. Therefore such types of malperformance as "underachievement," "poor classroom conduct," and "failure to adjust" are not identically defined, and aspects of pupil personality, performance, or ability at issue in one situation are not the same as those relevant in another.

Second, there are also many differences among schools in terms of their curricula, resources, teacher competencies, student bodies, and school organization. These variations produce wide differences in pupil learning environments, in opportunities for achievement or adjustment, and in conditions that shape the meaning of the school experience.

Third, significant differences exist among schools in their procedures for identifying and coping with pupil malperformance. In one school persons manifesting difficulty may become the targets for a full complement of remedial services. In another, pupils exhibiting similar behavior may encounter relative indifference or find that, when attention is given, the result is a loss of status or privileges, perhaps leading eventually to exclusion from classes and even suspension from the school.

Our theoretical framework for study of deviant behavior is similar to that of Cohen, Lemert, Friedson, and Erickson.[2] "Malperformance"

[2] See the following: Albert H. Cohen, *Deviance and Control* (Englewood Cliffs, N.J.: Prentice-Hall, 1966), pp. 1–48; Edwin Lemert, "Legal Commitment and Social Control," in *Human Deviance, Social Problems and Social Control* (Englewood Cliffs, N.J.: Prentice-Hall, 1967), pp. 67–71; Eliot Friedson, "Disability as Social Deviance" in Marvin Sussman, ed., *Sociology and Rehabilitation* (Washington: American Sociological Association, 1966), pp. 71–79; and Kai T. Erickson, "Notes on the Sociology of Deviance" in Howard Becker, ed., *The Other Side* (New York: Free Press, 1964), pp. 9–22.

is used to refer to behavior which violates valued norms in the school and/or community to the degree that, if it persists, will lead to assignment to a status having negative consequences for the person whose behavior is so defined. As Erickson suggests, these consequences may be of both a long- and a short-run nature:

> Deviance is not a property inherent in certain forms of behavior; it is a property conferred upon these forms by the audiences which directly witness them. The critical variable in the study of deviants, then, is a social audience rather than the individual actor, since it is the audience which eventually determines whether or not any episode of behavior or any class of episodes is labeled deviant.[3]

Pupil malperformance within this framework may be viewed as social or interactional in that it results from adverse interactions between characteristics of the student population and particular conditions of the school. Certain aspects of school organization and practice can contribute, often inadvertently and unwillingly, to the very problems they are designed to alleviate. For example, special classrooms for malperforming pupils serve to stigmatize these students and thus lead to informal discrimination or to foster organized stereotypical behavior. Thus any type of malperformance must be considered not as a unitary phenomenon, or as one inhering primarily in the attributes of the pupils, but rather as a result of the interaction between the school and the pupil.

Pupil difficulties are social in that they are manifested through the interaction with other pupils, with teachers, and with the academic tasks of the curriculum. These problems assume relevance as they are assessed in terms of the social objectives and values of school personnel. Such behaviors have their origin in and are currently shaped by the pupils' social relations and their experiences in the school and elsewhere. Once the pupil has been identified as a deviant, this social recognition may affect his identity and self-image in a variety of situations. It may induce him to seek compensatory approval through informal associations that support further deviancy. Finally, such identification has important implications for the manner in which the pupil is subsequently dealt with by the school, for the way in which his career is shaped, and ultimately for his life chances.[4] Thus we are concerned with the process of identification of malperformance and also with the ways in which malperforming pupils are managed within the school. With this knowledge it is

---

[3] Erickson, *ibid.*, p. 11.
[4] Aaron Cicourel and John I. Kitsuse, *The Educational Decision-Makers* (Indianapolis: Bobbs-Merrill, 1963).

possible to formulate strategies and approaches for coping with mal-performing pupils that will permit higher degrees of success vis-à-vis educational goals.

THE DESIGN FOR RESEARCH AND DEMONSTRATION

Preliminary investigations revealed that the reduction of malperformance was a complex phenomenon and that strategies for attack would require study of an intervention in many facets of organizational behavior. Four main areas for research were then delineated. The first was pupil characteristics, behaviors, and perspectives, assessed with particular reference to how these related to both educational achievement and malperformance. Second, in order to gain understanding of school organization and behavior, we studied curriculum design and the behavior and perspectives of teachers and other staff members, as well as organizational mechanisms for defining and coping with malperformance and for processing pupils into different curricular tracks. Third, study of the performance patterns of pupils over the three-year high school career provided us with opportunities to examine certain interactions between pupil characteristics and school practices. Lastly, we evaluated the processes and outcomes of group service methods.

Eight schools in five different communities were included in the major phases of the project. Contrasting communities were selected: a rural community with a kindergarten-through-high-school program housed on a single campus, a middle-class college town, a small industrial community, a residential suburb of a large metropolitan area, and an industrial community adjacent to a metropolitan area. Some of the school systems had initiated contact with the University of Michigan School of Social Work because of concerns about behavioral misconduct and underachievement.

Information from the U.S. Census and from local school censuses was used to ensure variation in school district and community characteristics. Although three elementary schools were included in parts of the study, greater attention was directed to the junior and senior high schools. The intervention strategy was designed primarily for males. Only two of the experimental groups were composed of girls, and therefore our generalizations for this population necessarily are very tentative.

Before a school was selected for inclusion, it was necessary that school officials agree to maintain the experimental service program as it was designed for a minimum of one academic year. In no case was this requirement difficult to meet, and arrangements were made whereby each school employed one or more social workers to provide the group service. These workers were assigned in each school as a part of its social work or special education program. The service program was conducted in each of the schools for more than two years, and since the termination of the project four of the five school systems have continued and expanded the effort.

In line with our interest in organizational change, it was believed essential that each school contribute to the development and support of the new program from the beginning. Far too often, innovations developed in demonstration projects are not adopted after the project ends, in part because special external resources are used to support the demonstration effort; little attention, if any, is given to assisting the organization to provide for the financial and other support of the endeavor.

Pupil Characteristics and Behavior

In all schools pupils were being identified and referred for underachievement and disruptive behavior; the introduction of group services apparently did not alter the schools' criteria for referral. Detailed information was collected about each pupil referred. Information obtained included grades, intelligence and performance test scores, family background, and school behavior reports. It was then possible to gain some understanding of the different kinds of pupils and behaviors "produced" by each school's distinctive organization and patterns. Later an attempt was made to systematize the selection of pupils receiving group service by use of standardized referral procedures for teachers, examination of school records, and observation of pupil behavior within the school setting by the research staff. Pupils were screened out whom the research staff judged as retarded, needing intensive psychological or psychiatric treatment, or so handicapped they could not participate in activities with their peers. This procedure was possible because many more pupils were referred than could be served in the groups. Systematic screening procedures were also helpful in identifying problematic conditions that were similar for many students. Although variations existed within and among the schools' systems with respect to the types of students referred for services, certain similarities emerged. Most students fell within the "average" range with respect to intellectual ability, but nearly all were "underachievers" relative to their capabilities. Most also manifested serious behavior problems, including disruptive conduct in the classroom or in other school areas; poor interpersonal relations with adults and peers; violation of school conduct norms, including frequent truancy and suspension; or withdrawn and isolative behaviors.

A control group design was employed in each school system to test the effectiveness of the group service strategy. Referred pupils were matched in pairs; one of each pair was then randomly assigned to the service groups, and the other became a "control" who received whatever attention was customary within each school *except* the group service. Another control group was randomly selected from the total population, excluding the referred malperformers, in appropriate grade levels. Matching procedures were slightly modified in one school because of service requirements during one year of the study. In the latter situation experimental and control groups were "matched" after selection. This modification was necessary because two natural peer groups were referred, and it was decided to provide service to these groups and then to select their controls.

The design of this study called for the use of a series of "before-and-after" measures, and comparisons between experimental groups and both matched and random control groups. It permitted us to identify outcomes that could be directly attributed to group work service rather than to pupil maturation or factors of chance. At the same time, the design allowed attitudinal and behavioral comparisons at a single point in time between malperforming pupils and a sample of the rest of the school population. During the second year of the project, data were collected on approximately 400 pupils in the service, matched control, and random groups, who were closely observed in the five school systems. Also, data were obtained on a slightly smaller number who were observed in the first year of the project. The demonstration phase took place between 1962 and 1965, with most of the data collection completed by 1964.

Three major sets of before-and-after measures were used to evaluate change. First, we developed an instrument to inventory teachers' assessments of pupil behavior in five areas—classroom conduct, academic motivation and performance, socioemotional state, teacher dependence, and personal behavior.[5] A second set of measures was composed of objective indices of school performance—grades, attendance records, and performance scores normally collected by the schools. The third set was derived from pupils' self-reports of behavior and attitudes. These were measured in interviews and written questionnaires. Dimensions studied included educational goals and expectations, academic and social skills, attitudes toward teachers, peers, and parents, and reports of school experiences. All of these data were collected on all pupils in the experimental and control groups and the random control group at the begin-

[5] Robert D. Vinter, Rosemary C. Sarri, Walter Schafer, and Darrel Vorwaller, *The Pupil Behavior Inventory: A Manual for Administration and Scoring* (Ann Arbor: Campus Publishers, 1966).

ning and the termination of service. Matched pairs were used to develop change score differences for the evaluation.

We also used the narrative records prepared by the group workers to evaluate change. This was done to see what practitioner behaviors were associated with pupil change. These records were analyzed with reference to targets of change, means of influence, and modes of interaction.

The before-and-after measures of pupil change served as the primary means for evaluating the modifications effected by group services. Means for assessment of the processes of change included systematic review of the practitioners' service records, independent interviewing of treatment groups in special group sessions, and direct consultation with service personnel. Practitioners were requested to obtain and record specific information about pupils during the period of treatment. With such information it was possible to assess elements of group processes and thereby to identify some of the key factors in change. This particular phase of the design was important because we were concerned with gaining somewhat greater knowledge about processes of change. Far too often evaluative studies of treatment programs have measured only outcomes, with processes of change remaining unknown or unidentified. Some members of the research staff served as consultants to school personnel actually working with the groups. Planning and problem solving conferences were held every six weeks with the practitioners to explore service procedures and examine preliminary study findings. Practitioners also undertook study and validation of project materials such as the practitioners' manual.

School Organization and Practices

This area of study involved school conditions and practices, including school size, staffing, and resources; school goals; curriculum design; grading criteria; means of identifying, labeling, and handling misconduct and malperformance; classroom practices; and teachers' orientations and perspectives. These dimensions were assessed through several procedures: directly observing classroom and other activities in the school; reviewing documentary and file materials; interviewing school administrators, teachers, and special service personnel; and administering questionnaires to all professional personnel in the sample schools. In addition, we made extended observations of the daily cycle of school activities; of board, faculty, and committee meetings; and of informal activities among pupils and teachers.

Data feedback sessions were held periodically with school administrators during the latter phase of the study. These sessions provided us with additional information about school practices and, in particular, about executive behavior. Continued observation of the several schools permitted us to gain some knowledge of planned organizational changes as attempts were made to implement some of the recommendations from the study. Unfortunately, the project ended before many of these changes were developed to the point where they could be assessed adequately.

Pupil Careers

Study of pupil careers over a three-year period was completed in two of the senior high schools. Here we were interested in identifying factors associated with curriculum placement, performance patterns including grades and test scores, and length of career. Grading practices were systematically analyzed. Other reward systems were also examined, although more superficially.

To accomplish the study of career patterns all pupils were identified who entered the tenth grade in the fall of 1961 in the two schools. This cohort was followed through the spring of 1964, when the majority completed the twelfth grade. Data abstracted from official files included grades, semester of and reason for leaving for those who did not continue, curriculum and curriculum changes for each pupil, intelligence and performance test scores, sex, race, father's occupation, and extracurricular participation.

Group Services

The initial intervention strategy, group services for malperforming pupils, was utilized in seven of the sample schools. Prospective group members were interviewed by the school social workers to review school difficulties, to explain why each had been selected for service and what would happen in the group, and to establish an initial "contract" for work together on specific problems. Workers frequently encountered resistance and skepticism in these interviews. Pupils often had had negative experiences in the school and frequently were doubtful that the school was really interested in helping them or in altering conditions that affected them adversely. The example of Bob White, a fifteen-year-old entering the tenth grade, is illustrative of initial contacts. The social worker reported:

> Bob was referred by his ninth-grade counselor for underachievement, rule breaking, and disruptive classroom behavior. He was on probation in the juvenile court for auto theft and stealing from a bowling alley. The counselor described him as one who elicited both adult and peer rejection. In the initial interview Bob expressed

a desire to work on some of his problems. He was negative about his probation experience but did reveal some understanding about his situation and school achievement. He agreed to give the group experience a try but wasn't optimistic about his future.

We will briefly describe the group work intervention. A set of principles for school practitioners who wish to employ this method of intervention was prepared in conjunction with the project.[6] Groups were typically composed of five to eight members identical in sex and grade level. Sessions were held one or more times a week during school hours and in the school buildings. Additional sessions were arranged for after-school hours in accordance with workers' plans and at the request of group members. The group sessions were the primary means through which changes were attempted, although individual services were provided as necessary, by the same worker who conducted the group sessions whenever possible.

Within the groups explicit public recognition was given to each pupil's difficulties and to the need for mutual assistance in resolving them. Emphasis was placed on mobilizing pupils' motivations to change toward improved academic achievement and appropriate conduct in the school. Workers deliberately sought to increase members' attraction to the group and to school, and they sought to help the students develop new skills and alternative methods for coping more effectively with stressful school situations. It was assumed that one of the special advantages of working with such pupils in groups is that powerful social forces can be developed to support the changes desired rather than covertly to encourage continued deviance.

We noted, as have many others, that pupils identified as underachieving and disruptive tended to seek each other out and to form associations that reinforce deviancy. A boy in one of the groups explained this tendency in these words:

> It depends on who you hang around with. Some guys' idea of fun is to see who gets the lowest grades, skipping school, classes, smoking in the bathroom. I started hanging around with guys like that. . . . The only reason me or anyone else did things like skip school was to make an impression on your friends. They'd think you're chicken otherwise. I feel if you can't get good grades, then brag about getting away with it.

[6] Rosemary C. Sarri, Robert D. Vinter, and Esther Goodman, *Group Work in the Schools: A Practitioner's Manual*, unpublished document, The University of Michigan, Ann Arbor, 1965.

In the sessions, the importance of general primary targets of change became apparent: specific academic skills and abilities, skills of social interaction with teacher and peers, and pupils' values, goals, and motivations. We frequently observed that the means and opportunities for successful performance were insufficiently or inaccurately perceived by malperformers. They were deficient in academic skills, some of which could be improved within the group (e.g., study habits, efficient use of time, or test preparation), and in readiness for successful interaction with teachers and other school personnel. We soon recognized that the social skills were particularly amenable to influence in the group sessions. Pupils' values, goals, and motivations often contradicted those supported by the school and were frequently the outcome of prior failures that resulted in pessimism and negativism toward school.

The workers often observed that legitimate opportunities for malperforming students were more limited than was equitable. In such cases, they intervened on behalf of the pupils with other school personnel. The views of one tenth-grader were typical of malperformers' perceptions of their situation:

> If Mr. Owen [the principal] had believed I was not the one who provoked fights, he would not have kicked me out for 3 days. Maybe kids like me won't get too far because of our actions in school, and we don't get good grades. He didn't seem interested in helping—kicks kids out real easy. Seems like he's looking for some of us kids to be doing something . . . .
>
> Should lower standards about getting on teams—lots of times you can't get high enough grades even if you try hard. Am not doing as good as I wanted to regarding grades—wanted to get into wrestling, but in the first marking period grades dropped, came up second period but not high enough and I had been trying real hard. I don't think it's fair—if you try hard enough should be able to get a good enough grade to do what you want to do. Don't know why got these grades—studied harder for tests but still dropped down . . . .
>
> (Regarding same chances as other kids of getting good grades) No—long ago I might have. At Carr School I don't think they taught kids half as much as other schools did because when us Carr kids got to junior high other kids were twice as smart as us—due to bad teaching at Carr.

Activities of the groups were largely determined by the goals set by workers and members together. Problem-focused discussion predominated, but all groups engaged in other activities as well. Groups with younger members tended to use discussion techniques less frequently. To teach new academic and social skills the workers employed simulation techniques and other procedures designed to improve study habits and test preparation and to increase ability to request assistance from teachers, obtain help from classmates, and complete assignments. Pupils were coached or coached each other in test taking, report writing, and the like. The workers recognized that each of these acts was a complex behavior that subsumed several specific skills. Where possible, attempts were made to define these skills so that generalizations could be made to other situations in and out of school.

Workers also became aware that the pupils' opinions about school materials and procedures had to be considered. Pupils often commented that required textbooks were dull and failed to "turn them on." For example, a twelve-year-old boy said, "Who wants to read *Elmer the Worm*—about a worm who talks to a boy?" To encourage malperformers to join the mainstream of school life and to associate with others beyond themselves, workers attempted to encourage and facilitate their participation in extracurricular activities.

The social workers made deliberate attempts to create cohesive and viable groups, but explicitly pointed out to the members that these groups were to be instrumental to individual change. In a few cases where the groups were oriented more to cohesion, problems were aggravated and few change goals were achieved. Changing the memberships of the groups, however, usually was effective in such cases.

In our estimate, the workers were able to guide the development of the groups to create desirable change conditions. In similar demonstration projects it has been reported that workers relied almost exlusively on the peer group and de-emphasized their own roles.[7] We did not find this to work successfully. Workers tended to be more effective, in our observations and evaluations, when they carefully structured the program of the group, using a variety of direct and indirect means of influence. The adult exemplified the roles he wished to have the members adopt even though he indicated his acceptance of the problematic situations of the pupils. It appeared that a climate was created in which members felt free to discuss and explore problems without fear of ridicule or rejection. They then were encouraged to try out new patterns of behavior in the group before displaying them outside.

Although most pupils seemed to perceive the groups as rewarding and satisfying, they were continuously aware of the serious purposes

[7] See, for example, Lloyd McCorkle, *The Highfields Story* (New York: Henry Holt, 1958).

of this experience and its relevance to school performance. In part this was accomplished by encouraging pupils to report incidents and difficulties they were currently experiencing in the school—and for most students there was no lack of such reports. The worker then involved the group in jointly exploring the situation, in considering cause-and-effect sequences, and in discovering more appropriate responses that pupils might have made. Because all pupils had witnessed or been involved in similar incidents, they were very effective in curbing each other's tendencies toward denial or projection and in proposing alternative ways for coping with situations.

Despite the positive learnings about the intervention strategy, critical limitations were also exposed. The school social workers soon discovered that many problems could not be successfully resolved by changing the individual pupil's behavior or attributes. School conditions hampered the attainment of desired change goals such as improvement in grades, increased participation in extracurricular activities, and reduction in dropping out. Malperforming pupils could not be helped when they were isolated or abstracted from the context of school events. The practitioners needed to have knowledge of curriculum, of teachers and their practices, of classroom climates, and of general school conditions in order to understand the particular circumstances that contributed to each pupil's problems. In addition to providing direct services to groups and individuals, the school social workers had to function as "mediators" and as consultants to teachers and other school personnel about the experiences and difficulties of particular pupils and of the malperformers in general. They also served as lobbyists in and out of school on behalf of malperformers, and they negotiated with families and agencies in the community.[8]

STUDY FINDINGS

Effects of the Demonstration

The results of the intervention were partially disappointing. Findings from the effort were evaluated at the end of each of the two years that it ran. The results after the first year indicated that there were no significant changes between the experimental and control groups

---

[8] Most of the social workers affiliated with the demonstration project engaged in each of these activities at one time or another, but among the different schools variations in emphasis were apparent. Apart from the direct work with service groups no attempt was made by the project staff to achieve uniformity in role patterns among the school social workers.

in grades received, absences, truancies and suspensions, or leaving school. Similarly, minimal change was observed for the random groups selected from the total population. One instrument, the Pupil Behavior Inventory, showed some positive change for the experimental group. This instrument will be described subsequently. It was designed to obtain teachers' ratings of pupil behaviors before and after the service program.

In attempting to understand what had happened, it became apparent that we needed systematic and detailed information about school practices and conditions. Procedures were then developed to study pupil career patterns, curricular design, teachers' perceptions and behaviors, and mechanisms for identifying and coping with various forms of deviancy in the school. We will now discuss these findings and report how they were used to modify the strategy for reducing pupil malperformance.

Characteristics, Perspectives, and Behavior of Malperformers and Randoms

Intensive study of the pupils referred in each school provided new insights. Data in this section are presented for the sample of malperformers identified in their schools as pupils who needed additional attention because of behavioral misconduct and/or underachievement relative to their ability. These data are compared with similar findings for the random sample (referred to hereafter as "randoms") of pupils selected from the total population of each school, malperformers excluded.

It can be observed in Table 1 that there were marked differences in overall grade point average and in numbers of absences between the two groups. No difference in mean IQ test score was noted, however. Below-average academic performance therefore must stem from factors other than deficiency in intellectual ability. The important findings can be summarized in five generalizations.

1. *Malperformers placed as great importance as randoms on achievement and success in school, as well as on long-term goals relating to employment and success in future life.* It is frequently asserted by school personnel that malperformers are not committed to educational goals and are not interested in school. Contrary to these beliefs, the data in Table 2 indicate that malperformers continue to maintain a basic commitment to succeeding in school and that they value educational goals even when experiencing personal failure. Because none of the differences between malperformers and randoms was statistically significant at the .02 level, it can be inferred that the two groups are alike in these basic attitudes.

Table 1   *Achievement, IQ, and Attendence Records of Malperformers and Randoms*

Grade point average, first semester of tenth grade
  Malperformers   1.84
  Randoms   2.63

Mean IQ
  Malperformers   107
  Randoms   107

Average number of single-period absences for year

	Excused	Unexcused	Total
Malperformers	3.9	2.4	6.3
Randoms	1.5	0.9	2.4

Average number of whole-day absences for year

	Excused	Unexcused	Total
Malperformers	11.5	1.3	12.8
Randoms	4.9	0.2	5.1

Although data were not obtained directly from parents about their attitudes and values, boys were asked what their parents thought about school and their school performance. Parents of both groups were reported as being strongly opposed to their sons dropping out of school (Table 3). Furthermore, malperformers reported much more often that their parents viewed their school performance as falling below parental expectations. Thus, the academic problems experienced by these pupils were not the simple outcome of a lack of interest in school, intellectual ability, or parental concern.

Table 2   *Pupils' Attitudes toward Educational Goals and Community Norms*

Percentage Saying Item Is Important	Malperformers	Randoms
Passing courses	76%	89%
Getting the most from school	57	68
Getting along with teachers	40	47
Going to college	67	70
Having a well-paying job when you are an adult	76	70
Having a steady job when you are an adult	92	94

Table 3   *Reported Attitudes of Parents toward School*

Percentage Reporting That:	Malperformers	Randoms	Level of Significance
Parents are against dropping out[a]	90%	98%	N.S.
School performance is below parents' expectations[b]	84	28	< .001

[a] "What do parents think about kids dropping out of school?"
[b] "How are you doing in your school work as compared with what your parents expect?"

2. *Malperformers engaged in a number of unacceptable activities more often than randoms. These were truancy, tardiness, leaving class, fighting, and being sent to the office.* Although malperformers were interested in and committed to educational goals, they reported that they did not put the same effort into school work as did the randoms. The findings in Table 4 reveal significant differences between malperformers and randoms regarding the violation of school norms. The former reported that they frequently engaged in a number of unacceptable activities, such as truancy, tardiness, fighting, and skipping school, and they often created trouble for teachers in their classrooms. Over a period of time, they increasingly failed to conform to school standards of conduct.[9]

Whatever the psychological mechanisms involved, malperformers seemed to devalue many school norms and standards of conduct. This

Table 4   *Pupils' Behaviors in School[a]*

Percentage Reporting:	Malperformers	Randoms	Level of Significance
Staying home when you could have come to school	57%	28%	< .02
Being late for class	80	54	< .01
Leaving class without a good reason	38	13	< .01
Getting into a fight	35	9	< .01
Being sent to the office	37	11	< .01

[a] "In the past two months how many times have you done each of the following things?" Figures are percentages of each group responding "1 or more times."

[9] The candor and truthfulness of the malperformers' self-reports, as measured in these and other areas and validated by school records, lent credence to their statements about their own and parental attitudes.

pattern may represent the gradual development of a general negative orientation toward the school as a crucial source of frustration and disenchantment. Of course, deviant behavior itself decreases the likelihood of achieving at a high level because of negative teacher reactions and falling further behind in class work as suspensions and other sanctions are imposed. In turn, low achievers may "try less hard" and thus get into further trouble. They also are likely to turn toward other boys in similar difficulty as referents in support of antischool attitudes and behavior.

3. *Marked differences between malperformers and randoms were noted in "acquired capabilites" such as study habits, in classroom conduct, and in perceptions of relationships with teachers.*

Malperfomers more frequently stated that they did not try as hard, lacked study skills, failed to complete assignments, and found it difficult to ask teachers for help. Table 5 reveals consistent and large differences

Table 5   *Pupils' Reports of Study and Classroom Habits*

Percentage Reporting That:	Malperformers	Randoms	Level of Significance
I try as hard as most other students in my class to do well in school work.	40%	77%	< .001
I can't seem to read as well as most other kids in my class.	34	42	N.S.
I don't seem to get very much done when I study.	56	28	< .01
I find it hard to keep my mind on school work.	78	57	< .05
I can't seem to remember much of what I have studied.	60	30	< .01
It's hard for me to sit still for very long in classes.	55	34	< .05
I fail to complete homework assignments once a week or more.	72	49	< .01
When schoolwork is hard, I ask teachers for help.	31	58	< .01
I ask friends for help when school is hard.	27	55	< .01
The way I do in school isn't much to be proud of.	59	32	< .01
I try as hard as most other students to do well in my schoolwork.	40	76	< .01

between the two groups of pupils in reports of their own behavior. Perceptions of teachers as unfriendly and not helpful seemed to be the result of repeated failure or continued difficulty in handling relationships with teachers. The findings in Table 6 are illustrative of the malperformers' reports of their views of teachers. Malperformers also were likely to report lower degrees of self-confidence and self-control in their transactions with teachers. Often they responded impulsively and aggressively to requests and to difficult situations.

Table 6 *Pupils' Perception of Teachers*

Percentage Agreeing That:	Malperformers	Randoms	Level of Significance
Most of the teachers at this school are friendly.	69%	91%	< .01
The teachers here don't deserve the respect they demand.	53	23	< .01
I have a fair or poor reputation regarding schoolwork.[a]	77	37	< .01
I have a fair or poor reputation regarding behavior.	37	19	< .05

[a] "What kind of a reputation do you have among teachers as far as your schoolwork (or behavior) is concerned?"

4. *Malperformers were often isolated from the mainstream of life in the school, but they were not isolated from peers.* Contrary to some observations, our findings indicate that malperformers were integrated into cohesive peer groups that supported behavior and attitudes largely inconsistent with conventional and acceptable norms. These peer groups exhibited much antisocial behavior in and out of school and provided encouragement for others to do likewise.

The findings in Table 7 reveal that malperformers as often reported having many friends as other pupils, but that they usually spent somewhat less time with these friends. They also generally reported that their friends were experiencing difficulties similar to their own and that they were not part of the dominant social system. These friendships were highly valued, perhaps, however, for compensatory reasons. In interviews with both groups of pupils each group indicated little contact with the other; randoms, in fact, reported that they deliberately avoided associating with malperformers. The latter reported similar behavior, and it is not surprising that pupils experiencing similar difficulties and

Table 7   *Pupils' Perceptions of Peers*

Percentage Reporting That:	Malperformers	Randoms	Level of Significance
I have five or more friends.	66%	73%	N.S.
Friends hang around together a lot.	57	19	< .001
Friends take part in a lot of school activities.	29	55	< .01
Friends study a lot.	29	47	< .02
Friends are concerned about grades.	69	87	< .05
Friends look for a good time.	67	34	< .01
Friends have a reputation with teachers as good students.	37	60	< .05
Friends are concerned about behaving as teachers think they should.	20	51	< .01

situations turn to each other and collectively adopt standards of conduct. The lack of support for positive achievement in school is demonstrated by the fact that malperformers asked their friends for help with school work less often than did randoms. These findings are similar to those of Polk and Richmond in a study of Oregon pupils. They suggest that students who fail are progressively shunned by achieving students, teachers, and the "system as a whole."[10]

5. *Malperformers perceived that they had far worse reputations than randoms and that, at least in part, as a consequence of their school experience they had few chances for success in school or adulthood.* Interviews with pupils, social workers, and counselors all pointed to the conclusion that malperformers were very pessimistic about the future as a consequence of their continued failure and lack of any positive reinforcement from the school. Table 8 clearly indicates their pessimism about success in school. When these findings are compared with those in Table 2, it is possible to see marked differences between goals and the perceived reality of their situations. It is not surprising, therefore, that malperformers turn away from desirable goals which they believe that they have little likelihood of ever achieving and accept alternative standards that may violate school or community norms. They are caught in a spiraling situation of diminishing rewards and increasing frustration

[10] Kenneth Polk and Lynn Richmond, "Those Who Fail," unpublished paper, Lane County Youth Project, Eugene, Ore., 1966.

Table 8   *Pupils' Attitudes toward Future*

Percentage of Pupils Who:	Malperformers	Randoms	Level of Significance
Expect to pass courses	24%	62%	< .001
Expect to finish high school	51	70	< .05
Expect friends to finish high school	42	64	< .05
Expect to have a good record when leaving school	16	53	< .001
Expect to have a steady job as an adult	28	60	< .01

and negative reactions. A tenth-grade student expressed his pessimism in these terms:

> I wanted a job out of school, but I wanted to get a good job. I dropped out in the fall . . . . I just didn't care. I wasn't getting good grades in the ninth grade. I figured out since I wasn't getting good grades then, it wouldn't change so I just didn't care.

It is, therefore, reasonable to assume that these pupils will view the classroom as confining and classroom tasks as uninteresting. Thus any effort to change, if it is to succeed, must direct itself not only toward developing the necessary capabilities in the pupils but also toward providing sufficient positive rewards and opportunities in the system. As the findings became known to the practitioners, the group service project was increasingly focused toward the latter ends. The workers emphasized the need to narrow the gap between measured capability and performance; the persistence of pupils' commitments to conventional values, including achievement and success; and the students' desire to reduce the adverse consequences of being regarded and handled as deviants. Experiences within the group sessions offered some opportunity for success and the development of additional skills for classroom accomplishment. However, the crucial condition was the extent to which these pupils could find new opportunities for positive achievement and could be rewarded for improved performance in the classrooms. In this regard it became apparent that teachers noted changes in pupils' behavior, but rewards such as grades showed little if any change. We will now examine some of the findings on teacher perspectives.

Teachers' Perspectives and Ratings of Pupil Behavior

Information obtained from teachers indicated that at least two foci were needed for the group work services. Unfortunately, much of this information was not obtained until the demonstration effort was underway and therefore could not be utilized fully. On the one hand, teachers regarded adequate pupil motivation as crucial to success. Three-fifths or more of the teachers in the schools studied reported that the single most important source of difficulty for most or all malperformers was their lack of motivation and interest in school. Motivation was thought to be an attribute that the pupil brought to school, and few teachers indicated an awareness of ways in which educational practices in school contribute to it.

Because of their perceptions it was difficult for school personnel to accept the study findings that revealed relatively high levels of commitment and aspiration among malperformers. Many (but not all) malperforming pupils were perceived as challenging the teachers' authority, and in some schools teachers were especially concerned about this problem. Had the findings about teacher perspectives been fully anticipated, we would have placed greater emphasis in the demonstration project on developing social skills relevant to the classroom and to pupil-teacher interactions.

That the work with the pupils had some positive effects, despite the weaknesses in the design of the intervention, is shown in the findings on the Pupil Behavior Inventory. Impressive gains were achieved, as indicated by the teachers' ratings of pupils before and after group work services. Those in the service groups, as compared to matched controls, showed improvement in many areas of performance.

Statistical analysis of the ratings given the students led to the identification of five major dimensions of student behavior.[11] They were (1) *classroom conduct:* twelve items, for example, disrupts classroom procedures, teases, provokes other students; (2) *academic motivation and performance:* nine items, for example, is motivated toward academic performance, is alert, is interested in school work; (3) *socioemotional state:* five items, for example, appears generally happy, seems isolated, has few or no friends; (4) *teacher dependence:* two items, for example, seeks constant reassurance, is possessive of teacher; and (5) *general socialization:* six items, for example, swears or uses obscene words, has inappropriate personal appearance. These dimensions indicate significant facets of pupil-teacher interaction patterns. They can be regarded as

[11] Vinter et al., *The Pupil Behavior Inventory, op. cit.*

sets of behavior about which teachers maintain expectations and toward which they focus judgments of pupils' conduct. It is within these areas that malperforming pupils apparently lacked sufficient skills and needed assistance in order to gain positive evaluation from teachers.

In Table 9 change scores are presented by dimension for the experimental and matched control groups in seven schools. The scores represent differences in ratings before and after the group services were offered. A positive score means that the treatment groups showed more positive change than their matched controls. Comparison of difference scores across horizontal rows in the table shows variations among schools. The final columns on the right indicate that experimental groups, considered together, made progress during the time they received service on all dimensions except one, "teacher dependence." The negative scores obtained in several schools on this dimension require clarification. It was reported earlier that many malperforming pupils had considerable difficulty in soliciting help from teachers. One objective of the group service was to increase pupils' skills in relating to teachers and in seeking and using their help within the classroom. The negative change scores indicate that pupils in the experimental groups were perceived as becoming more dependent on teachers at the end of the year. In view of the objective, these particular scores should be considered differently from the other negative change scores.

School Conditions and Practices

We have asserted that it is the interaction between certain aspects of the school and characteristics of the pupils which accounts for malperforming behavior. To clarify this relationship, three aspects of the school will be considered: grading practices, sanctioning procedures, and patterns of dropping out.

Grading Practices. Because so little change was observed in the grades received by pupils in the experimental, matched control, and random control groups over the period of a year, we decided to examine grading practices more systematically. The grades received by the entire cohort of pupils entering the tenth grade in two senior high schools were studied over a three-year period of time until they graduated, transferred, or dropped out of school. Important findings emerged that were relevant for the demonstration effort.[12] First, it was observed that grades were important determinants of location in the curriculum independently of factors such as IQ and reading scores. Second, when we analyzed

---

[12] More complete findings are to be published in a monograph on the entire study of pupil malperformance, pupil careers, and school conditions.

Table 9 *Change Scores Expressed as Differences between Treatment and Control Group Scores, by School and Dimension, 1963–64*

Dimension	School[a] A $T-C$[b]	B $T-C$	C $T-C$	D $T-C$	E $T-C$	F $T-C$	G $T-C$	Total Negative Values	Total Positive Values
Classroom conduct	−0.135	0.528	0.224	−0.259	0.542	0.243	−0.250	3	4
Academic motivation and performance	0.136	0.095	0.200	−0.568	−0.404	0.262	0.850	2	5
Socioemotional state	0.170	0.260	0.292	0.498	0.600	0.340	1.310	0	7
Teacher dependence	−0.127	−0.085	−0.100	0.770	−0.028	0.214	1.260	5	2
Personal habits	0.055	0.105	−0.067	−0.256	0.230	0.033	0.820	2	5

[a] School key: A = senior high school, B = senior high school, C = junior high school, D = junior high school, E = elementary school, F = junior high school, G = elementary school.
[b] $T - C$ = Treatment group score minus control group score.

grades with controls for curriculum location, we found that at both schools the distribution of course marks differed notably between college-preparatory and non-college-preparatory tracks (Table 10). Although we could not measure the performance of pupils apart from the grading practices of teachers, the data clearly suggest that differences in course marks are to some degree a result of different grading standards. In other words, if two pupils performed at the same level when measured objectively, their chances of receiving good grades would be different in the two tracks. Some of the differences in scholastic rewards might be thought to reflect the outcome of differences in reading skill. If this were the case, differences in achievement between curricula should decline across reading skill levels—but, in fact, every comparison revealed that pupils in the non-college-preparatory curriculum fared less well.

It appears that there may be an absolute or universal grading scale in the high schools with an arbitrary de-evaluation of performance within the non-college-preparatory track. Since a large proportion of the malperformers were enrolled in the general curriculum, the lack of any increase

Table 10   *Distributions of Course Marks by School, IQ, and Curriculum*

School, IQ,[a] and Curriculum	Course Marks						Number of Cases
	A	B	C	D	E	Total	
Industrial Heights							
High							
College-preparatory	20%	35	30	11	3	99%	(2102)
Non-college-preparatory	5	25	37	23	9	99	(363)
Low							
College-preparatory	3	19	39	29	10	100	(65)
Non-college-preparatory	2	13	34	40	10	99	(119)
Academic Heights							
High							
College-preparatory	27	35	28	8	2	100	(3553)
Non-college-preparatory	4	44	40	11	2	101	(166)
Low							
College-preparatory	7	25	43	19	5	99	(1946)
Non-college-preparatory	2	18	41	28	10	99	(1652)

[a] IQ cutting points are as follows: Industrial Heights, high, 109 and above, and low, 108 and below; Academic Heights, high, 109 and above, low, 108 and below.

in their grades over time becomes more understandable. Pupils were aware of the differential opportunity patterns, and it is not unlikely that this knowledge affected their motivation to perform.

Sanctioning Procedures. In addition to offering rewards and recognition to pupils for acceptable conduct or achievement, teaching personnel used a variety of negative sanctions to curb malperformance. Grades were, of course, the chief means for both reward and punishment. In the short run, poor grades serve as negative judgments, and in the long run they curtail pupils' future opportunities. We observed that sanctions often went beyond grades. Pupils were frequently exposed to a kind of double (or even triple) penalty. Those who performed below a certain standard received adverse grades and might also be denied, as a direct consequence, a wide variety of privileges and opportunities in the school. Also, policies in several schools explicitly provided for the arbitrary reduction of grades for smoking violations, suspensions, and other forms of behavioral misconduct not directly associated with academic performance. Pupils incurring these sanctions lost esteem among most of their classmates, were seldom chosen for minor but prestigious classroom or school assignments, and were excluded from participation in certain extracurricular activities. This process, in turn, often subjected such pupils to negative parental responses, representing a third penalty.

The linking of secondary rewards and sanctions to grades may result in far more than reinforcement of academic criteria, since it denies the poor performer legitimate alternative opportunities for recognition and success. His motivation to continue trying and his commitment to educational objectives are thereby jeopardized at the very time when additional supports may be needed to stimulate effort. In these situations the underachieving pupil receives little support for his efforts to improve, as continued failure subjects him to new deprivations. School personnel seldom indicated awareness of the negative consequences that could result when grading practices and sanctions for behavioral misconduct were interrelated.

Patterns of Dropping Out. Perhaps of greatest consequence for adult role placement is whether or not a person graduates from high school, for occupational and income ceilings are much lower for those who lack a high school diploma.[13] Successful completion of high school is increasingly essential because of technological and bureaucratic demands

---

[13] Burton Clark, *Educating the Expert Society* (San Francisco: Chandler, 1962), pp. 69–74; Herman P. Miller, "Annual Income and Life-Time Income in Relation to Education: 1939–1959," *American Economic Review*, Vol. 50 (December, 1960), pp. 962–986; J. K. Folger and C. B. Nam, "Trends in Education to the Occupational Structure," *Sociology of Education*, Vol. 38 (Fall, 1964), pp. 19–33.

in this society. Unfortunately many youth still leave school before they have completed the twelfth grade. And in this project the efforts of the social workers did not prevent several members of the target population from dropping out before graduation.

In both schools dropouts tended to be disproportionately represented in the following categories: boys, Negroes, those from working-class families, pupils with lower IQ scores, those lower on reading test scores and in overall achievement, those with lower grade averages, and those in the general curriculum. The data in Table 11 report the percentage of pupils who were dropouts in each of these categories in the two schools studied. Grade point average was the single factor most important in predicting who would drop out and who would not. Forty-one per cent of the dropouts at Academic High fell within the fourth quartile of the grade point average, and 63 per cent were in the same quartile at Industrial High. Dropouts also tended to show greater decline and less improvement in grades than did graduates.

Several studies have also shown achievement to be associated positively with remaining in school until graduation. As one writer suggests, this is not difficult to understand: "It seems entirely reasonable that any normal person would seek to escape as soon as possible from any situation in which he persistently found himself branded as incompetent."[14]

SUMMARY AND CONCLUSIONS

The findings from this study and demonstration effort provide substantial support for the proposition that pupil malperformance is most usefully viewed as a consequence of adverse school-pupil interactions. Both within-school and between-school variations were noted in teachers' perspectives, in group services, in curriculum placement patterns and outcomes, in grading practices, and in pupil careers. The findings further indicated that pupil careers are shaped in part by motivations, capabilities, and skills that are influenced by the opportunities and responses of the school through which cohorts and particular individuals pass. The school itself may maintain or even generate the very malperformance it seeks to eliminate by offering limited opportunity for educational attainment for some pupils, by judging pupils adversely because of attributes that are independent of their actions, by undermining existing motivation through unwise use of control practices, and by making

---

[14] H. H. Hand, "Who Drops Out of School?" in W. O. Stanley et al., eds., *Social Foundations of Education* (New York: Holt-Dryden, 1956), p. 236.

Table 11 *Percentages of Dropouts among Various Categories of Students*

| | Dropouts | |
Category	Academic Heights	Industrial Heights
Sex		
Boys	17%	24%
Girls	9	22
Race		
Whites	13	19
Negroes	38	27
Social class (based on father's occupation)		
Upper-middle	5	7
Lower-middle	11	11
Upper-working	20	15
Lower-working	32	31
IQ (quartiles)		
1 (high)	3	5
2	3	10
3	13	21
4 (low)	26	43
Reading score (quartiles)		
1, 2 (high)	3	13
3	8	26
4 (low)	25	24
Overall grade point average (quartiles)		
1 (high)	0	5
2	3	6
3	5	24
4 (low)	41	63
Curriculum		
College-preparatory	4	5
General	35	47

it exceedingly difficult for the pupil to "find his way back" once he has been defined as a malperformer.

Many of the findings about organizational conditions and behavior subsequently made were not available for utilization in the intervention effort. Had they been, much greater effort would have been directed toward modification of school policies and practices. As it was, the social workers tended to focus their major effort on providing group services to specified individuals. Limited positive results were thereby achieved. It is of interest, however, that since the formal conclusion of the project four of the five school systems have attempted to make changes on the basis of the study findings.

As was indicated earlier, the design for this research and demonstration project provided for two series of conferences to be held periodically over a two-year period. One series was conducted with practitioners to review study procedures and to systematize their interventions as far as possible. In general, the response of the practitioners was extremely positive, and they participated actively in review of preliminary findings and in using this knowledge to modify existing procedures.

A second series of conferences were held with school administrators— principals, superintendents, directors of special education, and so forth. The object of this series was also to review the study findings with reference to their implications for school policy and program design. These sessions were far less successful. Many administrators were reluctant to accept the findings as valid and reliable and maintained strong ideological perspectives about the causes of pupil malperformance. These views inhibited acceptance of the notions that school conditions contributed to malperformance and that basic policies and conditions needed re-examination.

The use of these conferences as a strategy for inducing organization change proved to be less potent and far more time-consuming than we had anticipated. However, after the conferences concluded, administrators in three of the five systems reinstituted contact with project staff members, who then provided come consultation about changes in school policies and procedures. In one community a new senior high school is being designed with a primary concern that conditions for the pupil in the general curriculum be improved. Modifications have also been made in grading practices and policies governing the application of negative sanctions. Changes in staff assignments have resulted in some of the more effective teachers being assigned to develop and teach courses in the general curriculum.

In a second community, utilization of the findings led to the design of a demonstration project that is just getting underway. This effort is directed toward modifying the policies, rules, procedures, and practices that serve to identify and label pupils adversely or to reduce opportunities for certain pupils to participate successfully in the academic and social life of the school. A second objective is to provide an opportunity for pupils to participate in educational decision making, and a third is to redesign existing curricula in the light of study findings. The third school system has begun to modify explicit policies and procedures that adversely affect malperformers.

It is now apparent that effecting innovation and change in today's public school is a complex and difficult task requiring attention not only to attributes of individuals in the system but also, and perhaps more importantly, to the behavior of the school itself. Our findings indicate that planned change can be effected, but that no single technique is likely to succeed unless it is addressed to the complexity of the total situation.

An Experiment in Urban Teacher Education

Bryan R. Roberts

INTRODUCTION

The crisis in American urban schools is an immediate one. Especially in underprivileged areas, urban schools face serious difficulties in recruiting and holding good teachers. It is apparent that teachers colleges must confront this problem with innovative programs designed to encourage their students to choose urban, problem schools rather than suburban ones with their higher proportion of fast learners and accelerated programs. In other words, future teachers must be encouraged to value the problems of slow learners and the culturally deprived child as well as the attributes of the bright, fast learners.

In this paper I explore the potential teacher education programs that actively encourage trainees to develop values suited to teaching in urban problem areas. This is a study of the development of professional attitudes within a college environment and seeks to show the importance of this environment for such attitudes.[1] The term "urban problem" areas will here denote urban living conditions of a very low economic level that offers children little encouragement to develop their learning potential. Traditional teacher education, concentrating on imparting subject matter knowledge and education skills, has given little attention to developing favorable teachers' attitudes toward the difficult and often culturally unfamiliar task of teaching slower learners.

The underlying proposition of the study was that the development of attitudes favorable to urban teaching depends as much on the nature

[1] For a full report of the study, see Bryan R. Roberts, "The Effects of College Experience and Social Background on Professional Orientations of Prospective Teachers," unpublished dissertation, Department of Sociology, University of Chicago, 1964.

of the college attended and the training offered as on the personal predispositions derived by trainees from their social backgrounds. Three basic sets of independent variables were examined: the policies and curricula of three colleges, the social environments within these colleges, and the social backgrounds of the trainees.

THE THREE COLLEGES

In 1961 an experimental teachers college was established in a large Midwestern city of the United States with the explicit aim of training teachers for urban areas. The aims of this college—which I shall call Newcity—were established by a committee of educators drawn from various parts of the nation by the city's superintendent of schools. In its report, the committee stated that the training program of Newcity must be such as to prepare teachers for the wide range of various kinds of teaching jobs and to produce trainees "free from the limitations imposed by ignorance, prejudice, and provincialism." To ensure that different subject areas would relate and to present something of a cohesive approach, departmentalization was rejected and four broad divisions were established. The titles of the divisions emphasized a broad approach to teacher education. Thus the Division of Interpersonal Communication of Ideas covered art, music, literature, languages, and mathematics. The Division of Teacher Education took care of professional preparation, but its courses were designed to relate as closely as possible to the work of the other divisions. Among the courses offered by the various divisions were ones specifically designed to broaden students' outlook through cross-cultural study and an emphasis on environment as a determining factor in social behavior and in intellectual ability. In addition, Newcity made arrangements with various social agencies throughout the metropolitan area to allow its students to work with these agencies in poor areas of the city. Specific arrangements were also made with city schools serving Negro and poor white areas to have Newcity trainees do their practice teaching in such schools.

To make comparisons with Newcity I studied two other colleges that were engaged mainly in teacher education and that drew most of their students from the same urban area. Unlike Newcity, however, they did not make a specific attempt through an innovative program to prepare trainees for urban problems. One of these—which I call Oldcity—was, like Newcity, a day college located in the city and a part of the city school system. This college, however, saw its role to be training teachers by means of traditional subject matter courses and teaching skills. Oldcity tended to emphasize vocational aims in a general education setting. Its catalogue stated, "Oldcity is a single-purpose institution, since all of its curricula lead to public school teaching. Nevertheless, all who graduate must have a well-rounded general education." In terms of courses, 50 per cent of Oldcity's courses were in relatively technical fields such as business, home economics, or industrial arts or in professional education. The comparable percentage of such technical and education courses in Newcity was 18.8 per cent.

State College—as the third college studied will be designated—had recently changed from a state teachers college to a state university and was located some sixty miles from the city. It drew many of its students from the metropolitan area and still had a large proportion of them in teacher education. As a state university it offered specialized courses in a wide range of academic and technical subject areas taught by qualified faculty. Thus the learning situation for prospective teachers was less vocationally biased than at Oldcity. In contrast to Newcity, however, no framework was provided in which all courses would emphasize the importance of new ideas and a readiness to face situations challenging to effective teaching. Being a residential college, able to offer a wide range of courses, State College had a good opportunity to affect students' attitudes broadly.

THE GENERAL PROCEDURE

To provide a test of the effects of stay at each of the colleges, cross-sectional analysis was used to compare samples of trainees starting their training with samples of upperclassmen. The questionnaire used contained a variety of questions concerning the trainee's social background, his views of his college, and his personal aspirations and attitudes on matters thought relevant to teaching in urban problem areas. On most questions the trainee was asked to check the one of a series of statements that most closely represented his own opinion or position. Opportunity was given for trainees to write in their own views about their colleges and about problems in teaching.

In addition to administering this questionnaire I conducted field work in the colleges. This work consisted mainly of forty-five interviews with Newcity faculty and thirty-one with Oldcity faculty. I sampled the faculty on a random basis and took care to ensure that all subject areas were proportionately represented. Personal observation and attendance at classes were used to obtain some feeling for the kind of college environment experienced by the students. The official publications of each college were analyzed to obtain statements on its goals and curriculum; such material was supplemented with research into the history of teachers colleges and into the backgrounds of these colleges in particular.

The Trainee Sample

In Newcity and Oldcity, the trainee samples were 25 per cent random samples of freshmen and of juniors and seniors.[2] No distinction was made between junior and senior year in my analysis since the trimester system in these two colleges made it difficult to distinguish between juniors and seniors in terms of length of stay. In State College, all teacher trainees at freshman and junior levels with home addresses in the city were used as the sample. State College juniors had the same average length of stay at college as did Newcity and Oldcity juniors and seniors. The choice of teacher trainees with home addresses in the city was made to ensure strict comparability with trainees in the other two colleges. To further ensure comparability between trainees in the three colleges, certain groups were eliminated from the sample for most of the analysis.[3] Male teacher trainees were unevenly distributed through the three colleges and were concentrated in State College and Oldcity. Their elimination from the sample also tended to ensure that the three colleges were comparable in the proportions of trainees wishing to teach in high school. (In both Oldcity and State College males were much more likely than females to aspire to high school teaching.) Trainees over 30 years old were eliminated from the samples on the grounds that their attitudes would be affected by factors in their home life not relevant to the present purposes. The other group eliminated for the major part of the analysis consisted of Negroes. They were concentrated in Oldcity, where they formed over 20 per cent of the sample. Where relevant, this Negro group was analyzed separately.

The Initial Hypotheses

My first hypothesis was that, with longer stay at college, trainees at all three schools would become more favorable to the teaching challenges of urban problem areas. The attitudes that these colleges were expected to encourage were of two kinds: first, a personal desire to teach in such areas and to see this opportunity as a challenge; and, second, more general professional attitudes that demonstrated flexibility and an understanding of the needs of children likely to be found in such areas.

[2] The sample of trainees obtained was as follows: 256 freshman and 270 junior-seniors at Oldcity, 210 freshmen and 297 junior-seniors at Newcity, and 352 freshmen and 108 juniors at State College. Excluding males, those over 30, and Negroes, the samples became thus: 142 freshmen and 118 junior-seniors at Oldcity, 192 freshmen and 214 junior-seniors at Newcity, and 215 freshmen and 66 juniors at State College.
[3] In all tables, unless otherwise stated, the sample of trainees will be white females under 30.

A second hypothesis was that the relative success of a college in changing these attitudes positively would depend on whether its training was based on a more professional or a more vocational concept of teacher education. The professional approach was defined as coordinating training in the various subject areas in a way that would emphasize the importance of receptivity to new ideas and new challenges for effective teaching. The vocational approach was defined as giving little attention to changing the attitudes of trainees and as emphasizing course work and the provision of technically qualified teachers. Thus, it was expected that, although all three colleges would encourage more favorable attitudes toward teaching in urban problem areas, the one that best fit the definition of the professional approach, Newcity, would be the most successful in doing so.

Third, trainees' social background attributes were expected to limit their receptivity to the challenging experiences of teaching in urban problem areas to the extent that they discouraged the trainees from facing new ideas and new challenges. Backgrounds of a low economic level and those offering narrow experiences were not thought likely to enhance the ability to meet uncertain situations. Consequently, I predicted that the lower the trainee's educational and occupational class, the lower the prestige of his ethnic group, and the more authoritarian his religion, the less ready he would be to accept the challenges of teaching in urban problem areas.

Finally, I expected that the extent to which trainees saw the faculty and college as interested in them would relate directly to their readiness to recognize college as a place where broad changes in attitudes could take place, including changes favorable to the challenges of teaching in urban areas. It was further expected that the professional approach to teacher education would be more likely to encourage a readiness to see college as a place where broad changes in attitudes could take place. Measures of trainees' involvement in college life, such as participation in extracurricular activities and their friendship ties, were also thought to be influential in determining the extent to which they would see college as a place where broad changes in attitudes could take place.

MAJOR FINDINGS

Trainee Questionnaire Responses

Trainees were asked a series of questions inviting them to evaluate teaching challenges found in urban problem areas in comparison with those more likely to be found in other situations. On one question trainees were asked to rank certain categories of children in terms of the importance of giving them individual attention in a classroom.[4] The contrasting rankings given "fast learners" and "children from slum neighborhoods" are especially relevant to our purpose (Table 1). An impor-

Table 1   *Preference for Fast Learner Rather than Slum Child*

Child Thought More Important for Receiving Individual Attention	Oldcity		Newcity		State College	
	Fresh-men	Juniors-Seniors	Fresh-men	Juniors-Seniors	Fresh-men	Juniors-Seniors
Fast learner	29.6%	48 2%	31.9%	52.1%	39.6%	72.6%
Slum child	70.4	51.8	68.1	47.9	60.4	27.4
Total	100.0%	100.0%	100.0%	100.0%	100.0%	100.0%
No. of cases	(142)	(114)	(188)	(213)	(212)	(62)

tant criterion for successful teaching in urban problem areas in a trainee's readiness not to overvalue the fast-learning situation in contrast with the challenges of working with the slower learner. Freshman trainees in the three colleges showed a decided readiness to acknowledge that, when the choice had to be made, a slum child needed individual attention more than a fast learner. By the junior-senior year, however, the majority of trainees had come to favor the fast learner over the slum child. Trainees in State College showed by far the greatest change in favor of fast learners.

Consistent with this finding were the results of a question that asked trainees to rank the importance of certain criteria for choosing a teaching post.[5] Some of the considerations, such as "the opportunity to help chil-

[4] The question: "In schools there is often the problem of finding time to give individual attention to certain groups of children. Please rank the groups below in terms of how important *you* think it is to give each individual attention (rank 1 to 7): (a) slow learners, (b) fast learners, (c) children who are discipline problems, (d) a child who talks and is restless in class, (e) a child from an ordinary home, (f) children from slum neighborhood, (g) a child from a well-educated family."

[5] The question: "Below are some considerations that might enter into your choice of a teaching situation. Rank them according to their importance to you (rank 1 to 5): (a) having enjoyable relationships with other teachers in the school, (b) having parents who will appreciate your efforts, (c) the presence of challenging teaching problems, (d) the likelihood of getting a good academic response, (e) the opportunity to help children who are difficult to teach."

dren who are difficult to teach," were thought relevant to teaching in urban problem areas. Another—"the likelihood of getting a good academic response"—was a criterion considered more suited to schools outside such areas. In all three colleges trainees became more likely to favor "getting a good academic response" as a job consideration by the junior-senior year. Other considerations that were more closely related to teaching in urban problem areas were also less highly valued by trainees by their junior-senior year. Thus, on these two questions, length of attendance at college was correlated with emphasizing fast-learning situations and discouraging teaching in urban problem areas.

Trainees were then asked to cite explicitly the types of school and the areas in which they would like or dislike to teach. Their responses were used to indicate their preparedness to teach in different areas of the city.[6] From responses to these questions, three groups of trainees were singled out as showing negative attitudes toward teaching in the city: those who wished to teach in the suburbs; those who said they did not wish to teach in a specific geographic area within the city (care was taken to include in this category only trainees citing areas that formed important segments of the city school system); and those who were specifically unwilling to teach in slum or other problem areas. On this measure, the trainees became significantly more negative toward city teaching by the time they reached their junior-senior year (Table 2). Except for Newcity, the results showed that longer training created more hesitancy in trainee preparedness to teach within the city. Once again State College's trainees became the most negative to the city by their junior year. At this point, the high percentage of Oldcity trainees who wished to teach in a specific area of the city should be noted. I shall discuss the significance of this below.

If trainees with longer training come to place greater value on the academic side of teaching and if they become more hostile to teaching situations within the city, then it might be expected that these trainees would become more favorable to suburban schools. This was the case. Responses to the question of what type of school was thought to provide

---

[6] The questions: "If a job was offered to you now, what kind of school and what area would you like to teach in? (Check *None* if you are prepared to teach in any school, and *Don't Know* if you are unsure about your preference)"; "If a job was offered now, what kind of school or area would you not want a job in? (Check *None* if you are prepared to teach in any school, and *Don't Know* if you unsure about your dislikes.)" Responses to these two questions were combined by categorizing trainees according to their specific like or dislike, or where trainees had no specific like or dislike, to "any school" when they had checked this response. The category "unsure" was used when this was checked on both items or when a conflicting response was given.

Table 2   *Range of Choice for Teaching Areas*[a]

Area Where Trainee Would Like or Dislike to Teach	Oldcity		Newcity		State College	
	Fresh-men	Juniors-Seniors	Fresh-men	Juniors-Seniors	Fresh-men	Juniors
Positive response to city						
Will teach in any school	8.5 %	10.5 %	13.3 %	20.6 %	8.3 %	9.4 %
Wants to teach in specific area of city	55.4	38.5	26.4	28.3	26.4	9.3
Unsure	9.2	10.6	22.3	14.5	17.8	6.3
Total positive response	(73.1)	(59.6)	(62.0)	(63.4)	(52.5)	(25.0)
Negative response to city						
Wants suburban school	3.8	8.7	15.7	10.3	16.3	23.4
Negative to one or more areas of city	6.2	11.5	13.3	15.1	14.9	26.6
Negative to slum or problem area	16.9	20.2	9.0	11.2	16.3	25.0
Total negative response	(26.9)	(40.4)	(38.0)	(36.6)	(47.5)	(75.0)
Total	100.0 %	100.0 %	100.0 %	100.0 %	100.0 %	100.0 %
No. of cases	(130)	(104)	(166)	(185)	(208)	(64)

[a] Differences between year levels and between institutions are significant at $p < .01$. Trainees with suburban homes were eliminated.

the best opportunities for three types of teaching experiences[7] showed that trainees in all three colleges became significantly more partial to the suburban school on each of the three items by their junior-senior year, despite the fact that none of these colleges provided any significant contact with suburban schools and two of them had close ties with good city schools (see Table 3). Their increasingly favorable attitudes toward suburban schools may thus represent a growing desire to avoid city school teaching situations. This rising preference for suburbs was, in fact, accompanied by a decrease in the percentage of trainees choosing a city school to provide the best opportunity for the preferred teaching

[7] The question: "Different types of schools offer different kinds of teaching experiences. Please indicate in the appropriate columns below the type of school which you think offers the best opportunity for the experiences listed:

Experiences	*Types of School*
Freedom to develop one's own ideas	Parochial school
Opportunity to experiment with new teaching methods	Suburban school
	City school in slum neighborhood
A great deal of intellectual stimulation	City school in middle-class neighborhood
	School in small town"

Table 3 *Preferences for the Suburban School*[a]

Type of School Chosen by Trainee	Type of Teaching Experience Sought					
	Freedom to Develop One's Own Ideas		Opportunity to Experiment with New Methods		A Great Deal of Intellectual Stimulation	
	Fresh-men	Juniors-Seniors	Fresh-men	Juniors-Seniors	Fresh-men	Juniors-Seniors
OLDCITY						
Suburbs	19.2%	28.6%	34.9%	53.8%	19.4%	43.4%
Other	80.8	71.4	63.1	46.2	80.6	56.6
Total	100.0%	100.0%	100.0%	100.0%	100.0%	100.0%
No. of cases	(130)	(105)	(129)	(106)	(129)	(106)
NEWCITY						
Suburbs	28.9%	37.0%	55.6%	61.1%	41.3%	60.3%
Other	71.1	63.0	44.4	38.9	58.7	39.7
Total	100.0%	100.0%	100.0%	100.0%	100.0%	100.0%
No. of cases	(190)	(211)	(189)	(211)	(189)	(210)
STATE COLLEGE						
Suburbs	29.5%	52.4%	51.2%	69.8%	37.6%	66.7%
Other	70.5	47.6	48.8	30.2	62.4	33.3
Total	100.0%	100.0%	100.0%	100.0%	100.0%	100.0%
No. of cases	(210)	(63)	(211)	(63)	(209)	(63)

[a] Differences between year levels and between institutions on all three items are significant at $P < .01$.

experiences. The percentage of trainees chosing "parochial school" or "school in small town" also declined from freshman to junior-senior year.

These results indicate that, in all three colleges, trainees consistently adopted attitudes more unfavorable to teaching in urban problem areas by their junior-senior year. I next examined whether trainees in Newcity experimental college were more or less likely to become negative to teaching in urban areas than trainees at the other two colleges. Summing the amount of change between the freshman and junior-senior years on the questions previously analyzed, I find that Newcity trainees showed the least amount of unfavorable change toward teaching in urban problem areas (Table 4). In fact on only one question—that concerning fast and slow learners—did the results deviate from this general finding. Equally consistent was the fact that State College trainees showed the most negative change; far more than other trainees, those at the residential college outside the city became less receptive to the idea of teaching in urban schools.

Table 4 *Changes between Freshmen and Juniors-Seniors on Various Measures*[a]

Measure	Percentage Differences between Freshman and Junior-Senior Year		
	Oldcity	Newcity	State College
Fast learner versus slum child	−18.6%	−20.2%	−33.0%
Academic response	−10.3	−7.1	−4.9
Types of area	−13.5	+1.4	−27.5
Choice of suburban school			
Freedom of ideas	−9.4	−8.1	−22.9
Opportunity to experiment	−16.9	−5.5	−18.6
Intellectual stimulation	−24.0	−19.0	−29.1
Total	−92.7%	−58.5%	−136.0%

[a] The minus sign (−) represents change negative to teaching situations in urban problem areas, and the plus sign (+) represents positive change.

Although Newcity did turn fewer trainees away from the idea of teaching in city schools, the results for this college were certainly disappointing. Despite its favorable emphasis on urban teaching situations, Newcity's trainees adopted attitudes more unfavorable to teaching there by their junior-senior year. Indeed on two of the questions (fast learner versus slum child and choice of suburban school), it was Oldcity trainees who remained most favorable to urban teaching situations by the junior-senior year.

Trainees in all three colleges became more ready to adopt flexible attitudes by the junior-senior year when the question did not involve evaluating urban problem teaching situations against those more likely to be found in suburbs or near-suburbs. This finding held true on a series of questions that asked the trainees their opinions of the educational potential of the slum child, whether a teacher should define his role in broad or narrow terms, and the importance of freedom from restrictions in contrast with security and stability as requirements for an ideal job. On these questions, too, there were statistically significant differences between the freshmen and the junior-seniors and between colleges. State College trainees, by their junior year, were most likely to adopt attitudes showing a more flexible approach to teaching on these general questions.

On the basis of the preceding information, it is possible to comment on the direction the findings are taking. On a whole series of issues, length of enrollment in college was a very important determinant of trainee attitudes toward teaching. There were considerable changes in the attitudes of trainees between their freshman and their junior-senior year. Furthermore, the three teachers colleges, with their distinctive individual approaches, showed large differences in their effects on trainees' attitudes. The problem then was not that teachers colleges were ineffective in influencing trainees' attitudes toward teaching; indeed, on certain issues that have been noted, the colleges influenced trainees in highly positive ways. In respect to preference for urban teaching problems, however, the colleges had a negative influence.

The data thus support the contention that there is need for further innovation in contemporary teacher education if trainees are to choose urban teaching situations. On the basis of the data for these three colleges, it appears that teacher education is apparently able to stimulate broader professional sympathies and a desire for independence in its trainees. Such sympathies and desires are channeled, however, into a preference for teaching situations most likely to be found in suburban areas. Newcity's experimental approach was not significantly successful in reversing this trend. To account for this finding and to analyze further possible determinants of trainees' rejection of urban teaching situations, I analyzed three possible limitations on the ability of teachers colleges to persuade trainees to choose urban teaching as a profession. The factors investigated were (a) the environment of teachers' colleges; (b) the trainees' social background; and (c) the position of the teachers college within the general system of local and higher education.

COLLEGE ENVIRONMENT

The Value of College

In all three colleges the learning environment seemed to encourage trainees to value their training in narrow subject matter terms rather than in terms of new experiences offered. Trainees' responses to the question of whether they thought it more important to give individual attention to the slum child or the fast learner were analyzed by college, correlating them with responses to another question asking trainees to rank five aspects of college experience in terms of the importance of each experience to them.[8] I look in particular at two of these five aspects—"enlarging your knowledge," which I assume reflects a more academic, nonprofessional attitude toward teacher training, and "exposing you to new experiences," a response more likely to be given by trainees who would value Newcity's experimental courses and the programs of practical experience directed at the problems of urban teaching.

In all three colleges and at both year levels, trainees were much more likely to see enlarging knowledge as a more important aspect of college than being exposed to new experiences. When responses to this question were correlated with trainee preferences for fast learners or slum children, the implications of this emphasis became apparent. Trainees who gave higher value to enlarging knowledge changed most in the direction of preferring the fast learner. A rejection of the conventional learning situation of a college by preferring to value new experiences had a definite relation by junior-senior year to a willingness to recognize the needs of a slum child.

Holding these two values constant made it possible to compare more precisely the effects of Newcity's approach to teacher education with those of the other two approaches. At the junior-senior level, when the effect of a college should have been most pronounced, it was only in Newcity that preferring new experiences was much more likely to lead to a preference for the slum child. When trainees with the academic bias of preferring to enlarge their knowledge were eliminated, the effect of Newcity's approach to teacher education was clearly to encourage trainees to develop attitudes favorable to teaching in urban problem situations.

Contrasting Oldcity and Newcity shows that, for those choosing "enlarging your knowledge," Newcity's environment was also more likely to encourage a preference for the fast learner. Thus the dual effect of Newcity's training is apparent. The result of both the presence of an academic bias in Newcity and an emphasis on an experimental approach to urban teacher education depends on which attitude an individual trainee adopts. For those wiling to be exposed to new experiences, Newcity's environment led to a decided preference for the slum child.

[8] The question: "Below are listed some of the ways in which college can be important to you. Please rank them in order of their importance to you (rank 1 to 5): (a) helping to develop important social skills, (b) providing a good training for your future occupation, (c) exposing you to new experiences, (d) enlarging your knowledge, (e) helping you to obtain a good job."

For those who accepted an academic interpretation of the college experience, the Newcity environment led to a preference for the fast learner.

This duality is also apparent when preferences of juniors and seniors for fast learner or slum child are correlated with choices of areas in which trainees wish and do not wish to teach. Newcity trainees choosing the slum child were the least likely of the three junior-senior groups to be negative toward some aspect of city teaching. Newcity trainees preferring the fast learner were more likely than Oldcity trainees who made the same choice to be negative toward some aspect of teaching within the city.

The environment of Newcity, when contrasted with that of Oldcity, is thus more effective in encouraging both trainees with and those without the "academic" bias of giving priority to fast learners to choose teaching areas consistent with their priorities. Perhaps the conflicting pressures of these two aspects of Newcity may account for the relatively small differences in impact between it and the other two colleges on trainees' attitudes toward teaching in urban problem conditions. (We should note that in State College choosing "new experiences" or "enlarging knowledge" made little difference to trainees' decided preference for the fast learner. Likewise junior trainees at State College were the most negative toward some aspect of teaching within the city, irrespective of the priority they gave to fast learner or slum child. This residential university consistently influenced its trainees away from city teaching situations.)

Trainee Perceptions of the College Environment

I found that the degree to which a college could change trainees' attitudes in a desired direction was likely to depend highly on its ability to gain the regard and involvement of its students. Two issues seemed relevant to the discussion of the problems facing Newcity's attempt to innovate in the field of urban teacher education. One concerned the extent of trainee involvement in Newcity and the other two colleges and included trainee attitudes toward college goals and faculty. The other concerned the effect of trainees' involvement in and attitudes toward their colleges on their readiness to adopt favorable attitudes toward teaching in urban problem areas.

The questionnaire data showed quite clearly that all three colleges face a basic problem in that trainee involvement in college is low and trainees do not perceive faculty and college goals are broadly interested in their development. One indicator of this feeling was the reaction of trainees toward faculty. To estimate whether trainees at the three colleges saw their faculties in favorable terms, they were asked to gauge the reaction of faculty when approached by students in a number of different situations inside and outside the classroom. None of the colleges could really be said to encourage students to be enthusiastic about the way in which faculty reacted. For instance, it was only on the item that purely concerned subject matter that anything like a substantial body of trainees saw faculty as being highly favorable to being approached by a student. Newcity trainees were the only ones to have a consistently more favorable view of faculty by the junior-senior level. In contrast, Oldcity trainees had a less favorable estimate of faculty reactions at junior and senior years on every single item.

Trainees were also asked to estimate how they thought they were treated by their colleges. Oldcity trainees became less likely to see themselves as being treated as very responsible and intelligent people by their junior-senior year. The other possible responses were all negative and implied that the college had little concern for the individual. In none of these colleges was a positive choice with regard to treatment made by the majority of trainees. Perceptions in Newcity and State College did improve from freshman to junior-senior level, but the improvement at State College must be set against an overwhelmingly negative response by its trainees.

In these and other measures, Newcity's curriculum, faculty, and official goals were shown consistently to encourage its trainees to attribute more favorable attitudes to their faculty and college than prevailed at the other two colleges. Yet in all the findings it was apparent that none of the three colleges was really successful in convincing trainees that it was interested in aspects of training broader than subject matter or vocational skills. This conclusion is reinforced by the fact that trainees themselves were not heavily involved in college life: when they were asked to estimate how many close friends they had at college and at home, their responses indicated that only at the junior level at State College—the one residential college—were they likely to have more friends at college than at home. Trainee participation in extracurricular activity was similarly low. Only in State College did the amount of extracurricular activity rise to a significant extent by the junior year. Approximately a third of Oldcity and Newcity juniors and seniors never participated in any extracurricular activity during the whole length of their stay. These findings are better understood when it is remembered that most of the trainees are forced to work part-time while at college and do not have the leisure to sit around and develop friendships or join in extracurricular activities after class. (In Oldcity, 61 per cent of trainees said that they either worked or would have to work part-time during college. The figure for Newcity was 55 per cent and for State College, 29 per cent.)

Certainly none of the colleges encouraged the trainee to see the value of his college experience as being much beside providing him with a channel to his future job. We can see this in responses to the question about the importance of five possible benefits of college experience.[9] Two of these had narrow vocational implications—"providing a good training for your future occupation" and "helping you to obtain a good job." The other three benefits stressed college experience in broader educational terms. Only Newcity increased the percentage of its trainees who firmly rejected the vocational definitions. In the other two colleges, trainees were more inclined to give higher ranking to the vocational benefits by junior-senior year. Once again, however, the percentage figures indicated that a substantial majority of trainees in all three colleges emphasized benefits of college experience that indicated little awareness of other than the strictly vocational functions of their colleges.

Stay at these three colleges did not enhance the prestige of the teaching profession in trainees' eyes. Trainees were asked to rank eleven occupations in terms of their relative prestige.[10] Newcity was the only college in which the trainees were less likely to rank school teaching in the lower half of the list by junior-senior year; in the other two colleges, trainees had a lower opinion of the prestige of teaching as an occupation by their junior-senior year. State College once again had the trainees with the most negative attitudes.

I tested directly the association between having narrowly vocational views of a college's purpose, being involved in college activities and friendships, and being persuaded that one's college is broadly interested in the individual student's welfare and development. There was a suggestion that a college environment which encouraged trainee involvement in college activities and convinced trainees that their college had a fairly broad interest in their welfare and development was also likely to encourage them to reject narrow vocational interpretations of the value of college experience.

Trainees were categorized by the rankings they gave to the two vocational definitions of benefits from college training to see whether those who rejected strictly vocational definitions were the most likely to have attitudes favorable to teaching in urban problem areas. Then their responses to four questions relevant to teaching in urban problem areas

[9] See footnote 8.

[10] The other occupations with which "school teacher" was compared were as follows: social worker, model, doctor, policeman, nurse, business executive, college professor, dentist, banker, and clergyman.

were analyzed in terms of the categories formed.[11] Overall a tendency appeared, by the junior-senior year, for those who placed most importance on the strictly vocational benefits of college to be the most likely to have attitudes unsuited to the teaching needs of urban problem areas. At the freshman level, however, the results showed no clear trend. These findings suggest that whether a trainee assigns a narrow or a broad definition to the purpose of college does affect, if only at the extreme limits, his readiness to be favorable to challenging teaching situations.

This section suggests, then, that the broader concept of teacher education espoused by Newcity could be an important factor in sponsoring more favorable attitudes toward urban teaching problems. Certainly a narrowly vocational definition of teacher education, with trainees seeing and using their college experience only as a source of subject matter skills and educational techniques, produces more negative reactions to the problems of urban teaching. A broader conception of teacher education, with an emphasis on the full learning experience that the college can provide, appears from the findings to be a necessary component of an innovative teachers college. As a consequence of this finding we can also state that an apparent limitation to innovation in teacher education is the low degree of trainee involvement in these types of teachers colleges.

SOCIAL BACKGROUNDS OF TRAINEES

Hyman and others suggest the hypothesis that students from blue-collar backgrounds or from narrowly religious or ethnic homes are less susceptible to attitudinal changes under the influence of their college environment.[12] I adopted a similar hypothesis and argued that the lower the cultural level of a trainee's home and the less its economic security, the more likely a trainee would be to choose a teaching position on the basis of the security and respectability that it provided. I had initially thought that, where a teachers college recruited heavily from such back-

---

[11] These four questions are the ones noted in footnotes 4, 5, 6, and 7.
[12] For a general discussion see among others: Herbert H. Hyman, "The Value Systems of Different Classes," in Reinhard Bendix and Seymour M. Lipset, eds., *Class Status and Power* (Glencoe, Ill.: Free Press, 1953), pp. 426–42; Morris Rosenburg, *Occupations and Values* (Glencoe, Ill.: Free Press, 1957), Chap. V; Martin Trow, Recruitment to College Teaching," in A. H. Halsey, Jean Floud, and C. Arnold Anderson, eds., *Education, Economy, and Society* (Glencoe, Ill.: Free Press, 1961), pp. 602–617. Specific to the effects of social background in a teachers college is the following: Earl Valentine, "Occupational Aspirations of Three Normal School Student Groups," unpublished Master's dissertation, Department of Sociology, University of Chicago, 1950.

grounds, therefore, it would have difficulty changing trainee attitudes in directions favorable to teaching in the problematic situations of urban areas. (In comparison with other full-time degree-granting higher educational institutions, these teachers colleges do recruit quite heavily from blue-collar backgrounds. This can be seen from Table 5, where for every grouping but one 40 per cent or more of the students came from backgrounds in this category.)

Table 5   *Occupational Background of Trainees*

	Oldcity		Newcity		State College	
Social Background of Trainee	Fresh-men	Juniors-Seniors	Fresh-men	Juniors-Seniors	Fresh-men	Juniors
Professional and managerial	22.0%	15.7%	19.9%	25.7%	29.8%	32.4%
Clerical and sales	27.3	29.7	38.2	37.1	27.9	24.6
Skilled worker	24.2	12.0	19.4	18.6	24.5	21.5
Semi-skilled, service, and unskilled worker	26.5	42.6	22.5	18.6	17.8	21.5
Total	100.0%	100.0%	100.0%	100.0%	100.0%	100.0%
No. of cases	(132)	(108)	(190)	(210)	(208)	(65)

When the social background of the trainee was correlated with the four questions thought relevant to attitudes favorable toward teaching in urban schools, there was little evidence that background had a significant effect on a trainee's attitudes toward urban teaching. This finding applied equally to parents' occupation, education, religion, and ethnic background. Similarly, on questions relating to general professional attitudes, the social backgrounds of trainees produced no significant differences. When these results were set against the large differences produced by length of stay in college, social background seemed to be a surprisingly unimportant factor in the development of trainees' professional attitudes. It is possible, however, that these findings may be a little misleading and that current changes in the social composition of the trainee body in the three colleges may have significant consequences for attempts to innovate in urban teacher education.

In the three colleges analyzed we were dealing with a selective sample of social backgrounds. Despite differences in the occupational or educational backgrounds of their parents, these trainees chose to enter a vocational undergraduate program in colleges with relatively low educational prestige. This action in itself suggests a certain homogeneity of cultural background that may be obscured by the social background classification used. I am suggesting that choice of college is in itself a powerful index of social background. Intracollege classification by crude indices of socio-economic status is thus likely to partially conceal the extent to which background factors limit the effectiveness of college training.

In this context, it is worth noting that the existence of differences in social background does not imply that trainees had had widely varying exposures to one of the central challenges of urban teaching—that of racial integration in schools. Only approximately 10 per cent of the white students in the three colleges had attended public high schools in racially mixed areas.

The data provide, however, suggestions of the kinds of background factors that are important in influencing the attitudes of trainees toward urban teaching. Freshman trainees from blue-collar backgrounds were the most likely to have attitudes suited to teaching in urban problem areas. At the freshman level, therefore, it was the trainees with parents in white-collar occupations or with some college training who, to a sta-tistically significant extent, were most likely to see the giving of individ-ual attention as more important to a fast learner than to a slum child. This same trend appeared on two other questions concerning teaching in urban areas.

The significance of these trends is clearer upon examining the re-sponses to a question concerning appropriate definitions of a teacher's role.[13] This question tapped trainees' views on school as an agent of social mobility. The narrower definitions of a teacher's role, especially the one concerning the value of honesty and hard work, implied that a teacher should encourage a child to accept the status quo. Conversely, the broader definitions, especially "helping the child get a better deal out of life," implied that a teacher should help a child improve his position. Initially trainees from higher occupational and educational backgrounds were significantly more likely to choose definitions implying acceptance of the status quo. At the freshman level, trainees from higher educational and occupational backgrounds were in a sense protecting

---

[13] The question: "Below are listed varying views of what a teacher's duties are, Which view do *you* feel teachers should have: (a) should do no more than assist the family to bring up the child in the way the family desires, (b) should be mainly concerned with teaching self-discipline, (c) should help the child to exercise his own judgement, (d) should teach the child that honest and hard work rather than critizing alleged injustices is the best way to improve position, (e) should concentrate on motivating and helping the child to get a better deal out of life than his parents?"

their own social positions by choosing definitions of the teacher's role that saw teachers as keeping children socially immobile. One reason why trainees from white-collar homes may react in this way is that training to become a teacher in one of these three colleges is not a step toward social mobility for themselves; in fact, for some trainees from professional homes, this kind of teacher training may even be felt as a movement downward on the social scale.

In contrast, trainees from blue-collar backgrounds were more likely to be familiar with the types of teaching situation found in urban areas than were trainees from white-collar backgrounds. At the freshman level they were likely to have many personal and family ties that bound them to urban areas. The low negative reactions noted earlier of Oldcity freshman, and even of Oldcity juniors and seniors, to urban teaching can be similarly explained. In comparison with Newcity, Oldcity recruited from areas that contained many of the old ethnic ghettoes of the city as well as many growing Negro ghettoes. The high percentage of Oldcity trainees wishing to teach in specific areas of the city is a reflection of their continuing close ties with these areas. Far more than was the case with Newcity or State College trainees, Oldcity trainees were unfamiliar with suburban areas of the city. It is likely that to them the realistic range of teaching opportunities was confined to the city.

These patterns can be highlighted by contrasting them with findings on the separate Negro sample. Negro trainees, who would find it difficult to teach anywhere but in their home city, became much more likely than other social groups to show a favorable inclination toward teaching in urban problem areas the longer they stayed in college.

By the junior-senior year occupational background made no difference to trainee responses. The effect of length of stay at these colleges "liberated" all but Negro trainees from the effects of their social backgrounds. Ties that bound trainees from Oldcity and blue-collar trainees in general to urban areas were likely to weaken. By eliminating the effect of social background on their attitudes, stay at college may also eliminate any attachment to urban teaching problems that they might have received at home.

If the foregoing suggestions are correct, they give added significance to the changes in social composition occurring at the three colleges. Oldcity, the most narrowly vocational of the three colleges, had the highest proportion of trainees from blue-collar backgrounds, but in the last three years it had successfully waged a struggle to de-emphasize its strictly vocational aspects, to upgrade its academic program, and to raise student standards. This is reflected in the lower percentage of trainees from blue-collar homes in the freshman sample than in the junior-senior sample. This trend is even sharper than would appear at first since between freshman and junior-senior years there was a disproportionate number of dropouts among trainees from blue-collar backgrounds. State College showed a similar trend with fewer trainees from blue-collar backgrounds in the freshman than in the junior year, reflecting its recent upgrading from a state teachers college to a state university with its vocational emphasis diminished. Newcity, which from its inception three years previously had consistently emphasized its experimental character and liberal arts approach, attracted the highest proportion of trainees from white-collar backgrounds. This proportion increased from the freshman to the junior-senior year. These colleges were in effect "socially mobile," catering to an increasing white-collar demand for college training and displacing blue-collar aspirants to lower rungs of the higher educational ladder—notably to the junior colleges.

The implications of these findings are clear. As teachers colleges become less vocationally oriented, their student body becomes more predominately white collar. Although trainees in this category tend initially to have a less favorable outlook on urban teaching than their counterparts with blue-collar backgrounds, the general findings indicate that trainees' social backgrounds do not have a very significant influence on their attitudes toward teaching. However, we also find that a personal familiarity with urban teaching problems, such as may be provided by a blue-collar background, could be an aid in encouraging trainees to have attitudes favorable to the teaching problems of urban areas. This finding, coupled with the results which show that students tend to be even less favorable to the idea of urban teaching after stay at college, presents significant problems for the concept of innovative teacher training for urban teaching.

HISTORICAL ANALYSIS OF TEACHERS COLLEGES

I noted earlier the presence of a subject matter bias in the learning environment of the three colleges and speculated on its consequences for trainee preferences for fast-learning teaching situations. It appears that such a bias is not a particular consequence of curricula or policies in these three colleges. This bias, and the general problems faced by these colleges in coordinating all aspects of their programs to consistently influence trainees' professional values, reflect the position of teachers colleges within the general structure of higher education. Teachers colleges have come increasingly to be assimilated into the system of academic higher education. As a result of these trends the three colleges, especially Newcity, face serious problems in reconciling the various tasks—professional, academic, and social—that undergraduate teacher education has undertaken.

The predecessors of teachers colleges were strictly vocational in emphasis. Like military schools, normal schools attempted, primarily through drill and discipline, to ensure the reliability of their trainees. By the end of the nineteenth century, however, social changes made the early normal school training inadequate for the needs of public school teaching. Rapid urbanization and industrialization put pressures on the public education system to provide a more varied and more extensive education for children, yet the narrow vocational bias of the normal schools gave them little means whereby to evolve a form of training suited to the changes demanded in public education. Claims of other higher educational institutions to train teachers increased. In particular, state universities had a direct interest in the quality of the public school system, from which they recruited their students, and soon established education departments. With their greater independence and research facilities and more diverse faculty, these universities tended to monopolize the teacher-training area. Consequently normal schools directly competed with universities for trainees and staff. By the beginning of the twentieth century, normal schools had a lower quality of faculty and students than in the midnineteenth century.[14] To survive, they gradually adopted university standards. From the end of the nineteenth century, normal schools began to add academic courses to their curricula and lengthened the required period of study, culminating in degree granting and in their conversion into teachers colleges in the 1930's. Teachers colleges thus became part of a unitary system of higher education in which institutional prestige was dictated by standards set by the academic universities.[15]

Gradually teachers colleges abandoned their position as single-purpose, narrowly vocational institutions. They began to provide training in the diverse subject areas taught in public schools, in general education subjects aimed at trainees' self-development, and in educational methods and skills. To fulfill these diverse functions, specialized courses, curricula, and staff were provided. This meant that teachers colleges were to be

[14] Jessie M. Fangburn, *The Evolution of the American Teachers College* (New York: Teachers College, Columbia University, 1932), p. 115.
[15] There is a relevant contrast with England. There the existence of the specialized academic high school, the state grammar school, and a large private high school sector meant that universities concerned themselves solely with standards in these institutions and left the bulk of state schools to teachers from teachers colleges. Teachers colleges in England were thus able to develop as a sector of higher education that was not in competition with, or judged by, the same standards as nonprofessional university education.

increasingly faced with problems in coordinating staff and curricula to their single purpose of training teachers. It also meant that these colleges were left with no distinctive professional function. They increasingly provided a training similar to the general system of American undergraduate education.

Significance of This Background for the Three Colleges Studied

This background has had evident effects on the colleges in this study. State College started as a normal school with a strictly vocational curriculum, but this curriculum gradually evolved until State College became a teachers college with degree-granting powers in 1921. Under pressure from increasing numbers of high school students seeking higher education, and with the desire to upgrade its own prestige, State College was transformed into a university in 1960. Slightly more than half its students still desire to become teachers, but every attempt has been made to play down its previous role as a teachers college. At present, it is rapidly obtaining all the accoutrements of a residential state university. Of the three colleges studied, its trainees showed the most uncertainty over their decisions to become teachers and a third of them indicated doubts about actually entering a teaching career.

Oldcity began as a city training school offering one or two years of additional preparation beyond grade school for those desiring to teach in the city schools. Its early vocational emphasis was gradually changed with the introduction of extracurricular activities and general education subjects, and by the 1930's its faculty had been increasingly trained in large universities rather than in teachers colleges, as had been the case earlier. For a long period it continued to emphasize special obligations to the city school system by courses designed for the vocational needs and educational problems of an industrial city. When the state began to provide funds for Oldcity in 1951, the city focus of this college was gradually de-emphasized. Student activities became stressed separately as an important part of Oldcity's functions. By 1957, the objectives of the college had been so rearranged as to place general education first and teacher training second in the catalogue. In 1964 with the active encouragement of its officials, Oldcity was removed from the city school system and became a state college. (Newcity, though only established in 1961 and specifically designed to service the particular needs of the city school system, also became a state college in 1964. The designation "teachers" was dropped from the names of both colleges.)

Newcity's experimental program was fashioned after the model of academic undergraduate education, especially that provided by liberal arts colleges. This appeared to be its basic problem. The administration of Newcity and the majority of the faculty were seriously concerned to provide a teacher training that stimulated students to value such challenges as urban teaching, yet the courses and faculty were basically of a kind found in nonprofessional education, with the emphasis on social science disciplines. This was due partly to the lack of alternative models for an experimental teachers college but also to determination on the part of Newcity's administration and faculty to provide an attractive undergraduate education that could compete for students with nonprofessional colleges and universities.

Given a greater diversity of courses than Oldcity and more specialized staff, Newcity in turn faced more problems in coordinating the staff and avoiding conflicts among members. Newcity had only 12.5 per cent of its total faculty trained in teachers colleges, while this figure reached 22.5 per cent for Oldcity. Consequently, a common vocational training was not present in Newcity to aid coordination among the various subject area specialists. Faculty members who had definite programs with which they wanted to experiment tended to see themselves in competition with other faculty for funds and time to carry on their projects. The original attempt at Newcity to coordinate the various subject areas by means of broad departments was breaking down, and departments under informal chairmen were proliferating, the number exceeding that at Oldcity.

These problems in coordinating a broad range of course offerings were exacerbated because Newcity faculty was less ready than that at Oldcity to reconcile academic standards to the exigencies of teacher training. Newcity had gone out its way to recruit faculty members highly trained in their own subject areas with interests beyond their fields and with a common realization of the importance of training teachers. But faced with competition for faculty, the best that the college could do was to recruit good subject matter specialists. To a greater extent than Oldcity faculty, thus, Newcity faculty members tended to see themselves as subject matter specialists rather than teacher trainers. Indeed, when asked what institution they would prefer to move on to next, they were more likely than their counterparts at Oldcity to cite liberal arts and other nonprofessional colleges. Newcity faculty members were likewise less ready than those of Oldcity to see themselves committing a large part of their careers to their present institutions. The sample of Oldcity teachers showed 44 per cent, as against 13.3 per cent of the Newcity sample, who estimated that they would remain for a considerable time at their college.

The less involved faculty members were with the concerns of the school classroom situation, the more pronounced was their refusal to accept other than academic standards for teacher training. At Newcity, in interviews, only one of the seven natural scientists did not complain that he was prevented from giving courses of a high academic content and that the academic performance of students was too low. Counselors at Newcity expressed alarm in interviews that natural scientists tended to be too rigorous in their evaluation of students. Natural scientists and to a lesser extent other teachers of nonvocational courses at Newcity were also critical of the academic content of courses in other departments. Many of the Newcity faculty, like their colleagues in universities, tended to be overconscious of the need to maintain academic standards and unwilling to compromise by recognizing other than academic aims for education. On the other hand, Oldcity faculty, teaching in a college with limited vocational goals, had little opportunity or motivation to be overconcerned with academic standards.

Despite the reservations, however, there was a genuine and widespread interest among Newcity faculty in the problems of urban schools and in encouraging trainees to teach in such schools. Various faculty members had sponsored student clubs concerned with social problems and encouraged students to work in action programs in slum neighborhoods. In conversations with faculty, it was clear that the large majority thought that teaching in urban problem areas was an exciting professional challenge. Many of the courses and practical experiences required were specifically aimed at encouraging trainees to value the educational potential of slum children.

In Newcity, then, there was a pronounced duality in the form of the teacher training offered—it was at the same time both a striving liberal arts college and a teachers college trying specifically to train its students for teaching in urban problem areas. I suggest that the presence of these twin emphases in Newcity was one explanation for its only partial success in interesting trainees in the teaching problems of urban areas when compared with the other two colleges studied.

CONCLUSIONS

It is apparent that teachers colleges can be meaningfully categorized in terms of their approaches to teacher education. Differences in official policies are reflected in differences in curricula and faculty. Specifically, a distinction can be made between a more professional approach and a more vocational approach to teacher education, where the more professional approach is seen as leading college and faculty to put a greater emphasis on attitude change in the trainee.

These differences, however, may be less important in influencing trainees' attitudes than is the academic orientation that appears to be present in the learning situation of these colleges. Factors in the history of the teachers college and the ambiguity surrounding the best approach to teacher education seem to have encouraged high specialization in subject matter areas. The consequence has been an emphasis on the importance of mastering individual subject matter that has led trainees to place less value on other professional challenges, such as those of the slower learning situations found in urban problem areas. The three colleges did lead trainees to become more flexible in regard to other, more general, professional attitudes that are relevant to the teaching needs of urban problem areas. Consequently, a distinction seems to exist between the ability of the teachers college to encourage general flexible attitudes and the effects of factors in the learning situations that channel such attitudes in directions unsuited to the needs of urban teaching.

Against this general trend, the college with the professional approach to teacher education, Newcity, appeared to be marginally more successful than the other two colleges in encouraging trainees to value the kinds of teaching challenges found in urban problem areas and to adopt attitudes suited to the needs of these areas. It encouraged its trainees to have favorable perceptions of the attitudes of their faculty and college and to see the value of their training in other than narrowly vocational terms. Trainees who valued their training in nonvocational terms were more likely than others to have a higher opinion of the prestige of their future profession and to be favorable to the challenges of teaching in urban problem areas. This suggests that both the formal and the informal aspects of the college environment must be taken into account when the development of trainees' professional attitudes is studied.

Especially important was the finding that parental occupation and education were not major determinants of the development of trainees' professional attitudes. Neither independently of the college setting nor in interaction with it were these social background attributes found to produce consistent effects on trainees' attitudes. Compared with the effects of differences in the approaches that the three colleges adopted to teacher education and with the effects of length of stay, the influence of social background seemed negligible. The major influence of parental occupation and education seemed to be reflected on the initial orientations of trainees. The findings strongly suggest, given the reservations made earlier, that even in Oldcity social backgrounds do not seriously limit the potentialities of education that the teachers colleges have. Other, more individual influences, such as contracts with persons already teaching, may be the most important determinants, outside of the colleges themselves, of trainees' professional attitudes.

The Impact of Community Action
Programs upon School Systems

Raphael O. Nystrand

It is generally accepted that change in educational organizations is more prevalent today than it has been at any other time in our nation's history. Journalists refer to the current scene as "revolutionary"; professors, foundation representatives, and government officials stress the importance of "innovation"; and many school administrators look to the establishment of new programs as the route to personal advancement. The rapid diffusion of Elementary and Secondary Education Act programs alone is sufficient evidence to indicate that Paul Mort's venerable assertion that fifty years is required for broad diffusion of a worthwhile innovation in American school systems has little relevance to the present era.

The assumption from which this paper proceeds is that the impetus for present-day educational change often comes from outside school systems. Newly published curriculum materials, activities in neighboring districts, state-mandated programs, peer relationships among school superintendents, and the availability of federal funds to support particular activities have had demonstrated influence upon local school programs.[1] Pressures to change school programs come from diverse

Editor's Note: Since the writing of this paper community action programs have lost their prominence as they have failed to withstand political pressures. But they have effects which continue to be important, for they introduced school personnel to a new set of outside agencies. The press for change, especially from other federal programs such as Title 1, continues to come from outside.

The research reported here was supported by a grant from the Office of Economic Opportunity under the provisions of Title II of the Economic Opportunity Act of 1964. Parts of the paper appeared in "Towards Participative Decision-making: The Impact of Community Action Programs," by Michael D. Usdan and Raphael O. Nystrand, *Teachers College Record*, 68 (November 1966), pp. 95–106.

[1] A compendium that summarizes several studies dealing with these and other factors related to educational change is the following: Mathew B. Miles, ed., *Innovation*

groups with varying degrees of authority and appeal to schoolmen. The legal sanctions and fiscal capabilities of government agencies give them great bargaining power. Citizen groups lack such obvious influence but have often developed effective strategies for dealing with schools in their areas.[2] Thus the traditional view that local authorities unilaterally determine the character of school programs is a limited one. To an important extent, the process of school innovation may be conceptualized as one in which school officials react to external influences.

The nature of this process undoubtedly varies from issue to issue and place to place, but it is pertinent, nonetheless, to inquire as to the conditions under which the maximum amount of change can be effected within school systems. The following pages treat this question as it relates to a particular federal program, the Community Action Program (CAP) established by the Economic Opportunity Act of 1964.[3]

Because the observations that follow are based on research regarding the effects of one program in only three cities, the traditional cautions about generalizing from small samples must be invoked. However, many of the conditions reported pertain to all of the cities studied, and variations appear to be explainable. It can also be noted that Community Action Programs are appropriate phenomena to study if one is interested in change relationships between schools and external agencies. Not only do such programs purport to introduce new ideas to schools, but also their structure is such that they involve schools in new relationships at both federal and local levels.

THE NATURE OF COMMUNITY ACTION PROGRAMS

Title II of the Economic Opportunity Act of 1964 established Community Action Programs to "provide stimulation and incentive for urban and rural communities to mobilize their resources to combat poverty."[4] The term "Community Action Program" means a program that:

---

in Education (New York: Bureau of Publications, Teachers College, Columbia University, 1964). Also see Roald F. Campbell and Robert Bunnell, Nationalizing influences upon Secondary Education (Chicago: Midwest Administration Center, University of Chicago, 1963).

[2] During the spring of 1966, citizens' groups in Detroit and Chicago pressured school officials for the removal of the principals from particular schools. Similarly, New York City residents forced school authorities to meet certain conditions for citizen involvement on the opening of a new school in September 1966.

[3] A more comprehensive treatment of the impact of this legislation upon schools is found in Raphael O. Nystrand, "An Analysis of the Implications of Community Action Programs for Educational Decision-Making," unpublished Ph.D. dissertation, Northwestern University, Evanston, Ill., 1966.

[4] Economic Opportunity Act of 1964, 78 Stat. 508, Title II, Sec. 201.

1. Mobilizes or utilizes resources, public or private, of any urban or rural, or combined urban and rural, geographical area (referred to in this part as a "community") including but not limited to a state, metropolitan area, county, city, town, multicity unit, or multicounty unit in an attack on poverty;
2. Provides services, assistance, and other activities of sufficient scope and size to give promise of progress toward elimination of poverty or a cause or causes of poverty through developing employment opportunities, improving human performance, motivation, and productivity, or bettering the conditions under which people live, learn, and work;
3. Is developed, conducted, and administered with the maximum feasible participation of residents of the areas and members of the groups served; and
4. Is conducted, administered, or coordinated by a public or private nonprofit agency (other than a political party), or a combination thereof.[5]

The potential scope of such programs was indicated by Section 205 of the law, which stated that the government would support programs in such areas as "employment, job training and counseling, health, vocational rehabilitation, housing, home management, welfare, and special remedial and other non-curricular educational assistance for the benefit of low income individuals and families."[6] Communities were quick to avail themselves of this funding opportunity; Congressman Gilligan (R. Ohio) told the House of Representatives that more than 1000 CAP groups were activated by local initiative within 100 days of the measure's passage.[7]

The range of programs that can qualify for CAP funding is great, and within this range educational programs have had high priority. In writing administrative guidelines to accompany the Act, the government gave broad interpretation to "special remedial and non-curricular educational assistance" by citing the following as examples of programs which could be funded:

1. Remedial programs that emphasize the correction of deficiencies in reading, language arts, spelling, and mathematics.
2. Programs that enrich the school experience beyond the normal curriculum.
3. Supportive services to increase the class room teacher's chance

---

[5] *Ibid.*, Sec. 202(a).
[6] *Ibid.*, Sec. 205 (a).
[7] *Congressional Record*, Vol. CXI, No. 32, p. 2984.

for success with children from low-income areas. Such services might include specialists in psychology, school social work, speech and hearing, and health.

4. Preschool day care and nursery centers for three- and four-year-olds.

5. Tutoring programs in which high school or college students and adults are used to tutor pupils in need of extra educational assistance.

6. Specialized in-service training for school personnel to make their efforts more effective in working with the children from low-income areas.[8]

Passage of the law presented an early opportunity (inasmuch as it preceded the Elementary and Secondary Education Act) to school districts in search of funds to provide services for disadvantaged children. This opportunity was seized in many ways and places: during fiscal 1965, 239 communities received CAP grants. The total cost of these programs was $118,879,418, of which $59,260,348, or approximately 50 per cent of the total, was allocated to education components.[9] Only 30 to the 239 communities did not establish educational components; the remaining 209 undertook 26 different types of programs. Included were preschool programs, remedial education programs, summer school programs, educational and cultural enrichment programs, special study centers, guidance and counseling programs, adult education, recreation programs, tutorial programs, training programs for teachers, use of aides and consultants, extension of school days, programs for non-English-speaking students, special education projects, precollege programs, library programs, increased home-school communications, education surveys, curriculum development, adjustment classes, model school programs, educational supplements, school breakfast projects, early school admission, school retention programs, and reading materials institutes.[10]

The most common way for school districts to obtain funds under the provisions of this legislation has been by working through a local Community Action Agency (CAA). Such an agency is overseen by a policy-making committee that includes representatives of major public and private agencies responsible for local welfare programs; other com-

[8] Office of Economic Opportunity, *Community Action Program Guide* (Washington, D.C.: Office of Economic Opportunity, 1965).

[9] Office of Economic Opportunity, "Report on the Educational Components Funded under Title II-A" (Washington, D.C.: Office of Economic Opportunity) June 30, 1965) (mimeographed).

[10] *Ibid.*

munity social, cultural, and industrial groups; and representatives of the population to be served by the program. More specifically, the *Community Action Program Guide* states that the following groups should be represented on the local CAP committee: the educational system, the housing system, the economic development system, the consumer information and credit system, the legal services, and residents of the area and members of the groups to be served.[11] If, indeed, all these interests were involved in developing proposals for educational components in Community Action Programs, significant changes in educational decision making would be occurring throughout the country. A committee is authorized to propose programs for government funding and to coordinate and make policies for component projects. The program guidelines allow day-to-day administrative decisions to be delegated to component directors (e.g., school superintendents) but place ultimate responsibility for local policy making with the CAP committee.

The relationship of a local CAA to the Office of Economic Opportunity (OEO) is that of an applicant to a funding agency; the power of the OEO is that of the purse. After a proposal for an educational component (or any other kind) is written and approved by the local CAP committee, it is sent to the OEO for review and possible funding.

In the minds of OEO officials, Community Action Programs are demonstration projects that must have potential for stimulating change in established institutions. The *Community Action Program Workbook,* the handbook for CAP authorities, states:

> "There is little chance for a successful community action program unless participating organizations and officials not only work together closely, but also welcome the chance to improve their internal operations and to change or discard those aspects of their programs which have proved ineffective in reaching and helping the poor."[12]

The philosophy of the demonstration project embodied in the administration of Community Action Programs has challenged public school decision making at two essential points. First, it has required school systems to spend some of their own funds for programs approved by the OEO; school officials thereby forewent other program options to which these funds might have been applied. In the districts studied, however, such commitments have been fairly small because of federal

[11] *Community Action Program Guide, op. cit.,* p. 17.
[12] Office of Economic Opportunity, *Community Action Program Workbook* (Washington, D.C.: Office of Economic Opportunity, 1965) (mimeographed), p. 11, B.2).

financing at the 90 per cent level and the legality of making local contributions in kind. The other and more important point on which the OEO has challenged public school decision making has been in the process of stimulating program change.

All of the programs studied were submitted to the OEO without prior advice from that office as to what kinds of components should be established. Although schoolmen sometimes met informally with OEO officials before the formal submission of their proposals, they received little more than encouragement to submit them as written. This was in marked contrast to the comments of analysts after the official submission. The point, however, is clear that government officials did not attempt to influence the nature of program proposals originally suggested by local leaders. Similarly, they made no attempt to monitor or influence the course of programs once they had been funded and reached the stage of implementation. In the intervening stage of negotiation, however, OEO officials made numerous and specific changes in proposed programs.

These changes took the form of conditions for funding. They included requirements for curriculum content, class size, teacher-pupil ratios, and recruitment of students. For example, a particularly strong-worded condition attached to the proposal of one city was the following.

> In the hiring of non-professionals, priority shall in all instances be given to persons who are residents of the areas or members of the groups to be served *and* who have had *less than* a high school education . . . . Where non-minority persons have been employed in non-professional positions, written justification must be submitted within thirty days.

Needless to say, the acceptance of this condition marked a departure from the criteria traditionally employed by the school system to which it was directed. This example and similar ones indicate that the OEO has imposed conditions during the process of negotiating contracts that limit local decision-making prerogatives at the later stage of implementation. Clearly, this is one effective means of introducing change into school systems.

It would seem that the development of CAP educational components poses a normative and operational dilemma for school officials. On the one hand, such programs are consistent with educational folk-thought in their advocacy of equal educational opportunity for disadvantaged elements of the population and citizen involvement in school programs. On the other hand, they apparently require schoolmen to relinquish what is often their closely guarded professional autonomy by actually sharing educational decisions with a CAP committee and the OEO. Additionally, such participation aligns schools in a common quest for federal funds with other local agencies, thereby challenging the popular, if fallacious, belief that educators must remain apart from the political world.

Whatever the attitude of school officials toward them, it has been shown that CAP agencies are quasi-legal bodies with legislative justification and financial capability to encourage change in school programs. We now turn to a more specific consideration of the relationships between these local agencies and public school activities.

RELATIONSHIPS BETWEEN SCHOOL SYSTEMS AND COMMUNITY ACTION AGENCIES

The relationships between public school systems and Community Action Agencies were studied in three cities, pseudonymously referred to as Van Buren, Winthrop, and Jefferson. Several similarities among these cities and the CAAs within them bear mentioning. All are located in a Midwestern industrial state, which means that all of the CAAs studied work through the same regional Office of Economic Opportunity. Each CAA studied is structured on a county basis and theoretically serves areas in its respective county other than the city being studied. Additionally, each of these agencies was originally formed under the auspices of a county-wide, not-for-profit group that functions as the coordinating unit for county charity, health, and welfare efforts. Finally, all of the cities employ a council-mayor-manager plan of government.

Important variations among the cities and their Community Action Programs relate to city and county population, size of the CAP as measured by the amount of federal funds allocated to it, proportion of these funds allocated for educational components in the school district studied, representation of the local school system on the CAP committee, and party affiliation of the congressmen elected from the local districts. These variations are summarized in Table 1.

The Van Buren public schools enrolled approximately 11,500 students in 1965–1966. The fact that almost 10 per cent were Aid-to-Dependent-Children recipients attests to the presence of poverty in the district. However, the district is well known for outstanding educational programs and excellent facilities. Many of its programs such as the school camp and the school farm are regarded as unique in educational circles. Although the district has long supplemented its regular classes with extensive special education for the physically and mentally handicapped,

Table 1 *Characteristics of Van Buren, Winthrop, and Jefferson Community Action Programs*

Characteristic	Van Buren	Winthrop	Jefferson
City population	50,000	85,000	180,000
County population	140,000	700,000	365,000
	(Capital County)	(Lafayette County)	(Crescent County)
Total CAP funds	$318,000	$2,500,000	$506,000
Percentage of CAP funds to district schools	35%	14%	39%
School district representative on CAP committee	Superintendent	None officially. Two board of education members belong in other capacities.	Superintendent
Affiliation of congressman	Democratic	1 Democratic, 1 Republican	Republican

it gave economically deprived students no special heed before the establishment of the CAP educational components.

At the time of this research, the district was under some pressure from local civil rights groups over alleged discriminatory hiring practices. They took issue with the fact that of the 500 professionals employed by the district only 15 were Negroes, and all of these were engaged in teaching rather than administrative duties. The superintendent publicly responded to this criticism by noting that the district had never had an application for an administrative position from a Negro, but that it was his intention to place one in charge of one of the CAP components if it were approved.

The seven-member Board of Education in Van Buren is made up of men who are engaged in local sales, manufacturing, and professional occupations. It is a "businessman's" board: Republican in politics, conservative in outlook, and accustomed to the patterns of delegated authority and fiscal responsibility that prevail in the business world. Although board members express pride in their school system, they hasten to assure the inquirer that the programs are excellent not because the public values education highly enough to tax itself heavily, but because the administration allocates the moderate revenues available to it efficiently.

Members of the board rely heavily upon their superintendent and rarely initiate program suggestions themselves or vote against his recommendation. As one community leader noted, "The Board of Education judges their superintendent by his accomplishments, not by his ability to follow directions." An incumbent of twelve years, the superintendent is one of the best-liked and most respected persons in the community. He is reportedly "a master administrator . . . a man who can do more things effectively at once than anyone I have ever known." The atmosphere is one in which the Board of Education follows the leadership of the superintendent, who, in turn, is sensitive to the general interests of the community.

The population of Winthrop contrasts with that of surrounding Lafayette County. The county is comprised primarily of affluent dormitory suburbs, but Winthrop, which is located at the edge of the county furthest from the nearby major city, is a small, self-contained city. Whereas almost 50 per cent of the county residents are white-collar employees, only 33 per cent of those in Winthrop can be so designated. The 1960 census reported that only 23,000 Negroes (3.3 per cent of the total state population) reside in Lafayette County. However, almost 19,000 of them reportedly live in Winthrop and thereby constitute 19 per cent of the city's population. A final contrast is seen in the 1960 report that the median level of schooling completed by all county residents was 12.1 years, and that of Winthrop residents was only 9.8 years.

The Winthrop public schools enrolled more than 23,000 students in 1965–1966. Relatively speaking, Winthrop is a wealthy school district—its per pupil valuation is third highest among county districts, and its per pupil expenditure of more than $550 compares favorably with figures for surrounding districts.

Citizens, members of the Board of Education, and school personnel regard the school program as somewhat conservative but sound. Perhaps the major program innovation of recent years came in 1962, when the district acknowledged the problem of disadvantagement in the schools slightly ahead of the national trend. As a result, it solicited and received foundation support to establish remedial and compensatory programs in the elementary grades. More recently, the district has considered the problem of *de facto* segregation and taken modest steps to deal with it, such as deliberately integrating field trips. The district has come under some criticism from local civil rights groups, but it generally enjoys strong support from both the local press and the public at large. The feelings of the latter were illustrated in the passage of a recent building bond referendum by a five-to-one margin.

The Board of Education is of a composition similar to the one in Van Buren except that it includes one Negro, a dentist and former president of the Urban League. The board also relies heavily upon the superintendent for leadership. No better example could be cited than its preliminary approval of the recommended fiscal 1967 operating budget. Although the matter had probably been discussed before in executive sessions, the superintendent took less than ten minutes to make his report to the open board meeting, after which the members gave their unanimous approval without raising a single question. The board president summarized their reasons for reliance upon the superintendent thus: "We are not educators; it is up to the superintendent to tell us what is needed for our youngsters."

Jefferson, with a 1960 population of 180,000, is the largest of the cities studied. The public school enrollment has increased rapidly during the past 15 years and is now in excess of 35,000 students. The racial composition of the student body has also changed dramatically; in 1940 less than 4 per cent of the student body was Negro, but by 1964 this figure had increased to more than 20 per cent.

The district has long practiced a neighborhood school policy, as indicated by the fact that every pupil in each of the 55 elementary schools goes home for lunch. This policy, in combination with city housing patterns, has created a situation of *de facto* segregation in the Jefferson schools. More than 95 per cent of the Negro students in the city attend 1 of 15 schools. (Both the incidence and concentration of poverty in the city are indicated by the fact that almost 60 per cent of the children enrolled in 4 of these schools come from families receiving welfare payments.) In a major step, the Jefferson Board of Education recently agreed to a request for a comprehensive study of school attendance districting patterns and their effects. Community and school leaders express confidence that the results of the study will be used as a basis for efforts to improve the school program and not to incite community groups.

The Board of Education has nine members and, like the boards in Van Buren and Winthrop, typically follows the recommendation of its superintendent. Although most of the board members are proud of their conservative fiscal policies, they are somewhat more progressive than the community at large. The district has a history of defeating bond and millage referenda. These defeats are apparently not so much repudiations of the school administration and its policies as they are evidence of general reluctance to support increasing levels of public expenditure. This public attitude intensifies the will of Jefferson Board of Education members to show something for every dollar expended. Against this background, it is interesting to observe that in October 1964, the board voted to use local funds to reduce pupil-teacher ratios, to employ eleven teacher aides, to employ a coordinator for inner-city programs, and to begin a limited preschool program (fifty students) in the city's disadvantaged areas. Thus the schools demonstrated a concern for the poor before a local CAP was begun.

In each of these cities, the Board of Education and the CAP committees acted independently of one another. There were no instances of joint planning or action, even in Winthrop, where the membership of the Board of Education and the CAP committee overlaps. The respective groups in each city approved programs on the assumption that their local counterparts either had already registered their approval or would soon do so. None of the groups that were studied initiated a program idea. Instead, all of them depended upon professional staff members to develop program ideas and to communicate with the two groups in their respective cities about program proposals.

As noted in the preceding paragraphs, each Board of Education that was studied tended to delegate to its superintendent the day-to-day tasks of running the schools and to heed his recommendations on matters of broader scope which he believed should be considered by them. Another similarity found among these boards was that their members are predominantly Republican in politics and conservative in their fiscal and philosophical positions. As both of these characteristics might indicate, not one of the boards studied suggested participation in Community Action Programs to its superintendent. The suggestion, in every case, was made by the superintendent to the Board of Education. Moreover, when presented with written proposals for educational components, no board suggested a single addition, deletion, or revision. In every case, the reliance of the Board of Education upon its superintendent for direction in the establishment and implementation of these programs was complete and unconditional.

Several of the members on each of the boards studied professed skepticism about federal aid to education, fearing the possibility of federal control. Significantly, however, not a single dissenting vote was cast in any of the cities studied on questions regarding participation in Community Action Programs. In each city, board members who were queried about their feelings toward federal assistance responded to the effect that the availability of funds to support programs deemed desirable by their superintendent superseded whatever philosophical reservations they might have about participation in a federal program.

The study also revealed that the same board of education members who expressed skepticism about federal control in abstract terms could not specify any federal limitations that participation in Community Action Programs had placed upon their own school district's decision-making prerogatives. Similarly, no member who was interviewed perceived any intrusions upon the domain of school decision making by local Community Action Agencies. This finding, combined with those reported elsewhere in this chapter. indicated that board of education members may, in fact, be unaware of the nature and source of some changes within the schools that are theoretically under their jurisdiction.

It is suggested that this unawareness is not so much a product of indifference on the part of board of education members to the responsibilities of their role as it is an indication of the manner in which they execute these responsibilities. In short, it offers substantiation for Dykes's forecast of increasing prominence for school administrators[13] vis-à-vis boards of education as educational decision makers. For the most part, it is the administrators who screen the conditions placed upon schools by external agencies and incorporate them into educational programs. Unless they are specifically reported as such by the superintendent, a board of education has little way of knowing which aspects of programs are locally inspired and which are the results of external influences.

In each of the cities studied, the CAP committee made decisions which indicated that board of education members underestimated its influence. In Jefferson, the proposal for educational components was written largely by persons outside the school system and under the direction of the committee. In Van Buren, the committee refused to accept a proposed home and family living nursery program as originally written by school personnel. In Winthrop, the committee passed resolutions that set forth requirements for the hiring of nonprofessionals and the integration of Head Start Programs. Another Winthrop resolution, the effectiveness of which remains to be tested, set limitations for the future development of school programs under Title I of the Elementary and Secondary Education Act.

In the main, however, the committees in all three cities were receptive to initial proposals for educational components submitted by the schools. There were two major reasons for this receptiveness. First, the schools, because of their local monopoly in proposal-writing expertise, were usually the only agencies to submit proposals in the early days of the Community Action Programs. At this time, various external pressures,

---

[13] Archie R. Dykes, "Of School Boards and Superintendents," *Teachers College Record,* Vol. LXVI (February 1965), pp. 399–404.

not the least of which was fear that the federal money would go to another locale, militated for rapid establishment of a local program. Second, committee members professed a lack of technical knowledge about education and deferred to the judgment of school officials regarding the nature of proposed educational components. With the exception of the second series of proposals submitted by Winthrop, none of the proposals studied that was of a completely educational nature received the slightest modification by CAP committees.

Two of the committees, those in Van Buren and Winthrop, did reject school-written proposals for components that were for programs essentially in the areas of health and welfare. At the instigation of health and welfare interests on the committees, these proposals were referred to subcommittees for revisions. This action indicated that, although CAP committees may have potential as agencies to encourage community cooperation, they can also serve as effective barriers to unilateral school actions in noneducational areas. While the committees have for the most part recognized the educational expertise of school officials and merely legitimated school proposals submitted by them, they have balked at attempts of these same officials to extend their influence into other areas.

The role of the committees, however, has been essentially that of legitimating the proposals and recommendations that have been brought to them. Except for the subcommittee referrals mentioned in the preceding paragraph, no CAP committee or subcommittee took any action except to approve the proposals or recommendations brought to it. The major variation in the processes studied involved the origin of these proposals and recommendations and will be treated in a subsequent section. The committees studied were broadly representative of social, civic, economic, and political agencies in their respective cities and reputedly contained members who were influential in virtually every sphere of community activity.

One group represented on the committees requires special mention because of the emphasis placed upon its involvement by the OEO. Section 204(a) of the Economic Opportunity Act required that representatives of the areas and members of the groups to be served be included on policy-making committees. Each of the committees studied included such representation, each was challenged on this point by local protests, and each was required by the OEO to increase the number of representatives from these groups. However, this study found no evidence indicating that the participation of these representatives had any effect whatsoever on the nature of the programs developed through the CAP committees. If the overall function of the committees was to legitimate decisions made by professionals, it may be said that the primary function of neighborhood representatives was to legitimate the good intentions of the committees to OEO officials.

The research indicated that, in legitimating proposals and recommendations placed before them, CAP committees performed two related functions. First, they encouraged the dissemination of information about programs throughout the community. It is in this role rather than that of policy makers that the representation of groups and areas to be served was found to be important. Indeed, success in reaching these groups would be considered a significant change in many school districts. Second, they provided an ostensible power base from which to approach individuals whose support could aid the program. Thus, congressional support for proposals was solicited by committee chairmen (or the vice-chairman in the case of the Jefferson mayor) rather than by the professionals who originated the proposals. For school people, this had the added attraction of allowing them to perpetuate their myth of nonpolitical involvement.

The most important finding of the study with regard to relations between boards of education and CAP committees was that these relationships were dominated by experts. In the case of relatively unsophisticated Community Action Programs, both agencies relied upon the same experts—the school district administrators. In more structured and extensive programs, the CAA had its own staff through which it dealt with school officials. The power of the experts had two dimensions. The first was general administration, based upon full-time attention to the programs and the assimilation of related information. The second was the more technical skill of proposal writing.

The possession of proposal-writing skills was a major determinant of the allocation of funds within the programs studied. These skills and the necessary free time to apply them were found primarily in the larger school systems within the counties in which research was conducted. Thus, the earliest proposals were submitted not only by school districts but also by particularly large school districts, thereby leaving unaffected a large percentage of poor children residing in outlying areas. Attempts to alleviate this imbalance included the hiring of a federal projects coordinator by one county intermediate school district and the expansion of the CAA staff in another county. It is suggested that passage of the Economic Opportunity Act not only marked the emergence of widespread concern for disadvantaged children but also introduced the "era of the proposal writer" for American school districts. It seems likely that such persons will play increasingly prominent roles as agents of change within school districts.

IMPLICATIONS FOR SCHOOL OPERATIONS

Participation in Community Action Programs brought about some internal reorganization in each of the school districts studied. For example, it was passage of this act rather than the Elementary and Secondary Education Act that stimulated all three districts to establish the position of a federal programs director. A basic duty of these directors has been to coordinate proposal writing in the districts. Another has been to assume responsibility for the financial reporting, program summaries, and requisitions stemming from the programs. Although each of the directors has coordinated these activities, their performance has required the involvement of other staff members as well. The point to be made is that participation in these programs required the addition of more than one full-time administrator to support the activities of those employed in the new programs. The expansion of federal assistance programs has created new administrative roles within participating school districts. The precise definition of these roles, as well as the recruitment and training of persons to fill them, is presently an important concern of professional educators.

In each city, the programs provided for the employment of additional personnel, many of whom were nonprofessionals. The acclimation of these persons to district policies and procedures required the design and provision of new in-service training programs. In Van Buren and Winthrop, where these nonprofessional personnel performed their duties during the regular school day, another pressure was created. Officials in these districts pointed out that the presence of teacher aides, more extensive instructional materials, smaller classes, and clerical assistance in federally assisted programs created educational status symbols and work conditions to which nonprogram teachers aspired. Officials agreed that these conditions made it easier to recruit teachers for disadvantaged students, and some suggested that they would be influential on future union demands. These reports indicated potential avenues for the future institutionalization of demonstration projects in the public schools.

Federal participation in Community Action Programs established a new agency with which the school districts studied had to deal. Ostensibly, the relationship was a profitable one for these districts because it provided another source of funds upon which they could draw. Reliance upon these funds, however, introduced an element of ambiguity that had not previously existed in the systems. The review and funding procedures of the OEO were such that the districts never knew until final notification came how much federal support they could receive for each proposal they had submitted. The tendencies of the OEO to extend the review process over a protracted period of time and to announce awards without regard to the beginning of school terms have created further ambiguities for school districts. Collectively, they have forced a new degree of administrative flexibility upon the schools that calls for continuous planning, personnel recruitment, and program initiation.

On the local level, participation in the Community Action Programs required establishing relationships with a new agency and its staff. The importance of this relationship was underscored by the role created for CAAs in the planning of Title I school programs by the Elementary and Secondary Education Act. The guidelines for developing programs under this act specify that local school boards must

> . . . develop projects under this title in cooperation with the public or nonprofit agencies responsible for any community action programs which may have been approved under the Economic Opportunity Act in their localities. Genuine working relationships should be established during the planning and development of a project under this title and maintained during the operation of the project.[14]

A memorandum sent to all CAAs by the OEO informed them of this requirement and went on to specify actions to be taken in the event of their objecting to locally proposed Title I projects. The recommended procedure established an appeal process involving officials from the state educational agency, the OEO, and the Office of Education.[15] The net effect is to invest CAAs with potential to delay local allocations of the largest part of the federal largesse available to school districts. Clearly, it is advantageous for school districts to maintain cooperative relationships with these new agencies.

This new relationship has created a forum through which demands can be placed upon the schools. The aforementioned Winthrop resolutions were examples of such demands; other examples included requests to develop county-wide school programs in Van Buren and Winthrop. Although unacted upon to date, the introduction of these requests in

---

[14] U.S. Department of Health, Education, and Welfare, Office of Education, *School Programs for Educationally Deprived Children: Basic Facts for School Administrators* (Washington, D.C.: U.S. Government Printing Office, 1965), p. 13.

[15] Office of Economic Opportunity, "Community Action Memo No. 28" (Washington, D.C.: Office of Economic Opportunity, 1966), p. 2.

such an influential forum suggests the possibility that demonstration efforts such as Community Action Programs and regional laboratories established under Title IV of the Elementary and Secondary Education Act may provide a vehicle for encouraging permanent consortiums or consolidation among public school districts.

Participation in Community Action Programs increased the vulnerability of the school districts studied to social protests from existing interest groups. In Van Buren, the submission of Community Action proposals provided the local chapter of CORE with an opportunity to gain widespread publicity by calling for a federal investigation of the local schools that were to receive CAP funds. Conversely, the CAP committees were the actual targets for the protests in Winthrop and Jefferson. However, because the programs of these agencies were essentially educational in nature, the school districts were associated with the committees in reports of the incidents.

Because the OEO has established its willingness to investigate the protests of dissident minority groups, local CAAs have become a target for these groups. As far as school administrators are concerned, this has not only prolonged the time they must spend negotiating for program acceptance but has also established the need to justify the innocence of the district to both the OEO and wide-ranging local groups.

A similar but more general point is that all of the programs studied were conducted very much in the public eye. The attention of local news media to federal fundings and related protests, the efforts of CAA publicists, and the strong national emphasis upon the mitigation of disadvantagement have collectively assured these programs public visibility out of proportion to their status as a part of the total school program. Inasmuch as schools are public agencies, this has meant that administrators at all levels have devoted a disproportionate amount of their time to developing, coordinating, and publicizing these programs.

If we define politics as the process through which patterns for the allocation of scarce resources are determined, the findings of this study support the contention that school administrators are involved in the process. The political demands of participation in the Community Action arena are especially great. Unlike dealing with state legislatures for revisions in aid formulas, seeking support for millage increases, or applying for Elementary and Secondary Education Act entitlements, seeking Community Action funds must be done without any guarantees of receiving something at some time. Furthermore, applicants must gain approval at both local and federal levels for the allocations sought. On the local level, schools compete with other school districts and health and welfare agencies that are also eligible for funding. On the federal level they compete with similar institutions that have also won "trial heats" at the local level.

It has been emphasized that among the school districts studied the technical expertise of school administrators was the most effective policy determinant. The school administrators who succeeded in having themselves heard by CAP committees found that their knowledge of educational matters was respected by those groups. In short, their expertise was a source of influence.

A necessary supplement to this expertise, however, was the establishment of access to the committees by school officials. In other words, the administrator must be assured of sufficient contact with the committee so that he can bring his influence to bear. The committees in Van Buren and Winthrop were established through the efforts of the superintendents, who thus enjoyed great access to them at an early date. In Van Buren, the superintendent has remained active on the committee, preserving his access through participation. Although the Jefferson superintendent was not instrumental in founding the local committee, he was appointed to it and has remained active on it. In contrast, the Winthrop superintendent discontinued his participation on the Lafayette County committee soon after the first set of proposals was submitted. As a consequence, the Winthrop public schools have lost their "voice of expertise" on the committee and, with it, much of their power to influence local Community Action policy.

Although the administrative expertise of the districts studied was also important for dealing with federal program analysts, it was apparent that local school and CAP officials were not willing to rely on it entirely. In every instance the support of local congressmen was sought for proposals submitted. However, this support was always solicited through a committee officer, even though the proposals were for educational programs. The use of such intermediaries gave the requests additional legitimacy and also set school administrators one step away from soliciting congressmen's favors. Nonetheless, the nature of the process was such as to make clear both its political character and the involvement of school officials.

It can be noted that the study found no reason to believe that congressmen, mayors, or other political figures played any role in the establishment and implementation of these programs other than that of attempting to expedite the negotiating process. It should not be inferred, however, that no political official experienced any personal gain from the role that he did play. As Banfield and Wilson have noted, the strategy for building political coalitions has shifted from providing specific in-

ducements to individuals on a precinct level to providing general induce-
ments to large population groups.[16] Community Action Programs in
general, and educational components in particular, are general induce-
ments. The Winthrop newspaper article headlined, "Congressman _____
Announces Grant of $225,613 to Schools," and others like it had two
results. First, it bolstered the image of the congressman as a supporter
of education for the disadvantaged, thereby encouraging those with
similar concerns to support him. Second, it very probably linked the
public schools with the congressman in the minds of many readers.
Although school administrators may continue to proclaim the independence of schools from political concerns, the participation of their districts in federal programs promises to inform the public otherwise.

EDUCATIONAL COMPONENTS IN VAN BUREN,
WINTHROP, AND JEFFERSON

The preceding sections have discussed the implications of participation
in Community Action Programs that were common to the school systems
in all of the cities studied. It is now appropriate to shift our attention
to differences in these cities, their school systems, and their CAAs. The
theme to be developed is that these differences contributed to variations
in the processes through which the respective educational components
were established. These variations in process will be linked, in turn,
with differences in educational practice. Comparative analysis of the
latter relationship is of particular interest, for it suggests the characteristics of processes that are most conducive to educational change.

As noted earlier, the cities, school districts, and CAAs that were
studied varied in terms of the following characteristics: (1) population
of cities and their containing counties; (2) total federal funds allocated
to the program; (3) percentage of the total federal funds allocated
for educational programs in the district studied; (4) the representative
of the school district on the CAP committee; and (5) the party affiliations of congressmen serving the respective cities.

The affiliations of congressmen had no differential importance for the
processes in the three cities studied. All of them apparently contacted
the OEO on behalf of the proposals submitted by their constituents,
but none seemed to enjoy more success than the others in expediting
the approval of proposals. Moreover, none of them attempted to influ-

[16] Edward C. Banfield and James Q. Wilson, *City Politics* (Cambridge, Mass.:
Harvard University Press, 1963), p. 337.

ence the nature of local programs when they became operational. Although the situation may be different for other locales, this study contributed no evidence to suggest that the role of congressman is important for explaining variations in the processes by which educational components were established.

The percentage of funds allocated to educational programs in the district appeared to be a resultant indicator of process variations, rather than a factor contributing to these variations. That is to say, whether schools received greater or lesser percentages of the funds depended on the extent to which the schools were given prominence in the deliberations of the CAP committees.

County population figures and total federal allocations were closely related. This can be attributed to the fact that the OEO guidelines for the allocation of funds are based upon the number of poverty level residents within an applying target area. It is suggested that large populations in applicant regions and large amounts of funds available encourage the employment of a professional staff to administer the CAA.

City population figures were important only insofar as they were an index of the prominence of city institutions in the county. They suggested, for example, that Jefferson agencies are the most prominent in Crescent County. This prominence was reflected in the membership of the Community Action leadership committee. More than three-fourths of the members chosen reside in Jefferson, and the remainder live in adjacent suburbs. A similar situation exists in Capital County, where Van Buren is the center of what is otherwise a predominantly rural area. Almost two-thirds of the members of the Community Action Division reside in Van Buren. The membership of the two committees differed, however: that of Crescent County had a larger number of reputed civic and business leaders than that of Capital County, which included the heads of more service agencies.

Winthrop constitutes only a small part of Lafayette County, which is a metropolitan county with a multitude of service and governmental agencies. For example, the county contains thirty-one school districts, six of which have enrollments of more than 12,000 students. It would be impossible to represent all major agencies on a leadership committee of any reasonable size. The committee was constituted, therefore, primarily of lay citizens who were active on the boards of directors of various county agencies rather than the technical heads of those agencies.

To summarize the data, the committees established in Jefferson and Winthrop, although for different reasons, were both heavily representative of persons accustomed to managerial activities. Minar has noted that such persons traditionally delegate much responsibility to staff members in their employ.[17] The added incentive of relatively large amounts of available funds probably encouraged them in this direction. In any case, it is clear that the committees in these two cities relied heavily upon their capable and expanding staffs.

In contrast, the Capital County committee included many service agency heads whose work was limited to a relatively small geographical area and who knew one another well. The funds available to committee members were comparatively limited and precluded the employment of a highly qualified professional staff even if they had wished to have it. Although they did employ a director, his influence has been limited, and the committee has done little but serve as a channel of funds for school districts submitting proposals through it.

It is suggested, therefore, that characteristics of CAP committees which can be explained at least partially by demographic and socio-political factors, together with the amount of funds available to support programs, determine the way in which CAAs will be staffed. Since findings reported earlier noted that, in the cities studied, the committees themselves did not initiate decisions but legitimated the proposals and recommendations brought to them, it is further suggested that the strength of the agency staff is a crucial dimension of variation in decision-making processes. A strong staff is one that develops proposals and recommendations for consideration by the CAP committee. Among the subjects on which it makes recommendations are proposals submitted by outside agencies.

A TYPOLOGY OF DECISION-MAKING PROCESSES

The interrelation of these two dimensions suggested a typology for viewing decision-making relationships between CAAs and boards of education in the cities studied. This typology is represented in Figure 1. Although it must be emphasized that the figure represents ideal types and that the variations in the processes studied were relative, the cases to which the research was directed can be described in terms of the typology.

Type I Processes (Weak Staff—Low School Access). None of the cases studied was of the Type I variety. Such a process would be characterized by a weak agency staff and a low level of access to the committee for school officials. The establishment of educational components

[17] David W. Minar, "Community Characteristics, Conflict, and Power Structures," in Robert S. Cahill and Stephen P. Hencley, eds. *The Politics of Education in the Local Community,* (Danville, Ill.: Interstate Printers and Publishers, 1964).

Access of school superintendent to
the Community Action committee

		Low	High
Strength of CAA staff	High	Type IV	Type III
	Low	Type I	Type II

Figure 1 A typology of decision-making processes.

in such a situation would require that the initiatory actions be taken by either a nonschool agency or the committee itself. The investigation of processes in other cities to determine the possible existence and implications of Type I situations would seem warranted.

Type II Process (Weak Staff—High School Access). The processes utilized in Van Buren and in Winthrop during the development of the first set of proposals can be classified as Type II situations.[18] In both instances, the superintendent of schools was instrumental in establishing the CAA. Other agencies were not sufficiently staffed to develop proposals, and the CAP committee had no staff that could assist it. Thus, the CAA was totally dependent upon the schools and the technical expertise of school officials for proposals. These officials developed the proposals unilaterally, presented them to the CAP committee, and saw them receive perfunctory approval.

The programs begun in this way were essentially modifications or extensions of things that the schools were already doing. Preschool classes that looked very much like kindergartens were started for four-year-olds in disadvantaged neighborhoods. Similarly, reading specialists and high school counselors were added to school staffs to do virtually the same things that had been done by other specialists and counselors in the past. The major change promulgated by these programs was a reduction in the student-professional ratio in schools serving disadvantaged areas. In effect, schoolmen employed the funds available from the OEO to implement the long-popular panacea of educators—reduction of class size.

The other and most innovative program undertaken in both Van Buren and Winthrop was a neighborhood school program. The integral concept

[18] The processes studied in Winthrop included those associated with the first establishment of CAP components and the subsequent refunding of the same components.

in such a program is that the school should be open in the late afternoon and early evening to serve neighborhood residents, including adults. The idea for the programs was rooted not so much in the experiences of Van Buren and Winthrop as in those of a nearby city. For many years, this other city has enjoyed national acclaim for its neighborhood school program, which is made possible by foundation support. Thus, the establishment of these components in Van Buren and Winthrop can probably be attributed to professional communication among administrators. As established in these two districts, the neighborhood school programs were dominated by such traditional offerings as classes in typing, basic English, arithmetic, and physical education. Although these classes were held during evening hours and taught by professional teachers, their enrollments were not as large as many school and CAP leaders wished. Indeed, a common observation by leaders in both cities was that many of the people who could benefit most from the program did not seem to be aware of it.

In summary, the components developed through Type II processes looked very much like existing school programs. School officials given the freedom to choose unilaterally the programs they wish to establish are likely to opt for extensions of traditional school activities. The CAP will be treated simply as a supplementary source of funds for school programs directed toward disadvantaged children.

Type III Process (*Strong Staff—High School Access*). The process through which the CAP was established in Jefferson can be classified as a Type III situation. In this instance, a leadership committee composed of influential city citizens was established without impetus from the schools. This committee employed an executive director in its earliest days and encouraged him to develop proposals. The school superintendent was placed on the committee, and indications that his educational expertise was acknowledged were seen in the routine way in which the committee approved Head Start and summer enrichment program proposals submitted by him.

Because the superintendent belonged to the CAP committee, he knew that the members strongly approved of the volunteer program on which the CAP proposal was being modeled by the executive director. He also had high regard for the community-wide influence of the committee and did not wish to gain its disfavor. In this sense, he was co-opted by the committee. Although he had reservations about some elements of the proposal, he did not voice them but encouraged his staff to co-operate in proposal development and pledged the support of the schools to it.

The program established in Jefferson resembles the neighborhood school programs that were established in Van Buren and Winthrop. That is, it uses school facilities and provides some of the same components (e.g., counseling and remedial and enrichment education). However, it differs organizationally in that it is not a school program. As the superintendent stated, "It is a Community Action Program, and the schools are subcontractors for a portion of it."

The program has a broader scope than the programs in Van Buren and Winthrop. Because it is not solely school-administered, cooperation with such agencies as the Planned Parenthood Association and the Methodist Community House is facilitated. Subcomponents related to the schools include classes in job development for the unemployed, in homemaking for women, and in home living for men; guidance and counseling for potential dropouts; remedial and enrichment education for grade-school children; and Saturday morning physical education classes. Programs not subcontracted to the schools but run in conjunction with them include evening care for preschool children (so that mothers can attend classes), family planning, several skill and tutoring classes staffed by volunteers and held at the request of neighborhood residents, and an organizational component that provides staff members ("urban agents" who canvass the target area to identify problem situations and refer needy individuals to programs that are in existence). Thus a major difference of the Jefferson program in contrast to the others is its far greater reliance upon nonschool personnel.

Those close to the program are of the opinion that it has awakened an interest in and a respect for education on the part of residents in the neighborhood which it serves. Although hard data on such attitudes are not yet available, and perhaps never will be, the continuing increase in program enrollments offers some support for the generalization just made. The fact that there has not been a window broken in the school which houses the program since its inception is perhaps testimony that the program objective of bringing children closer to the school is being realized.

Although the effects stated are somewhat ambiguous and difficult to document, there is no question that the decision-making processes through which the program was established and implemented created a rivalry between old-line school personnel and those involved in the CAP. This rivalry can be traced to an early disagreement between Community Action representatives and school officials regarding the degree of "educational structure" to be included in the program. At the base of the dispute was a difference in social and educational philosophy.

As the CAP executive director stated, "We were interested in grass-roots involvement and participation; they wanted educational soundness."

Some teachers and principals saw this difference in philosophy reflected in administrative procedures of the CAP and complained about the apparent lack of structure and student discipline. As one principal stated,

> . . . They should not let students make noise, talk, and walk out if they want to. You cannot have children cavorting in the halls when other students are really making an effort. One of our crying needs is for good work habits, and this is violating that need. What image does the school have—should it be a place where you can run around the halls or a place where you come to study?

The development of the program outside the school hierarchy undoubtedly contributed to the basis for such feelings. They will probably continue, for the executive director has said, "The long-range effectiveness of Community Action Programs will depend upon what modifications boards of education and other agencies make in their administrative structure and procedures as a result of participation."

Consideration of the circumstances surrounding the Jefferson CAP suggest the generalization that interagency cooperation at the planning level will encourage interagency conflict at the operation level. Teachers and principals were found to resist the attempt of an external agency (the local CAP) to establish educational programs that differed from their notion as to what schools should be. A compounding irritant was the employment of former school personnel in positions of authority within the external agency. Thus, teachers and principals not only perceived a challenge to their professional expertise but also suffered the additional discomfiture of seeing former peers and subordinates gain status in the new agency.

There is no doubt that the existence of a "we-they" syndrome has impeded the coordination of the Jefferson CAP with the everyday school program on the building level. However, central office administrators, although possessed of some philosophical reservations themselves, see evidence of cooperation developing and have fond hopes for the future. Indeed, in many instances teachers and principals have worked with CAP personnel to help meet family needs that the schools are not equipped to serve. Additionally, there have been more than 200 referrals by school personnel to the CAP and several cases in which the CAP counselor has worked jointly with teachers. However, perhaps the most valuable contribution made by the program has not been in what was done but in what was avoided.

Many writers have noted that the potential for conflict between school personnel and inner-city residents is great.[19] For the most part, school employees are products and representatives of a middle-class culture that is alien and some times suspect to inner-city residents. Schools often convey the image of being hierarchical and impersonal service agencies to middle-class aspirations, thereby erecting barriers that discourage communication and understanding between school personnel and local residents. Similarly, cultural differences sometimes prevent teachers and administrators from carrying their views to the public in meaningful and understandable terms. This lack of communication can create misunderstandings that provide the basis for wider and deeper conflict.

Several examples of action by urban agents or the local CAP coordinator have suggested that these persons provide a communications link which mediates potential conflict situations. For example, one principal halted a school-sponsored program of free immunizations in her building because many students did not return the first parental permission slips sent home with them. Some Negro community leaders were outraged at this stoppage and went to the CAP coordinator with their grievance. The coordinator telephoned the principal and offered to print new permission slips in his office if she would reopen the program. She reluctantly consented, protesting, "There is a limit to how many times you can expect professional people to do things over."

The new permission slips stated that "lockjaw shots" rather than "tetanus inoculations" (the phrase used on the original slip) were being given. This time, almost the entire student body responded. As a result, everyone involved, including the principal, lauded the activity, and the possibility of community conflict was averted.

Several times, urban agents, who are residents of the inner city employed by the CAP agency to visit and service neighborhood residents, have convinced parents that they should send their children back to school after the youngsters have come home complaining of prejudicial or unfair treatment by teachers. "Teachers are not always wrong; they want to help your child" is the theme that the urban agents carry into the neighborhood. Their effectiveness in such situations appears to be maximized by their positions outside the school hierarchy.

In review, Type III processes were characterized by strong CAP staff

---

[19] Events since this manuscript was prepared, most notably those in Ocean Hill-Brownsville, make it clear that this is important.

influence and high access of school officials to CAP committees. Because this is the only situation in which both the schools and strong nonschool interests (represented by the CAA staff) have joint potential to influence the committee, it is suggested that this is the one most likely to produce cooperatively planned programs. Moreover, the representation of nonschool interests serves as a check upon educational traditionalism and encourages the possibility of establishing programs substantially different from those already in the schools. Success in this endeavor, however, requires that the support of school officials for CAA staff proposals be co-opted, as it was in Jefferson.

Type IV Processes (Strong Staff—Low School Access). The co-optation of school officials is more likely to be accomplished by the CAP committee than by its staff. Consequently, it is more likely to occur in Type III processes, in which the superintendent has access to the committee, than in Type IV situations, where he does not.

Two related possibilities must be noted. The first is that, by cooperating with the CAA in furthering proposals initiated by the agency staff, the superintendent can win CAP committee support for other educational programs suggested by the schools. This happened in Jefferson. Although the development of the program discussed above followed the Type III process, the CAP committee and staff deferred to and supported the educational expertise of the schools in processing Head Start and Elementary and Secondary Education Act proposals.

The other possibility is that, rather than leading to cooperatively developed programs, a Type III situation could lead to conflict between the CAA staff and the superintendent in which the CAP committee supported the former. Should this occur, however, it is probable that the schools would withdraw from the CAP arena, shifting the situation to that classified as a Type IV process. After clearing the original set of proposals through the local committee, the Winthrop superintendent had no more dealings with the committee. School officials began to deal instead through the executive director and later the deputy director for educational programs within the CAA. These staff personnel have subsequently screened all school proposals and made recommendations regarding them. By following these recommendations of its burgeoning staff, the CAP committee has simultaneously decreased the percentage of funds that it will apportion to school programs and increased its interest in affecting all local educational programs for disadvantaged children.

Resolutions which the CAP committee has passed include the following:

1. That schools be notified in writing that the Lafayette County CAP committee guideline for hiring teacher aides is to hire the resident poor. . . . Head Start teacher aides are (to be) hired from the resident poor from the respective communities when available for neighborhood communities when not available locally.

2. That field trips and other activities appropriate for Head Start provide an opportunity for socially integrated activities (i.e., field trips can be jointly planned by schools of racially different groups). The planning and execution of this matter *must be done by the CAA staff.*

3. That the CAP committee instruct the director to investigate the population being served by Title I, P.L. 89-10 (Elementary and Secondary Education Act) monies allocated to the school boards of Lafayette County. The question to be answered, are the poor being identified and served? (*sic*)

4. That school districts applying for funding of any programs under the Economic Opportunity Act submit their total programming under Elementary and Secondary Education Act to the CAA prior to application for OEO funds.

5. That over-all federal expenditures for poverty school districts be considered when OEO allotments are made for school community action projects with the objectives of maximum feasible participation by the poor and maximum efficiency of federal funds to serve the poor.

The lack of access to the CAP committee by the Winthrop superintendent impeded his making the official school position on these points known to the committee before its action. Because the resolutions were passed without consultation with school men, they took the form of unilateral directives to the schools.

It would not be inaccurate to say that the Winthrop schools have resisted implementing these directives. For example, when the CAA deputy director requested the twenty-nine school districts in the county to submit information about the economic status of students enrolled in Title I programs, only six districts responded. Similarly, when asked about CAA charges that Title I programs ignore economic deprivation and had not involved adequate coplanning with the CAA, Winthrop school officials took refuge in the state Title I guidelines. These guidelines, they said, make no reference to the need for programs to be concentrated on children of poverty, but merely require them to be conducted in schools located in disadvantaged areas. Indeed, one school-man noted that a state department had referred to the act as "general aid to education in disguise." Thus, the attempt of the CAA to influence the development of Title I programs apparently faces local opposition that may be ameliorated only by the issuance of revised guidelines or perhaps even a court test.

The characterization of Type IV processes by strong staff influences upon the CAP committee and low access by schoolmen to the same body suggests that this situation is more likely to generate interagency conflict than any of the others studied. This conflict may arise over either of two issues: the blockage of an attempt by the schools to submit a particular proposal, or the attempt of the CAA staff acting through the CAP committee to affect existing school programs.

In either case, the central prerequisite is the development of a strong staff within the CAA that manifests greater devotion to the amelioration of poverty than to continual stability in educational programs. A neces-sary corollary is the lack of effective access to the CAP committee by school superintendents and staff members. Thus the agency staff medi-ates all proposal requests from schools and conveys them with recom-mendations to the committee, which legitimates them.

The likelihood of significant educational changes resulting from such an arrangement is questionable. In the first place, it is unlikely that very many local CAAs have the political power or community prestige that would enable them to emerge victorious in a public dispute with the local schools. Although the Winthrop CAA may temporarily succeed in having Elementary and Secondary Education Act funds withheld from the schools, it must be doubted that the agency could survive the pressure of being recognized as responsible for halting the program altogether. Thus, in any showdown situation, it is hypothesized that entrenched public school interests will survive any frontal attack by a relatively young and politically unstable CAA.

Second, CAA staff members, in such situations, will probably reject what they consider the traditional approaches embodied in school pro-posals. Schoolmen, on the other hand, will reject the resolutions of the CAP committee as unwarranted intrusions upon their domain by an ex-ternal group. The lack of interaction between CAP policy makers and school officials will not permit the former to demonstrate their sincerity and strength of support for particular ideas, nor will it allow the latter to draw sufficiently upon their expertise in responding to the concerns of the committee. Without such exchange, impasse is the most predic-table outcome of the decision-making process.

CONCLUSION: PROJECTING THE IMPACT OF COMMUNITY
ACTION PROGRAMS UPON SCHOOL DISTRICTS

Although educational components vary in the extent to which they deviate from previous school programs, they can be considered curricular innovations. As such, there are at least two reasons to indicate that they will gain permanency in school programs.

First, they have been widely and favorably publicized by nonschool as well as school sources. It may be argued that school programs which gain local publicity of a favorable nature are rarely discontinued. Schools being public agencies, their officials are loath to terminate popular programs, regardless of personal feelings or educational merit. In a more particular sense, educational programs for the disadvantaged constitute a special interest of spokesmen for this group. At this point, such programs have a strong ally in the civil rights movement. The most pointed lesson of this movement for school administrators has been that they cannot insulate themselves from the demands of minority group spokesmen, who are also, by and large, the spokesmen for the disadvantaged. Thus, school officials can be expected to take a long look at alternatives and possible repercussion before discontinuing educational components.

A second force working for the continuation and even extension of educational components is the attitude of teachers. Many of these components introduce what may be considered teaching luxury or convenience items into school districts. Such prerequisites as small classes, teacher aides, special materials, and funds for field trips become desirable to teachers to whom they are not customarily available. As teacher organizations continue to gain strength and the scope of negotiable issues increases, it is not unlikely that teachers will make bargaining points of such matters. Thus, boards of education could be forced to allocate local funds to the extension of programs that were initiated with federal subsidies. Such developments not only would place further strictures upon the decision-making prerogatives of school boards but also would constitute new demands upon local and state revenues available to support education.

These generalizations suggest that school innovations promulgated by external groups or agencies and funded by them on a limited or temporary basis will ultimately be put before the general public as budget items for their approval. It would seem prudent for schoolmen to cultivate citizen support for these innovations before such referenda are required. The structural and procedural characteristics of Community Action Programs that encourage this kind of action constitute, in themselves, important innovations in many school districts.

By encouraging the participation of lay citizens, including those who are poor, and officials of nonschool agencies in decisions regarding educational components, Community Action Programs suggest that education is becoming a community process rather than the exclusive domain of professional educators. The culmination of this point of view is seen in OEO support for educational programs administered by agencies other than schools. School officials have voiced, and probably will continue to express, concern about these "nonprofessional competitors." In so doing, they may be overlooking a worthwhile by-product of such involvement.

It is suggested that a major effect of increased lay participation in either advisory or administrative capacities will be to strip schools of some of the institutional mystique and aloofness attributed to them by disadvantaged citizens. When new voices aid in shaping schools policies, ears in disadvantaged areas will become increasingly attentive to the messages proclaimed. Greater involvement of lay citizens in school programs will increase the dialogue between schools and their surrounding communities, thereby encouraging concomitant increments in both educational effectiveness and citizen appreciation. The ultimate benefits to administrators may extend beyond any particular program and be manifested in community willingness to support schools at higher tax levels.

As Community Action Agencies and/or similar non-school units gain power, they will strongly challenge the unilateral decision making by school officials that has become the norm in many districts. They promise to contribute to the erosion of boards of education as policy-making bodies. The Community Action people and those affiliated with them will deal with administrators, not board members. This liaison activity will increase the knowledge base and consequently the influence of superintendents vis-à-vis boards of education.

Although participation in Community Action Programs may increase the influence of superintendents in dealing with their boards, it simultaneously threatens to reduce their influence over the educational program. Establishment of program conditions by federal officials, recommendations of lay advisory committees, and resolutions by local Community Action committees all impinge on what previously have been considered matters of professional concern and administrative discretion.

Impingements on the local level may result from involvement solicited by administrators through the establishment of advisory committees. They may also come from the efforts of a strong CAA staff that speaks through the Community Action committee and seeks to determine program policies for disadvantaged students. In either case, superintendents will find that the role to which they have grown accustomed requires alteration.

Community Action Programs are testimony to the increased prominence of schools as agents of social change and the emergence of education as a community process. In such an atmosphere, the role of a superintendent can be limited neither to that of an executive agent administering policies of a board nor to that of a technical expert determining policies for a board. Rather, his role must be structured to ensure viable relationships with many community groups and agencies in addition to his board of education. The pressures created by Community Action Programs suggest that this role must move increasingly toward that of an educational broker. The incumbent of such a role will acknowledge, weigh, and coordinate the sometimes conflicting educational demands of various interest groups, including his own professional staff and the board to which he is responsible.

The Use of Nonprofessionals in Large-city Systems

Timothy Leggatt

During the past ten years nonprofessionals, both paid and volunteer, have been introduced into many public school systems in auxiliary teaching roles. This paper is concerned with identifying the factors that account for this particular type of innovation, or the lack of it, in large-city systems and with assessing its scope and ultimate consequences. This instance of innovation has been chosen because of its evident importance for the interrelations of school systems and their constituent communities.[1]

The many social pressures to which public school systems in American cities historically have been exposed have in recent years been greatly intensified. To the perennial problems of teacher shortage, expanding student enrolments, and the need to reduce class size and replace uncertified or ill-qualified teachers have been added those due to sustained rates of dropout from school at a time when the society's need for more highly educated employees is also growing and to prevalent attempts of educators to provide more programs of "enrichment" and more social and psychological care.[2] Two further factors are yet more pressing. The handicaps from which schools and children suffer in inner-city and slum areas, as contrasted with those in suburban areas of relative affluence, have been forcefully brought out and clearly documented by many commentators.[3] And this imbalance in educational provision is further

---

[1] This paper is based upon material presented in full detail in the writer's Ph. D. dissertation. See Timothy W. Leggatt, "The Use of Non-professionals in Public Education: A Study in Innovation," unpublished Ph. D. dissertation, Department of Sociology, University of Chicago, 1966.

[2] See Morris Janowitz and David Street, "Final Report, Russell Sage Foundation Project," University of Chicago, June 1965 (mimeographed).

[3] See the following: James B. Conant, *Slums and Suburbs* (New York: McGraw-Hill, 1961); Patricia Cayo Sexton, *Education and Income* (New York: Viking Press,

complicated by the factor of race—the compelling evidence of Negro deprivation. Hence the tasks of the schools have become intrinsically more difficult to handle, and school systems in cities of both the North and the South have become the object of mounting civil rights activity and of increased public attention. Finally, since the initiation of Project Head Start in 1965, the massive input of federal government funds under the various education acts and the Economic Opportunity Act has added a further powerful stimulus to public scrutiny, city government pressure, and the clamor of community action groups.

This is the context in which the introduction of nonprofessionals into public education has to be viewed. It is clear that educators must search continually for means of adapting the schools to changing demands, that they must experiment and innovate. The role of the teacher and the relations of schools with their communities need to be thought out afresh, and new ways of organizing the teaching process in its changing social context should be carefully considered in view of present circumstances.[4]

Three distinguishable instances of the use of nonprofessionals in education are examined in this paper on the premise that they are all parts of one innovative movement: the employment of paid aides in schools, the use of volunteers in schools, and the work of volunteers in out-of-school situations. The research upon which this paper is based took the form of comparative case studies of educational systems of five major cities: Chicago, Detroit, New York, Pittsburgh, and Washington, D.C. Within these cities the magnitude of the innovations varies. In New York in-school volunteers amount to only 1.6 per cent of public school teachers, but in Detroit they constitute over 12.5 per cent. In Washington paid aides constitute 5 per cent of teaching staff members; in New York, 14 per cent.

Any study of the internal organization of a school administration and of the relations between the professional staff and their lay superiors on the school board inevitably falls within the tradition of the sociological analysis of bureaucratic organization. This perspective leads first to a focus upon the performance of the holders of power in an organization hierarchy—in this context the superintendent of schools and the

1961); Janowitz and Street, op. cit.; and Frank Riessman, The Culturally Deprived Child (New York: Harper & Row, 1962).
[4] Aides were first introduced into schools in their current usages in 1952 and volunteers in 1956. According to Miles, by 1960–1961 9 per cent of elementary and 18 per cent of secondary schools were using aides in some way. See Matthew B. Miles, "The Nature of the Problem," in Miles, ed., Innovation in Education (New York: Bureau of Publications, Teachers College, Columbia University, 1964).

members of the Board of Education. Second, it gives attention to the response of subordinate staff—in this instance teachers. Third, it requires an analysis of organizational format—here of the school system. However, as the environmental context of school systems is so clearly relevant to the introduction of nonprofessionals, the theoretical perspective must be broadened by the use of concepts derived from the study of interest groups. Members of boards of education may be elected or appointed, but in any event their sources of authority are external to the school system and in effect political. In addition, various interest groups—of teachers, parents, volunteers, civil rights workers, and other citizens—are concerned in the determination of school policies. This second perspective emphasizes the importance of taking into account the political bases of school board decision makers and their accessibility, as well as the strengths and weaknesses of external groups. This theoretical orientation served to guide the collection of data in the five cities and also the analysis that follows.

THE SEQUENCE OF INNOVATION IN THE FIVE CITIES

The developments in the use of aides and volunteers can be clearly perceived when data from the five cities are directly compared and contrasted, and when it is shown how the systems differ in their innovative qualities.[5] Some of the effects of using nonprofessionals are already readily observable, and these are similar in all the cities. There are considerable contrasts between the cities in their structures and strategies of innovation, however, and it is from an analysis of these differences that three models of innovation have been constructed: a model of administrative management to fit the cases of Detroit and Pittsburgh, a model of competitive enterprise for Chicago and Washington, D.C., and a composite model for New York City.

The clearest way to present the sequence of innovations in the five major cities is in tabular form, as set out in Table 1. In all the cities volunteers have also been active in out-of-school locations. These programs have multiplied at different rates and are not easily compared. Nevertheless, those in Chicago and Washington may be distinguished from the others. In these cities the programs were well established before volunteers were introduced into schools—as indeed they still had not been in Chicago up to the close of the 1965–1966 school year. In these cities the programs have been to some degree coordinated and brought into contact with each other by one agency; in Chicago this is the Com-

---

[5] Full details of programs in the five cities are given in Leggatt, *op. cit.*

Table 1   *Sequence of Innovation in the Use of Nonprofessionals in Five Major Cities*[a]

Date	City	Innovation
	The Use of Aides	
1959	Detroit	Great Cities Project
1960	Pittsburgh	Team Teaching Program
1963	New York	First use of aides
. . . .		
1965	Washington	First use of aides
	Chicago	First use of aides
	The Use of School Volunteers	
1956	New York	Public Education Association School Volunteer Program
1959	Detroit	Great Cities Project
1961	Pittsburgh	First use of volunteers in Compensatory Education Programs
1962	Washington	Urban Service Corps Programs
	New York	School volunteers taken under school administration
. . . .		
1964	Detroit	Department of Volunteers established
1965	Pittsburgh	Expansion of volunteer program
1966	Chicago	Director of volunteers appointed

[a] In both parts of the table a dotted line indicates the time at which federal funds became available for use in the programs.

mittee on New Residents, which is part of the Mayor's Commission on Human Relations, and in Washington it is the Office of Tutoring Services of the Health and Welfare Council. Volunteers in Chicago and Washington, more than in the other three cities, have provided competition with the schools.

When aides and volunteers are considered separately, no simple pattern of innovation emerges for the five cities. However, when the two are considered together, there are two clear conclusions. First, when the innovations are managed by the school administration itself, they come about earlier than in systems where there is a situation of what may be called competitive enterprise; the sequence is also different. Second, federal funding plays a more important role in initiating programs in cities in which the administration takes no initiative; and in all cases external funds rather than reallocated existing funds have supported school programs using nonprofessionals, with only one exception.

In both Detroit and Pittsburgh the use of aides preceded that of volunteers and occurred in these cities before the other three. The aide programs were embodied in projects financed in part by the boards of education and in part by foundation funds. In these two cities volunteers were invited into the schools by the administrations, and the programs involving volunteers were also financed by administration or foundation funds. When federal funds became available, they were utilized for the expansion of existing programs.

In contrast, Chicago and Washington were the last of the five cities to introduce aides, and they did so only after federal funds became available. They were also the last to use volunteers; as pointed out previously, by the end of the 1965–1966 school year Chicago had not advanced beyond an expressed intention to use them. In Washington the administration has contributed nothing toward the funding of the volunteer programs; foundation funds were superseded by federal monies in 1965–1966. In both cities volunteer activities outside the schools preceded all other developments, and these have grown to greater importance than in the other cities.

New York presents still a different case, reflecting the appropriateness of describing it by a composite model of innovation. An internal initiative was taken to introduce aides in New York, but this occurred after an outside group, the Public Education Association (PEA), had been responsible for bringing volunteers into the schools. It took six years before the administration was prepared to assume responsibility for the supervision and funding of the school volunteer program. Although New York is similar to Chicago and Washington in that the initiative for using volunteers came from outside the administration, it is dissimilar in that it developed its aide program earlier and in advance of the availability of federal funds, which it has used only in order to add to its program.

The Role of External Funds

Federal funding for the introduction of nonprofessionals and for the expansion of existing programs is clearly of prime importance. However, other sources of external funds have also played a major role. In New York the school volunteer program was started with funds from the Public Education Association, the New York Fund for Children, and the Fund for the Advancement of Education. In Washington the Eugene and Agnes Meyer Foundation supported the early years of the Urban Service Corps, the agency of the administration that introduced volunteer programs into the schools. In Detroit the John F. Kennedy Memorial

Fund financed the start of the Department of Volunteers. In Detroit, Pittsburgh, and New York the Ford Foundation played an essential part in the development of programs using nonprofessionals.

The only program that has been developed without any reliance on external funding is the New York school aide program (and this has used some federal funds since 1965–1966). Not one of the programs introducing volunteers has been launched without external funding. In short, innovation is dependent upon new sources of funds becoming available, whether or not they are actively sought, rather than upon a reallocation of existing funds.

THE EFFECTS OF THE USE OF NONPROFESSIONALS

Some obvious effects of the strategy of innovation upon school systems are already evident. The introduction of nonprofessionals has an effect on the teacher's role, on the internal structure of school systems, and on school-community relations.

Effects on the Teacher's Role

It is certainly premature to make a complete assessment of the full effect of the introduction of nonprofessionals on the teachers with whom they work.[6] However, although some teachers are found to be ill suited to work with aides and volunteers, there is no evidence that nonprofessionals are incompatible with the professionalism of teachers. To the contrary, it seems more probable that the status and professionalism of teachers are enhanced by the use of aides and volunteers. Of the five cities, only in New York, Detroit, and Pittsburgh can the effects be commented on; in Chicago and Washington programs are in too rudimentary a stage of development, although the intentions of the Washington program deserve comment.

There are three ways in which the use of nonprofessional personnel may affect the teacher's role. First, it may merely provide a supplementary academic service for students and teacher, without noticeably affecting the teacher's range of work—unless, that is, it adds to it. The use of nonprofessionals for enrichment purposes exemplifies such a service. Second, this innovation may save the teacher from performing many

[6] For other published discussions of this subject see, *inter alia*, John J. Howell et al., *Teacher Assistants* (New Haven, Conn.: Yale University and Fairfield, Conn., Public Schools, 1959); T. Margaret Jamer, *School Volunteers* (New York: Public Education Association, 1961); Arthur D. Morse, *Schools for Tomorrow, Today* (New York: Doubleday, 1960); and Judson T. Shaplin and Henry F. Olds Jr., eds., *Team Teaching* (New York: Harper & Row, 1964).

subprofessional chores, so that the most demeaning of her former duties are taken care of by a nonprofessional. This may be termed the mopping-up function of nonprofessionals, when they are employed principally for clerical and custodial duties. Third, the use of nonprofessionals may involve a genuine restructuring of the teacher's role, a vertical rather than a horizontal (as with "mopping up") differentiation of work. The regular use of aides or volunteers inside the classroom, working with groups of children under the guidance of the teacher, is such an instance of a new form of specialization or internal differentiation.

In the case of volunteers, all three usages have been practised, and the use of volunteers might be expected to have an effect of a structural nature upon the division of labor in teaching. However, since volunteers are rarely in a position to give of their time on a regular day-to-day basis, this actually is not a likely development. The use of volunteers in schools should be regarded rather as the provision of a supplementary service. Another result of the occasional nature of their work is that volunteers do not pose a threat to the continuing authority of the teacher, and teachers who have been prepared to use volunteers have not lost any prestige from having lay persons share their jobs in certain ways. Although two accusations that volunteers in schools fall down on their duties and that their taking holidays causes a disruption of the programs in which they work are continually made against volunteers, no evidence to substantiate these charges was found during this research.

Because aides are commonly employed on a daily basis, they become a part of the school staff to an extent that the more occasional volunteers cannot hope to equal. They may have a more profound effect upon the teacher's role, but this is far from necessarily the case. In New York aides are used for "mopping-up" functions, and these are also the principal duties of aides in Detroit. Those in Washington—at least the ones introduced by the Center for Youth and Community Studies at Howard University—may in due time, if it proves possible to offer them genuine career development, allow restructuring of the role of the teacher. In Pittsburgh, the use of aides in the context of team teaching has already led to this development.

In New York the availability of aides to save teachers from unprofessional custodial and clerical chores clearly enhances the status of teachers to some degree. In Detroit and Pittsburgh the aides are used as an integral part of special programs and are allotted specific duties that are also supportive of enhanced status for teachers. The team-teaching program in Pittsburgh has certainly raised the prestige of master teachers (team leaders).

Should the developments that are anticipated in Washington occur and should those in Pittsburgh be still further extended, there will in time develop a need for these innovations to be taken into account in programs of teacher training. This development is at present not past the talking stage.

Effects on the Internal Structure

The strategy of innovation seems likely to involve certain structural changes in school systems that will give stability to the new programs. The new or adapted structures that owe their existence or adaptation to the innovation ensure its continued implementation at least throughout the period for which it has been scheduled.

In Chicago and Washington there has been no fundamental change, up to 1966, although the appointment of a new superintendent of schools in Chicago may lead to innovation. The appointment in Chicago of a director of volunteers is certainly no more than token. The Urban Service Corps in Washington, through which volunteer programs have been introduced, remains an addition to the normal administrative structure, rather than an integral part of it; this supplementary quality is enhanced by the corps' dependence upon volunteers in supervisory roles. The New York volunteer program has resulted in only a minor change, since the system has absorbed the PEA personnel who were previously supervising the program outside the school system and has thereby created a new department.

The structural changes in Detroit and Pittsburgh, however, are of a larger order. In Detroit the development of new programs has involved the establishment of the Division of Special Projects in 1964 and of the Department of School Volunteers in the same years. Outside the downtown office several new roles have been created at the local level, including those of school-community agent and school service assistant. In Pittsburgh the development of team teaching has itself constituted a structural change, as has the initiation in 1965 of the volunteer program, involving a hierarchy of administrative staff, both locally and in the downtown office, of school-community agents, community coordinators, and a director of volunteers. The Compensatory Education Section, responsible for all these programs, and Detroit's Division of Special Projects are in effect new structures designed for the introduction of programs of innovation.

Effect on School-Community Relations

The impact of using nonprofessionals may be examined in yet another way: in regard to its effect on the relations of school systems with their constituent communities. In this instance two alternative outcomes are possible. Either the innovation means that the school system has extended its reach beyond its former limits out into the community, or it means that the community has discovered the need for a new educational service, not provided by the schools, which it finds itself having to provide competitively. The new and increasing demands of the public upon the schools have been noted earlier, and with this in mind the alternatives may be differently expressed. If the system is responsive to external needs and demands, it will develop a program to extend its reach; if it is not responsive, it will take a "four-walls" attitude and leave the community to cope with its own resources.

Detroit, through its Extended School Program and the Great Cities School Improvement Project, and Pittsburgh, through its program of team teaching and its appointment of school-community agents and community coordinators, have both clearly extended the services of the school system out into the community. In Chicago, where all volunteer effort is outside the school system, and in Washington, where the outside program is more vigorous and larger than that inside the schools, federal government decisions and competitive services have been required to respond to the new-found needs of the schools' clientele. The situation in New York is once again intermediate. Here the externally devised program of the PEA was at least given the blessing of the New York City Board of Education from the beginning, so that the ideal type of competitive situation was impossible. Yet the program has remained relatively small, and much competitive activity is carried on by external agencies with large educational programs.

THE STRUCTURE OF INNOVATION

The next question to be considered is central to the interests of the paper: what features of the school systems (or indeed of the five cities) determine that innovation will occur in one rather than another, that it is abetted here and resisted there, and that its forms of occurrence are various? Three dimensions of the context in which the innovations take place need to be considered: socioeconomic factors, factors that relate to the internal structure of the school systems, and environmental factors.

Socioeconomic Factors

It would seem on first reflection a probable hypothesis that differences in the socioeconomic characteristics of cities might be of relevance to an understanding of the introduction of nonprofessionals in the five cities. There are marked differences among the cities in their racial compositions, ranging from Pittsburgh's 17 per cent to Washington's 55 per cent of nonwhites in the total city populations. The economic resources also vary. Yet there is no evidence that factors of this nature are of value in explaining the comparative lag of Chicago's introduction of nonprofessionals as against Detroit's, or any of the other differences among the cities.

It is true that the internal allocation of resources within school systems is closely related to socioeconomic composition. The new programs designed to assist children in deprived neighborhoods are directed at the poor, and the bulk of the out-of-school volunteer programs have the same aim. Furthermore, the federal funds that have contributed so vitally to the programs considered have been specially earmarked for the benefit of the poverty areas of the cities. Hence socioeconomic factors do determine the allocation of resources of programs once they have been set up or even envisaged. Nevertheless, they do not explain differences in the actions of school systems of the kind that have been noted. Either, therefore, socioeconomic differences are of no consequence, or (what in this context amounts to the same thing) they are too small or refined to be of relevance to the rather gross differences being considered here.

Factors Relating to the Internal Structure of School Systems

Janowitz and Street have pointed out three consequences for large systems of the combination of centralized decision making in the central office, inadequate resources to supervise the carrying out of decisions, and poor communications between the central office and the schools. First, policy making is undifferentiated for the needs of different districts. Second, there is a lack of central control, which makes possible the development of local initiative and local variations. Third, there is a lack of information in the central office about what is occurring at the school level. As Janowitz and Street comment, this situation is ill-adapted to innovation.[7]

This analysis closely fits the situation in New York, as well as that in Chicago, from which it was derived. Washington seems to be more heavily centralized, with the administration exercising more control, though policy is not differentiated for different areas. The conditions for the model are not found in Detroit and Pittsburgh, where decision making is centralized but both communications and control are more adequate, especially in relation to the programs using nonprofessionals. In these two cities special departments are in complete control of the

[7] Janowitz and Street, *op. cit.*

programs, dealing directly with the schools and providing a communication link between school principals and the superintendent. In Detroit and Pittsburgh, therefore, the organizational format of the administration has been adapted to facilitate innovation. In the other three cities the lack of an adaptive format has been one factor that has certainly hindered initiative and responsiveness to opportunities for innovation.

A second factor, though of lesser importance, has been the attitude of staff toward the introduction of nonprofessionals. The position taken by unions has had at least some effect on change. In New York the United Federation of Teachers has supported the introduction of aides and succeeded in obtaining a massive expansion of the program at one point. In Detroit also the union has backed the program fully. By contrast, in Chicago the CTU has played only a negative role; it has steadfastly opposed any use of volunteers in schools and seems only to have endorsed the employment of aides, though not with conspicuous vigor, as a countermeasure to what it perceives as the threat of volunteers. In this instance the attitude of the union has coincided with that of the administration and therefore suited it.

Principals also have an important effect upon the introduction of nonprofessionals. In all five systems studied, principals have a certain measure of autonomy, so that a program is not likely to have great success if they oppose it. Volunteers are not placed in any schools unless principals request their services, or in any class in which the teacher is opposed to them. The same is true of aides to a great extent, although a few unwilling principals have been obliged to accept team teaching in Pittsburgh (in the latest expansion of the program), and no doubt Detroit principals have not had a real opportunity to reject parts of a package of special projects.

The importance of staff attitudes is clear, but at the same time it remains unlikely that the behavior of individual teachers and principals will be so uniform as to constitute either a positive force for innovation or a barrier against it. Different teaching staffs hold different positions, so that in every city there are some in favor of nonprofessionals being brought into schools and others opposed. Even the Chicago union's opposition to the use of volunteers does not constitute a monolithic objection among all teachers. Even more diverse among staff are the reasons for the positions taken and the roles approved of for nonprofessionals. As a result, although school administrations and external advocates of change have to take into account the views of teachers and principals, their role in the innovative process may be said to be of no more than secondary importance.

This consideration of the role of staff has excluded that of the superintendent. However, the professional perspective of the superintendent of schools is the third internal factor of importance in innovation. School systems no doubt vary in the scope that they afford to individuals, but in all five cities under consideration much importance attaches to the leadership style of the superintendent. At least in these cities Keppel's words are true: "His sense of policy and his estimate of the wise path to follow is the key to school development."[8]

The fourth important factor for innovation is the personal leadership quality or charisma of the superintendent. It is not always possible to separate the aspects of a superintendent's style of leadership that are due to his professional orientation from those that reflect his personal charisma. Nevertheless, the categories are clearly separate and will be distinguished as carefully as possible.

In Washington, Superintendent Hansen has not proved to be a vigorous executive; his tenure of office has been characterized by a lack of decisive leadership. He does not possess charismatic qualities, nor has he revealed in his attitude to the schools and the public a professional attitude conducive to innovation. In Judge Bazelon's words, "The poverty of the system is visible in the precedence that administrative goals have over what should be the ultimate goal—teaching."[9] In Detroit, Pittsburgh, and Chicago, however, there has been no lack of decisive leadership. Superintendents Brownell (over 10 years), Gross and Marland (over 8 years), and Willis (over 13 years), respectively, have been of critical, even decisive, importance in these cities. Brownell, Gross (when in Pittsburgh), and Marland have been innovative, accessible to outside views, and active in seeking new sources of funds. All have displayed a professional perspective conducive to innovation, but they have not been equally effective in leadership. Brownell and Marland have possessed this quality, but Gross despite his innovative intentions seems to lack it. In Pittsburgh he was in a favorable situation and showed himself very effective as an innovator. In New York, however, Gross failed. Notwithstanding the structural barriers to change within the New York administration, this failure cannot be explained satisfactorily without note of the personal shortcomings Gross manifested: indecisiveness and a neglect of reaching a satisfactory relationship with the New York Board of Education.

In Chicago Willis showed very strong leadership and a definite style

[8] Francis Keppel, *The Necessary Revolution in American Education* (New York: Harper & Row, 1966).
[9] U.S. Congress, House Committee on Education and Labor, *Hearings, Investigations of the Schools and Poverty in the District of Columbia,* 89th Congress, 1st and 2nd Sessions, 1965 and 1966, p. 868.

that guaranteed him support from the majority of the school board and from his subordinates in the central office. However, he was inaccessible to outside proposals, hostile to criticism, and little concerned with programmatic innovation. He clearly did not have the professional orientation conducive to the innovations now being considered. As Keppel has written, "The superintendency implies the role of leadership, and part of its function is to take responsibility . . . for the relevance of the schools to the social issues of the day."[10] This professional orientation was foreign to Willis.

Environmental Factors

At the outset of the research it was assumed that the formal legitimacy of the school board—its mode of appointment—would be of importance for the process of innovation. Of the five Boards of Education that have been considered, two, those of Chicago and New York, are appointed by the Mayor of the city; two, those of Pittsburgh and Washington, D.C., are appointed by judges; and one, that of Detroit, is elected. However, nothing was discovered in the course of the research to suggest that different behaviors of boards are attributable to this one factor; nor has previous research been conclusive on this point.

Equally, the size of the boards, which varies from Pittsburgh's fifteen persons to Detroit's seven and includes eleven for Chicago and nine each for New York and Washington, discloses little. Crain's argument that large boards are likely to be in greater agreement than small and are less liable to divisive rifts is certainly persuasive, but what is the cutoff point?[11] The matter is speculative, and it can be no more than guesswork to consider that of the five cities Pittsburgh alone has a board large enough for its size to be a significant factor in the present context, especially perhaps for its ability to mobilize in response to new demands from its community.

In any event, it is still necessary to examine each of the five cities as a separate case in the light of its history. The circumstances of each are in some way special, and in particular they are different in the political base of the school decision makers and in the attitudes displayed by the boards of education to their duties and their public.

The New York Board of Education emerged from its last period of ignominy only in 1961, when a new "reform" board was appointed. In the five subsequent years the board has not been accused of any mal-

[10] Keppel, *op. cit.*
[11] Robert L. Crain et al., *School Desegregation in the North: Eight Comparative Case Studies of Community Structure and Policy Making* (Chicago: National Opinion Research Center and University of Chicago, April 1966), p. 251.

practice; instead, it has been in a position from which it has been unable adequately to determine policy. The nature of the bureaucracy is such that effective power is shared between a number of interest groups within the administration and thereby diluted to the point where none has dominance. The superintendent is as handicapped in exercising executive control as is the board in determining policy. It is well understood by all parties that the initiative resides in the Livingston Street office (and not, for example, in City Hall), but it is an initiative that eludes the grasp of any one person or group. The result is that, although the New York administration is free of political manipulation, it does not have open and effective channels of communication with its public.

In Chicago, where the board is also appointed by the Mayor, the situation is quite different. For many years Chicago, like New York but to a greater degree and over a longer period, suffered from the plundering of its Board of Education. However, when this period finally came to an end in 1947, the outcome was different from that in New York. The board was shorn of its power, but the superintendent became more powerful having at last obtained control over the business management of the system. Although the scandals of the past involved the Democratic political machine, the changes of 1947 did not wholly weaken the power of the Mayor to appoint to the board candidates who would be loyal to himself. The setting up of a new Commission on School Board Nominations hampered outright political control however, and it has accorded with Mayor Daley's administrative style to accept this situation and operate within it. Therefore, while the Mayor's influence over the Board of Education remains important, the principal change in recent years, as mentioned previously, has been a great increase in the power of the superintendency. During the period of Willis' dominance the board was unable to pursue policies contrary to his wishes. The administration has not been regarded as accessible to public demands in a meaningful way, nor has it been seen to be free of the political influence of the Mayor.

In Pittsburgh the tradition of appointment has been nonpolitical. The judges, who take advice from the board itself, appoint members of Pittsburgh's powerful civic elite, which has taken the initiative in many of the city's postwar programs; this elite has been self-perpetuating but not exclusive, and appointments have been made to "balance the ticket" among important groups in the city, including trade unions, Negroes, and religious groups. As already noted, the board is large enough to make this appointment system readily workable. The result has been a strong, responsive, and civic-minded school board that allows a wide range of representation. This board has traditionally sought to appoint strong and capable superintendents, and recently it has succeeded. However, unlike the Chicago board, it is not in a position of relative inferiority vis-à-vis its superintendent. At the same time it has remained open to outside critics, especially to civil rights groups.

The school board in Washington, D.C., is also appointed by judges, but the result has been different from that in Pittsburgh; the city does not have internal self-government, and hence no tradition of self-leadership has been established. The city lacks industries and conventional politics; as many as a third of the employed population are in government service, and the politicians of the U.S. Congress have their prime responsibilities to their constituents elsewhere. Washington, therefore, has no civic elite of the Pittsburgh variety. The city is ruled directly by Congress, which has delegated none of its substantive power and holds decisive control over the budget; the Board of Education is as a result inherently weak. It is the only board that is formally subordinate and responsible to an external authority. Although it is formally accessible to members of the public, it has not paid obvious attention to the views of outside persons in shaping its policies.

Detroit is the only school system of the five considered that has an elected school board. This might *prima facie* suggest particular responsiveness to community interests. However, school board elections evoke little interest, so that the mere fact of being elected does not *ipso facto* make the board more representative of the community than one that is appointed. Nevertheless, there is a history in Detroit of the school administration having to count on the electorate for tax votes and hence being accessible to the public. In Detroit, it is also customary to give the superintendent the opportunity and the authority to run the system as he sees fit. The board has maintained its independence of partisan politics.

The implication seems to be clear that those school boards are more inclined toward innovation that have real stength, whether derived from their own civic standing or the backing of political power, and that show a commitment to their duties and their community through wise choice of a superintendent and an accessibility to members of the public. In other words, the factors that are important are the independent base of the decision makers and their communications with their client public.

The final environmental factor of significance in innovation is the availability of external sources of funds. These may be sought for the development of new programs; but even if they are not, the mere availability of large federal monies may exercise significant pressure for innovation on school administrations. The accessibility of these funds under the Economic Opportunity Act and the Elementary and Secondary

Education Act is public knowledge, and as a consequence any neglect of these substantial sources of funds constitutes an obvious point of attack for critics of a school system. Benson has described the pressure that this legislation exerts:

> ". . . What happens when a federal act is passed is that the prestige of the central government is placed behind the programs and activities specified in the act, and national publicity is focussed on the efforts of various state and local bodies that seek to comply with the intent of the law."[12]

The effects of federal legislation on the development of programs involving nonprofessionals in Chicago and Washington, D.C., and on the expansion of programs in Detroit and Pittsburgh have already been remarked.

All the environmental factors noted appeared during this research to have an effect on the behavior of school administrators and on their innovativeness. In addition these same factors affect the behavior of interest groups outside the school administrations. This relationship may also work in another direction; on occasion an interest group may directly affect the administration. The outstanding instance of this process in the five cities is the influence of the Public Education Association upon the New York school administration. It is at least highly probable that the administration would not have listened to suggestions coming from any other sources. However, the PEA had already been active in New York education for sixty years and had won respect for its single-minded concern for improvement. In addition, it had a tradition of research, and it was in a position to provide the necessary funds to finance the proposed program on an experimental basis. It may be speculated that only a group with such outstanding credentials is in a favorable position to exercise a direct influence upon the school administration of a large-city system.

THE MODELS OF INNOVATION

The preceding analysis has shown that socioeconomic factors have not determined which school systems are innovative in bringing nonprofessionals into education. Four internal structural factors are, however, important: (1) the organizational format of the administration,

---

[12] Charles S. Benson, *The Cheerful Prospect: A Statement on the Future of American Education* (Boston: Houghton Mifflin, 1965), p. 105.

(2) the professional orientation and (3) the leadership effectiveness of the superintendent of schools, and (4) the behavior of staff. All these influence the administration's attitudes to its duties and responsibilities. There are also three factors of importance in connection with a school administration's environmental relations: the strength of the school board, its relations with interest groups and the public, and the availability of external sources of funding.

The three models of innovation that have been proposed are based upon this analysis. According to the *model of administrative management,* innovations involving nonprofessionals are introduced on an administration's own initiative. Hence aides are introduced before volunteers, since this development does not rely on outsiders and represents an extension of the reach and responsibilities of the school system out into the community. The strategy of innovation is assisted by the establishment of new internal structures, that is, departments; and the institutionalization of innovation is abetted by the development of additional structures, that is, new roles or organizations. Although external funds are utilized and indeed sought, funding is taken as an internal responsibility, and this may be seen as signifying the acceptance and stability of the programs. The model of administrative management is also associated with superintendents who have a professional orientation conducive to innovation and responsive to community needs. Given this orientation, a superintendent with exceptional qualities of leadership will actively abet the use of nonprofessionals. Finally, the model of administrative management is associated with a board of education that has strong community standing and maintains good communications with its public.

In contrast to these characteristics are those that have been found to be associated with the *model of competitive enterprise.* According to this model, the school system is slow to accept the use of either aides or volunteers and does not spontaneously promote programs for either. In the case of aides a program is introduced as a response to the need to make proposals in an application for federal funds which of necessity involve the employment of "indigenous" aides; here the federal government has taken over the decision-making role. In the case of in-school volunteers, programs develop (perhaps in merely a token fashion) only after some or many others have already developed in out-of-school settings, hence in the face of competitive enterprise. In this situation volunteer programs outside the system become solidly stable and institutionalized. According to this model, innovation is not aided by structural changes, nor does it lead to them to a meaningful degree. Reliance for developing programs is placed upon external funds.

The model is associated not with innovative superintendents but rather with either weak or obstructive superintendents holding a different professional orientation from those who welcome innovation. In this instance school boards appear to lack independent strength, whether or not this is due to some involvement with city politics.

The *composite model* exemplified by the New York situation is not so clear-cut. The early introduction of the PEA volunteers may seem to suggest an instance of competitive enterprise. However, there was at the time no other program, and the PEA program was from its beginning sanctioned by the system. It cannot be said that the system has extended itself into the community or that structural changes have been associated with the innovations. On the other hand the system has funded its programs from its regular budget. It does not appear that the role of the superintendent has been of consequence, though in recent years no holder of this post has demonstrated personal charisma. The school board has been weak largely because of internal features of the organization of the administration. Since New York presents characteristics of each of the other two models, it is appropriate to place it in a third category, that of a composite model.

It might plausibly be thought that the influence of the factor of size was ignored in this analysis and that the experience of smaller systems would differ from that of the major cities discussed. This does not seem to be the case, except perhaps in relation to the composite model. Four smaller systems were examined, and the two principal models described were found to fit closely.[13]

THE FUTURE OF NONPROFESSIONALS

One final question remains to be considered in this paper: What are likely to be the scope and the ultimate consequences of the use of nonprofessionals in auxiliary teaching roles? Here also the same factors as before are of importance: the balance of influence between the professional leadership, the political leadership (the school board and those it represents), and external interest groups, and the intervention of the federal government through the supply of new funds.

In the school systems in which nonprofessionals have been used, programs have so far been of limited scope; the use of volunteers in

[13] The four small systems were those of Benton Harbor and St. Joseph, Mich.; South Bend, Ind., and Winnetka, Ill. For further detail see Leggatt, *op. cit.*, pp. 162–191.

particular has been modest. Nevertheless the developments have been meaningful. They have appeared in many different forms and have shown their value in supporting new services and in giving school programs more flexibility. School officials are firmly in control of these programs and so are able to hold them to the size that they choose, although the continued provision of federal funds is likely to be a powerful stimulus toward expansion.

In less innovative systems the strongest coercive pressure toward the use of nonprofessionals has been the availability of federal funds tied to programs that require the employment of indigenous personnel. The various interest groups that have supported the use of nonprofessionals are too weak to achieve more than they already have in most school systems, without the support of what amounts to federal intervention; the stability of volunteer groups in particular is always limited. Alternatively, changes in the superintendency or in the constitution of school boards may lead to innovation. This could occur with the appointment to a powerful superintendency of a man with a professional orientation inclined toward organizational innovation and responsive to external community demands. It could also occur as a result of a realignment of political influences that lead to a united and socially aware school board capable of giving firm direction to its professional staff or of making appointments of innovative officers.

The Use of Volunteers

No school volunteer program is of significant size. The New York program, which is the one most publicized, involves 700 volunteers and 33 schools. Contrasted with the system's 44,000 teachers and more than 800 schools, these figures are unimpressive. Volunteers are not a stable population, and they cannot be fitted neatly into standard administrative organizations and procedures. No doubt also school officials do not wish to permit the expansion of programs over which they have less than their accustomed control. By allowing a modest volunteer program into the schools an administration can benefit both from the direct contributions of the volunteers in broadening teaching programs and freeing teachers from chores and also from the indirect advantage of meeting one form of community criticism: they can seem to be responsive to community interest and to be taking advantage of willing offers of service. The volunteers in turn derive immediate satisfaction from their work and acquire closer acquaintanceship with the schools. If established amicably, this two-way process can significantly contribute to school-community understanding. Certainly there are some schoolmen who see volunteers in school as a Trojan horse planted by the community in their private professional domain; but even in cases where this viewpoint is valid, the horse is largely under Trojan control.

In cities such as Chicago and Washington, D.C., in which volunteer activity has occurred exclusively, or almost exclusively, outside the schools, it has acted as a challenge of initiative to the administration and a situation has arisen that has been described as one of competitive enterprise. This activity constitutes for the school system unequivocal evidence of community concern for education and disappointment with the performance of the schools. At least it is a source of friction, and perhaps it is even a goad provoking the system to undertake new programs and to recognize new responsibilities to the community. In this way volunteers make a positive contribution to the expression of community needs and the development of programs to meet them.

The long-term stability of out-of-school programs is in doubt, but so far their contribution has been substantial. Should they prove unstable, school administrations might be able to withdraw to attitudes of further diminished responsiveness, at least for a period. But as long as these programs maintain vigor, their pressure for change increases. Whether in or outside the schools the most important effect of volunteers is that of a community goad on the system, which cannot in the long run be ignored by an institution with public responsibility. The problems for the future are whether and how far this function can be institutionalized.

The Use of Aides

The use of aides has the potentiality to lead to far more profound changes than the use of volunteers in schools. Their numbers are larger and are likely to increase as federally funded programs continue. They can be employed on a daily basis and as either full- or part-time help in accordance with the requirements of a particular program: hence their deployment is flexible. Their functions may be very varied, from freeing teachers from nonprofessional duties to supporting teachers in classroom roles. They are also a part of the system, drawing wages and subject to discipline. Like volunteers, they can add to school-community understanding. They may also make possible a more refined division of labor in teaching, and they may be expected, if widely used, to enhance the status and professional standing of teachers.

Riessman advocates rigorous definition of the new nonprofessional roles, clear career prospects, and organization of nonprofessional employees; the last of these measures, he argues, is important for developing the power of the aides, their feeling of identification as a group, and the formation of role identity and job identity.[14]

If Riessman's proposals were followed (this does not seem likely to occur), a career line might be developed for aides so that some of them could graduate to become teachers. However, although aides will undoubtedly continue to play their part in school programs, there is at present no evidence that changes in this direction will occur. The conservative characteristics of teachers and of the teaching situation that so effectively limit change in schools are likely to prove too strong to allow aides to affect the division of labor seriously.[15] Educators are firmly in control of all the programs that employ aides, and they will surely not allow this group to infiltrate further into territory that can be defined as reserved for professionals. They will tolerate an increase in numbers of aides, but not a development of the role likely to affect the structure of the profession in ways that cannot wholly be foreseen and that they may presume to be adverse to their interests.

Hence Riessman and those who think like him are in several respects asking for the impossible, at least on the evidence of this writer's research. First, they assume or they seek to arouse awareness of particular problems (which they identify) likely to be met with by supervisors (in this instance teachers) and aides. However, excepting the effort of the Institute of Youth Studies in Washington, D.C., there is so far no evidence of this kind of awareness, either of the special problems of the nonprofessional roles or of the need for special training for teachers in working with aides. Second, the facilities and resources that would be needed for continual supervision of aide programs, if the developing career concept were brought forward, are neither available now nor built into the future of existing programs. Third, the present approach to the use of aides is administration- rather than research-oriented. Questions raised about the programs concern whether they work and are useful and manageable; they are approached from the pragmatic viewpoint of the administrator, and not from the experimental viewpoint of the researcher. Fourth, a too rigorous definition of the

[14] See Frank Riessman, "Strategies and Suggestions for Training Non-Professionals" and "Some Specific Suggestions for Training Non-Professionals," (Mental Health Services, Lincoln Hospital, New York, (both mimeographed). See also Arthur Pearl and Frank Riessman, New Careers for the Poor (New York: Free Press, 1965), pp. 55–73, and Center for Youth and Community Studies, Howard University, Training for New Careers (Washington, D.C.: President's Committee on Juvenile Delinquency and Youth Crime, June 1965).

[15] For detailed discussion of resistance to innovation among educators see Leggatt, op. cit. 13–34.

roles of aides might inhibit their inventive use at the school level and tend toward loss of flexibility of the programs in which they are employed. These points show something of the distance between present programs and thinking and the Riessman approach.

A fifth and final point may be made concerning whether any programs of the future are likely to fit the prescription better. Although Riessman is primarily concerned with how those responsible for programs should structure and organize them, he is also in favor of the aides developing some power and autonomy of their own; as already mentioned, he suggests unionization. Of the five cities on whose experience this paper is primarily based only in New York are the aides unionized, and this is within the State, County, and Municipal Employees' Union. This is obviously an unsuitable union from the Riessman perspective, since it lacks experience in the educational area and the know-how to abet the kind of step-by-step development to the position of teacher that the career concept requires. In other cities unionization, when it occurs, is more likely to come about within the teachers' union, and this would effectively nullify the Riessman goal of achieving an independent power base for aides. In all of the five cities the administration has the aide program firmly in hand and can surely avoid sharing control with any new union organization. School administrations plainly do not wish aides to achieve power and will not espouse any developments, including career development, that are not necessary to the maintenance of programs.

If it is remembered that Riessman and those who think like him have been acting as champions of the poor, which school administrators are not, it may be understood that their views on career development for aides are not matched by those that school administrators can be expected to hold. Considering that aides are recruited from a new source and have low educational qualifications and little prestige, it is surely quite unrealistic to imagine them acquiring independent power.

Despite these limitations upon future developments, there is no reason to doubt the stability of programs of the type and variety already established. It is likely that two innovations in administration are necessary for the effective institutionalization of the use of aides in schools. First, some restructuring of the central administration is needed, either the creation of a new administrative section or the adaptation of an existing one, so that the role may become institutionalized and at least in some measure defined and delimited. Second, a measure of autonomy must be allowed to school principals as a means of ensuring programs flexible enough to satisfy the different requirements of different neighborhoods. These two moves will go far to establish aides as part of the school system and to define their roles, at least loosely, while at the same time providing for the exact nature of the role to emerge or be determined at the school and neighborhood level. A third step to assure stability would be the incorporation of aides into the teachers' union, and this is likely to follow upon clear long-term recognition of aides by school administrations.

The Use of Nonprofessionals

From an organizational perspective there are two prime functions of nonprofessionals working in the field of education. On the one hand, they permit great flexibility in the development of programs and a modification of old routines; in this way they can in some measure contribute to debureaucratization. They are able to take menial tasks and chores away from the teacher and to contribute to the nurturing and socialization of children in school. Thus they assist the teacher and make possible new programs that the unaided teacher could not undertake. This development may even in the long term have the effect of raising the status of the teacher. On the other hand, nonprofessionals provide a stimulus from the community that, together with others, is moving school administrations to commit themselves to a larger role and to closer cooperation with lay people; and this is a trend that it will prove difficult to reverse. This stimulative function can be carried on either inside or outside the schools, and indeed it seems important that it should be. There is clearly a continuing role for agencies external to the school system to perform in the field of education, which is not and should not be the monopolistic preserve of schoolmen.

These principal functions of nonprofessionals need to become institutionalized, but a move in that direction entails the danger that the uses made of nonprofessionals will become routinized and will lose much of their value. For aides, who are easiest to absorb into the school system, the threat of unimaginative and dull programs is especially real. Eisenstadt has suggested,

> "The development of a bureaucratic organization in the direction of debureaucratization seems to be connected mainly with the growth of different types of *direct* dependence of the bureaucratic organization on parts of its clientele."[16]

If this hypothesis is correct, then clearly the more aides and volunteers become representatives of the schools in which they work rather than

[16] S. N. Eisenstadt, "Bureaucracy, Bureaucratization, and Debureaucratization," *Administrative Science Quarterly*, Vol. IV (1959), pp. 302–320.

of the outside community, the less they will contribute to the flexibility of programs and to debureaucratization. In the interest of flexibility it seems equally important that aides not be offered careers, as Riessman advocates, so that they are not absorbed too fully into the system. Although these dangers are not so apparent in the case of out-of-school volunteer activities, here also there is a need for vigilance to avoid the development of dull routines.

It was noted at the beginning of this paper that school systems are under increasing pressure from external demands. The social responsibilities of education are continually being redefined, and the changes make heavy demands upon educators and school boards. These cannot gain in the long run if they look on their communities as instruments of opposition and thereby fail to respond to the needs of the publics that they purport to serve. This paper should give support to the belief that school administrations should meet with imagination and even anticipate the changing needs of their communities, and should deploy for programmatic and organizational change their newly emerging resources.

The Local Board in New York City:
A Personal Document

Martin Mayer

For the last five years the opening of school has meant for me a constantly ringing telephone, a round of meetings, and a burst of duty visits to PS this-or-that. As a school-board chairman in a district with more than 30,000 children of all races, creeds, and colors, I was supposed to know what was happening in my district and somehow to reconcile the professional staffs of its schools and the parents whose kids attended them. Mine was by no means a unique experience—there are at least

Editor's Note: Martin Mayer's works often have bridged the social sciences and journalism, and as the author of *The Schools*[1] *and Social Studies in American Schools*[2] he has had a long-standing professional interest in education. His concern became personal, and all-engrossing, in 1962, when he became chairman of a local school board on the East Side of Manhattan. The appointment was part of a city-wide effort to reform the New York public schools through decentralization, revitalizing moribund local citizens' boards. As it turned out, the boards have had good intentions but little authority. The following paper is a personal narrative of the severe frustrations and limited accomplishments that emerged in Mr. Mayer's role over a five-year term of office. It is adapted from an article that appeared in *The Saturday Evening Post*[3] and reports not only the author's experiences but also the sharply pointed set of criticism of big-city education that he developed over the years. As such, the paper might be classified as a "polemical life history document." But the paper can be read for more than pathos and polemic. It documents the powerful resistances to change that are built into the New York City schools, and it indicates ways in which overcentralization and overcommitment to universalism in decision making

[1] Martin Mayer, *The Schools* (New York: Harper & Brothers, 1961).
[2] Martin Mayer, *Social Studies in American Schools* (New York: Harper & Row, 1963), based on a report commissioned by the American Council of Learned Societies.
[3] "What's Wrong with Our Big-city Schools?", *The Saturday Evening Post,* September 9, 1967, pp. 21–23, 66–68.

make it extremely difficult for the schools to operate in a reasonable manner at the local level. It shows the gap between citizen and parent on the one hand and professional and decision making on the other. And it demonstrates the inadequacy of essentially *pro forma* attempts to bring the school "back to the people." Mr. Mayer's occasional successes should be read in light of the reputation his board acquired as one of the most successful in the city. Its accomplishments derived more from the personal contacts that local board members had with powerful figures in the central headquarters then from the structure of the innovation itself. Such accomplishments were even more unlikely in neighborhoods where there were few persons vocal and influential on a city-wide basis to be recruited onto the local board. The paper calls for a genuine and truly radical decentralization of big-city schools, and I gather elsewhere that Mr. Mayer has been in many respects in sympathy with the most recent (since his paper was written) plan for decentralization of the New York City schools, the Bundy report,[4] which calls for breaking the system into a large number of almost completely autonomous districts, and with the intention of the new experimental districts actually launched. Yet, as he recognizes, such proposals threaten to enlarge inequalities (for example, in teacher recruitment) and to strain the educators' sense of professional competence and security beyond the breaking point. His writing, done more than a year before the tumultous events and teachers' strikes over the Ocean Hill decentralized district in the fall of 1968, thus anticipated these events to some degree. In the dilemmas of decentralization it is obvious that the New York, Chicago, Los Angeles, and other city systems are too monolithic and too far removed from the local citizenry, and that such an innovation as Mr. Mayer describes is insufficient remedy. It is not clear at all, however, that such complete and diffuse turnover of school matters to neighborhood groups as Marilyn Gittell advocates[5] could lead to other than the kind of chaos that New York has subsequently seen. Sadly, decentralization has been transformed into a simplified public issue concerned only with dispersing lay control and not with decentralizing the bureaucratic machinery and maintaining some appropriate balance betweeen relatively autonomous professionals and local citizen groups. Thus, developing opinions in New York City ignore what is perhaps the most important idea about decentralization contained in Mr. Mayer's account. This is the notion that improvement in the decentralized school district comes not so much directly from local lay decision-making as from a process in which lay agitation creates an area of freedom for the local administrator to do something sound for his district—and also embarrasses him into testing this freedom. Thus we can go beyond a simple formula of deprofessionalization to one of coupling increased lay control with the building of a drive for educational entrepreneurship, so often lacking in the inert middle ranks of big-city schools, among the professionals. In this formulation, the schoolman acts not only as responsive administrator but also, with reference to the headquarters staff and board, as an advocate for his area.

---

[4] Mayor's Advisory Panel on Decentralization of the New York City Schools, *Reconnection for Learning* (New York: The Panel, 1967). Mr. Mayer has published a comprehensive report on the Ocean Hill-Brownsville controversy and the resulting 1968 New York school crisis in *The Teachers Strike* (New York: Harper and Row, 1969).

[5] Marilyn Gittell, *Participants and Participation* (New York: Center for Urban Education, 1967).

23,000 school-board chairmen who enjoy similar rewards of prominence every fall. The experience was unusual in one way, however, because there was almost nothing I could do for the people who called me, and little of substance that could come out of our meetings. That parents kept calling us and coming to the meetings shows how desperately the people who have children in America's big-city schools want someone who will at least listen to their troubles.

All big-city school systems suffer from a kind of deafness that keeps them from hearing what people are saying. When a working mother suggests that it might be a good idea to open a school at 8 rather than 8:30 so women like herself could leave their children in a supervised place before going to work, the answer is that there's no budget for that. When mothers whose children ride a disorderly bus to and from school volunteer to take turns keeping peace on the vehicle, the answer is that the system's insurance policy covers only children supervised by licensed personnel. These are supposed to be real answers, but what they mean, obviously, is that nobody's listening.

Parents don't realize that teachers get the same sort of answers. At one of our meetings a junior-high teacher came forward to complain that she had spent the summer working at a university on the problems of teaching illiterate 13-year-olds to read. Now she had a class of illiterate 13-year-olds, and her principal wouldn't let her give her children the books she had learned to use; he said they weren't on the Board of Education's "approved list" of materials that could be bought for the classrooms. The teacher, who had been conditioned to obeying silly rules, was prepared to accept this answer, but she was puzzled about why the books hadn't been approved. When she checked up, she found that they really were on the approved list, but they were new and her principal had an old list. Then the principal told her all the money was spent, so she still couldn't have the books that she was sure would help her desperate class.

Actually, in the case of the teacher and the books, I had enough status to pry the money loose and get the materials into the classroom. It was one of those little triumphs that an honest attempt to listen can bring if you're a board member. But the day comes when you can see you're bailing the bay with a thimble, and after five years I am done with official listening: on June 30, 1967, I resigned. The bay is too big for my thimble.

The New York City school system consists of over 900 schools manned by about 55,000 teachers and educating, more or less, almost 1.1 million pupils. Though nearly a third of the city's children are in private or parochial schools, our public schools have more children than 40 of the

50 states. About $1.4 billion, 5 per cent of all the money spent on public elementary and secondary education in the United States, is spent annually by the New York City Board of Education—on about 2.5 per cent of the nation's students. Though everybody poor-mouths all the time, the one problem New York does not have is money. Our expenditures per pupil are one-third greater than those of the next richest big-city school system, and higher than those of such luxurious suburbs as Cleveland's Shaker Heights, St. Louis' Clayton, or Boston's Wellesley. Of all the teachers in the United States who make $10,000 a year or more, one-quarter work in New York City.

The system is almost completely insulated from public control. The nine members of the Board of Education, unpaid, are appointed for seven-year terms by the Mayor, and they are just about unremovable except by the state legislature. About 60 per cent of the operating money for the schools comes from the city's general budget, about 33 per cent from the state's general budget, and about 7 per cent on special programs from the federal government. New Yorkers almost never vote on school budgets or taxes. (Once they got a chance to vote on a half-billion-dollar bond issue to build new schools, and turned it down.) It is literally true that nobody knows where the money goes. I once cornered the then-president of the Board of Education in the men's room of the Bankers Club, and he said, "Only two people know where the money goes—God and Ferris [John J. Ferris, then director of the school budget]. And when Ferris dies, God will know a great deal more than he does now."

Our Board of Education relies for its information about the schools on an unbelievably harassed superintendent, who in turn depends on a headquarters staff of literally thousands of drudges, most of them in a twelve-story rabbit warren of an office building in downtown Brooklyn. There millions of documents that may not be thrown away creep out into the corridors in filing cabinets covered with years of filth. The members of the headquarters staff spend their time, not unpleasantly, attending meetings with each other: it is a rare occasion, calling for polishing of all the brass and threats of instant damnation to any teacher or child who says the wrong thing, when anyone from headquarters actually designs to visit one of the city's schools. All authority resides in the Board of Education and is exercised exclusively by the superintendent. No power is ever finally delegated to the people who must do the work—anyone who feels aggrieved can always appeal to the superintendent, and anything in the least original must have the superintendent's personal approval. Thus, for example, during the last school year, in addition to supervising an operation larger than all the television networks put together, Superintendent Bernard Donovan had to decide whether boys could wear their hair long in a high school, whether a little elementary school in an economically mixed neighborhood had enough poor children to qualify for a Head Start program, where precisely to draw the lines in rezoning two Queens high schools, how to use seventy ladies who never finished high school but had had a year's training to prepare them to be "assistant teachers," and whether or not certain magazines were suitable for school libraries.

The superintendent's power is exercised primarily through the by-laws and regulations of the system, books of printed rules which fill a bookcase in the office of the secretary of the board. Because nobody really knows what is in the rules, almost any expenditure of money or assignment of personnel or change of curriculum can be blocked by a bland statement that it violates the regulations (or the union contract, or the state education law, itself such a mess that the majority leader of the state senate had to commission a computer center in Pittsburgh to try to make sense out of it before he could begin proposing amendments). The regulations serve another function, too. With only a handful of exceptions, all positions in the New York schools are filled, on civil service principles, by people who have passed exams which "license" them for the job.

We have more than 1000 different "licenses" in New York—some teachers collect them like stamps, so they can apply for several different possible promotions as jobs become vacant. The exams are drawn up by an internal but almost independent Board of Examiners with a budget of about $2.5 million a year. Among the subjects of the exams are the regulations of the New York City system, guaranteeing that outsiders cannot apply for leadership positions in New York—and also supplying to the existing supervisors more than $1 million a year in added income from fees paid by teachers "coaching" for the next exam.

The main purpose of all the regulations, of course, is to make sure that everything is done the same way everywhere. Headquarters rules that classes in slum schools must average 28.3 children each, and every school so situated is promptly awarded enough ordinary classroom teachers to achieve that average—plus a ration of OTPs ("Other Teaching Positions"), to give classroom teachers rest periods during the day and to offer art or music or counseling or physical education or remedial reading or corrective reading (the difference between remedial reading and corrective reading is that the remedial reading teacher holds a special license and the corrective reading teacher doesn't). A school is not permitted to use some of its OTPs to form new and smaller classes, or to put classroom teachers on specialized duty. The big "reform" of the fall of 1967 is the assignment of additional teachers to first and second grades to reduce the ratio of pupils to teachers. (Class size may actually go up, but larger classes will have two permanently assigned teachers, who will presumably both be working at the same time.) A school with a crackerjack first-grade teacher who doesn't want anybody else in her room cannot use the extra teacher to handle third- or fourth-grade problems, because headquarters insists that all the extra positions be assigned to doubling up in the first two grades.

Now, this sort of organization simply doesn't work. Even if one accepts the very arguable premise that the people at headquarters are infinitely wiser than the people who actually work in the schools, it remains true, as an Irish philosopher once put it, that the parish priest knows more about his parish than the Pope does. There is a limit to the number of real decisions that can be made on a city-wide basis anywhere—and this is New York, the richest city in the world, with the largest welfare budget; home to more people who buy opera tickets than anywhere else, and to more people who buy heroin; where the Stock Exchange and Harlem are separated by six quick stops on the subway. In New York any decision which is good for one part of the city is sure to be bad somewhere else.

What keeps the school system running at all is that nobody at headquarters knows what is going on in the schools, so principals and teachers—if they don't make too much noise about it—can get away with a fair amount of rule breaking. Some of the teachers assigned to first- and second-grade double-up duties will undoubtedly work in the other grades, and nobody at the central office will ever hear about it. Sometimes the ignorance at headquarters is really devastating: in the spring there was a series of picketings and boycottings and sittings-in connected with the opening of a new school in West Harlem, not far from Columbia University, and the focus of the disturbance seemed to be the principal appointed for the new school by the routine operation of the personnel machinery. A member of the Board of Education asked Superintendent Bernard Donovan whether the principal was any good or not; and Donovan replied, honestly, "I don't know. I'm trying to find out."

To a degree, the system is self-correcting, because every once in a while the combination of tight rules and ignorance generates a public scandal. The most delightful one in recent years was the revelation in 1963 that the janitor of Boys High School in Brooklyn was the third most highly paid public official in the United States—his income from custodial duties around the building was running better than $50,000 a year. The most important of the scandals, however, was one which emerged in 1961, when an assistant in the Board of Education's construction division happened to wander into a room where the deputy superintendent in charge of construction was opening sealed bids from contractors. When these bids were ties, established procedure called for flipping a coin. Most of the contracts that were being awarded on this day, it turned out, had drawn identical bids from the construction companies that specialized in school projects. (Only a few companies are willing to build schools, because the Board of Education pays its bills so slowly.) The assistant noted approvingly that his boss was indeed flipping a coin after opening each set of bids. But then he saw that *the boss was not looking at the coin after he flipped it!* This was very disturbing, and on the advice of his wife the assistant took his tale to the District Attorney—and presently the deputy superintendent in charge of construction had dramatically retired (on full pension), and the state legislature was in special session to do something to clean up corruption in the school system.

This is where I come in. The main purpose of the bill the state legislature passed was to throw the rascals out: the entire Board of Education was dismissed by legislative act, and the Mayor was told to pick a new one from a list of candidates who would be nominated by a panel of distinguished citizens, including the presidents of the local universities, bar associations, and so forth. But the legislature also took notice of the fact that the school system seemed to have almost no points of contact with the people who live in the city. Knowing more about politics than about education, the legislators (unlike the city's schoolteachers) had heard about the city's "local school boards"—some fifty-two honorary bodies with no defined duties, whose members were appointed by the city's five borough presidents, appeared at school graduations and the like, and got their names on brass plaques on new buildings. Under the new law, these appointments were taken away from the borough presidents, and among other reforms the new Board of Education was told to accomplish was the "revitalization" of the local school boards.

Doing something about the local school boards could not be a first-priority item for the members of the new Board of Education who took office in the fall of 1961. They had to find a new superintendent—the old superintendent, John J. Theobald, had been mixed into the construction scandals by the newspapers, which uncovered a story of a pleasure boat that had been made for him at one of the city's vocational high schools (several people in the school system, declaring themselves absolutely unwilling to step into any boat made in a vocational school, thought this incident should be chalked up to

Theobald's credit, but the editorial writers thought otherwise). The new board had to con increased budgets out of the legislature and the Mayor (which it did with spectacular success: from 1961–62 to 1967–68 the New York schools' operating budget has doubled). As civil libertarians, the new board members felt a need to spend endless hours on the cases of some teachers who had been dismissed for failure to sign non-Communist affidavits (a requirement which the Supreme Court later threw out as unconstitutional, anyway). And there were a couple of board members who were crusading, with admirable single-mindedness, to restore the magazine *The Nation* to the school libraries, from which it had been banned as the result of Paul Blanshard's articles attacking the Catholic Church.

Because the board was busy with other things, the job of setting up new local school boards was turned over to a young lady named Andrea Wilson, a former economist for a Wall Street investment banking house who had never before in her adult life (except as a mother) had anything to do with schools. She quickly discovered that the system was divided administratively into 25 "districts," each with about 40,000 pupils and a "field assistant superintendent," appointed by headquarters and assigned, in the dreary language of the by-laws, "to supervise such schools or groups of schools or to such professional duties as the Superintendent of Schools shall determine." Mrs. Wilson decided there should be one nine-member local board for each district superintendent, and she duplicated on a smaller scale the appointing system mandated on the Mayor by the state legislature, organizing "screening panels" of civic groups, settlement houses, religious leaders, and parents' associations to consider nominations for the local boards.

Then Mrs. Wilson went out to get unusual people to apply. Having written a book called *The Schools,* in part highly critical of the way the New York schools were run, I was in her mind (if not in the minds of all others) a natural candidate. It is, I suppose, a reasonable measure of Mrs. Wilson's efficiency that I said "No" and shortly thereafter found myself a local school board member. I was one of a rather large number of unexpected and unusual appointments (among the others, for example, was the village anarchist Paul Goodman), and Mrs. Wilson had some trouble getting us through. The vice-president of the new Board of Education was James B. Donovan, who had negotiated the release of the Bay of Pigs prisoners for the Kennedys and who was about to run for the Senate against Jacob Javits. He had personally explored this question of who should serve on the new local boards and had come back with a list of Knights of Columbus, B'nai Brith, deserving politicos, and tame clubwomen. In a tense, not to say raucous, session of the board, Mrs. Wilson's list went through.

The district for my local board ran up Manhattan's East Side from 10th Street to 106th Street. This includes the northern four blocks of the old immigrant Lower East Side; the enormous middle-class and upper-middle-class white housing projects Stuyvesant Town and Peter Cooper Village north of 14 Street; the elegance of Gramercy Park; the fanciest part of the city's business district; the UN headquarters; the most expensive housing in American on Park Avenue and Fifth Avenue in the 60s, 70s, and 80s; the second-generation and first-generation German-Polish-Czech-Hungarian immigrant communities in Yorkville (east of the rich housing in the 60s through the low 90s)—and, above 96th Street, which is a kind of Chinese Wall, the teeming slum of East Harlem. There is no more varied slice of urban life anywhere in the world.

One of the strengths of the New York schools, even in their present extremities, is that this district, where most people with money send their children to private or parochial schools, could supply from its public school constituency a board of the quality of ours. Mark McCloskey, the only other man in the group, had started life as a tough kid in Hell's Kitchen; and among his mature services had been a term as a trustee of Vassar College. In between, courtesy of a settlement house, he had been graduated from Princeton; he had known and was admired by every politician and social worker in New York for the last 50 years; he had been State Commissioner for Youth; and he had a glorious brogue and a gift of gab which enabled him to get us out of the stickiest and angriest meetings with a benediction in the form of a story. At 75, incidentally, he is still active, teaching at Manhattan Community College.

Among the seven ladies on the board were Mary Fisk, daughter of former Governor Averell Harriman and director of the imaginative School Volunteers Program, which sends unpaid citizens into New York classrooms a day or two a week to help selected children, mostly with reading problems; Nanette Berman, then associate counsel to the New York Civil Liberties Union and now a family court judge; Peg Eddy, herself an ordained minister, wife of the man who founded and runs the East Harlem Protestant Parish; and Frances Low, ex-newspaper-woman and wife of City Councilman Robert Low, who may be the next Mayor of New York.

We met together for the first time on October 2, 1962, in the district superintendent's dark and dirty meeting room behind the auditorium in an antique school in the East 30s, and I was elected chairman (by a 5–4 vote). This did nothing to ease the worries of our district superintendent, Edward Scalea, a lean, almost military man with a lined face, neatly combed iron-gray hair, and mustache to match. Scalea's bearing, his rather harsh voice, and his schoolteacher's manner of wagging his finger at people while instructing them on why they were wrong gave him a quite misleading appearance of inflexibility. Brought up in the now-fading Italian section of East Harlem (which for years sent the radical Vito Marcantonio to Congress), Scalea was the son of a bandmaster and, when not overwhelmed by school duties, was a dedicated amateur violinist; and though he was good at choking it down he had a high sense of humor that sometimes burst through into an explosive laugh. Much as he disapproved of me (I learned much later that he had begged Mrs. Wilson not to put a writer on his local board), he was determined to make the board a functioning and significant body. He and his wife (a principal in a Brooklyn school) had worked in the New York system all their lives. They had no children themselves; they cared about what happened to the children whose education they supervised; and if that meant getting along with the irreverent likes of me and Mark McCloskey, it was a price Ed Scalea would pay.

Scalea had prepared for each of us a map of our district, on which were marked the location of every school and the boundary of every school zone. A fact sheet for each school told us the capacity of the building, the date of its construction, and the number of children in it; the number of teachers and their special functions if any (remedial reading, art, physical education, etc.); the relative proportions of Negro, Puerto Rican, and "other" children; and the average measured IQ. It took only the most casual browsing of these documents to see that we had bad troubles.

Though our district's resident population was more than three-quarters "mainland white," the schools were five-eighths Negro and Puerto Rican. Of our 18 elementary schools, 2 which were more than 90 per cent white had two-fifths of all the white children in the district; and 6 were more than 90 per cent Negro and Puerto Rican. In most of the schools with a majority of Negro and Puerto Rican students, more than half the children in the classrooms in September would move elsewhere before June. In many of the schools in the slum area, a third or more of the *teachers* left every year. Nearly all the schools in Negro and Puerto Rican neighborhoods were badly over crowded, in poor repair, short of books and equipment, staffed primarily by "substitute" teachers (without a regular license) or by very young teachers with 3 years' experience or less. More than half the sixth grade in our two upper-middle-class overwhelmingly white schools were working nearly 2 years above grade level as measured by standardized tests; more than half the sixth grade in our slum schools were working nearly 2 years below grade level.

The worst single disaster was a junior high school at 100th Street and First Avenue, facing the block which the New York *Times* had recently labeled the worst street in the city. The building had been put up 50 years before as an elementary school to house 1200 children, and conversion to a junior high—with larger auditorium, gyms, and a library—had reduced its capacity; but there were 1800 children in the building. Portable classrooms to house 360 children had been promised for the opening of school that year, and would eventually relieve the situation a little—but in October they had yet to arrive. And the Negro and Puerto Rican children in this school were about as badly battered by the fates as any in New York. Only 1 in 20 of them were up to grade level in reading or in math; half of the seventh grade and probably a third of the ninth grade were for all practical purposes illiterate—a condition which meant, incidentally, that they could not decipher the incredibly complicated schedule cards which told them where to go each period in a building where classes were held in different rooms on different days to keep every room in use in every period. There were always lost kids wandering in the halls.

My second evening as chairman of a local school board, Scalea and I went up to a meeting at the auditorium of this school, and sitting in uncomfortable dignity on a platform I very earnestly agreed with the speakers, in Spanish and in English, that something would have to be done. A few days later I spent a morning at this school, found a very few bright spots (chiefly an experienced and motherly art teacher who had very firmly put her ninth graders to doing precise architectual drawings of the details over the windows and doors on the local tenements) and an ocean of gloom. I shall never forget the principal of this school ushering me into the auditorium to look at six classes' worth of children—180 kids—herded here for a "study period" because there was no classroom in which they could sit. The principal was a decent, not unkindly, not unintelligent man who had been head of the science department in a middle-class white high school before he passed the junior high principal's exam which fatuously pronounced him "qualified" to run this desperate school. He waved at the 180 boys and girls huddled in varying attitudes of dejection, boredom, and rebellion, and he said, "We just have to face the fact that half of these children will never hold a job in their lives."

Scalea managed to get us a new principal for this school, a little man with leadership qualities less subject to shell shock; but in most situations our resources for making any changes at all were frighteningly slight. Though new money was already pouring into the New York schools, it was all allocated by central headquarters; teachers were examined, qualified, appointed, and assigned by central headquarters; all schools were required to follow city-wide "courses of study" to the point where the most common single answer to a child's question in a class was, "We don't learn that in this grade." If our staff or our board got any bright ideas, in short, we had neither the means nor the authority to do anything about them; as a local board, we were empowered merely to "advise" the Board of Education, and we were supposed to explain and defend the board and its policies to the community (which, however, we flatly refused to do). Despite all the restrictions we were in fact occasionally able to accomplish something, but it is impossible for anyone who has never had to operate in the atmosphere of a bureaucracy as all-encompassing and power-hungry as the New York public schools to imagine the time that has to be taken to shake free of even an obviously stupid rule proclaimed by the superintendent of schools.

An example that sticks particularly in the memory grew out of the New York transit strike of January, 1966. As part of a district program to ease overcrowding and provide a little integration, we were busing about 300 Negro and Puerto Rican children from East Harlem down to white schools in Yorkville. The school buses kept running through the strike though they were of course late and fantastically slow in the massive traffic jam every morning. Superintendent Bernard Donovan had announced that high school students, who normally rode the subways and the public buses, would be permitted to attend the school nearest their homes for the duration of the strike—but elementary school children would be required to report every day to their usual schools. After all, the school buses were still running.

I had a call from East Harlem complaining about children waiting an hour or more for their delayed buses in the cold and snow and slush of January. (The man who made the call, in the new tradition of self-destructiveness in the civil rights movement, "demanded" that we solve the problem by closing all the schools in Yorkville for the duration of the strike.) Now, near the collection points in East Harlem where these buses stopped we had two elementary schools involved in an experimental More Effective Schools (MES) program, which meant that no classroom in the school was much more than half full, and some rooms were used only part of the day. A member of my board pointed out that nothing could be easier than to notify the children at the bus stop that instead of waiting in the weather they could go to one of these two nearby schools and keep going there until the strike ended.

Scalea said, "I can't do that."

"Why not?"

"Because our orders are that all elementary school children are to go to their regular school."

"Supposing we could get your approval from headquarters to let these children go to the MES schools—would you do it?"

"Yes; it's a good idea."

I got on the telephone to Lloyd Garrison, then president of the New York Board of Education, and explained the situation; and he said he would see what he could do. Superintendent Donovan was in Albany trying to pry money from the state legislature, and Garrison would have to clear it with Executive Deputy Superintendent John T. King. A superb example of how thoroughly even an able Negro must conform to get ahead in a school system, King had advanced to the post of executive deputy by absolute unbending and unthinking adherence to the rule book. The rule in this case was that elementary school children had to go to their regular schools, regardless of how late their buses might be running. Garrison called me back and said we couldn't let the kids go to the MES schools. I asked why, and Garrison, an unusually sweet-tempered and upright man, lawyer, head of the War Labor Board during the Second World War, said, "Martin, I don't understand why." At my urging, he tried again.

Some hours later he called a second time and explained the reasoning. Our district was in an unusual position. In most districts, there were no seats available in the schools near the bus stops: "King says that if we let you do it, we'd have to let everybody do it."

At this point I became somewhat upset. "That's exactly right," I said. "Then those district superintendents who *can* get the kids off the street corners will do so; and those who *can't* will be man enough to tell the parents that they can't and tell them why."

Garrison agreed, but there was yet another call, this one about 9:30 at night. Was I sure that Scalea really wanted this authority? Yes, I was sure. Well, if Scalea would personally call King and ask him, King would give him a go-ahead, provided it wasn't publicized and wasn't regarded as a precedent. I called Scalea; Scalea called King. Presently we had an interesting demonstration of what an able administrator can do. In 15 minutes on the telephone after 10 o'clock that night, Scalea organized a group of teachers and parents to go to the bus stops the next morning at 8 and send the children off to the schools around the corner. The activist leaders, incidentally, continued to denounce us all for not closing the Yorkville schools, so all school children might be penalized absolutely equally by the transit strike. Not being parents of school children themselves, they had never thought that the East Harlem families had enough trouble from the strike without keeping the kids home, too.

We had lots of these hassles with headquarters. Once it was necessary for us to lead a group of parents and teachers to the Borough President of Manhattan to get him to block (in the city's Board of Estimate, which must approve all school construction funds) a carelessly planned "modernization" of a crowded school which would have substantially reduced its capacity. Once we had a month-long battle to retain at her job an "acting" assistant principal, the only Negro or Puerto Rican staff member in a school more than half Negro and Puerto Rican, who was to be transferred by headquarters *because she had passed her exam for a regular assistant principal's license!* Under the rules of the system, the publication of a list of newly licensed assistant principals meant that all positions held by "acting" assistant principals were automatically declared vacant, and anybody with seniority or a higher score on the exam could push our very popular and successful lady out of her school—even though she was now, for the first time, legally qualified for the job she was doing. We won that one. In another school, however, a very able "acting" principal, who did not hold a principal's license, got pushed out (to the serious detriment of the school) because headquarters had to find jobs for people who had passed exams. To our and Scalea's great annoyance, we could do nothing about it.

I think (perhaps it's local pride) that New York has the nation's champion rule-bound bureaucracy, but most of the big-city school systems are run in very much the same manner. Sociologists advising the Chicago schools have found *de facto* centralization every bit as extreme as New York's. Talking about his Philadelphia study of possible "education parks" (groups of schools clustered together to which students from different parts of town would be bused, to defeat the educational consequences of segregated housing), the consultant Cyril Sargent said recently that he thought their greatest advantage would be their better chance of achieving some independence from the Philadelphia central office.

The superintendent of schools doesn't live who won't talk about the flexibility of his leadership and the unfairness of critics who accuse his school system of rigidity, but this line of gab usually vanishes when some specific reform is proposed. I remember a national meeting where I pointed out that at least a third and maybe more of the big-city "transiency," the moving around of children from school to school, was caused by families whose new home was in the same general neighborhood but across some artificial school district boundary line. If the school systems would encourage children who still could walk to their old schools to continue going there, the teachers would have a better chance to remedy a fair fraction of the failures in the slums. The then-superintendent in Detroit, who had just berated most of us at the meeting for our intolerance of superintendents, immediately proclaimed that it couldn't be done—all the safety procedures and crossing guards were planned for children who lived within the district, some schools would become overcrowded, and so forth. I suggested that at least the people on the scene, the principals and district superintendents, could be empowered to decide whether a stay-in-the-same-school policy made sense in their neighborhoods; but the Detroit superintendent wouldn't hear of it—that sort of policy had to be made city-wide. . . .

Similarly, the instinctive reaction of the big-city school system to demands for integration is some sort of city-wide program. The usual approach, tried out in New York, is random busing, by which children in the ghetto who apply can ride to white neighborhoods to go to school. In some cities, of course, housing is so segregated that only a city-wide effort offers any hope at all. But random busing emphasizes and perpetuates the rootlessness which is part of the disease that cripples the in-migrant big-city poor. To the extent that integration can be achieved by small units of the city, far more important benefits of community involvement become possible. Our district all by itself was 60 per cent Negro and Puerto Rican and 40 per cent mainland white in the schools—we didn't need to import colored children to integrate our schools.

New York's "open enrollment" program was doing little good in our district. Colored children from all over Harlem and northern Manhattan were being shipped individually into our schools, without any thought for a sending community with which a school might establish a relationship. There was no neighborhood which would know that a bused child had won a prize or appeared in a play or been elected to an office or got into trouble. Moreover, because city-wide policy had pronounced that busing was "a right, not a privilege," applications had to be accepted in the order they were received and the "receiving schools" could not reject even the saddest and most dangerous misfits. The principals of the "sending schools" were under almost irresistible pressure to use open enrollment as a way of dumping children they couldn't control. Some principals urged the parents of "disturbed" children to try their luck in the new surroundings of a white school; at least one, to our certain knowledge, forged a parent's signature on a request to bus a juvenile arsonist. Every so often a Harlem mother would hear about the local school boards, and I got a few calls asking me if I couldn't do something to get some psychotic child off the bus the caller's child had to take every day; I had to tell the mother there was absolutely nothing the local board or the local staff could do.

Ed Scalea, studying the rule book eagerly, found a way to get some of our underused white Yorkville schools out of the open enrollment program and into something the district could run itself. The excuse was the overcrowding of our East Harlem schools: integration in Yorkville would be a by-product of relieving the crush in East Harlem. In the fall of 1963, we started a joint "East Harlem-Yorkville" project which was unquestionably the most significant accomplishment of our district. Because we never sought publicity for the project, we never got any; and because it was an invention of the district, rather than of the Board of Education, the board in its frequent breast-beatings has never boasted about it. The result, oddly, is that our little project acquired a considerable underground reputation among those civil rights leaders who did hear about it. In the fall of 1966, one of the most bitter of the Negro leaders in town used our project in his standard "you should be ashamed of yourselves" speech as the example of what the city could have done if the Board of Education really cared. In fact, it wasn't that good—but it was interesting.

The plan had three main components. The first was concentration on first and second graders in our two most overcrowded East Harlem schools, to be sent to the two Yorkville schools which had the greatest number of unused seats. (One of them was the school where my boys went.) By busing about 150 younger children about a mile and a half downtown, we could make the first and second grades in each of these Yorkville schools about one-third Negro and Puerto Rican. We were, of course, bound by the city-wide policy that busing was a right—but because both sending and receiving schools were in our district, Scalea could with a few well-chosen phrases make sure that the principals of the sending schools discouraged any applicants who looked like a bad bet on the bus.

One of the difficulties about open enrollment had been the "homogeneous grouping" of children in the New York schools, where the best pupils are put in a "top" class, the next best in the next-to-top class, and so forth down to the worst pupils in a "bottom" class. The grouping when we started our project in 1963 was done by IQ tests (today, in a loudly trumpeted reform, it is done by reading scores, which slot children just about where they fit on group IQ tests). The usual result was that the bused-in children wound up in segregated bottom classes, which did not greatly help them as individuals or race relations as an ideal. It is hard to avoid this horror when you pick up your students for the first time in fifth or sixth grade, at the age of ten or eleven: no purpose is served by trying to teach in one class two groups of children the same age who are on the average two to four years apart in reading ability. But we were taking children at ages six and seven, when there just wasn't much visible difference in what they could do: the grouping problem could be made manageable.

Scalea, in what must be called a stroke of genius, decided that he could keep administrative procedure pure and still gain our ends by scoring the selection tests separately for the East Harlem and Yorkville contingents. Then, if there were three first grades to fill in the receiving school, the top third in both groups would be put in the "best" class, the middle third in the "average" class, the lowest third in the "slow" class. In fact, few of the East Harlem children scored as well as the average Yorkville child on the test, but the teachers weren't told that. So far as they were concerned, they had "homogeneously grouped" classes which happened to be about one-third Negro and Puerto Rican.

That was part one of the plan: physical integration in the classrooms. Part two was to use the fact that we had a "community transfer" rather than an "open enrollment" program—all the children who rode the buses lived in the same neighborhood. The receiving schools could keep in touch with the community which sent the children, the sending schools could be influenced by what was happening in Yorkville, the parents from both groups could work together on what had become, to some degree, shared problems. A "four-schools" association was set up to give people a framework for their efforts.

This sort of two-community action project is not easy to operate, and we knew we would need outside professional help. Fortunately, an alert group of women in the Yorkville Civic Council had been study-ing educational problems as a matter of personal interest, with the oc-casional guidance of a level-headed professor of education at Bank Street College. We talked over with him what we were planning to do. He investigated, found that the four existing separate parents' associations were all active and intelligently led (the presidents of both of the East Harlem parents' associations are now working in supervisory jobs in the poverty program), and decided that the East Harlem Schools Com-mittee, already formed under the aegis of the Protestant Parish, could balance the better organized but less involved Yorkville ladies. He also found that Scalea's district staff included a quiet but effective "commun-ity coordinator," who had the confidence of all the parent leaders. If we could find some money, the Bank Street professor said, he would put in a day a week helping the parents and the four schools work together. The Alfred P. Sloan Foundation, which had previously specialized in university-level (indeed, graduate-level) scientific studies, gave a grant of $10,000 a year to pay the expenses. In the city-wide system, $10,000 is less that 1/100,000 of the budget and not worth looking at twice—but in a district with no other discretionary funds, you can cherish and do a lot with $10,000.

This little chunk of money made possible the third basic feature of the plan, which was my baby. I had only limited faith in the proposition that physical integration and human relations programs would by themselves improve the performance of the East Harlem children, or give the Yorkville parents any feeling that something was being done for the benefit of *their* children. I thought it essential that the teachers who were working in these classrooms should not be thinking race-color-creed all day long. If we simply offered the standard New York course of study, the teachers would know how children "should" react from their past experience in these middle-class white schools. But if we brought in some new stuff for the kids to do, we could protect the teachers from their own expectations, give both Yorkville and East Harlem something to talk about other than skin colors—and, I thought, improve the performance of the children by substituting something interesting for the rather soggy New York course of study.

A new reading program would tread on teachers' toes: that's the one thing the first- and second-grade teacher thinks she can do now. We considered a new math program, and David Page, the infinitely imaginative inventor and director of the University of Illinois Arithmetic Program, came to our district for a week to teach an integrated demonstration class before an audience of about fifteen of our teachers. This didn't work: Page was too good. The dazzled teachers, few of whom knew enough math themselves to understand *why* Page was teaching children how to jump around a number line according to increasingly tricky formulas, came out of the week saying that it was amazing what the kids could learn but they could never teach it. Also, Scalea got into trouble: headquarters found out somehow that Page had been in New York without the consent or participation of anybody who worked in the superintendent's office, and ordered that this sort of thing must never happen again.

I knew a lot of new programs, because I was a member of a continuing White House panel on educational research and development; and I had just completed a report for the American Council of Learned Societies on new developments in the teaching of social studies. Scalea and

I and some other members of the local board talked over a number of possibilities, and decided that on all counts the best bet would be the new elementary school economics course being developed by Lawrence Senesh of Purdue in the schools of Elkhart, Indiana.

The Senesh program is especially ingenious because it uses much of what is in the usual social studies programs for the early grades—daddy at work, mother in the kitchen, "community helpers"—but uses them to teach economics rather than just to pass time. Children learn about the division of labor, the way the marketplace determines what is produced in the factories, how we pay for public services, why people are sometimes unemployed (very important in the slums, where unemployment often seems a kind of punishment from God, spreading shame through the family).

I knew Senesh personally. An ebullient Hungarian with a heavy accent, who escaped to this country before the war and served in the U.S. Army, he had used the GI Bill to pick up a degree in art in Denver and another in economics in London. He wanted to try out his materials in integrated conditions in a big city. Chicago was closer to Purdue, but Chicago hadn't asked. He would come to New York and help our teachers (who would need help to present the material properly) in return for his out-of-pocket expenses, which took only a small chunk of our $10,000. Later, the Sloan Foundation put up another $10,000, which—thanks to very generous budgeting by Purdue—paid travel expenses, room and board, and fees for seventeen New York teachers for a summer seminar in Indiana on the Senesh program.

Scalea played this one safe and told central headquarters Senesh was coming to work with six of our teachers in the first phase of the program. One of my worst moments on the local school board was sitting in the library of a Yorkville school with Senesh and the principal and the six teachers, and watching a deputy superintendent and four headquarters assistant superintendents take over the session at which Senesh was to give our teachers their start in figuring out what they were supposed to do. With all this brass in the room, of course, the teachers were scared to ask questions themselves; and when the superintendents left they took with them five of the six packets of material Senesh had brought for the teachers. Fortunately, the teachers were pretty, Senesh thought the incident was funny, and after we'd had a drink together at my house he telegraphed home to Indiana for more books.

The first year of the East Harlem-Yorkville project (1963–1964) was a delight to know. This was the year that the civil rights groups ran two massive one-day boycotts of the city's schools, pulling out about half the pupils, as part of giant agitation for all sorts of new nostrums.

It was a pleasure for all concerned to feel that while others were yelling we were actually doing something. The teachers at the Yorkville schools found the classes manageable, and most of the bused-in children seemed to be doing well. We never had anything resembling "objective" verification of the program—I doubt that honest verification would have been possible, anyway, using the blunt instruments of educational research—but Senesh dug out an odd and encouraging fact. He found that his material was being presented in greater detail and depth in the "top class," and that the East Harlem kids were mostly following along fine. When he asked the teachers of the "middle" groups why they weren't trying some of the things the top group was doing, he was told, "Our children aren't as good as they are—they're the top group." In fact, most of the East Harlem first graders in the top group had scored below the average Yorkville child in the middle group. But we had given our teachers a new table of expectations—a new stereotype, if you like—which had persuaded them to treat some of the "disadvantaged" children from East Harlem as *better* than most of the pupils from Yorkville. And as a result of this change in image the East Harlem children did better work.

There was to be a fourth step in this project, but we could never take it. I had hoped that as we expanded the program some of the teachers who had succeeded with East Harlem children in the integrated classes would be willing to take a year in East Harlem schools, trying out their techniques and expectations with segregated classes. Meanwhile, teachers from the East Harlem schools could come down to Yorkville to work in integrated surroundings; and through rotation we could spread over much of our district whatever lessons came out of our experiment.

Of course, before we could even ask the Yorkville teachers for this favor, we had to be able to guarantee to them that after their year in East Harlem they could get their old jobs back—and here the headquarters Bureau of Personnel said a firm "No." Any teaching position vacated in a desirable Yorkville school would have to be advertised as vacant and filled on a permanent basis by teachers elsewhere whose seniority gave them the right to transfer. Later it turned out that we had put a bug in the bureau's ear; and the next contract between the Board of Education and the United Federation of Teachers contained a clause specifically permitting what we had wanted to do the year before. But by then the steam had gone out of our project, and though it is still officially alive it just twitches occasionally to remind people that what was tried here was very different from the other busing projects in New York.

Many reasons can be assigned for the loss of momentum after the second year of the East Harlem-Yorkville project. My personal favorite reason is that we tried to expand it without expanded resources. For the second year, we added three more Yorkville and two more East Harlem schools. It turned out to be impossible to create a "nine-schools" parents' association, and some of the vitality of the "four-schools" association was sapped by the fact that the children from the two original East Harlem schools were now spread over five schools in Yorkville. Meanwhile, two new buildings were opened in East Harlem, relieving some of the overcrowding at our sending schools, which meant that both the parents and the staffs of the East Harlem schools were much less eager to bus children. The normal high transiency of East Harlem affected our project just as it affected the local schools: instead of advancing up the grades with the group that had started young, we were necessarily recruiting older children, many of whom were behind the level of work at the Yorkville schools.

Much of the energy that might have gone into constructive planning for the project had to be diverted to a series of fights. In early 1964, someone sold the Board of Education a bill of goods about the Princeton Plan, under which two schools of different racial composition would be "paired," all the children taking their first three years at one school and their next three years at the other. Two such pairings were suggested for our district. As nobody was able to provide any reason why this device would be of benefit to anyone, the parents' associations of all four schools suggested overwhelmingly rejected the pairings (the Puerto Rican mothers at one of them were particularly outraged at the idea that they would be forced to send little children some distance from their homes), and then we had the struggle to get our district off the board's gig list, which we did. (Other local school boards were equally effective in this effort, by the way, and the twenty-odd "pairings" originally proposed by the Board of Education were reduced to four, which still survive, all overwhelmingly colored, as a kind of monument to the folly of our central leadership.)

Another wrestle with headquarters came over its insistence that we save seats at the Yorkville schools for open enrollment children as well as the children of our project. Yet another, the most infuriating of all, grew out of the rezoning of the city to provide 30 instead of the original 25 local districts. The man charged with making up the new maps was given only one requirement that the new lines had to meet—all the new districts had to be exactly equal in student population, so the burden on district superintendents would be the same everywhere. The easiest way to reduce our district to the new city average was to lop off East Harlem. I was in Europe when this war broke out between ourselves and headquarters, and could merely contribute an angry letter; but my board held a series of meetings with puzzled members of the Board of Education, who didn't know anything about any East Harlem-Yorkville project, and in the end our district was cut from its southern rather than its northern border.

Our most enervating fight, however, came in our own constituency. Our district includes the New York school with the wealthiest student body, PS 6, in the heart of the high-rent district, the most advertised public school in town. It was about 95 per cent mainland white in "ethnic distribution." Its zone was long and narrow, covering a strip of about a mile and a half along the row of the city's fanciest apartment houses. Apartments for rent or for sale are listed in the paper as "PS 6 district." We redrew the famous "six district" to reduce the school's enrollment by about 200 and make room for children from East Harlem. Scalea had done a first draft of the rezoning and brought it to us at an executive session of the local board with a big block-by-block map of the area, showing on each block the number of children sent to PS 6. I remember borrowing a compass and tracing out on the map equal distances from PS 6 and from the other schools to which the 200 PS 6 children could be sent, to make sure that in every (well, almost every) case the child's new school was closer to his home than PS 6 was.

This care did not, however, do us much good with the parents whose children were to be reassigned. They got up at public meetings and denounced us for violating the sacred principles of the neighborhood school, and threatened us with lawsuits and worse. I went to a meeting of the PS 6 parents' association (which stood by us loyally but uncomfortably) to hear grim rich people who were standing in the aisles. I told them that the schools to which their children were being assigned were at least as good as PS 6 even though they never got in the newspapers (which was true, by the way), but there wasn't much satisfaction in that for people who were paying higher rents to live in the "six district" and were now being taken out of it without any reduction in their rents. They did sue, finally—the case was *Van Berklom v. Donovan,* brought officially against the president of the Board of Education, though Scalea had to defend it. And our care paid off when the court ruled, "Each of the involuntarily transferred children . . . will travel the same or in most instances a shorter distance to his new school. Their newly assigned schools are 'neighborhood' schools." But it didn't make a wholesome atmosphere for the growth of the East Harlem-Yorkville project.

The good will that permeated the project survived its loss of momentum. When a three-day strike of school bus drivers left our East Harlem children without transportation, ninety-odd Yorkville mothers got in their own cars to pick them up in the morning and deliver them home in the afternoon. Yorkville ladies put up posters in East Harlem, went to meetings, and even rang doorbells in one of the city's most publicized "dangerous slums" to urge Negro and Puerto Rican parents to send their children. Negroes are buffeted about too much and too often by a hostile or patronizing white community ever to lose all their suspicion of what a white group may be up to, but I was touched this spring by the degree to which the parents' associations of East Harlem fought off the Black Power types—refusing to attend their meetings or sign their petitions and insisting that East Harlem still had reason to hope for progress through integration. This took a good deal more courage, moral and physical, than people who are not living in the ghetto can easily imagine.

It also took faith. We have, I think, played square throughout. We nearly always said in our monthly public meetings exactly what had been said in our twice-a-month private "planning meetings." When Scalea grabbed an abandoned elementary school in midtown for conversion to a seventh-grade annex to relieve the overcrowding at our wretched junior high school at 100th Street, we fought successfully to make the new building an administrative unit with our Yorkville rather than with our East Harlem junior high school. In other words, we eased our numbers pressure not by expanding the capacity of the segregated school where the pressure was worst (which is what headquarters wanted to do) but by expanding the capacity of the integrated school and assigning 400 East Harlem children to it. In planning the new junior high which would permanently end overcrowding, we demanded a site south of 96th Street and in the luxury housing area, so we could make two integrated junior high zones. We met twice with the Mayor, led a delegation of several hundred parents (mixed Yorkville and East Harlem) to a Board of Education hearing, and organized some publicity for our problems by marching around our chosen site (an old armory used mostly for policemen's horses and occasional polo games) led by a junior high school band and a city councilman dressed in Rough Rider costume. And we got the site.

We did not try to gain credit with the activist groups by waving simple black-and-white banners for meaningless or impossible integration. As I wrote in a memo for a planning meeting in 1964, "The Bowery is integrated, too, and who needs that?" (This was, I think, the only time my board forbade me to say at the public meeting what I had

said at the planning meeting—my only ally in the vote was the only
Negro member of our board.) We talked to people in terms of what
we thought could be done with profit to the children, not in terms
of slogans; and we honestly said flat out that there was no point even
thinking about busing white children north to East Harlem. A civil
rights spokesman started in our district the complaint, "Why is it always
our children who ride the bus?" which has driven the Board of Education
into paroxysms of guilt and dishonesty. I told him what seemed to me
to be the inescapable truth: "It's because they're disadvantaged. One
of their disadvantages is that they ride the bus." This hurts, of course;
but it hurts a lot less than being lied to.

We had our little triumphs. In five years I came to know—to relish
and at the same time to fear—the disturbingly wild joy of telling grown
people what to do, and of leading them in a public fight for what
then became *their* proposals. I will be warmed on cold days in future
winters by the memory of letters I received when I first tried to resign
from the local board in the spring of 1966, and of some statements
by East Harlem mothers at the final public meeting last June, after
I had at least succeeded in resigning. But there should be, I think,
a limit to the number of Brownie points one accumulates simply for
trying one's best. And the fact seems to be that we have not been
able to do much for the great majority of our Negro and Puerto Rican
students, who still attend the segregated schools of East Harlem.

I say "seems to be" because one of the many sins of the New York
Board of Education is its failure to gather or present information in
a usable fashion. Up to this year, when ridicule (mostly from our local
board) forced a change, the Board of Education would even present
the reading scores for a school in terms of "averages." In fifth grade,
where the test New York uses has a bottom score of 3.0 (i.e., start
of third grade), one bright lad reading at eleventh grade and three
total illiterates will produce a meaningless "average" score of 5.0
$(11 + 3 + 3 + 3 = 20 \div 4 = 5)$—fifth-grade level, by golly, we aren't
doing so bad after all! But even with this nonsense removed, and scores
presented on a more meaningful basis, we get little indication of how
we are doing. In most of our East Harlem schools, the turnover of
pupils is 50 per cent or more every year—but the machinery is not geared
to give us separate averages for the children we have worked with
all year as against the children who have just arrived. Most of our
East Harlem schools, again, are half Puerto Rican. It is, of course, just
as important that our Puerto Rican children read English as it is that
our Negro or mainland white or Chinese children read English—but
a test score report presenting an average that mingles together the per-

formance of English-speaking and Spanish-speaking children does not give much information to people on the scene.

Test scores, of course, are a dangerous measuring tool—indeed, we have already entered an era when insistence on high test scores warps both the program and the ethics of a number of schools. There is, after all, no difficulty about delivering somewhat better test scores from your class or your school: you simply give the children an hour to take a timed test which is supposed to be limited to forty minutes. A few years ago, the junior high school division of the New York schools began pushing the principals to deliver better reading test results—and today no high school in New York will attempt to advise a student on program until he has been retested on the spot: the data from the junior highs are too often totally unreliable.

And of course there is much more to education than success on standardized tests. I am dubious about the validity of test scores as a measurement of how well children really function when confronted with a practical or intellectual problem which seems worth working at. I am prepared to believe in the possibility of programs which would improve the real performance of children without improving their test scores. But on the basis of dipping into occasional East Harlem classrooms at various grade levels, I am not prepared to believe that we have in our district accomplished anything of the sort. Our sixth graders test a year and a half behind in reading because they are a year and a half behind.

The state and the city have added more than half a billion dollars a year to the operating budget of the New York school system since the new Board of Education was installed in 1961. Our local board now meets in a clean new meeting room for its planning sessions, not in a dark hole behind an old auditorium. Our buildings are no longer crowded; our classes are smaller; we have more teachers in every building for fewer children, lots of shiny new textbooks and movable tables where once there were screwed-down desks, Head Starts and kindergartens and full-time instead of double-session first grades, and psychological and sociological jargon till you could scream—but more than half the children in our East Harlem schools are simply not making it by any definition.

What the principals and teachers of our district have wanted from our local school board is that we should say this failure is not their fault. I walked into Scalea's office shortly after the test scores were delivered last fall and found him slumped at his desk: "It's so hard on the teachers," he said; "they're terribly depressed." Many, perhaps most of the teachers in East Harlem work as hard as they know how to work, every day. The thrill of watching a child respond and grow is equally great whatever the skin color or home background of the child. The parents themselves do not hope harder than the teachers that this year the spark will catch in more children. (The very strength of this hope is the reason why we cannot avoid the use of standardized tests, because hope powers the great human factory of self-deception.) Not many people are close enough to sainthood to work as hard and as hopefully as our teachers work, and then to blame themselves when their efforts fail. They cannot bring themselves, of course, to blame the children, so they blame the community, the street, the "culture of the disadvantaged." Then they wonder why the community sometimes mistrusts them.

The last few years have been fertile with excuses. The enormous popularity of Head Start among educators, for example, traces at least partly to its obvious implication that there isn't much the schools can do for children already in the classroom who didn't enjoy such advantages. In the spring of 1967, one of the most popular subjects of discussion among New York schoolmen was the Civil Rights Commission report, *Racial Isolation in the Public Schools,* which announced that compensatory education plans could not help colored children in segregated schools. Impeccable federal authority, liberal-minded as all get out, thereby justified the failures of the principals and teachers: now, why bother?

What made the commission's report especially infuriating was that its assertion was meaningless—even if it could be demonstrated that all the half-dozen incomplete compensatory programs the commission investigated had not worked, that evidence said nothing about what might be accomplished with more solidly based and imaginative programs. Anybody who has looked around knows that compensatory programs work well in some schools but not in others. Considering the very obvious fact that most Negro children in nearly all our big cities will be attending segregated schools for the foreseeable future, it would have been far more responsible of the Civil Rights Commission to investigate the differences between successful and unsuccessful schools and not to average down the test scores for the purpose of telling the nation's urban teachers (and taxpayers) that they might as well quit.

What we have told the staff in our district is that we are not interested in who is to blame for current conditions. At one meeting of our local board with our twenty-odd principals. I asked them to consider the East Harlem mother who sees an 18-year-old unemployable part-time thief lounging against the wall up the block, and remembers what he was like 10 years ago—and then looks at her own 8-year-old playing in the gutter and can see nothing that makes his chances much different from those the older boy had 10 years ago. There is no question of saying that teachers have caused this horror—but to tell this mother that it is all her fault is an unthinkable insult, a disgusting cruelty, and a lie.

The school is almost the only handle society has with which to help these children, and the schools are not resented and hated in the slums as the current fashions say they are. A majority of the Harlem sample queried about a year ago for the House Education and Labor Committee told (Negro) interviewers they thought it was the kids' own fault that they didn't learn in school. In his investigation of the juvenile gangs in Brooklyn some years ago, Harrison Salisbury of *The New York Times* reported that the dropouts did not have hostile attitudes toward school—they felt that the school was the only institution in their lives that had ever cared what happened to them. The one thing we as a school board have asked from our principals and teachers is that, if the school program didn't work last year or this year, for God's sake don't do the same things the same ways next year. Don't expect miracle drugs, and don't worry about fancy words like "innovation" or "creativity." Look around, there are lots of different sorts of material in print these days, especially for teaching reading. Try something new that looks good to you; see what happens.

To say that this attitude has not been supported by the Board of Education would be an understatement. Indeed, the board's new and loudly touted "decentralization" program specifically forbids the districts to vary from the city-wide curriculum or the approved list of books, "to insure the large numbers of pupils who annually transfer from school to school and district to district the ability to adjust properly and to pick up at the point of the program that they had left." Behind this fatuous pronouncement lies the fact that virtually all our highly transient children are years and years behind in their work—and are surely not encouraged by finding in a new school the same stuff they had failed to learn in the old one. If the educational psychologists have proved anything at all (which is, of course, arguable), it is that children do not learn in a smooth, steady way: they learn, as they grow, in jumps. The Board of Education won't let individual districts try to make jumps: "If that happened," one particularly insensitive board member once told me, "all the other districts would be angry that they didn't have the same program. . . ."

One of the things I tried to do, being on a lot of mailing lists, was to bring the new reading programs (and other programs, in math, science, and social studies) to the attention of the professional staff, which does not have time to go exploring. If we had enjoyed a discretionary budget in the district, I would have fought to put much of it into paying teachers to go to summer institutes which would prepare them to teach new materials, and into purchasing for the children for the next year the materials the teacher had just learned to use. But it's nonsense to force new teaching approaches on teachers who don't understand why the topics are being presented in a different way. A fine demonstration of how little is accomplished in most subjects by just throwing books at teachers and children is the city-wide degradation of the Senesh program, which the Board of Education later tried to put into all the city's schools without giving teachers any preparation for teaching it. Nobody at central headquarters, of course, thought of demeaning himself by consulting a mere district staff or local school board to learn how we had been handling the Senesh program for two years. And bringing any substantial variety of new materials into the districts, unfortunately, requires the disarmament of central headquarters and also of the district supervisors, who insist that nothing can be taught unless they like it. Imagine the power of the lady who sits behind a desk at school headquarters and because she doesn't like the method or the author or the publisher says, "No you can't use that in New York City"! It would never occur to me that I should deny a teacher the chance to use something new that the teacher thinks might help, just because I feel it's no good. Teaching is a more complicated art than that. Unwillingness to trust the judgment of the people who have to do the work is, unfortunately, built deep into the beliefs of nearly all those who have made it to supervisory positions in the New York school system—and, I fear, in the school systems of the other big cities, too.

The combination of bureaucracy, failure, and the race problem has created a mental disease in education in the big cities. Teachers are distrusted by principals, principals by district or other lower-level supervisors, district staff by central office, and the system as a whole by many of the most concerned and articulate leaders of the community. We are suffering from a loss of nerve, which will be fatal to the public schools in the big cities if prolonged. To be sure, we cannot achieve in the schools world peace, perfect justice, and a high income for everybody. But where we now fail with 60 per cent of a neighborhood's children, perhaps if we try very hard we can fail next year with only 50 per cent, and the year after that with only 40 per cent. Moving one step at a time, trusting out destinies to the old human procedures of trial and error, we can equip for a better life large numbers of children who are now doomed to irrelevance in our society. I can see no way to advance toward this goal in our cities other than by giving the highest possible degree of freedom to the people in the schools and the classrooms who must do the work. A year ago, at a meeting with the Board of Education, I said that what we in the neighborhoods wanted was simply the right for our board and our district superintendent to make our own mistakes—we thought it was unfair for the Board of Education and the superintendent of schools to insist that they had to make all the mistakes. This was taken as a joke, but I meant it.

For five years, I have been shouting about this sort of "decentralization," and last spring I had the bittersweet experience of seeing the word become a political slogan in New York: everybody is now for decentralization. The state legislature has ordered the Mayor to produce a recommendation for decentralizing the New York school system, to be delivered before the end of the year, and the Mayor has appointed McGeorge Bundy as chairman of a blue-ribbon committee to prepare a plan for him. But nobody on this committee has ever served on a local school board or a district staff, or (with the exception of Al Giardino, the new president of the Board of Education, who inevitably represents other interests) has ever had occasion to think about the problem.

Both the Mayor and the Board of Education, moreover, have joined their policy statements on decentralization with a commitment to reorganizing the school budget according to the Program-Planning-Budgeting-Systems design pioneered by Secretary of Defense McNamara—which, whatever its applicability to buying bombers, has little relevance to education and is totally incompatible with significant decision making out in the field. The current enthusiasm among the politicians is for a "decentralization" which would leave budget and curriculum control at the center but place the choice of principals and district superintendents in the hands of community groups and local boards, who have no qualifications whatever to exercise such authority. This is something worse than just a fake. Nothing could do greater damage to what morale remains in the school system than the predictable flood of smooth educational and political con men who show a great face to the public, leaving the people in the schools who actually have to do the work looking at their unimpressive backs.

There is work to be done. To insist that the professionals listen to the community and interpret its needs rather than their own theories is entirely different from subjecting them to all the cross currents of neighborhood "power." People who should know better have been filling the press with statements that the slum activist groups are really asking for no more than middle-class parents already have. Lloyd Garrison, then president of the Board of Education, told the local school board chairmen last fall—in the middle of nationally televised rioting over the choice of principal for a new school in Central Harlem—that, after all, parents' associations in wealthier neighborhoods are very effective in controlling who gets hired and fired as principals in their schools. This statement came as a great surprise to the wealthiest such group in my district, which has been trying desperately and unsuccessfully to get rid of its principal for all the five years I have known the situation. Commissioner James E. Allen of the New York State Department of Education recently described the suburbs as places where "middle-class white families . . . can go to the school board and pound on the table and get the kind of schools they want." It has never been my good fortune to meet anyone who lives in a suburb where this situation prevails. The professional staffs run the schools everywhere—nobody else can.

The function of a lay board of education is to improve the performance of the professionals by feeding into the system information about what the community thinks is wrong and by asking the questions which force the professionals to look for intelligent answers. A central big-city board of education is no good for this purpose, in New York or anywhere else, because its members can't know enough about what is going on. New York lucked into a device which might have been useful, but its Board of Education, which has had four presidents during my five years on the local board, has lacked the desire and very probably the capacity to think through the question of the kinds of authority it should delegate to make the system work.

So far as I am concerned, the battle is over and I lost. I resigned from the local school board effective June 30, 1967. To say that the five years were a complete failure would be unfair to the hundreds of people who worked so hard with me on the many things we tried to do. But the fact is that the schools of my district are still in trouble, that the program for most children has changed little, and that the quality and performance of the teaching and supervisory staff have not noticeably improved. I cannot imagine any other potentially useful activity into which I could have put 2500 hours (my wife says 5000) and seen so little result. Ed Scalea, who has become a friend (sometimes an estranged friend), is also gone this fall, under doctor's orders to take a sabbatical leave. He will probably return: he says I am too impatient. It seems to me there is a minimal degree of impatience involved in being alive.

Five years on a school board is of course enough. (Indeed, I was at my departure the last surviving member from 1962.) You get to know too much, especially about what "can't be done," you begin to think all the meetings you attend mean something, and you come to "understand" too well the problems of the staff. Last winter, City University proposed that the Board of Education turn over some Harlem schools to its professors and see how they could do with a separate little slum school system completely independent of city headquarters. Mrs. Rose Shapiro, now vice-president of the Board of Education, called several of us local school board chairmen to lunch with her. She wanted us to oppose the City University plan (which in the end the board licked without our help), and when we asked her why she said, "They'll be free of all those restrictions we have—of course they'll do better." We exchanged some glances at the lunch table, and then I told Mrs. Shapiro that I thought she was probably right, and that was exactly why I supported the City University proposal. Mrs. Shapiro was almost abashed.

I never became so negative as Mrs. Shapiro, but I was on my way. It's impossible not to resent the newcomer, who arrives full of notions that you know are crackpot or don't match the problem or the reality or the resources. What the professionals really need on their lay boards (though it isn't what they want) is the hotheaded dreamer, not the experienced and sobered practical man. I was coming too close to the latter category for my own satisfaction or for real service to the schools.

I feel no pain (just a little discomfort) at the thought that others may succeed where I failed. My successor as chairman of the local board, Mrs. Leola Hageman, is a friend, a bright and lively resident of East Harlem, colored (which will help), a graduate of the University of Chicago (which will help even more); she already has a number of ideas which for one reason or another I would never have thought of trying out. Pessimism about the future of the big-city school systems makes sound logical argument and good newspaper copy, but in the end it is a foolish attitude. The texture of all our children's future lives is at stake in the struggle for education in the big cities. If enough people can remember that there is work to be done, not just arguments (or elections or lawsuits) to be won, we can get ourselves out of this morass. As a start, of course, it would be useful to stop sliding in deeper every year.

Conflict over Educational Change in an Economically Depressed Negro Community

Robert J. Parelius

The principle of local control over education is widely accepted in the United States. The thousands of school systems that are spread across the nation attest to this fact. However, the meaning of local control varies widely. In suburban and rural areas local control is essentially control by the local community, but this is not the case in big-city school systems.

It is clear that school government is not nearly as close to the people in large cities as elsewhere. Urban school systems have developed into massive, conservative, consensus-oriented, and largely ineffective bureaucracies. They have generally been insensitive to variations in the needs and demands of the multifarious subcommunities that they serve. In recognition of these problems and a wide variety of related ones, plans have recently been developed for the radical decentralization of some metropolitan school systems. The pendulum seems to be swinging back in the direction of local community control.

In view of this trend toward decentralization, it is essential that we understand the dynamics of school-community interaction under conditions of control by poverty-stricken communities. If this understanding is to be achieved, detailed case studies that describe how the schools are influenced by local politics, economics, and values are necessary. This paper will explore relationships of this type. It will focus on the schools and social structure of a single small, poverty-stricken town on the outskirts of a major metropolis. Special emphasis will be placed on

The research reported here was performed under a contract with the U.S. Department of Health, Education, and Welfare, Office of Education, under the provisions of the Cooperative Research Program. Additional support was provided by the Institute for Juvenile Research, Chicago, and the Center for Social Organization Studies, University of Chicago.

the conflict that was engendered by efforts to modernize the community's schools.

RESEARCH PROBLEMS AND METHODS

The research I will describe did not begin as a study of educational change. Its original concern was with family influences on the scholastic achievement of children in a lower-class Negro community and with family-school interactions. In the course of gathering background information for this study, it became clear that the community was divided into two hostile factions, and that this schism greatly affected perceptions of the school. It became apparent that controversial programs for modernizing the schools were important issues in community conflict. Therefore the research focus was broadened to include community problems arising from educational change.

This report draws upon a wide variety of data.[1] One major body of information derives from semistructured interviews with 201 mothers of fourth- and sixth-grade children. They represented over 90 per cent of the mothers of children in those grades in the three local schools. Other data come from school board election campaign materials, local newspaper stories, school records, questionnaires filled out by teachers in the schools, and extensive unstructured interviews that I conducted with school personnel, members of the school board, workers in welfare organizations serving the community, and other significant community actors.

THE RESEARCH SITE

The Impoverished Central Village

The research was conducted in 1966 and 1967 in a small (population approximately 5000) Negro community located within easy commuting distance of Midwest Metropolis. To preserve its anonymity and to reflect its primary characteristic, extreme poverty, I give it the pseudonym of Low Water. Despite its proximity to a major northern industrial center, a visitor is first struck by the great similarity of the village to small farming towns in the Deep South.

During the late summer, a wall of corn hides Low Water from the view of travelers on the nearby highway. The village is almost com-

[1] For a complete discussion of the research problems and methods see Robert J. Parelius, "The Schools and Social Structure of an Economically Depressed Negro Community," unpublished Ph.D. dissertation, University of Chicago, 1967, pp. 1–14.

pletely surrounded by farm land. Although Low Water can no longer be rightly classified as a farm town, it still depends on the land to an important extent. The wages from work in the fields and the vegetables grown in plots next to their homes are crucial to the budgets of many local families.

A large percentage of the dwellings in the center of Low Water are no more than tarpaper shacks that were erected by their owners. They have no running water or indoor toilet facilities and often hold families of ten to twelve persons. The charred remains of similar shacks that have burned to the ground are scattered throughout the center of Low Water. Slightly over 65 per cent of the housing in the community is substandard. However, two large public housing projects furnish relatively comfortable living quarters for some of Low Water's poor.

Within the central village are a number of small groceries and churches. However, there are no supermarkets or impressive new churches, such as are found in the prosperous suburbs nearby. The community has bars and restaurants, but no medical or dental facilities, drug stores, or movie theaters. Because they have no parks or other recreational areas, Low Water's many children play in empty lots, dirt and gravel streets, and abandoned cars.

The Working-Class Periphery

Not all parts of Low Water, however, are economically depressed and deteriorated. A few attractive and well-built houses can be found here and there throughout the central village. Furthermore, there are three developments of low-cost private homes located on different edges of the village. All of these have attracted working-class Negroes from Midwest Metropolis.

The first housing tract, Douglass Homes, was completed in 1960. Its prefabricated houses are very small and inexpensive. For a number of reasons, including inadequate sewage facilities and activities of fraudulent mortgage payment collectors, many of the persons who first bought these homes have left the area. At present, some houses are vacant and others have been rented to the poor. The area is badly deteriorated.

Within two years of the completion of Douglass Homes, Woodcreek Estates was built. These houses are larger and somewhat more substantial. Although none has been abandoned, many are poorly kept.

The newest development, Sunny Acres, is ecologically separated from one of the poorest parts of the village by a plowed field. As in the other developments, all the houses have small lots and look very much alike from the outside. However, about one-third are somewhat smaller than the others and have no basements. They are cooperatively owned and share a single mortgage. The rest of the houses are privately owned and are kept in better repair. Sunny Acres is different from other parts of Low Water in that well-groomed lawns and flower gardens are common, while abandoned cars and vegetable plots are rare.

THE SOCIAL STRUCTURE OF LOW WATER

It is impossible to understand the controversy over educational change in Low Water without first gaining some insight into its social structure. Thus I will describe the major features of this social structure and their historical bases before proceeding to the community's school politics.

The Villagers

The majority of Low Water's residents settled there long before any of the new tract developments were erected. They came at the beginning of World War II as part of a great migration of Negroes from the South to the urban North. These migrants were attracted by the promise of work in the burgeoning wartime industries and a less oppressive racial system.

Low Water was on one of the major routes of migration. Although the great majority of the local population was white when the migration began, Low Water served as a stopping-off place for many Negro families. Others decided to settle there rather than to continue into the crowded ghetto of Midwest Metropolis. As more and more Negroes decided to stay, the whites began to leave. By 1950 virtually all of the whites were gone. The situation persists today with about 85 per cent of the population being Negro and practically all of the rest being Mexican.

Low Water became a true pocket of poverty. A few statistics from the 1960 census should make this clear.[2] At that time more than a third of its families lived on incomes of less than $3000, the government's criterion of poverty.[3] Median family income was only $4421. The unemployment rate of 12.8 per cent was three times the national average. Of persons over 20 years of age, less than 4 per cent had completed high school. The median number of grades completed was 7.9. The infant mortality rate was among the state's highest, at 39.74 per thousand births.

However, many features of Low Water were attractive to these people,

---

[2] The following statistics were reported in a document prepared by the Regional Office of Economic Opportunity, 1966.

[3] The study employed a more sensitive index of poverty, one developed in James N. Morgan et al., *Income and Welfare in the United States* (New York: McGraw-Hill, 1962), pp. 188–190. In terms of this measure, almost 80 per cent of the families in the study sample lived below the subsistence or poverty level.

whom I shall call the Villagers. It was uncrowded. There was land enough for families to build homes and plant gardens. No building or zoning laws hindered them. The community was close to new factories and to rich suburbs. Thus, jobs as laborers and maids were available. Furthermore, Low Water had many physical and social similarities to the residents' former homes in the South. Ties of friendship and kinship that had held many families together in the South continued to do so in the North. Many of Low Water's present residents had come from the same small southern towns.

As far as I can reconstruct the situation, Low Water was a socially homogeneous environment within which these low-status members of society could live without being constantly reminded of that status. It appears that stable social order developed within which even the poorest could participate. However, the Villagers were not effectively integrated into the major institutions of modern industrial society.[4] At that time Low Water resembled Redfield's ideal-typical peasant society in that it was ". . . small, isolated, nonliterate and homogeneous, with a strong sense of solidarity." There were further similarities in that behavior tended to be highly conventional and personal rather than impersonal.[5]

The indigenous leadership structure that developed was conservative and, as we shall see later, perhaps corrupt. However, these leaders were attractive in that they laid no claim to being better than anyone else in the community.

The Suburbanites

Low Water did not remain an isolated, semirural pocket of poverty for long. It was soon caught up in the spread of Midwest Metropolis across the hinterland. The construction of low-cost private housing developments on the peripheries of the community brought about dramatic changes. It became what Dobriner has called a "reluctant suburb." According to him, such a community

> . . . is a going concern before the suburban assault begins. It has evolved a social system that works for a population of a certain size [and, we would add, character]. But once the restless city discovers the little village and pumps a stream of suburbanites into its institutions, the social system soon develops a split personal-

[4] In this respect Low Water displayed a "culture of poverty" described by Oscar Lewis in his *La Vida* (New York: Random House, 1966), p. xiv.
[5] Robert Redfield, "The Folk Society," *American Journal of Sociology*, Vol. 52 (1947), pp. 293–308.

ity. Where a Levittown faces the problem of creating a community from scratch, the sacked village has a community already—but it is soon divided between the pushy, progressive, and plastic world of the newcomers on the one hand, and the accustomed world of the old-timers, the villagers, on the other hand.[6]

During the last seven years a process similar to the one described by Dobriner has gone on in Low Water. However, his use of the term "sacked village" implies that the villagers inevitably lose in an unequal battle. This has not been the case to date in Low Water.

A two-step pattern of migration brought most of the newcomers, the Suburbanites, to Low Water. Like the Villagers, virtually all of them had been born in the South. However, they were more likely than the Villagers to have been born in urban areas. When they moved to the North, they settled in the large Negro community in Midwest Metropolis. There they lived for several years until they could save enough money to buy a house in the suburbs. The new homes that they purchased in the housing tracts on the edge of Low Water represented very substantial investments for them. The Suburbanites became most heavily concentrated in the Sunny Acres section of Low Water, but some came to live in other new areas.

When asked why they came to Low Water, these families stress the advantages for their children. They were attracted by its relative openness, quiet, and safety. They were also misled by the real estate salesmen, who claimed that the schools were of superior quality.

Few of these families were solid financially. As a group the Suburbanites would have a relatively low status within American society as a whole. However, in Low Water they were at the top of the socioeconomic hierarchy. Whether consciously or not, by remaining in Low Water, they chose to be big fish in a very small pond.

Background Characteristics of Low Water's Present Population

The preceding discussion suggests that two dimensions, length of residence and level of economic welfare, are central to understanding the social structure of Low Water. These dimensions can be employed in the analysis of data gathered from the survey sample to produce a more precise picture of the social background characteristics of the residents of Low Water.

For the purpose of this analysis, 1960, the date when Douglass Homes were occupied, was used to differentiate the population in terms of

[6] M. Dobriner, *Class in Suburbia* (Englewood Cliffs, N.J.: Prentice-Hall, 1963), pp. 127–128.

length of residence. Those who settled in 1959 or before will be referred to as the Oldtimers. The others, naturally, will be the Newcomers.

The ratio of a family's need to its total income can be called its "welfare ratio," and this is the second major dimension used in this analysis. Following Morgan, the poor were distinguished from the others in the community by having a welfare ratio of .9 or less.[7] An additional cutting point of .5 or less was used to separate the truly destitute from the rest of the poor.

When the two variables are combined, six statistical categories emerge, as illustrated in Figure 1. The concentrations of the two major social

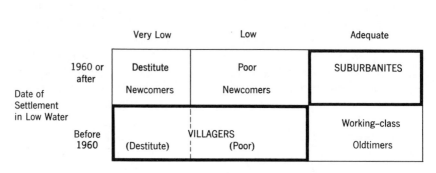

Figure 1   Low Water's social structure and social types.

types, the Suburbanites and Villagers, are indicated by the way these categories are set off by heavy lines. The former group consisted mainly of Newcomers above the poverty line. The Villagers were predominantly poor, or destitute long-time residents. The three remaining statistical categories are mixed.

All six categories can be used to examine the social background characteristics of the study sample, which are summarized in Table 1. Section (a) of the table shows stark contrasts in the family structures of the Villagers and Suburbanites. The families of the latter group are smaller, more stable, and more isolated from kin than are those of the Villagers. The contrasts between the Suburbanites and the destitute Villagers are very great indeed. As section (b) of the table shows, the great majority of all the mothers in Low Water come from rural backgrounds. However, long-term residents at all levels of welfare are more likely to be from farms than are the Suburbanites. Because the measures of social class

[7] Morgan et al., *op. cit.*, pp. 188–190.

Table 1   *Position in the Social Structure and Social Background Characteristics*[a]

Social Background Characteristic	Destitute		Poor		Working Class	
	Newcomer	VILLAGER	Newcomer	VILLAGER	SUBUR-BANITE	Oldtimer
(a) Family Structure						
Family has more than six children.	53 % (17)	**64 %** **(31)**	42 % (30)	**48 %** **(60)**	6 % (18)	15 % [c] (40)
Father is absent from home.	41 (17)	39 **(31)**	13 (31)	**27** **(64)**	11 (18)	12 [b] (40)
Mother's age is 40 or more.	19 (16)	**42** **(31)**	27 (30)	**33** **(60)**	33 (18)	38 (40)
Parents have one or more relatives in Low Water	53 (15)	**64** **(31)**	52 (25)	**71** **(62)**	37 (18)	59 (39)
(b) Urban-Rural Background						
Mother has lived on a farm for 1 year or more.	71 % (14)	**82 %** **(28)**	71 % (28)	**65 %** **(51)**	36 % (14)	57 % [b] (30)
(c) Measures of Socioeconomic Status						
Total family income is $4000 or more.	38 % (16)	**48 %** **(14)**	68 % (19)	**85 %** **(46)**	93 % (15)	97 % [c] (35)
Breadwinner's occupation is semiskilled or above.	36 (11)	**18** **(22)**	41 (22)	**54** **(48)**	43 (14)	66 [b] (32)
Breadwinner has more than 8 years of education.	47 (15)	**46** **(26)**	36 (28)	**52** **(58)**	86 (14)	73 [c] (27)

[a] Base numbers are given in parentheses in this table and the following ones.
[b] Chi square significant at 0.05 (d.f. = 5).
[c] Chi square significant at 0.01 (d.f. = 5).

reported in section (*c*) are strongly related to the measure of economic welfare, this section yields few surprises. Perhaps the most interesting finding is that more than half of the Suburbanites hold unskilled jobs. Thus, it is quite clear that this is more a working-class group than a middle-class one.

CONFLICT AND RESISTANCE TO EDUCATIONAL CHANGE

There have been four major distinct stages in the recent natural history of school-community relations in Low Water. First, there was a long period of consensus and quiescence. Then there was a sudden and dramatic takeover by Reformers, most of whom were Suburbanites. This was followed quite closely by a resurgence of the Villagers. Finally, there has been a period of consolidation of power by the Villagers and of the demoralization of their opposition.

Stage I: Consensus and Apathy

Vidich and Bensman give an extensive and graphic description of politics as they existed in Springdale, a small town in upstate New York.[8] There are many similarities between the politics of Springdale and those of Low Water during this period. Within both towns local elections were dull, drab affairs with little campaigning, few real contests, few votes, and candidates running more or less on "whim" rather than on backing from strong political organizations. Decisions tended to be made in a caucus fashion with much of the discussion of issues going on in private. Public decisions tended to be unanimous.

However, Vidich and Bensman do not discuss the type of corruption alleged to have been common in Low Water. True, they note that school affairs tended to be manipulated by a behind-the-scenes economic dominant. Still they do not allude to misappropriation of funds, the acceptance of "kickbacks," featherbedding, or nepotism. These conditions are said to have been rife in pre-Reform days in Low Water.

A few examples of the allegations regarding school politics should suffice. First, there was the controversy over the construction of a second school for the community. Irregularities were said to have occurred in the bidding for the construction contract. Despite the objections of the architect and some citizens that the cost of the school would be far out of line, the board authorized the construction. Within two years of completion of the school, a major structural defect appeared in the gymnasium, necessitating discontinuation of its use. Many local residents felt that the head of the school board and the superintendent of schools had received large kickbacks from the contractor. Similar charges were made regarding the purchase of school supplies and furniture. Also, it was rumored that school teachers bought their jobs for $500 from the head of the school board.

During this stage, which lasted from approximately 1950 to 1963, the charges of corruption were not raised effectively. Only a few of the working-class residents of the community were concerned about school affairs. Their power was miniscule compared with that of the entrenched leaders. This situation, however, was soon to change.

[8] Arthur J. Vidich and Joseph Bensman, *Small Town in Mass Society: Class, Power and Religion in a Rural Community* (Princeton, N.J.: Princeton University Press, 1958), pp. 174–201.

Stage II: The Reformist Takeover

The Suburbanites provided the stimulus for change in Low Water's school system. Shortly after settling in the village, they began to participate in a wide range of community affairs. It was not long before they became convinced that the village government and the school system were backward and thoroughly corrupt. Some left in the face of this disappointment, but others accepted it or stayed to fight for modernization.

In order to promote reform the Suburbanites moved quickly to establish a coalition with the few dissatisfied long-time residents. The members of this coalition will be referred to as the Reformers. Using effectively the element of surprise as well as their relative legal and political sophistication, the Reformers were able to gain control of the nominating convention of Low Water's only major political party. The Suburbanites nominated prestigious long-term residents for offices in both the village government and the school board. The Old Guard leaders were left out in the cold.

The Reformers won the next elections after fierce contests in which printed campaign literature appeared for the first time in the village's history. Central to their programs were the goals of eliminating corruption and modernizing the community. The Reformers who were elected to positions in the village government pushed through a major reorganization of the governmental structure and codes covering building, sanitation, and zoning. They also pressed for general improvements in fire and police protection, street lighting, and recreation. Once in control of the school board, the Reformers moved quickly to replace the white superintendent, whom they felt was incompetent and corrupt. After an extensive search they selected a young, vigorous, and experienced Negro to fill the vacant position. Dr. Neuman was the first Negro school superintendent in the state's history.

Acting with the board, Dr. Neuman sought many changes in the administration and operation of the schools. His conception of the superintendent as a relatively independent administrative advisor to the board was highly unpopular with the Villagers left on the board. Instead of inviting board members to join with him in screening teachers or other employees for the district, as had his predecessor, Dr. Neuman acted alone and then made recommendations to the board. The ferocity of the Oldtimers' opposition to this policy seems to add weight to the charge that school jobs had been purchased in the past. The new superintendent felt that many of the community's teachers should return to college in order to make up deficiencies in their training. In addition, he sought to establish a uniform salary scale in order to eliminate the practice of paying on the basis of friendship and loyalty. These actions incurred the wrath of some teachers who formed the core of a developing teachers' union in the district. Finally, Dr. Neuman and the Reformers on the board shared a modern view of education that stressed the need for close cooperation between the school and the family in caring for the child's psychological and physical needs. The resultant programs of psychological testing, health care, counseling, and family visitation, which were carried out by newly appointed personnel, were attacked as expensive and useless educational frills.

Stage III: Resurgence of the Old Guard

From the time the new superintendent, Dr. Neuman, took office in 1964, opposition to him grew stronger and stronger. It came not only from the Old Guard leadership of the Villagers, but also from the teachers and from other school employees, such as cafeteria and janitorial help. The school system was then, and still is, the largest employer in the community. The nonprofessional jobs were dispensed as patronage, and so they were endangered by this changeover in administration.

With this widespread opposition it was not surprising that the Reformers soon lost their majority on the board. Many of the Reformers claim that votes were bought in these elections. Indeed, 16 mothers in the study sample said that they had heard that bribes were offered. Each of 5 said that she personally had been offered $5.00 for her vote. The board attorney said that he was approached by the leader of the Old Guard for a "campaign contribution" of $60.00. It is also alleged that at least one Reform leader was bought off by the opposition with a patronage job within the school system.

In 1965 and 1966, there existed a 3-to-3 split in the board with one independent or "swing" vote. Pressure continued to build up on the superintendent. His proposals were blocked at every turn, and, after he had won two fights by threatening to resign, his third threat was accepted. The independent member had become convinced that Dr. Neuman really wanted to leave.

The new Negro superintendent, Mr. Lane, was chosen from within the ranks of the teachers of the district. His leadership experience was not great nor was he trained for administration. Indeed, he had been the school's music director before he was appointed. The Oldtimers fiercely supported Mr. Lane. The Newcomers were fiercely opposed. The issue of qualifications was brought up openly. In private many suggested that he was chosen because he would be a tool of the Old Guard.

Indeed, one rumor has it that the superintendent actually pays part of his salary back to one of the leaders of the Old Guard. An administrative assistant was chosen, creating a new post. The Old Guard says that this was done because they had the opportunity of getting two good men instead of just one. Their opponents say that the position was created because Mr. Lane is not capable of administering the district by himself.

At any rate the Villagers did not take long in reasserting their control over the school system. Since they have regained power, new controversies have developed. The school district has long been in financial trouble and has been forced to sell tax anticipation warrants. According to the board attorney, these warrants were not sold on a legitimate bidding basis. Instead they were sold at a rate well above the competitive one, to an out-of-state company that has a very shady reputation in the business world.

Another issue developed over the activities of the Congress of Racial Equality in Low Water. A group of the Suburbanites residing in Sunny Acres called this group in from Midwest Metropolis to help in expressing grievances about the school situation. The CORE organizers advised the Suburbanites to stage a sit-in at the office of state officials of education. This last suggestion was too militant for the Suburbanites, however. The circular shown in Figure 2 was distributed as part of CORE's activities. The group's involvement was brief, but it caused quite a stir.

The biggest scandal in the recent period developed over an alleged case of misappropriation of school funds. It was charged that a leader of the Villagers had taken an unauthorized companion with him to an out-of-state convention and used school funds to pay her expenses. That the companion was a woman other than the man's wife added spice to a rumor that spread like wildfire through much of the community. This controversy led to the Villager's resignation as head of the school board.

The Reformers had a difficult time finding someone who would bring charges against this powerful leader. However, finally someone was found; a trial began. Postponement followed postponement. Both sides accused the other of stalling. After many weeks had passed the case was finally heard and promptly dimissed. The leader of the Villagers claimed that he was fully cleared. The Reformers, however, alleged privately that the dismissal of the case was a direct result of bribery. They pointed out that the judge was a close relative of the school board attorney of pre-Reformist times. According to their account, the trial delays were designed to stall until this particular judge took the bench.

WHY SHOULD NEGRO CHILDREN IN LOW WATER SCHOOLS GET INFERIOR EDUCATION???

WHY DO LOW WATER CHILDREN LEAD THE DROPOUT LIST AT TOWNSHIP HIGH SCHOOL???

WHY SHOULD LOW WATER CHILDREN BE MADE THE INNOCENT VICTIMS OF CORRUPT AND INEFFICIENT SCHOOL ADMINISTRATION???

WHO IS RESPONSIBLE FOR INFLICTING AN INCOMPETENT SCHOOL BOARD ON LOW WATER'S FAMILIES???

* *

Midwest Metropolis CORE (Congress of Racial Equality) has received complaints from concerned parents of Low Water children who are anxious to overcome the causes of second-class education in their schools. Among the grievances these parents brought to the attention of CORE are the following:

1. The superintendent of schools does not have the educational background and training or other qualifications necessary for a first-class school system.
2. There are some members of the school board who use the school system for personal gain and advantage.
3. There has been no accounting of school funds.
4. There are inadequate facilities in the schools, including the lack of a library, showers, lunchroom, and landscaping which were supposed to have been paid for.
5. There is an unexplained shortage of school books.
6. The continuation of a "Voodoo Witch" gun-totin' principal in one school.
7. The teachers and parents do not want an alcoholic physical education "floater" seen in a drunken condition by their children in the schools.
8. Concerned parents do not want to send their children to classes with absentee teachers.
9. Teachers and parents do not want to see the Head Start Program abused this year.
10. Teachers, parents, and school system employees want an end to political hiring, firing, and transfers.
11. Concerned parents and taxpayers want to get unqualified teachers and incompetent help off the school system payrolls . . . NOW!!!

* * * * * * * * * *

Midwest Metropolis CORE is ready to support the concerned teachers and parents in Low Water to develop a first-class system for the children of Low Water.

The CORE program includes (1) Research, (2) Education, (3) Negotiation, and (4) DIRECT ACTION!!!

"We shall Overcome"

Figure 2   Midwest Metropolis CORE circular attacking Low Water's school system.

Stage IV: Demoralization of the Reformists

The Reformers had never had an easy time of it in school politics in Low Water. Personal attacks and other forms of harassment had plagued them from the beginning. Their initial successes were due largely to the elements of surprise and bureaucratic expertise. Now the Villagers are retrenched and are as powerful as ever. There had been a series of recent defeats, but the acquittal of the leader of the Villagers on the issue of misappropriation of funds, as just described, seems to have been the straw that broke the back of the opposition.

The results of the last two school elections are shown in Table 2. They indicate that in these elections there was very little support for the Reformist candidate. What little there was, however, came mostly from the Suburbanites. Although the trends are slight and the numbers relatively small, the table also shows a reduction in the percentage of the total vote for Reformers between 1966 and 1967, and a loss of support from among the community's poor.

Table 2   *Position in the Social Structure and Per Cent in Study Reporting Having Voted for Reformers in Recent School Board Elections*

	Destitute		Poor		Working Class	
Election Year	Newcomer	VILLAGER	Newcomer	VILLAGER	SUBUR-BANITE	Oldtimer
1966: two vacancies	25 % (8)	**22** % **(9)**	13 % (8)	**10** % **(30)**	**50** % **(16)**	17 % (18)
1967: three vacancies	00 (6)	**00** **(8)**	00 (6)	**13** **(30)**	**43** **(7)**	13 (15)

In short, the Reform movement in Low Water has disintegrated. In better times there was a highly cohesive leadership core with a kind of missionary zeal. It used to have frequent social as well as political meetings, but that is no longer the case. Now there is even great trouble in finding anyone to oppose the Old Guard in school board elections.

Many of the leaders of the Reformers have given up. They have removed their children from the school system and sent them to local parochial schools. Some have moved out of the community, and many other are talking about doing so. A feeling of deep depression and alienation is present: "Our situation here has gone from bad to worse . . . . Nobody cares about the problems of a small Negro village . . . . Fighting just doesn't do any good. I really feel that only God's hand can solve that problem now . . . . The corruption stretches from here all the way up to the governor's mansion. We can't fight that." These are some of the ideas that are expressed over and over again in conversations with the ex-leaders of the Reformist opposition.

These, then, are the four major phases that have emerged so far. It might seem that events have gone full circle and that a new period of consensus school politics is about to begin. This is probably not the case, however, because of a new development.

A New Force: The Teachers' Union

Although its role has yet to become completely clear, a new force has begun to show itself. This is a militant local union affiliated with the American Federation of Teachers. The teachers who belong to this union are not residents of the community; most of them commute from Midwest Metropolis. They have a stake in the schools of Low Water, however, since these schools are their source of livelihood. Of late these teachers have sought a greater voice in school affairs.

The union has been gathering strength since the time when the Reformers installed Dr. Neuman as school superintendent. Apparently several of the teachers whom Dr. Neuman wanted to send back to school for further training turned to the union for help. Some of these teachers are now leaders of the local union. Over the last three years the AFT has won the support of the vast majority of teachers. Lately it organized a successful strike in order to force an election for the sole bargaining agent of the teachers. In this election the rival State Education Association got less than 5 per cent of the votes cast.

Over the last few months the union has been engaged in negotiations with the school board over a contract for the teachers. One line from the introductory section of the union's initial draft of the contract suggests that the potential influence of the union may go far beyond the usual concerns for better wages and working conditions: "It is our sincere feeling that through such an agreement . . . significant contributions may be made in the areas of student welfare, wise use of tax funds, and over-all educational excellence."[9] The Villager who is presently head of the school board feels that this threatens the board's power. This statement forebodes another stage of an on-going struggle for control over school affairs in Low Water.

Already alliances are beginning to form. Many of the Reformers have

---

[9] Draft of American Federation of Teachers contract, Low Water Public Schools, December 20, 1966.

supported the union recently because they see it as a possible source of change for the better in the schools. Their support is somewhat ironic, for many of the union leaders are the very teachers whom the Reformers tried to remove through the activities of CORE. As a result there is an element of ambivalence on the part of the Reformers with regard to the union. The Villagers on the school board are split on the union issue. The present head of the board strongly opposes the union's contract as it is worded. He sees it as a threat to the central functions of the school board. However, the past president of the board strongly favors the union's position. Some Reformers suspect that he has made a deal with the union leaders on this issue.

THE OPPOSING FACTIONS VIEW ONE ANOTHER

It is appropriate to go into greater detail about the types of issues involved in the conflict. By piecing together information gathered from a variety of sources, I will describe the conception that each faction has of the situation. It is not at all surprising to find that the two factions have very different opinions about the qualifications and motives of the school administration, school personnel, and the opposing school board members.

The Reformers point critically to the nonacademic backgrounds of the present superintendent, his assistant, and one of the three principals. The Oldtimers retort that the backgrounds are adequate and that length of employment within the system is a primary consideration. The following quotations from election documents will illustrate the opposing positions.

Reformer Position

First, this is not for confusion. This is an organization of parents who are aware of inefficiencies within our area, and we know that the two head administrators are not in their proper working fields. Mr. Lane has a degree in music and Mr. Steele has his masters in Physical Education. What a choice! . . . We have one principal in the Woodburn school who never has nor ever will be efficient. Why isn't she replaced? Her masters is in Physical Education . . . .

Villager Defense

(1) The two leading administrators who, you say, are working out of their field are, according to the state, quite capable and well qualified. Your top administrator has a masters degree in Elementary Education from the University [of a neighboring state]

plus many other awards in the field of education, which is an honor and a credit to our local Board of Education. (2) The other "head" is a product of [neighboring town] and formally trained at State University. We refuse to try to list his many accomplishments, for you are aware of them. He had served as a State Supervisor in the Department of Public Instruction before coming . . . . (3) . . . the superintendent has been in the district longer than anyone . . . . When you are first in an area, you can't be ill-prepared and it is the reason for the exceptional (sic) high standards the district has now . . . .

With regard to the quality of school personnel and of the schools in general, the Reformers are generally more critical than the Villagers. Indeed, the Villagers use the criticisms of the Reformers as evidence that they are out to tear down the community. In private, however, some who are part of the conservative faction say that the school system is in terrible shape and that its teachers are the dregs of the Midwest Metropolis school system. One such person said in despair, "It's a miracle that the children get what little education they do get here!"[10] This was a comment not only about the quality of the schools per se, but also about the effect of the community controversy over the schools.

Reformist leaders charge the Old Guard members of the school board with legal and moral corruption, backwardness, lack of education, selfishness, and inefficiency. The Villagers, in return, charge the Reformers with being Communists or Communist dupes, wasteful, snobby, pushy, irreligious, power hungry, and selfish. In their campaign appeals the Reformers emphasize the education, sincerity, and community service of their candidates. The Oldtimers do not stress education, for they have less of it, but emphasize religious activities, being well known in community activities, and pride in the community and its schools.

BROADER PERSPECTIVES ON THE CONTROVERSY

From a macrosociological point of view it is crucial to realize that Low Water has only very recently been caught up in the sprawl of Midwest Metropolis across the countryside. A few years ago it was clearly a rural town. Now it is on the rural-urban fringe. It is certain that in the long run urban influences upon the life of Low Water will in-

[10] Low Water's children do very poorly on standardized achievement tests. Less than 10 percent of the fourth- and the sixth-grade children performed at or above their grade levels in reading or arithmetic. The mean IQ score of sixth graders in the sample was only 83.88.

crease, not decrease. That social conflict has accompanied this rapid social change should not be surprising. Several recent studies have shown that such conflict is often reflected in school affairs.[11]

Coleman has suggested that community conflicts appear in four major areas: (1) economic, (2) power and authority, (3) values or beliefs, and (4) persons or groups.[12] In Low Water and other reluctant suburbs the major schism seems to exist between two groups, the Villagers and the Suburbanites. These groups have come into conflict on issues of economics, power, and values or beliefs.

Economic Factors

Low Water's school district is by far the largest and richest employer in the community. It is much more important than the village government in that regard. The school district boundaries include a major automobile fabricating plant, whereas the village boundaries do not. This plant provides more than one-half of the tax revenues for the schools but employs only a handful of local residents. The schools, on the other hand, provide jobs for over thirty members of the community.

When the Reformers charge that the schools are run on a basis of corruption and patronage, they pose a threat to vested economic interests. Their proposals for expensive new school programs threaten the poverty-stricken Villagers with a heavier tax burden.[13]

Minar found conflict over school taxes and school board elections especially common in low-income areas with a relatively strong tax base and low school tax rates.[14] This is, of course, the situation in Low Water.

[11] James S. Coleman, *Community Conflict* (Glencoe, Ill.: The Free Press, 1957), *passim.;* Dobriner, *op. cit.,* pp. 113–117, 137–149; Benjamin Fine, "Educational Problems in the Suburbs," in William M. Dobriner, ed., *The Suburban Community* (New York: G. P. Putnam's Sons, 1959), pp. 317–325; Ralph B. Kimbrough, "Development of a Concept of Social Power," in Robert S. Cahill and Stephen P. Hencley, eds., *The Politics of Education in the Local Community* (Danville, Ill.: Interstate Printers and Publishers, 1964), pp. 99–103; Burton R. Clark, *Educating the Expert Society* (San Francisco: Chandler Publishing Co., 1962), pp. 129–133; and Grace Graham, *The Public School in the American Community* (New York: Harper & Row, 1963), pp. 283–284.

[12] Coleman, *op. cit.,* pp. 5–7.

[13] See Robert E. Agger, "The Politics of Local Education A Comparative Study in Community Decision-Making," in Donald E. Tope, ed., *A Forward Look—The Preparation of School Administrators, 1970* (Eugene, Ore.: Bureau of Educational Research, University of Oregon, 1960), p. 166. This study shows that better-educated voters are more likely than poorly educated ones to favor increased spending on special education programs.

[14] David W. Minar, "The Community Basis of Conflict in School System Politics," *American Sociological Reveiw,* VOL. XXXI (December, 1966), pp. 822–835.

Interpretations of the conflict differ, however. Fine and Dobriner suggest that it is a result of population change and is primarily a battle between Suburbanites, who want to spend more for schools, and Villagers, who want to hold the status quo.[15] Minar, on the other hand, hypothesizes that the conflict is due to the lack of middle-class citizens skilled in conflict management. The experience of Low Water supports the interpretations of Fine and Dobriner. There are some sophisticated middle- and working-class persons within the community. The skills that Minar speaks of are available. However, the persons who possess them are rejected. What appears to be happening is a genuine power struggle wherein the Villagers are protecting vested interests, and the Reformers are attempting to establish "clean government" in the schools.

The Struggle for Power and Authority

It was not long after Dr. Neuman was brought into the superintendency by the Reformers that controversy arose about the respective limits of the authority of the superintendent and the board. According to a Villager leader, then president of the board, "He went about everything ass backwards. Instead of having reports, budgets, and hiring go through the board and then to him, he wanted to do everything without consulting the board . . . ."[16] Clearly, in the past the superintendent had let the board have a great deal of authority in matters of hiring, firing, and purchasing. The separation between the policy-making function of the board and the administrative function of the superintendent was just not maintained. When Dr. Neuman took over his proper functions, he threatened the power that the Old Guard was used to exercising.[17] He and the other Reformers menaced what these Villagers perceived to be the organizational integrity of the school board. If the Reformers' charges of corruption are true, a strong independent superintendent was an economic threat also.

Thus, part of the conflict between the Suburbanites and the Villagers may be seen as a struggle for power and authority in school affairs. The Refomers wanted the power for their superintendent. The Villagers

---

[15] Fine, op. cit., p. 320; Dobriner, Class in Suburbia, passim. See also other references cited in footnote 11.

[16] Interview with the chairman of the school board, Low Water, December 22, 1966.

[17] See an excellent review of the research literature on school board-superintendent relations by C. E. Bidwell, "The School as a Formal Organization," in James G. March, ed., Handbook of Organizations (Chicago: Rand McNally, 1965), pp. 994–1003. This review illustrates the fact that Low Water's problems in this area are quite common.

wanted it for themselves. Both groups argued that they had the children's interests at heart. Beyond what was probably a genuine concern for the betterment of the educational system, it is probably true that the Reformers wanted to achieve control of the schools for some less altruistic reasons. These persons had been denied positions of authority in Midwest Metropolis. They had felt helpless when confronted with the huge bureaucracy of the schools and the city government. As Wood puts it, the new Suburbanite seeks to ". . . re-enter the civic life of a small community, no longer a faceless member of a mass rally, but a citizen . . . whose political participation makes a difference."[18] Some Reformers may have valued political activity in and of itself.

Conflicting Values and Beliefs

Schools are major agencies of socialization. As such they serve the function of inculcating community values and attitudes in the young. Just what values and attitudes should be taught in the schools is often a focus of controversy. Sometimes this has to do with religious values.[19] At other times political orientations are at the center of disagreement.[20]

In Low Water it seems that many of the value conflicts between Oldtimers and Newcomers or Reformers involve oppositions between rural and urban, traditional and modern, local and cosmopolitan, and conservative and liberal value systems.[21] Like the residents of Vidich and Bensman's Springdale, the Villagers dislike the city and all that it stands for in their minds—corruption, irreligiosity, liberalism, crime, modernity, etc.[22] The new residents are symbols of these things to the Villagers. Especially salient are concerns that these people represent the encroachment of socialism or even communism upon this small bastion of traditional American values. The Old Guard pointed out that one of the major supporters of the Reform candidates, Mrs. Redmond, is a white, Jewish woman whose Negro husband was accused in the *New York Times* of being a Communist. Candidates who are backed by this politically sophisticated couple are likely to be stigmatized as "Communist dupes."

[18] Robert C. Wood, *Suburbia: Its People and Their Politics* (Boston: Houghton Mifflin, 1958), p. 166. See also David W. Minar, "School, Community, and Politics in Suburban Areas," in B. J. Chandler, Lindley J. Stiles, and John I. Kitsuse, eds., *Education in Urban Society* (New York: Dodd, Mead, 1962), pp. 90–104.

[19] Dobriner, *Class in Suburbia*, pp. 113–117.

[20] One study of attacks by arch conservatives can be found in Mary Ann Raywid, *The Ax-Grinders: Critics of Our Public Schools* (New York: Macmillan, 1962).

[21] Clark, *op. cit.*, pp. 124–132, and William M. Dobriner, "Local and Cosmopolitan as Contemporary Suburban Character Types," in his *The Surburban Community*, pp. 132–143.

[22] Vidich and Bensman, *op. cit., passim.*

The ex-school board head is really convinced that the Reformers are out to take over control of the schools so that Communist doctrine will be taught in them. This leader is also quite concerned with the introduction of War on Poverty funds into the community to support a day-care center. He feels that the Reformers have too much power over the center and that too much government control is being exercised in the area.

Educational Concern

As the preceding material has implied, the Villagers and Suburbanites are quite different in the nature of their involvement in the education of their children. Low Water's teachers make a sharp distinction between the small minority of "active" or "interested" parents and all others. Some of these teachers identified the Suburbanites as an outstandingly concerned group. There was general agreement among the teachers that one good measure of parental concern is whether or not the parents ever visit a teacher on their own volition. Table 3 shows the Suburbanites to be outstanding in this measure and on two related ones, expectations that their children will go to college and voting in school board elections.[23]

Social class differences aggravate the conflict of values in Low Water. Some of the Reformers are upwardly mobile parents who want their children to have the best modern, progressive education. They are likely to look down upon the poverty-stricken long-time residents who do not share these values and attitudes. In turn, the Villagers are very sensitive to slights on the part of the Newcomers. It was not uncommon to hear

Table 3   *Position in the Social Structure and Educational Concern*

Measure of Educational Concern	Destitute		Poor		Working Class	
	Newcomer	VILLAGER	Newcomer	VILLAGER	SUBUR- BANITE	Oldtimer
Family had one or more parent-initiated contacts with one school.	43 % (14)	**31** % **(24)**	37 % (30)	**29** % **(56)**	**73** % **(15)**	54 % [a] (35)
Mother expects child will attend college.	56 (15)	**39** **(30)**	60 (25)	**58** **(50)**	**80** **(16)**	80 (16)
Mother voted in last school board election.	60 (17)	**55** **(31)**	52 (29)	**78** **(59)**	**90** **(18)**	66 (39)

[a] Chi square significant at 0.01 (d.f. = 5).

[23] The measure of parent-teacher contact derives from questionnaires that the teachers filled out. Interviews with the mothers provided the other measures.

a Villager remark, "They think they are just too good to pay attention to us."

CONCLUSIONS AND IMPLICATIONS

Educational Change in Suburbia

This case study suggests that the receptivity of suburban communities to modern, progressive educational programs varies in part with the social-structural chracteristics of the communities. Reluctant suburbs like Low Water are likely to have bifurcated social structures with severe splits between groups comparable to the Villagers and Suburbanites or Reformers. In such areas resistance to educational modernization is likely to be just one part of a broader attempt to defend the established economic, political, and value systems. There will be some long-term residents who have a vested interest in the status quo and who will therefore actively oppose change. This is no problem in newly established suburbs simply because there is no status quo to defend.

Resistance to modern educational practices would be expected in working- and lower-class suburbs, however, even if they happen to be brand new and socially homogeneous. Among the poor, Riessman has pointed out,

> The progressive approach . . . does not catch on. It has too many features that are essentially alien to the culture of the deprived; the permissiveness; the accent on self—the internal—the introspective; creativity and growth as central goals of education; the stress on play; the underestimation of discipline and authority. All these values are contradictory to the traditional attitudes of the deprived.[24]

It is also true that in poorer areas local residents are more likely to depend on the schools as important sources of income, power, and prestige since few alternative sources are available. Thus, there is likely to be strong resistance to bureaucratization, professionalization, and other changes that will probably decrease local control of the schools.

Implications for Urban Systems

It is dangerous to generalize from small social systems to large ones and from case studies to other situations. Nonetheless some of these

[24] Frank Riessman, *The Culturally Deprived Child* (New York, Harper & Row, 1962), p. 72.

findings seem to have tentative but broad implications that should be stated.

This study accents some of the problems and advantages associated with control of educational institutions by the local community. Small, suburban school systems are especially vulnerable to external influence. In rich suburbs the pressures come from highly educated parents, both as individuals and in organized groups.[25] In poor communities like Low Water, most parents are apathetic. Therefore, the way is opened for control by a self-serving oligarchy.

The urban areas have a quite different problem. There the school systems have become such massive public bureaucracies that they tend to be inflexible, invulnerable, and unresponsive to demands emanating from the local community. Until recently these demands have not been forcibly expressed. However, there are indications that the militant actions of minority-group parents in New York and Chicago may become more widespread.[26] Proponents of decentralization of city school systems feel that this will bring an improvement in the educational achievement of children from deprived minorities. This consequence is anticipated from the increased innovation, experimentation, and research in teaching methods and curriculum, as well as closer integration of school and community, resulting from decentralization.

However, with decentralization may come debureaucratization. As government moves closer to the people, pressure for educational decisions on the basis of qualities rather than performance may increase. For instance, the concept of Black Power may be extended to the schools, resulting in an increased emphasis on race in matters of personnel and purchasing. The safeguards provided by the civil service system and city and state laws may be inadequate to resist strains toward political intrigue and corruption of the sort found in Low Water.[27] "Balkanization" may be another result of decentralization.[28] Already tense race relations may be strained further. The schools may be lost as assimilating agencies when they seek to combat self-hate by teaching Negro history and Swahili rather than American history and European languages.

The plans for decentralization have come at the same time that mili-

[25] See C. E. Bidwell, op. cit., pp. 1009–1012.

[26] Stokeley Carmichael and Charles Hamilton, Black Power: The Politics of Liberation in America (New York. Vintage Books, 1967), pp. 42–43.

[27] Clark, op. cit., has pointed out, "The historic and extreme decentralization of education in this country has made control a problem of state and local government, and until recently these have been the locales of nearly all the conflict of interest" (p. 123).

[28] Joseph Featherstone, "Community Control of Our Schools," The New Republic, January 13, 1968, p. 17.

tant professional unions of teachers have begun to make their demands felt. A power struggle seems to be developing between parents, teachers, and bureaucrats. The demands of local communities for a voice in school affairs are pitted against the needs of the school to maintain its organizational integrity and of the teachers to maintain their professional integrity. Maintaining a balance between these forces has become, and probably will continue to become, increasingly difficult. It is a problem that various other public bureaucracies, such as police departments, universities, and welfare agencies, are also facing. It is too early to predict the outcome.

Pupil Mobility and IQ Scores in the Urban Slum: A Policy Perspective

Thomas S. Smith, C. T. Husbands, and David Street

Residential transiency is a significant feature in the demographic profiles of low-income urban neighborhoods. Below-average achievement and intelligence test scores are just as prominent in the educational profiles of the schools in these areas. Some researchers have investigated the possibility that there is more than an ecological correlation between these characteristics, but these studies have in general failed to demonstrate the hypothesized relationship.[1]

This paper will present evidence to demonstrate that high levels of pupil mobility are in fact related to school ability, as measured by IQ scores. The finding will become strongly apparent when we analyze the data making a methodological innovation: looking at the effects of mobility on IQ test results *over time*. We shall investigate also the extent to which pupil mobility reflects not only residential transiency but also administrative policies that are potentially manipulable. In this way we shall assess the policy implications of the research.

DATA AND METHODS

The data we are to analyze were collected in 1964 from nine public elementary schools on the South Side of Chicago.[2] The attendance areas

---

The research on which this paper is based was conducted with the cooperation of the Chicago Public Schools, principally through the good offices of Dr. Curtis C. Melnick, then superintendent of District 14.

[1] James L. Lehman's "Pupil Mobility and Its Relationship to Age, Intelligence Quotients and Achievement," unpublished doctoral dissertation, Northwestern University, 1963, is illustrative and contains a review of other studies.

[2] This data collection was part of a larger project involving information on all third-, sixth-, and eighth-grade pupils in District 14 of the Chicago Public Schools,

256

involved were mostly in the East Woodlawn community but also included one census tract from each of the South Shore and Greater Grand Crossing community areas. We are here concerned only with third- and sixth-grade pupils, of whom there were 795 and 803, respectively. These grades were selected because they are levels at which the school system administers standardized tests on a uniform city-wide basis. The basic variables derived from the records covered histories of pupil mobility (both residential and interschool), ability and achievement scores, and a variety of background characteristics. Complete information was not available for a large number of pupils, but there is no evidence that the omission of cases with incomplete information systematically biases the sample or affects our findings.

At the time of our data collection the whole area where the schools are located was largely a Negro slum. The school racial census conducted in October, 1964, revealed that six of the eight schools from which our third-grade sample is drawn and five of the seven schools with sixth graders had student bodies that were over 98.0 per cent Negro. Three schools formed very minor exceptions: one, providing only third graders, was 92.2 per cent Negro; a second, furnishing only sixth graders to the sample, was 93.1 per cent Negro; and in the third, where both grade levels are represented, 96.9 per cent of the student body was Negro. In the 1960 census the total population of the area was 86 per cent Negro, a figure that had undoubtedly increased by the time we collected data, and 29 per cent of the households had family incomes of less than $3000. None of the school attendance areas, as approximated by the aggregation of census tract data, had a median family income as high as $5000. Because the school records provided no information on the race of individual pupils, we have been unable to control for the effects of race.

That mobility can be dramatically high in the urban slum is shown in Table 1. It can be seen, for example, that by the sixth grade 59 per cent of the pupils had had more than two different home addresses and 29 per cent had had five or more addresses. Interschool mobility is often even more pronounced; by third grade almost 85 per cent of the pupils had attended more than one school.[3] It would certainly be

which covers East Woodlawn, Hyde Park, South Kenwood, and northern South Shore. Information was collected on each pupil from records maintained by school officials. Findings on the other schools, which had higher socioeconomic characteristics than those considered here and which in some cases contained substantial numbers of white pupils, will be reported in subsequent papers.

[3] This contrasts with findings in nine nearby middle-income schools, where the comparable figure was 53.7 per cent.

Table 1   *Numbers of Chicago Public Schools Attended and of Home Addresses*[a]

Numbers	Third Graders		Sixth Graders	
	Schools	Addresses	Schools	Addresses
1	15.6%	32.7%	15.8%	18.4%
2	36.4	27.4	22.8	22.9
3	21.5	18.3	19.9	18.0
4	12.9	11.6	14.6	11.7
5	6.8	5.5	10.7	11.5
6	3.4	2.2	6.5	4.7
7	2.2	1.3	3.5	5.2
8	0.4	0.4	2.7	2.5
9+	0.8	0.7	3.5	5.1
Total	100.0%	100.1%	100.0%	100.0%
No. of cases	(775)	(763)	(751)	(768)

[a] Since entering any of the Chicago public schools.

extraordinary if such levels of transiency had no deleterious effects on the academic achievement of the children subjected to them.

FINDINGS

The approach taken in this analysis is initially to follow the methodological practice of earlier related research by seeking an association between current IQ scores and the number of schools attended. Subsequently we shall introduce the refinement of considering changes in IQ measurements over time in order to be able to make inferences about the nature of the dynamics of pupil mobility. We shall address such topics as the stage of a pupil's career where the consequences of mobility are most pronounced, whether and in what circumstances earlier moves are more damaging than later ones, and whether any particular level of initial IQ affords some protection from the consequences of small degrees of mobility.

Table 2 cross-tabulates current IQ scores with the number of schools attended in the Chicago public school system for both third- and sixth-grade pupils. The third-grade data show a very clear association between current IQ and interschool mobility: the more frequently a child has

Table 2   *IQ Scores by Numbers of Schools Attended in the*
            Chicago Public Schools

IQ Score	Number of Schools			
	1	2	3	4 or more
Third graders				
70 or less	—	0.4%	2.5%	1.0%
71–80	8.7%	5.9	12.6	16.1
81–90	20.0	27.2	28.3	31.1
91–110	62.6	59.9	52.8	49.3
111–120	6.1	5.1	3.8	2.6
121 or more	2.6	1.5	—	—
Total	100.0%	100.0%	100.0%	100.1%
No. of cases	(115)	(272)	(159)	(193)
Sixth graders				
70 or less	9.3%	10.6%	5.4%	10.1%
71–80	13.9	11.1	18.5	22.6
81–90	17.6	24.2	24.6	26.8
91–110	43.5	48.5	46.2	35.5
111–120	13.9	5.1	3.1	3.1
121 or more	1.9	0.5	2.3	1.7
Total	100.1%	100.0%	100.1%	99.8%
No. of cases	(108)	(198)	(130)	(287)

changed schools, the greater is the probability of his having a low IQ. However, no such clear pattern prevails in data on sixth graders.

Analysis of Change over Time: Rationale

We will find that the analysis of the effects of interschool mobility on changes in intelligence scores reveals the hypothesized relationship even more strongly for third graders and, more importantly, enables us to be more precise about the effects of pupil mobility on sixth graders. The use of changes in scores between two points in time has other very important advantages that do not accrue when using merely raw scores. In the first place it is conceptually more elegant, as the phenomenon measured by intelligence tests is far from being a stable and nonreversible attribute of each individual. Rather each person should be seen as having an intelligence potential whose development or retardation is very greatly determined by environmental conditions experienced in the early part of his life.[4]

The most significant advantage of using over-time data is that this analysis provides an implicit control for the contaminating effects of background variables, which the school records used in this study were very weak in providing. All research in the correlates of intelligence measures has to be mindful of a considerable body of literature on the relation between socioeconomic status (SES) and intelligence measures.[5] Our exclusive use of pupils from a low-income neighborhood minimizes the relevance of a control on the consequences of difference in SES. Yet it should be mentioned that the area where the schools are located is far from completely homogeneous in this respect: about 23 per cent of the male labor force was classified as white collar in 1960. Using changes in scores rather than raw scores does enable us, however, to obviate the complications that this fact might otherwise cause, because we can separate preschool from school influences on intellectual development. Presumably, the continued influence of socioeconomic factors (or, more precisely, the home environment characteristics with which these tend to be at least moderately associated) is limited after the child has entered the school system; much of the impact of SES has exhausted itself by this stage, and this variable is increasingly superseded by other influences specific to the educational environment. A final benefit of using over-time data is that a comparison of the role of mobility in two different effect periods makes it easier to assess with what strength this variable continues to operate in the later period of the school career and how much of its impact is lost after third grade.

The underlying conception of the effects of interschool mobility that forms our rationale for the particular way in which we execute this analysis is as follows: High levels of mobility produce a tendency in a pupil to lose IQ points, and low mobility or none at all permits the action of influences that stimulate intellectual progress and lead to a gain in IQ points. It is not difficult to see how mobility may lead to a child's intellectual degeneration. He has to adapt himself to numerous disturbances in his educational environment; new peer groups within the school have to be cultivated, often at a time when concomitant residential mobility means he is also in a socially isolated position among age-mates outside school. In addition, he often has to come to terms

[4] See, for example, Benjamin S. Bloom, *Stability and Change in Human Characteristics* (New York: Wiley, 1964), pp. 68–76.
[5] One of many books summarizing the conclusions of several such studies is the following: Anne Anastasi, *Differential Psychology*, 3rd ed. (New York: Macmillan, 1958), pp. 515–522.

with different organizational procedures in his new school, and the general effect of such experiences, especially on the younger child, is likely to be traumatic, meaning a reduced ability and motivation to cope with the intellectual challenge of school work. The low-mobility pupil in a slum school is usually in something of a minority and may even suffer indirectly some of the consequences of mobility, such as reduced peer support, because he has a large proportion of highly mobile age-mates. Nonetheless, even in slum schools low-mobility pupils do acquire such advantages as personal recognition and perhaps encouragement from teachers, who may come to know these children well enough to develop more than a strictly formal relationship with them.

We will base most of our data analysis on comparisons of differences between the proportions of pupils who lose IQ points and of those who gain points among our different control groups at various levels of mobility. This difference shows the relative tendencies to point losses or gains induced by particular degrees of pupil mobility. Operationally a significant loss or gain has been set at 5 or more points. There are two reasons for this: first, it is hardly realistic to view a change of 1 or 2 points over a 2- or 3-year period as meaningful; second, and more pertinent, the school district that we sampled does not employ the same types of test at all grade levels. In the first grade most IQ scores were obtained by the Kuhlmann-Anderson test; in other cases, the California Test of Mental Maturity or, occasionally, the Stanford-Binet was used. The scores not obtained by the Kuhlmann-Anderson test represent children who moved into the area studied from places where other tests are used. All current third graders were measured by the Kuhlmann-Anderson test. Almost all current sixth graders had been measured by the Kuhlmann-Anderson test when they were in third grade, although a few pupils had been given the California Test of Mental Maturity or the Stanford-Binet. All sixth-grade scores were from the California Test of Mental Maturity. Although all tests have been standardized in terms of their means and deviation IQs,[6] they do not correlate perfectly and so to some extent may even be measuring different aspects of intelligence. The Chicago public school administration operates on the principle that these tests are comparable in the range of 85 to 125 and vary somewhat in the tails of their distributions.[7] In view of this element of noncomparability between types of test, a change of at least 5 points was considered essential if it was to be regarded as meaningful.

We will also use IQ score at the beginning of each effect period,

[6] For an explanation of this term see Anne Anastasi, *Psychological Testing*, 2nd ed. (New York: Macmillan, 1961), pp. 95–97.
[7] According to Dr. Melnick of the Chicago Public Schools.

considered as a further control. In view of the relationship already mentioned between SES and intelligence measures, this is to some extent also a proxy control on the effects of social class variables. However, the primary concern in introducing this variable is to see whether various initial IQ levels afford differential protection against the effects of earlier mobility. Because our procedure is to compare differences between tendencies to point losses and point gains at various mobility levels, this procedure does introduce an element of spuriousness of which the reader must be warned. It arises from the fact that intelligence tests do not have equal units at all points of their scales. The implications of this phenomenon have received some attention from Benjamin Bloom, who has concluded from a survey of currently available literature that the relationship between initial IQ and absolute change from this score is almost nonexistent among very young children, but attains significance after the child is about 7 years old. The association is negative. The scores of people with initially high IQ, in conditions favoring an improvement, have a propensity to rise less in absolute value than those of similarly situated people with initially low IQ. This Bloom ascribes to a ceiling effect, in which persons with initially high scores may make smaller changes less easily than those with initially low scores.[8]

In the population under consideration the overall direction of change is downward: the mean IQ falls from 95.8 in the first grade to 93.6 in the third grade for contemporary third graders, and from 92.8 in the third grade to 89.5 in the sixth grade for contemporary sixth graders. We may hypothesize the operation of a "floor effect." Our method of defining IQ change has the inevitable drawback that it arbitrarily captures in the loss category an excessive number of initially high IQ persons, merely because they have further to fall, while disproportionate numbers of pupils with initially low IQ escape being classified among those who lose merely because it is harder to fall the necessary 5 points. When we subtract proportions who lose from those who gain we therefore weight the category of initially high IQ persons with an excessive tendency toward point losses. We are warranted in attempting to show that various categories of initial IQ are differentially vulnerable, not to the composite effects of mobility, but merely to particular ordinal moves. If high-IQ pupils lose points by frequent moves, so will the less gifted, though the latter, having less to lose, will lose less.[9]

[8] Bloom, op cit., pp. 62–63.

[9] This statement assumes that we are dealing with levels of IQ found among children of normal development potential. The excessively retarded child and the genius are probably beyond the redemptive or degenerative influences of their environment, pupil mobility being considered among these factors.

Change over Time: Results

Third-Grade Data. Table 3, a turnover table with initial IQ controls, reinforces the conclusion about the third graders that we had already reached using raw IQ scores. Within each of the three control categories, extra mobility results in the proportions who lose points increasing and the proportions who gain points decreasing more or less *pari passu.* It is immediately observable that proportions losing are higher among those who were above 110 in first grade, a finding that can be ascribed to the lesser susceptibility of this group to the "floor effect."

The most revealing part of the analysis is the comparison of the relative effects of different degrees of mobility toward point losses and point gains. The results of subtracting the proportion who gain points from those who lose are shown at the bottom of Table 3. They are arranged graphically in Figure 1. We may now readily answer questions concerning what the overall strength of the effect of mobility is, whether a particular ordinal move is more than usually damaging, and whether the effect is attenuated after a child has moved among schools some critical number of times.

The lines in Figure 1 represent the initial IQ control categories. Our concern is with their shapes rather than their ordering above each other in the graph; the latter illustrates what Table 3 shows about the delayed action of the "floor effect" among initially-high-IQ pupils rather than their greater vulnerability to mobility. That this is a valid conclusion receives a measure of support from the fact that in their general direction the lines do not show marked departures from the parallel as mobility levels increase; the "floor effect" operates to the same extent among pupils with five moves behind them as among those with no moves.

Figure 1 shows that the ordinal move likely to be most damaging in its consequences varies according to initial IQ. Furthermore, within the amounts of mobility with which the numbers of cases allow us to deal, there is no critical number of moves beyond which the effect of mobility is attenuated or disappears for all sections of the population. However, it is clear that a critical level does exist that is peculiar to each class of initial IQ.[10] Differentials between initial IQ levels are partly explicable in terms of the floor effect, which operates more quickly for persons of initially low IQ. For them earlier moves produce the most dramatic decline, and the influence of mobility is curvilinear, with in-

---

[10] It is reasonable to suppose that certain other variables, which we did not have adequate data to consider, are pertinent in this respect, for example, what the home environment is like and whether school moves are accompanied by long or short residential moves.

Table 3 IQ Change of Third-Grade Pupils since First Grade by Interschool Mobility and First-Grade IQ Score

First-Grade IQ:	Below 90				90–110				Over 110			
Number of Schools Attended:	1	2–3	4–5	6+	1	2–3	4–5	6+	1	2–3	4–5	6+
Loss of 5 or more points	16.7%	23.1%	32.4%	33.3%	42.1%	45.1%	54.1%	70.8%	71.4%	61.8%	83.3%	100.0%
No significant change	—	32.0	35.2	25.0	36.8	41.4	39.4	16.7	—	23.6	—	—
Gain of 5 or more points	83.3	44.9	32.4	41.7	21.1	13.6	6.6	12.5	28.6	14.7	16.7	—
Total	100.0%	100.0%	100.0%	100.0%	100.0%	100.1%	100.1%	100.0%	100.0%	100.1%	100.1%	100.0%
No. of cases	6	78	34	12	38	162	61	24	7	34	6	1
Difference between proportion losing and proportion gaining	−0.67	−0.22	0.0	−0.08	0.21	0.32	0.48	0.58	0.43	0.47	0.67	1.0

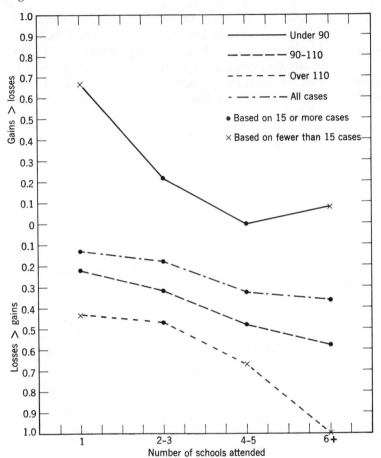

Figure 1 Differences between proportions with point losses and point gains by interschool mobility and first-grade IQ for third graders.

creasing attenuation in the upper categories. The actual reversal of the trend in favor of point gains among pupils who have attended six or more schools is an irregularity for which it is impossible to provide an adequate explanation; we must view it as a likely product of random error among the small numbers of cases on which it is based.

High-IQ pupils, on the other hand, are apparently able to resist the retarding effects of earlier moves, but as the number of schools attended increases, the negative consequences of mobility rapidly become apparent. Part of the protection afforded by high initial IQ against the effects of earlier moves may actually be due to SES variations in the sample, since pupils in this group are likely to be of somewhat higher SES. If such is the case, however, the protecting role of SES is confined to the lower levels of mobility. In the classes of mobility with which we deal, the relationship for high-IQ children is curvilinear with an increasing downward gradient, although this doubtless tends to horizontality at some critical number of moves too high to appear on this graph. Among pupils with average initial intelligence, mobility operates linearly, and this line must also flatten at some higher level of mobility than can be considered here.

Sixth-Grade Data. We can reconsider the sixth-grade data using changes in score between third grade and sixth grade as the dependent variable. This procedure clarifies to some degree the weak relationship that Table 2 showed between raw IQ and pupil mobility by demonstrating to what extent and among which groups an association exists. Two prefatory observations are in order, however. First, we did not record the dates of particular moves between schools, and so we are relating IQ change between third and sixth grade to the number of schools attended in the pupil's entire school career. It is therefore necessary to make the largely reasonable assumption that moves between schools are not concentrated in any particular period of a child's school career. However, this limitation in the data makes it impossible to consider whether particular ordinal moves are equally damaging irrespective of which effect period they occur in, and we are not able to view the sixth-grade data as representing in all respects a continuation of the experiences of the third graders already examined. The second observation is that, when discussing the development of intelligence, it must be remembered that during certain periods of childhood a pupil is more susceptible to the environmental influences that will determine his IQ at maturity than he is at other times. Susceptibility decreases with age. Bloom concludes that "in terms of intelligence measured at age 17, at least 20% is developed by age 1, 50% by about age 4, 80% by about age 8, and 92% by age 13."[11] Arranged graphically, these figures show that in the 2 years between first and third grade an extra 10 per cent of mature IQ is determined, while during the succeeding 3 years the figure is only about 7 percent. Thus we would expect less extreme reactions to differentials of our independent variable at the sixth grade.

Table 4 relates changes in the IQ scores of sixth graders between third and sixth grade to the number of schools they have attended, controlling on IQ at the beginning of the effect period. Among the bulk of the sample, those with initially average IQ, the hypothesized

[11] Bloom, *op cit.*, p. 68.

Table 4 IQ Change of Sixth-Grade Pupils since Third Grade by Interschool Mobility and Third-Grade IQ Score

Third-Grade IQ:	Below 90				90–110				Over 110			
Number of Schools Attended:	1	2–3	4–5	6+	1	2–3	4–5	6+	1	2–3	4–5	6+
Loss of 5 or more points	36.0%	38.8%	34.9%	38.5%	19.6%	46.6%	50.0%	51.1%	71.4%	62.5%	71.4%	100.0%
No significant change	40.0	47.5	46.0	32.7	43.5	32.8	26.8	33.3	28.6	18.8	—	—
Gain of 5 or more points	24.0	13.8	19.0	28.8	37.0	20.7	23.2	15.6	—	18.8	28.6	—
Total	100.0%	100.1%	99.9%	100.0%	100.1%	100.1%	100.0%	100.0%	100.0%	100.1%	100.0%	100.0%
No. of cases	25	80	63	52	46	174	82	45	7	16	7	2
Difference between proportion losing and proportion gaining	0.12	0.25	0.16	0.10	−0.17	0.26	0.27	0.36	0.71	0.44	0.43	1.0

relationship clearly holds, though with less strength than was the case with the equivalent third-grade data. Among those with initially extreme IQ scores, the existence of a relationship is rather more doubtful. For those starting with scores less than 90 in the third grade, the influence of mobility is quickly attenuated, and the cases in the over-110 category are too few to mean much.

Figure 2, in which are examined differential propensities to lose or gain with mobility, as was done with the third-grade data, allows the particular nature of the mobility effect to be seen more clearly. Certain conclusions are immediately obvious: all lines except the one for those

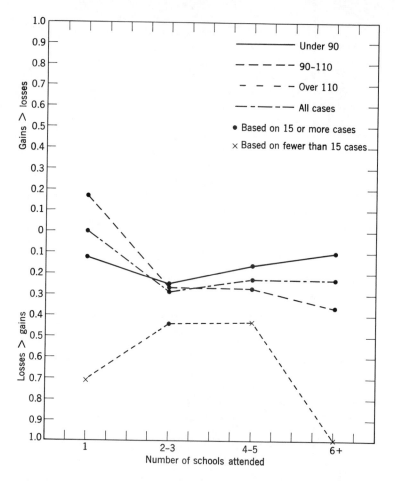

Figure 2   Differences between proportions with point losses and point gains by interschool mobility and third-grade IQ for sixth graders.

under 90 in the third grade have an overall downward direction, but their average gradient is less than among the equivalent third-grade categories. The whole sample shifts from no tendency either to lose or gain points with no mobility to a tendency to lose after attendance at more than five schools. Mobility, we may conclude, has less impact between third and sixth grade than it has in the first period of the school career. With the exception of the line for those of initially high IQ, which in any case is based on too few pupils for significance, lines are closer to the point where the tendency to losses equals that to gains. They are also closer to each other, and it is likely that there is a phenomenon of regression toward the mean for estimates of loss and gain tendencies, caused by lesser susceptibility of pupils to influences tending to alter IQ after they reach third grade.

The trend to horizontality in the line for those of initially average IQ concurs with expectations concerning the operation of the "floor effect," although the rising tendency toward point gains among pupils in the under-90 group as mobility increases is an irregularity difficult to understand. Since the figures for schools attended on the horizontal axis are in most cases greater than the mobility actually experienced during the effect period, it seems plausible to suggest, from the sharp decline in lines representing students with initial IQs of 110 or below between one school attended and two or three schools attended, that only one or two moves after third grade are necessary to produce the full retarding effect of mobility, after which subsequent moves cause very little or no extra decline. Undoubtedly this is especially true if the pupil has already moved between first and third grade.

CONCLUSIONS

The Major Findings

We must assert the conclusions of this study with caution because of the incomplete quality of some of our data. Replications of this study that have accurate information on exact dates of all moves between schools, scores at several grade levels based on the same types of tests through-out, and perhaps individual SES should enable the conclusions presented here to be given greater test and elaboration.

Nonetheless, we can say with confidence that during each effect period pupil mobility has significant retarding influences upon intellectual advancement among slum children. This relationship is greater before third grade than afterwards. After a certain level of mobility the effect tends to disappear, and this point is reached more quickly by those with initially low IQ. At least before the third grade pupils of low IQ are more than usually susceptible to the negative consequences of early mobility.

It is our contention that the system of mobility effects can be deduced from a set of more general sociological ideas. Contrary to arguments that mobility is merely an epiphenomenon of other social processes which are themselves the real causes of observed educational effects, it is useful to recall an extensive tradition of research pointing to the fact that mobility itself has basically disruptive properties. To acknowledge the causal antecedents of mobility is not to eliminate the importance of considering it as an intervening event, with special properties and special effects of its own.

Policy Considerations

One does not need further speculation and research to recognize the plausible implications of these findings and interpretations for the policies of urban school systems. Most mass school systems, and certainly Chicago's, have preserved rigid definitions of pupil attendance areas even in neighborhoods where mobility is high and where schools are located very closely together because of high population density. Whether this rigidity arises largely as an accommodation to the demands of the opponents of integration for a sanctification of the "neighborhood school principle" or mainly from an overcommitment to traditional administrative practice, the result is the same: the slum schools are apparently encouraging a deterioration in academic levels by their administrative policies.

This contention of course rests not only on the evidence presented in this paper on the association of pupil mobility and IQ change, but also on evidence that a considerable amount of the mobility is what we can call "administrative mobility," deriving wholly or largely from school policies. As the data in Table 1 indicated, many students have changed schools more often than addresses. This conclusion is demonstrated more directly when the variables of home addresses and numbers of schools attended are run directly against each other.

Additional Findings on Moves. Approximately 46 per cent of the third graders had had more schools than addresses, whereas about 16 per cent of them were in the opposite situation. About 31 per cent of the sixth graders had been in more schools than homes, and 29 per cent in more homes than schools.

The movement represented by excess of schools attended over home addresses is "pure" administrative mobility, resulting from the operations of "natural transfers" from one school to another at given grade levels (a set of procedures that produces very complex attendance area maps with overlays of different grade levels) and from frequent administrative changes through the opening of new schools, shifting of boundaries, installation of new mobile units, etc. Attendance administration is rigid in denying exceptions to rules about which pupils must attend what schools, but flexible in redrawing attendance area boundaries affecting whole city blocks. The effects of this kind of mobility are moderated by the facts that "natural transfers" at the end of the school year are less disruptive than those coming during the year and often involve the movement of the same school population. Also, under conditions of population stabilization the amount of opening and shifting of facilities and the numbers of within-year administrative changes would be reduced.

More important in the policy sense is within-year mobility stemming directly from the fact that even very short moves—and these are characteristic of the slum—are likely to result in changes of school. This is especially apparent from estimates, made on large maps with rulers, of the as-the-crow-flies distance in numbers of city blocks involved in the most recent residential move of each of the pupils sampled. Moves were very often just a few blocks. Over 60 per cent of all moves by third and sixth graders in the nine schools were of less than one mile, 50 per cent of them were under four blocks, 43 per cent were under three blocks, 34 per cent were under two blocks, and fully 21 per cent were under one block.

It must be remembered that the school attendance areas in this neighborhood are usually quite small, often two blocks by three blocks. In order to provide a rough indicator of the effects of short moves under these restrictions we estimated the hypothetical percentages of pupils making a residential move of average length in each school attendance area who would have to change schools because they crossed attendance boundaries. The labor involved in this operation limited consideration to a 20 per cent sample of the pupils.[12] We estimated the average length of move for each school's population by the distance of the most recent move of its pupils, and we made the simplifying assumption that we could treat each school's attendance area as a circle, although the usual shape was that of an irregular polygon. Under this procedure we estimate that, except for one school having an unusually large attendance area, 49 per cent or more of average moves are likely to result in a change in schools. In the exceptional school the figure was 40 per cent. Six of the other eight schools had estimates of over 55 per cent, and the highest was 79 per cent. When it is remembered that a great many

[12] This sample included eighth graders as well as the third and sixth graders.

of these moves involve only one to four blocks, these rough estimates take on substantial meaning.

Implications. The data clearly suggest the need for change in the administration of attendance rules in slum areas. At the minimum, when moves are only of a few blocks, transfer to another school could be postponed to the end of the semester or academic year, and parents could be informed of the potential benefits of requesting this delay.

The findings also imply the need for reflection on and innovation in the ways in which unavoidable school transfers are handled, with a view toward minimizing disruptions. Observations in several schools indicate that children who are transferring into them tend to be incorporated into their new schools in a relatively superficial manner. The child's character is defined only on the basis of the sketchy official record of previous semester grades received and of test scores or, with the record often delayed in shipment, such information as he is able to communicate shyly to a school official in a brief encounter or two. These bases and the relative crowding of various classrooms largely determine into which grade level, ability-grouping level, and classroom he will be placed. There the sensitive teacher may inquire further, integrate him into the classroom curriculum or ask that he be moved to a more appropriate room, and if he remains work to incorporate him socially; the insensitive teacher may simply find him a chair and give little attention to the sequence of his learning. Certainly the schools need to explore ways to be more sensitive to the newcomer's academic preparation and readiness and to utilize welcoming rituals and other means to ease his disorientation and trauma.

Finally, the data bear on the question of the "community school." The high rates of movement in the slums make it nearly impossible to explore the benefits predicated in the progressivists' notion of the school operating in close interdependence with its community. Paradoxically, rigidity in administering the neighborhood school policy mitigates against interdependence. The innovations in administration suggested seek to enhance the community school, particularly at the lowest grade levels. However, they should not be taken as arguments against transfers and busing to promote racial and social integration or against proposals for educational parks. Mobility is a problem to be addressed, not a fatal condition, and the community school should not be defined in a completely localized manner. The genuine notion of the community school seeks to extend the definition of "community," an extension that is compatible with pupil movement when it is properly phased and handled in an appropriately sensitive manner.

Institution Building in Urban Education

Morris Janowitz

THE SLUM SCHOOL AND CONTEMPORARY SOCIETY[1]

By the middle of the 1960's sociological categories had come to pervade popular and professional thinking about slum schools and education of the lower class. Militant demands for improving the effectiveness of inner-city education incorporated a rhetoric of practical sociology because of the realities of social class and race relations. Terms such

[1] In preparing this paper, I have drawn on the published and unpublished studies of experimental programs in mass education, and on the various surveys and proposals for reorganizing public school systems. I seek to include the experiences of a variety of experts, especially curriculum development specialists and entrepreneurs of automated and electronic teaching equipment. The concepts are derived from the research program on mass education of the Center for Social Organization Studies, which has been organized by David Street and his collaborators. My work was aided by a United States Public Health Service Training Grant, 5 T1 MH 8933, given to the Department of Sociology, University of Chicago. This analysis also encompasses my personal experiences with research and development programs since 1961, which range from small-scale volunteer tutoring programs to comprehensive experimental inner-city school districts under the Delinquency Control Act and more recently the Model Cities Program. My experiences with the South Commons development on the Near South Side of Chicago, which seeks to integrate urban renewal planning with the activities of the Board of Education, are also incorporated. The paper draws heavily on the materials collected by Gayle Janowitz in her demonstration work with volunteers in education, entitled "After-school Study Centers: Experimental Materials and Clinical Research." The policy implications of these research efforts were stated in a report to the superintendent of the Board of Education of the city of Chicago, "Innovation in the Public School System of the Inner City: A Policy Perspective," Working Paper No. 48, Center for Social Organizational Studies, June, 1965. A thoughtful summary, based on these materials, of the organizational difficulties of innovation in public education was published by Nicholas von Hoffman in the *Washington Post*, January 15, 1967.

as "cultural deprivation" and "deviant behavior" were no longer technical jargon but the language of political debate. The persistent criticism of intelligence and psychological testing and the growth of awareness of the social and normative problems of the slum school facilitated a rapid introduction of sociological analysis into policy issues. Education as a psychological model also gave ground during this period as there was a parallel increase in concern with economic modes of analysis of the school system.

It was inevitable that the first phase in the application of the sociology of education would focus on empirical findings about the social and cultural characteristics of the student body. There has been a long tradition that the more the teacher knows about the psychology of the pupils, the more effective the school system will be. In turn, educators have developed an interest in the social characteristics of their pupils. It would be difficult to argue against this perspective, especially if such inquiry is pursued in a sympathic fashion and practical purposes are fused with worthwhile intellectual goals. More often than not, however, the introduction of special courses on the culturally deprived and manuals on the social characteristics of inner-city children degenerates into a search for another set of schematic principles for imposing order on an intractable social environment.

A second step in the utilization of sociological findings has been the construction of curricular materials for the inner city. Obviously, to know more about the social environment of the school is an aid in the preparation of teaching materials. However, the sociology of education can be disruptive if it leads to the development of a specialized and distinctly separate curriculum that is designed to meet the needs of low-income children. Whatever relevant findings field researchers develop about the culture of the poor, the teacher who stresses the human differences between lower- and middle-class pupils, rather than their similarities, is certain to complicate his professional tasks and to further contribute to social separateness.

Fortunately, the sociological contribution to educational policy and practice has broadened to include a concern with the school as a social institution, that is, as a social system. The terms "social institution" and "social system" can be used interchangeably, although the latter is coming to replace the older term "social institution." I prefer not to lose sight completely of the concept "social insitution," because for me it includes a more concrete dimension. To think of the school, especially the slum school, as a social institution is to encompass its empirical realities. One sees the physical structure, the community setting, and the human beings involved, as well as the persistent patterns of behavior.

The tasks of this paper are to explore the basic characteristics of the school as a social institution and to determine the relevance of sociological categories for institution building in education, that is, for transforming it and adapting it to meet contemporary requirements.

"People-Changing" Institutions

The problems of institution building for inner-city schools are not unique. There is, strangely enough, a powerful analogy between the mental hospital or the correctional institution and the slum school. It makes a great deal of sense for sociologists to refer to all of these as "people-changing" institutions.[2] Ideally, the school in the lower-class community should supply a link by which youngsters are able to enter the mainstream of American society. The school has been assigned the task of socializing or resocializing the motives and values of its pupils, in a manner comparable to that of the mental hospital or the correctional institution.

It is relevant to note that during the last two decades sociological analysis has played a creative role in efforts to transform the goal of mental hospitals, juvenile correctional institutions, and even to some extent the adult prison from "custody" to "treatment." Once the goal of sheer custody was abandoned, the contribution of sociological thinking was conceptual and analytic. It assisted in broadening professional practice from a limited concern with restructuring individual motives to the development and management of a more meaningful institutional and/or organizational milieu, whether labeled as treatment or rehabilitation.

As a result, there has developed a body of research literature on these "people-changing" institutions and a common language of discourse between social investigator and selected administrators. Of course, it is an open question whether, in terms of rigorous input-output models or even more limited quantitative measures of performance, transformations have drastically improved the "efficiency" of such institutions. However, it is clear that the social and moral climate of mental hospitals or training schools can be altered to become more compatible with the standards of a humane society that stresses self-respect and dignity.

Clearly, progress in the mental health field has been in part the result of a broad political and social movement propelled by humanitarian impulses. However, the social sciences and sociology in particular have made a conceptual and analytical contribution in helping to clarify the

[2] See David Street, Robert Vinter, and Charles Perrow, *Organization for Treatment* (New York: Free Press, 1966).

requirements for an appropriate milieu. Empirical findings of research on "people-changing" institutions have helped to identify the organizational variables that make possible more rational and effective management of such institutions.

A custodial institution is one in which the relations between staff and clients are based on mutual mistrust and hostility. In many crucial respects, the slum school has such a character. Paradoxically, the slum school has not had a transformation parallel to that of the mental hospital or correctional institution, either in organizational concepts or in effective administration and professional practice. This is strange because the schools are a much more vital institution to society than is the mental hospital or the correctional institution. Moreover, it is also strange because one would have assumed that to adapt and creatively improve the school, with its much younger and more malleable student body, would have been more feasible. It would seem harder to deal with problems of the mental hospital or the correctional institution, whose clients may have deeply fixed personality structures and patterns of deviant behavior.

By any measure, the amount of progress in the transformation of inner-city schools during the last twenty years of social ferment is not impressive. In fact, our argument is based partly on the assumption that the level of performance, relative to the new societal demands on public education, is lower. Basically, there has been no fundamental conceptual or analytical transformation in professional thinking about the organizational format of public education comparable to the development of the organizational milieu or organizational climate in the mental hospital. Social science researchers, and especially sociologists, have not developed a similar common discourse with practitioners, which would contribute to more effective management of inner-city schools. Clearly a first step, although only a partial one, is greater agreement on the sources of the present "crisis."

The "Crisis" in Education

A decade of vigorous intellectual criticism from 1955 to 1965, plus extensive professional and experimental efforts, did not produce educational development in the inner city that satisfied the demands of public pressure. Nor were many professionals satisfied with the rate of progress. But to evaluate the school crisis in the inner city, it is necessary to separate contemporary issues from those that have persisted over the last half century. It is best to assess the crisis by first focusing on the long-term growth in effectiveness of the system. For the nation as a whole, the retention rate of youngsters in high school has risen continually in recent decades. For example, out of every 1000 pupils who entered the fifth grade in 1945, 525 later graduated from high school. By 1957, 710 fifth graders out of every 1000 were eventually able to graduate from high school. The figure has continued to rise; of every 1000 fifth graders in 1965, approximately 800 ultimately graduated from high school. This expansion in retention rates is not merely a custodial enterprise, for results of achievement tests suggest that the levels of overall academic performance of elementary and secondary school populations have risen during the last two decades. Of particular note has been the sharp upgrading of college preparatory programs in the United States to the point where an important minority of high schools offer work on first- and second-year college levels. In the mid-1960's these increased standards of academic performance in secondary education had reached the point where educators were questioning whether high school students had the emotional maturity to comprehend, in meaningful terms, parts of the improved curriculum. Mental health specialists were also concerned with the emotional impact of high school social climates in which new academic standards narrow the basis for personal and social maturity.

Given this expansion, the new crisis in public education is linked to the transformation and organization of the labor market under advanced industrialization. In the past, at least up to the Great Depression, the socialization of youngsters from European immigrant families and of migrants from rural areas was in good measure accomplished through work experiences—part time and full time. This is not to overlook the fact that the comprehensive high school served as a powerful mechanism in stimulating students from low-income families to acquire academic skills and social orientations required for college education. Since 1945 in the United States, high school graduation or its equivalent—not only in terms of academic and vocational requirements, but also in terms of social attitude, interpersonal competence, and maturity—is being defined as a desirable and indeed required goal for all, including the lowest income groups. No society has ever exposed its lower class to such a process of socialization and to such opportunities. The public school system never had to cope with such societal demands. Actual work requirements, changed standards of employment and trade unions, and new legislation about minimum wages account for this transformation. Public educators have been prepared to follow these trends and to extend high school education as a desirable goal per se. Therefore, it makes little sense to speak of a decrease in the effectiveness of the high school system in catering to the needs of lower-class youths. The inner-city comprehensive high school has been weakened, and in this sense there has been an actual deterioration in the quality of available public education. However, the "crisis" in education is a "new crisis" because schools must now accept responsibility for all youngsters who are not college bound until they develop levels of personal maturity sufficient for them to enter the labor market at an age level equivalent to high school graduation or even beyond. The present resources and practices of the inner-city school system are inadequate for this expanded task.

These trends have special relevance for Negro students, who are concentrated in the inner city and are particularly vulnerable to the impact of technological change in the labor market. It is well known that these technological changes are complicating the process of assimilating the Negro into the mainstream of society. Jobs in the semiskilled category that in an earlier period afforded the major opportunity for other minorities to enter the labor market and become socialized into the larger society are declining. Access to these jobs is also complicated for Negroes by residential location and transportation problems.

However, the educational "crisis" for the Negro student in the inner city reflects more than economic and technological change; it has cultural and psychological dimensions as well. Race prejudice has made the experience of the Negro in the public school system different from that of other minority and immigrant groups. In this sense the crisis is an old one. As early as the 1930's, as a result of the work of E. Franklin Frazier, sociologists pointed to the profound disarticulation between educational institutions and the social organization and culture of the Negro family, which was fashioned by slavery and by postemancipation segregation. Negro schools, both in the North and in the South, were traditionally inferior. Until about 1960, professional educators did not show impressive initiative in seeking to deal with these problems. To speak of the "old crises" in public education is not merely to draw attention to the traditional inferiority and ineffectiveness of Negro schools, but also to refer to other such long-standing pockets of inadequate education in older working-class communities serving selected second- and third-generation European immigrants, in southern white Appalachian families, or in chronically depressed rural areas. The old crisis is the persistence of gross inequalities in educational resources that derive from the local organizational format of public education and the absence of minimum national standards. If the tradition of American public education has been adapted to the social, cultural, regional, and religious diversity of the United States, this advantage has been purchased at the cost of highly uneven minimum performance. In one sense, the old crisis and the new crisis fuse as low-income and Negro populations concentrate in the older central cities. But institution building in public education confronts not only the issues of equality of opportunity (the extension of the old crisis) but also the formulation of new practices (the consequence of the new crisis).

Efforts at Segmental Change

As a means of dealing with the old and the new crisis, innovation in the inner-city schools has been highly fragmentary. Leading experts have been concerned with specific practical problems or particular aspects of school administration. There has been considerable inventive thinking about the pacing of the classroom curriculum, namely, in the development of various schemes of nongrading, multigrading, or continuous education. There has been a vast effort in the production of administrative schemes for achieving racial integration both of teachers and of pupils. In fact, some sociologists and psychologists have argued that social and ethnic heterogeneity of the school is the key dimension in the reconstruction of the inner-city school system. There have been various formulations of new roles in the educational system ranging from the master teacher to the school-community agent. But all of these approaches must be considered to be partial models of transformation, especially in contrast to the comprehensive and holistic analysis that has been developed for other "people-changing" institutions.

One of the rare efforts at comprehensive reformulation of inner-city education is found in the writings of Robert J. Havighurst.[3] The import of his approach rests in the fact that he directly approaches the policy issues of both social class and racial segregation in urban education. He places high emphasis on achieving racial integration, thereby seeking to continue what he believes to be our tradition of social heterogeneity. But in the contemporary context of metropolitan urbanism, he is prepared to trade off social class heterogeneity for progress in racial integration. He is fully aware that integration is most likely to be achieved in middle-class groups, or under conditions in which social class differences are not stongly operative.

The core of his framework for restructuring the inner-city public school system is organizational and not interpersonal. In his view, the metropolitan public school system needs to be reorganized into larger organizational units, four or five super units at most. In each unit there should be an appropriate racial balance ensuring managed integration, but each educational sector should have a distinctive social class com-

---

[3] See especially Robert J. Havighurst, *The Public Schools of Chicago: A Survey for the Board of Education of the City of Chicago* (Chicago, 1964).

position and an educational program to serve the needs of its student population. The comprehensive high school gives way to a greater degree of educational specialization along socioeconomic lines.

Havighurst is seeking a comprehensive restructuring of public education in the inner city. He believes that he is continuing the pragmatic tradition of American education. Yet the assumptions of his approach are so at variance with the social and political goals of the articulate public that, although his thinking has been incorporated into many official documents, it has quickly disappeared with little lasting impact.

In the absence of an appropriate administrative or educational concept for strategic innovation, efforts to improve the effectiveness of inner-city school systems can best be described as segmental change. Reform in public education since the end of World War II started with a concern for increasing the quality of high school education for college-bound students. In part, it was the result of new definitions of education for scientific and educational careers. In part it was a reflection of a social structure that was making education a more and more important criterion for social mobility, and in part it was a response to competition with the Soviet Union.

This trend can be called the Europeanization of American public education. It represented principally the efforts and agitation of university professors to improve American society politically and culturally by training youngsters both earlier and more thoroughly in basic disciplines. It was an American aspiration for the German gymnasium, spearheaded by university professors who were, in effect, seeking to demonstrate that they were "effective men" and who were outrightly hostile to much of the existing leadership of American society. This drive for Europeanization of the secondary school was being developed during a period when, paradoxically, social democratic governments of western Europe were struggling to introduce the American comprehensive high school in an effort to transform and modernize their social structure. This impetus of academic change in the United States led to elaborate efforts to reform the curriculum, not the organizational format. The result may well have been to weaken the comprehensive high school system. It advanced the decision to prepare for college, especially for entrance to a superior institution, to an earlier age and restricted it to a smaller range of schools. This is not to deny that the curriculum reform movement brought a select number of high schools back to higher levels of academic performance such as existed in 1920 and 1930, when many competent adults entered high school teaching only because of the absence of college-level teaching opportunities. The curriculum reform movement continued to exist because of the vested interest it rapidly

created and because of the increased prestige and income it afforded
a group of university experts and specialists in managing nonprofit
organizations.

After 1960, the goals of reform in public education were transformed
by political intervention, by the basic problems of the civil rights movement, and by political pressures to reduce poverty. The focus shifted
to the slum school. The economic and fiscal context has become well
known. Discrepancies in the level of educational expenditures and the
quality of public education in the inner city versus the suburbs have
become so well known as to generate profound political tensions.[4] The
source of these economic differences rests in the variation in the amount
and type of tax base and in the difference in costs of municipal services
between the central city and the suburbs. Because of the superior political
position of rural and suburban areas, the allocation of state aid had
tended to work against the inner city. Moreover, suburban areas have
their socioeconomic position enhanced by the services rendered to them
by agencies in the central city. Thus, for example, it has been estimated
that for some metropolitan areas expenditures for central-city education
could be raised by at least $50 per pupil if the full cost that the residents
pay for services rendered to suburbanites employed in the central city
was returned to the city.

The financial problems of inner-city public school systems have been
made more difficult by the pattern of federal aid to education. Until
1965, such aid was almost exclusively directed to the support of higher
education, rather than to primary or secondary levels. This was a result
of explicit political decisions by Congress. The first efforts at federal
aid to education in the inner city were proposed not by a liberal, but
by a conservative, Senator Robert Taft of Ohio, in 1948. But Congress
refused to act because of tensions and conflicts over aid to religious
schools. Support for higher education was more feasible since the con-
tending parties were less divided. The result of the emphasis on higher
education meant greater benefits to middle-class and suburban families
than to lower-class or central-city families.

Since 1965, expenditures for federal aid to primary and secondary
school education have been growing, with some priority to inner-city
requirements, but they have not been of a magnitude to cause the fundamental reallocation of public expenditures required to close the gap
between the suburbs and the central city. Moreover, changes in federal
allocations must be balanced against the willingness of state legislatures

[4] "The Rich Get Richer and the Poor Get Poorer . . . Schools," *Carnegie Quarterly*,
Fall 1966, pp. 1–3.

to give high priority and allocate extensive sums of money to higher education at the expense of increased state aid to the inner city. Again, these expenditures on higher education disproportionately benefit high-income and suburban families. It has been carefully documented that even the curriculum development programs financed by the federal government have disproportionately benefited the suburban and the upper socioeconomic communities.[5]

A dramatic but typical example can be seen in the construction of the University of Illinois Chicago Circle Campus, a state university that was designed for the urban community and symbolically located in the heart of the inner city, but that in effect draws its student body heavily from the surrounding suburban areas. During the period 1960–65, while the Chicago Board of Education had extremely limited funds for essential high school construction, the state of Illinois invested almost half a billion dollars in the University of Illinois Chicago Circle Campus. As of 1965, only about 3 per cent of the students at this campus were Negro, and the prospect of more than a token increase during the subsequent 5 year period was very remote. Political pressures generated by this experience have led the administrator of the University of Illinois system to propose a second "specialized" university community west of the existing campus that would emphasize remedial college education.

As new funds have become available, inner-city school systems have sought in one fashion or another to develop new experimental programs. Funds were initially made available by private groups and by specialized government legislation, such as the Delinquency Control Act of 1961, which, had it been implemented, would have been more comprehensive than any subsequent legislation. The second stage began with the passage of various programs of the Office of Economic Opportunity and involved new but unstable allocations of funds for educational development. With the passage of the Elementary and Secondary School Act of 1965, there emerged a more permanent basis for institution building, since federal funds were specifically designed to assist city school systems with immediate fiscal problems and to stimulate innovation. In addition, special funds were made available for experiments in desegregation plus a variety of other special purposes, all of which had long-term implications for school development. In fact, it could be argued that the variety and complexity of federal funds created a difficult and unwieldy administrative formula. Congressional leaders, however, initially believed that legislation should be drawn to stimulate innova-

[5] Roald F. Campbell and Robert A. Bunnell, "Differential Impact of National Programs on Secondary Schools," *The School Review,* Vol. 71, No. 4, pp. 464–476.

tion. In due course, Congress moved away from such an approach to more blanket funding and a return to the support of state and local leadership.

In a short period of time, by 1967, most school systems of the United States had had some experience with these conscious efforts to improve the quality of their educational programs. Such efforts ranged from limited programs of new libraries to "saturation" programs in selected schools.

It was anticipated that mass education in the inner city had an institutional character which would produce resistances to change even when new resources were made available. All evidence at hand has confirmed this expectation. It is not easy to identify the real barriers to organizational innovation in public education. It is clear that the typical slum school is part of a large central-city system. The typical suburban school is part of a much smaller system. This dimension by itself facilitates change. The sheer size of the central-city school system becomes of overriding importance when one considers the logistics of change. But clearly resistance to change is more than a matter of organizational size, for large-scale organizations do institute drastic and basic changes. In fact, in the military establishment change has been so institutionalized that some observers believe the organization is weakened in its capacity to achieve immediate goals. Resistance to change is rooted in basic decision-making and authority structures of the public school system.

First, experience since 1960 seems to underline the conclusion that the infusion of new funds into existing or only partially modified organizational structures does not produce higher levels of performance. Even significantly higher levels of expenditure appear to have limited consequences. The per pupil costs of education in New York City are the highest in the United States, but there is no evidence that the level of performance is discernibly different. Of course, it can be argued that the measures of performance are not precise or broad enough. It can also be argued that in New York City the levels of expenditure are not really high enough to make a crucial difference or that the problems are so pressing that without these higher levels of expenditure the situation would be even worse. Although these are relevant counterarguments, they do not reverse the basic contention that increased expenditures have not produced clearly discernible results.

This proposition can be highlighted by even a limited examination of the manner in which increased funds have been used. Aside from increased teacher salaries and higher operating costs for existing programs, the major thrust has been on the reduction of class size. This is true for most large metropolitan systems. In short, the basic response has been to continue the same procedures but on a more intensive basis. Such a response would be expected of an organization under pressure. In the city of Chicago, federal funds were actually used to increase the length of the school day; the system that produces a 40 per cent dropout rate and massive academic retardation by third grade was given another hour to demonstrate its limitations.

There exists a respectable body of literature to the effect that class size per se is unrelated to teaching effectiveness.[6] This is not to argue that there are no desirable upper limits in size class but rather to emphasize that limited reduction in class size without fundamental changes in classroom management is perhaps an uneconomic allocation of resources.

Second, federal funds that have not been absorbed by higher teaching costs have been allocated for segmental change mainly in the form of demonstration projects rather than planning for fundamental institution building. The fate of demonstration projects, including large-scale ones, points to their inherent limitations. At the research level, there is little agreement about the scientific findings of many demonstration projects. Widespread differences of professional opinion exist about the meaning and validity of criteria of success and failure as well as the adequacy of research design. Often there is a generalized reaction that the "big factors" like the organizational setting of the school and the quality of leadership are left uncontrolled. As a result, research generated by demonstration projects frequently seems to focus on trivial variables. There is reason to believe that careful comparative analysis of organizational records, including cost benefit analysis, will probably be as rewarding an approach as the evaluation of the limited demonstration project. The advantage of research on demonstration projects flows from an emphasis on detailed clinical and case study analysis of teacher and student reactions and their definitions of the situation, rather than from the systematic and quantitative data that are generated.

Even more fundamental is the life history of demonstration programs. They have tended generally to be small scale and short lived, with professionals learning that results are not cumulative but rather seem to be disjunctive. There is a high turnover of personnel so that the consequences of a particular demonstration face gradual extinction. The most critical argument is that, when there is a decision to spread the demonstration project throughout the system, it faces death by diffuse and partial incorporation. In addition, there is an absence of training to

[6] For a summary of this literature see Neal Gross, "Memorandum on Class Size," August 15, 1961 (unpublished).

ensure the implementation of new procedures, nor are there effective devices of inspection and audit. In the end, there is a considerable degree of frustration as old practices and procedures are given new names.

Although the typical demonstration project is of limited scope and short duration, selected instances have grown in the amount of resources that are involved. The highly publicized and well-financed Higher Horizons demonstration project of the New York City Board of Education suffered the same fate as the typical small-scale demonstration enterprise. In a limited area effective work was undertaken in 1959. Higher Horizons sought to emphasize cultural pursuits, counseling, and involvement in extraschool activities as a means of stimulating school involvement and academic performance among lower-income public school youngsters. The next step in the demonstration was extensive publicity and the development of popular expectations. Extras expanded to include 100,000 students in 52 elementary and 13 junior schools at a cost which reached $250 per pupil. As the project was enlarged, it lost its vitality and in 1966 the special apparatus for conducting this demonstration project was abandoned.

The limits of segmental programs of change can also be inferred from the case of the New York City More Effective Schools Program, which was clearly the most ambitious and comprehensive demonstration program to improve "urban education." In 21 program schools, per pupil costs were raised to almost twice the average instructional levels. It is true that the bulk of the increased costs were allocated for reduced classroom size. The program with its special character and widespread publicity should have developed and probably did result in some Hawthorne effect—producing results merely because of the attention generated by an experiment. However, an evaluation study of the More Effective Schools Program was most discouraging and symbolized the end of a phase in urban education demonstration that began in the early 1960's with the allocation of private foundation funds.[7] The program put into practice many segmental innovations that had been recommended, but it was able to carry them out only with large-scale funds and resources. In the fall of 1967, the evaluation report was issued after 10 of the schools had been in operation since 1964 and 11 others since 1965. The report concluded that the program had had no significant impact. The overall school climate, staff attitudes,

[7] David J. Fox, *Expansion of the More Effective School Programs; Evaluation of New York City Title I Educational Projects, 1966–1967*, The Center for Urban Education, September, 1967.

and community relationships had improved, but there was no significant effect on the academic achievement of the pupils. The major weakness of the demonstration effort was the "inexperience and lack of preparation of teachers," factors in part outside the scope of the design of the demonstration. In effect, this evaluation study, like many others, pointed to deficiencies in larger organizational factors, in this case the demand and supply of teachers and their preparation and professional career development.

But this project, like most efforts at educational innovation, needs a more penetrating evaluation than it received. The focus was on academic achievement, and on short-term consequences at that, although there also was a concern with staff-school climate attitudes and school-community relations. But clearly, the significance of the demonstration programs, as in the case of the transformation of mental health institutions, rests primarily in its ability to create a social and moral climate in the school compatible with the values of the larger society. Therefore, as long as academic grades are used as the basic criteria of success, the evaluation studies of slum schools are either naïve or self-defeating. The development of the appropriate social and moral climate should be an end in and of itself. It should be a demonstration that the school system has accepted the responsibility of treating its pupils with fundamental dignity and of enhancing their self-respect. It would imply that the school is fully cognizant of the gap between the family and social backgrounds of low-income groups and the behavior desired by the school. Vocational and academic success may well be delayed. But the establishment of the appropriate school setting is of the highest pragmatic importance if youngsters are to develop in time their vocational and academic skills and interests. In fact, such experiences are not likely to be achieved within the confines of the school but require group recreational, cultural, and work experiences outside of the school in the larger society.

Thus, in the broadest terms, the evaluation of the More Effective School Program and a great variety of other such programs has helped to bring the first phase in "inner-city" experimentation to a conclusion. This first phase, roughly designated as covering the period from 1960 to 1967, emphasized piecemeal change, the demonstration project, and the process of change from the bottom up or by lateral diffusion. It is not to be concluded that no progress was made. There has been a great deal of social and organizational learning, but of course this whole first phase might well have been avoided or more readily terminated by more rational analysis and more forthright leadership.

The emerging second phase is that of strategic innovation, or institutional building, which focuses on the system as a whole. It involves a strategy from the top down, it is more comprehensive in scope, and it is concerned with the realities of authority and decision making. The purpose of this analysis is to explicate sociological concepts that may help in the organizational transformation of public education.

Obviously, more than a conceptual framework is required. Political and professional leadership is central, but the contribution of social scientists remains that of supplying a conceptual framework. The initial step in formulating a change-oriented conceptual framework is to present a characterization of the school system of the inner city as a bureaucratic structure. The school as a social institution has characteristics and features that conform to generalized notions of a large-scale organization, but it has also very distinctive characteristics arising out of its particular goals and its operational logic.

ORGANIZATIONAL FORMAT: IMAGE AND REALITY

The public school system of the inner city, and especially its administrative apparatus, have come under severe and repeated criticism. These criticisms have produced a set of popular images about school administration that are based on a sense of frustration rather than on careful analysis of organizational realities. The result is that the urban public school system is viewed by citizen leadership and even experts as an excessively rigid organization that has great difficulty in dealing with innovation, whether the issue be academic policy, vocational program, or social climate. The rigidities of the system mean that it has a low capacity to meet the needs of whole groups of students as well as of individual youngsters. At least three images grounded in sophisticated notions of administrative behavior are repeatedly applied to the public school. Each image requires elaboration and refinement if it is to articulate with actual practices.

Centralized Organization

First, in the image of the alert outsider, the inner-city school system is a highly overcentralized organization, which is a core factor in accounting for the lack of innovation and the absence of flexibility. Thus the Booz, Allen, and Hamilton management survey of the Chicago system, prepared in 1967 as Dr. James Redmond assumed the post of general superintendent, repeated this point of view:

From an organizational viewpoint, the Chicago system is highly centralized. Central office personnel have responsibility for the implementation of these programs in the schools. Relatively few decisions of substance are made in the field. Generally, only routine action is taken without central office approval (p. 11).

In describing the relationship between the Chicago Board of Education and the general superintendent, the report concluded on the basis of recent history that "out of it has emerged an organizational structure where responsibility and authority are concentrated in a relatively small number of people who administer the programs of the school system on a highly centralized basis" (pp. 1–2).

The term "overcentralization" as used in this sense is too imprecise to characterize adequately the decision making in the big-city public school system. There is a profound limitation in the term "overcentralization" if a distinction is not made between decision making about long-term goals or organization of the school system and the procedures for administering the organization on a day-to-day basis. It is of course abundantly true that in short-term allocations of resources, in the management of personnel, and in the modification of operating procedures the approval of a few officials is required, and in this respect decision making is highly centralized. However, centralization of authority at the top levels of the big-city school system is greatly reduced by the statutory and legal restraints that narrow the scope of authority of the board of education and its superintendent in the strategic management of the organization. Thus, state law has developed a web of rules and regulations that limit the scope of change by rigidly defining many organizational procedures and setting professional standards. The superintendent is even limited in the appointment of his key assistants. The impact of schools of education has removed from the superintendent effective jurisdiction over the training of personnel. Professional associations and commerical groups have strong influence on curriculum and educational procedures.

Moreover, the concept of centralization fails to reflect the diffuse process by which educational goals are established. Although the typical operating school is a relatively self-contained organization (a relatively closed institution in organizational terms), the top management of public school systems is subject to continuous and variegated restraints and pressures that limit its effective authority. The board of education typically can be viewed not as an integrated group able to impose its will on the superintendent, but rather as a legislative-type forum in which varying community groups are engaged in a process of balancing conflicting interests. Only in a rare case can the board, through a coalition of political party interests and business groups, develop sufficient cohesion to make a fundamental policy change.

Superintendents often present the image of strong figures and are at times able to dominate their organizational apparatus personally. But the administrative format of the typical large-scale system defies the emergence of a truly overcentralized system. The lines of authority are generally vague, and the central staff lacks the information, resources, and training to make for truly effective centralized decision making. Compared to industrial corporations, the school system is truly a "primitive" organization.

Central planning in the educational system is done by ad hoc committees. In the absence of effective staff work, these committees are usually manned by line officers who are removed from their operating responsibilities for a few hours or a few days. An atmosphere of constant turmoil and instability, of rushing from one crisis to the next, pervades the system. Fundamentally, the limits on centralization derive from the lack of adequate information available at the top levels, due in part to the diffuse criteria of judging educational performance and to the sheer absence of adequate internal information systems.

Uniform Organization

In the popular image, the inner-city school system is seen as a highly uniform and routinized enterprise that has little capability for change or flexibility. There can be no doubt that this image reflects the reality of limited effectiveness. Direct observation of the actual working of a big-city school system, however, highlights the wide variation in practices and approaches from school to school. A more accurate and precise statement, perhaps, is that such a system permits considerable deviation from routine practice. Large-city school systems are very highly centralized with regard to particular academic matters and the formal standards for recruiting and utilizing personnel. However, in day-to-day operations, urban schools display weak articulation between the individual school and the central office. Individual principals have considerable operational latitude to make decisions to mobilize resources if they are so inclined. The principal plays a crucial role in what variations do exist and in the higher levels of teaching performance that can be found. The principal affects the recruitment, retention, and morale of the teaching staff, as is well known. He enjoys considerable power and can institute a variety of changes, even if they are only temporary, that is, for the duration of his tenure. It is not unknown for a principal to alter radically the grading and tracking procedure in a manner at variance with customary practice in the system. In particular, the principal can have a considerable role in shaping the social milieu of his school. If he operates successfully, the reason is that he is a vigorous entrepreneur and is able to mobilize additional resources both within the system and in the community at large.

But this type of "freedom" does not make for long-term development. Each school is a relatively isolated institution characterized by vertical communication patterns. There is a relative absence of lateral communication among principals in the large urban school system. Since district superintendents generally operate without adequate staff, there is little planning at the district level except that which can be done in an informal way or at the expense of temporarily removing the principal from his school and his area of direct responsibility. In many cities, because of the pressures of their work load and their high mobility from school to school, principals are not as deeply involved in professional or local neighborhood associations as are their counterparts in suburban systems. Instead, urban school principals frequently are oriented toward pursuing higher degrees in graduate schools of education, where unfortunately the program content seems to bear only a limited relationship to the immediate operating problems facing them in the inner city. The principal operates without adequate group, professional, or organizational support for effective innovation. He is much more an isolated specialist than is the doctor or lawyer, in whose field formal and informal networks supply the effective cohorts of professionalization.

In turn, principals, if they wish—and this is more typically the case—can resist change and innovation. Each school principal operates as a kind of local chieftain. It would be more accurate to describe the inner-city school system as fractionalized than as overcentralized. Perhaps the most striking feature of the local school, in the United States, in contrast to most European systems, is the absence of a policy of meaningful on-the-spot inspection that operates both as a means of audit and control and at the same time as a device of assistance and communication to the local principal. The result is a weak and disarticulated system that is subject to continuous crisis and of necessity must develop a defensive and reactive stance when confronted with new public demands. The operating logic of this fractionalized system is to defend existing practices, rather than to generate clear-cut statements about the resources required to achieve the tasks assigned to it by its clients and by the larger society.

The notion of overcentralization and uniformity is paralleled by a popular and vague image of overprofessionalization of teachers. This image is supposed to describe the excessive concern with formal education, formal certification, and professional status. Again, this concept of professionalization is too arbitrary to supply a meaningful basis for understanding the dilemmas and strains that the classroom teacher must face. Rather than speak of overprofessionalization as the pathology of the classroom teacher, it is more accurate to highlight the excessive professional isolation of the classroom teacher in an inner-city school, an isolation even greater than that of the school principal.

The public school teaching profession has been heavily concerned with formal requirements as a basis for raising professional status and income. This pressure has led to an emphasis on rigid entrance and training requirements often unrelated to actual teaching requirements. The teaching profession has resisted the introduction of subprofessionals and other labor-intensive approaches to mass education. The very notion of professionalism is difficult to apply to public school teachers. Some writers concerned with the problems of overprofessionalization have sought to introduce the term "craft" to describe more adequately the skills involved in elementary and secondary school teaching.

But these concepts should not obscure the realities of classroom teaching in general, and especially classroom teaching in a tough slum school. Teaching youngsters is a profoundly enervating task. It is not an exaggeration to emphasize that under the pressures of the slum school environment the task has debilitating elements. Adults must gain their gratifications from interaction with other adults, for the responses that youngsters can offer are both consciously and unconsciously incomplete for adult psychic needs. In earlier historical periods and in small communities with stable residential populations the grammar school teacher developed her basic job gratification from the fact that she maintained contact with her pupils as they grew up. She could see them through their letters and return visits as adults, and their behavior and accomplishments in maturity were important ingredients in her work satisfaction.[8]

The sheer wear and tear on the teachers and the resulting drain on their energy constitute powerful pressures. It is a cruel public indifference and an administrative inertia that denies to teachers, especially women, a recognition of these realities. Classroom teaching is more of a personal and psychological strain than nursing. Retreat into indifference and excessive detachment is clearly an understandable response. Thus teachers require the professional support of their colleagues in order to meet these pressures. But in its current organization teaching is in

[8] The social history of the teacher, especially the old-fashioned but highly effective spinster, needs to be written. These women were able to develop satisfactory gratification from working with youngsters. But old-fashioned spinsters (and often repressed, hysterical teachers) have passed from the scene because of the new personal freedom which eliminates that particular characterological type.

practice a solo profession, in contrast to many other professions that emphasize group practice or at least close relations with colleagues. The teacher operates independently in her classroom. In the typical slum school, she does not have close personal and social contacts with her colleagues. Direct supervision and the opportunity for staff conferences are limited. The result is not overprofessionalization in the actual performance of the job, but rather professional isolation and excessive vulnerability to the impact of the social and administrative environment.

Standards of Performance

Third, the public school system is viewed as an organization that suffers because of the absence of standards of performance, that is, it lacks criteria for judging effectiveness and efficiency. The comparison is frequently made with industrial and business corporations, for which economic cost and profit supply clear-cut standards. As a result, there is increasing pressure to construct more meaningful standards of performance that would incorporate or at least parallel the procedures of cost effectiveness. Educators are able to offer powerful counterarguments that the standards of performance in education are diffuse and are of necessity very difficult to operationalize.

There can be no doubt, however, that marked improvement in factual reporting in public education is required. The public image of inadequate reporting and accounting systems has an essential validity. Moreover, the search for more valid quantitative measures of performance is a challenging intellectual task. But it is a grave error to overlook the existing system of reporting and the existing standards of performance. A great deal of effort is expended in public education on record-keeping, and the record-keeping system has powerful influence in developing rigidities.

Public education suffers because it makes a major effort to evaluate the individual student, rather than to evaluate the teacher, the principal, the school district, or the educational system. The record-keeping system of public education is based on extensive intelligence testing, most of which is of doubtful validity. It also involves massive efforts at academic achievement testing which are either unfair in that they do not measure actual progress or are self-defeating in that they serve as devices for thwarting the interests and energies of youngsters from inadequate backgrounds.

The results of various academic testing procedures are made available to the student with the naïve hope that such information will in some way influence his performance and stimulate his involvement in the educational process. Actually, the testing system has on the whole a negative impact for inner-city school students, since it serves to lower the aspirations of those who are performing inadequately. But the system is even more rigid and distorted since research indicates that in high school the same level of performance leads to different grades depending on social background; students from families of lower background, with similar measured potential, receive lower grades than do students from families of higher social background.[9] The ranking system is part of a system of social control that maintains social inequality. The grades are a reward system, and their distribution becomes a technique for managing and controlling the student body. Dropouts are not limited to inferior students. Once students with adequate IQ scores at the high school level recognize that they are not likely to be adequately rewarded, they withdraw; to do otherwise would almost be irrational. In the slums youngsters who are unprepared to perform in terms of national standards enter the school with relatively positive attitudes toward the system. By the end of the third or fourth grade, a great many have failed at least one grade; many have failed twice. The result is that failure becomes the norm, with negative results for both teacher and pupil.

Much of the grading system, because it is oriented to reporting on the student rather than on the teacher or the school, is not easily used as a management tool. The basic question in standards of performance is therefore twofold. The first task is to convert the testing and record-keeping procedures into a system for evaluating teacher and organizational effectiveness. The question becomes not the particular student's grades but, for example, the relative capacity of a school to lower drop-out rates or to produce progress in academic achievement levels. Second, the record-keeping system and criteria of performance need to be developed as devices for ensuring the rights of the pupils, that is, for guaranteeing a system of due process. Because the public school system is a relatively closed one without appropriate grievance procedures and without adequate channels of review, parents must individually negotiate on behalf of their youngsters, if they have the skill and motivation, and often in a most indirect fashion. In the case of a slum school, the public presence is very limited as parents either have withdrawn or are excluded.

Thus, the image of the school system of the inner city as an organization that operates on the basis of (a) overcentralization, (b) organizational uniformity, and (c) the absence of criteria of performance, gives way to a more differentiated view of its organizational format. Such a view is a starting point for a conceptual model of change.

[9] See the paper by Rosemary C. Sarri and Robert D. Vinter, pp. 91–119 of this book

ALTERNATIVE MODELS OF CHANGE

One underlying assumption of this analysis of the inner-city school system is that a crucial barrier to strategic change and increased effectiveness of public school systems is the absence of comprehensive conceptual models.[10] To speak of the importance of conceptual models of education is obviously not an academic exercise that is oblivious of the political and social elements required to produce actual change. Institution building in public education cannot be accomplished by any single drastic or dramatic act. Schools cannot be transformed by boycotts or parents' strikes, although these demonstrations may accelerate the process of reform. School systems are too complex to respond to the mere appointment of a new superintendent. Likewise changes in the system of recruiting board members or plans for decentralization may be essential for organizational development but are only preconditions.

In the American scene, there have been powerful constraints against a positive and direct involvement by elected municipal officials in the management of the school system. Profound and explosive religious differences have threatened public education whenever the management of the school system became directly involved in partisan politics. The highly pluralistic nature of American politics has meant that elected political leadership exercised narrow and only indirect influence on educational institutions.

During the last decade, elected officials have cautiously expanded their involvement in educational policy. The sheer increase in local, state, and federal expenditures has required their more active participation. Elected officials have had to confront questions regarding the adequacy of the contemporary framework of local, state, and national governments for administering fiscal aid to education. They have had to search for standards of need and meaningful standards of performance. In fact, isolated elected officials have questioned fundamental notions about which aspects of mass education belong in the public or private sector or what new combinations are required. Conceptual models are designed in part to supply political leaders and educational professionals with a more common language of discourse.[11]

---

[10] This is but an alternative specification of the idea that increased financial resources alone will not produce the type of school which is able to meet the demands of society.

[11] If there has been an absence of holistic models to assist innovation and change, there is no shortage of broad-scale attacks on the public schools as social institutions. From the radical left and from conservative sources, writers of considerable force

The Mental Health Model

Because of the extent of professional concern with the slum school, it was inevitable that efforts would be made to impose the strategy of the mental health movement directly on the school system, to develop an organizational model fundamentally paralleling the therapeutic setting. Numerous reservations can be formulated about such an approach, but these efforts are noteworthy because of their comprehensive intentions.

This approach assumes that the resources of the family in the slum are so limited or its values so at variance with the goals of the school that the school must seek to become responsible for the total social-space of the child. The model falls just short of formulating a residential institution, but every effort is made to come as close as possible to a residential approach. (In Great Britain, there has been discussion of governmentally financed boarding schools, which would make available to working-class children the same advantages offered a middle-class child at boarding school.) Within existing public systems there are individual principals who seek to implement such an approach of the school as a "home away from home."[12]

This approach calls for a drastic reduction in teacher-pupil ratios to about one to fifteen or even one to ten. The teacher becomes the teacher-counselor in a manner not dissimilar to that of the residential treatment center, as, for example, the Orthogenic School.[13] The teacher-counselor rejects or at least reduces reliance on a complex division of labor and must personally intervene to help ensure that the needs and services required by each child are made available. The housing, feeding, and clothing of each child is a school responsibility that must come under the surveillance of the teacher. The teacher and the principal take whatever steps are necessary and possible. Likewise, the teacher sets the pace and guides the formal educational program, but only in the light of the interpersonal need and social reality of the child. The

---

have offered both searching criticisms and educational utopias. These writings carry considerable weight in the public debate concerning American education. For the radical left, see Paul Goodman, *Growing Up Absurd* (New York: Random House, 1960). For the conservative approach to the reaffirmation of fundamentals, see Hyman Rickover, *Education and Freedom* (New York: Dutton, 1959).

[12] Bruno Bettelheim and E. Sylvester, "Milieu Therapy—Indications and Illustrations," *Psychoanalytical Review*, Vol. 36 (1) (1949), pp. 54–68.

[13] Elements for such an approach are described in the profile, "The Principal," *The New Yorker*, May, 1966, pp. 52 ff., which deals with the work of Elliot Shapiro at P.S. 119, New York City; reprinted in Nat Hentoff, *Our Children Are Dying* (New York: Viking Press, 1966).

teacher is truly the substitute for the parents, with the clear recognition that the parents have been and continue to be unable to meet the needs of the child. It is not by accident that those involved in such programs have had experience as staff members in mental hospitals or institutions.

Criticism of such a model derives not from its costly nature. The costs of such an approach may well be the basic price that society has to pay. There is no adequate knowledge about the societal costs of alternative programs or the current costs of not having effective educational programs. Reservations and limitations derive from two other sets of considerations.

The first is the theoretical issue of the impact on the socialization of youngsters that would result from such an educational model; what types of interpersonal strengths and dependencies are likely to be generated? These issues are highly speculative. The teacher-counselor model is a modification of the classic two-person psychotherapy, but it is an approach that is still grounded in notions of transference or at least the necessity for strong interpersonal identifications as a basis for changing personal motives and gratifications. The teacher-counselor model seeks to manage the total educational environment in order to facilitate the restructuring of motives and to broaden the opportunity for interacting with adults and peers who can serve as stimulants for positive response. The basic thrust is to establish stable and gratifying interpersonal relations, and in effect there is a built-in proclivity toward seeking to extend and enlarge the relations between the teacher-counselor and her particular group of youngsters. Such stable and gratifying relations are seen as prerequisites to educational involvement.

The advocates want to maintain these relations for as long a period as possible. The critics point out that, given the mobility and disruption of social life in the slum, there is a strong element of unreality in these efforts. Only a small number of youngsters are likely to develop such relatively enduring relations with a teacher-counselor. The counter-argument is that a teacher-counselor may introduce an element of stability into the lives of these youngsters. For example, there is case material to demonstrate that effective teachers can help youngsters persuade their families to give up the practice of repeated and pointless residential mobility, nurtured by frustration and boredom. Advocates hold that such attachments are essential for the process of maturation. Critics argue that the impact of such intense relations with teachers would produce an adjustment to the school and not to the large society. It would be equivalent to the prisonization syndrome, whereby the model prisoner performs well under custody but fails when he is returned to the outer world.

Second, and more to the point, critics are concerned with the problem of translating the model into an organization system. The problems of staffing such an educational enterprise seem immense, but the basic dilemma is deeper than the sheer supply of appropriate personnel, difficult though that may be. How would such a system operate and maintain its effectiveness? An organization cannot function on the basis of the sheer energy of its constituent elements, but requires a division of labor and a system of effective support. Any conventional administrative apparatus would by its very nature tend to thwart many positive elements of the approach.

But one has only to observe directly the social climate of a classroom or a school in which these notions are operative to recognize that any system of improved academic effectiveness must rest on the creation of a classroom climate based on mutual respect or value sharing, to use Harold Laswell's terminology. A school based on these conceptions—either as a planned demonstration or by personal accident—is a useful element in any system. The existence of a number of such efforts in any school system can operate as a public yardstick and serve as criteria to be taken into consideration by educational administrators. Even if the teacher-counselor model is not generalizable, it is an important element in a comprehensive effort at institution building.

The Early Education Model

The difficulty of applying the teacher-counselor system or other equivalent notions on a comprehensive basis has led to efforts to formulate partial strategies based on dynamic psychology. The early education movement is clearly the most massive expression of such a compromise. It is based on the assumption that the earlier the school intervenes, the more effective will be its work. There is special relevance for the youngster of the slum family wherein parental impact has been demonstrated to inhibit and retard intellectual and cognitive processes. Early education has had the administrative advantage that progress could be made without having to deal with the fundamental problems of school organization. Most programs were established outside of existing structures or with their minimal cooperation. Again, one has only to observe the vitality of many of the preschool education programs initiated by federal funds to appreciate their validity and to anticipate that such experiences will gradually become part of the educational background of youngsters.

Over the short run, early education efforts were very costly to develop. They failed to have maximum impact because children who had such experiences subsequently entered conventionally organized school systems. Perhaps one of the most powerful direct results of these efforts was the stimulation of parents' interest in the education of their youngsters. To speak of interest is not to imply direct involvement in the actual education of the children. The results of such experiences for adults were to develop stronger political interests and even political activity related to education.

At best the early education movement can be considered another partial strategy. At worst it was a basic error in priorities. A partial strategy of change that allocated highest priority to the preschool youngster is a reflection of a concern for the management of the individual rather than the management of the slum community. The counterstrategy of intervention with the oldest school-age groups is more plausible. In a slum community, the 14- to 18-year-old males have the greatest impact on the moral and social climate of the school. In this group are opinion leaders in the slum youth culture and the effective bearers of the culture of the slum from one generation to the next. If these youngsters develop a sense of frustration and a group life in opposition to the goals of the school, as they generally do, they are able to thwart innovation. The case can be made, therefore, that this group, not the youngest group, represents the highest priority if comprehensive change is to be effected.

At this point, it needs to be emphasized that the absence of strategic models of change which see the school as a social institution or a social system is due in part to the fact that administrators have been operating with limited resources. They have developed such strong defensive postures that they are inhibited in formulating strategic conceptions. A whole generation of top administrators seems destined to retire or circumvent, rather than reorient. The successful big-city superintendent is the man who can bargain in advance for the conditions to eliminate the old guard. In part, we are also dealing with the absence of an effective intellectual and research tradition about school administration.[14]

The present state of writing about educational administration, despite the large number of available books, offers little special stimulus. Since the 1950's, graduate schools of education have concerned themselves with the intellectual basis of the profession. The approach has been to infuse social sciences into their training. Although the quality of educational administrators has increased markedly, there is no extensive body of scholarly or research literature that commands serious attention.

---

[14] For a useful and realistic overview of the field, see Roald F. Campbell, John E. Corbally, Jr., and John A. Ramseyer, *Introduction to Educational Administration* (Boston: Allyn & Bacon, 1966).

This absence of an effective body of literature on educational institutions has been repeatedly noted by research scholars. In 1956, Neal Gross reported that there was no systematic study of school organization.[15] A decade later, Charles E. Bidwell concluded his comprehensive review of the organizational research literature with the same pronouncement.[16] Willard Waller's *The Sociology of Teaching*, published in 1932, can still be cited as a pioneer classic that has remarkable enduring value because of its realism and vivid insights.[17] Perhaps one of the most pointed observations that can be made about the literature of educational institutions concerns the absence of autobiographical materials by administrators, in contrast to revealing and insightful documents produced by business, political, and military leaders. Although school administration is a verbal and literate profession, it has not developed this mode of self-study.

The Specialization and Aggregation Models

Basic decisions about educational policy are being made and will have to be made without a rich body of comparative organizational studies. Therefore, the strategy of this analysis is to present two contrasting models of organizational change in educational institutions: the *specialization model* and the *aggregation model*. Both of these models see the school as a social institution. They supply criteria for judging and evaluating specific research findings and particular innovations. They are offered as a basis for describing many current practices and for assessing efforts at strategic innovation. It is not enough to point out that both are hypothetical constructs. The specialization model is in effect an expression of the major trends of innovation programs over the last decade. This model encompasses a variety of segmental as well as administrative changes.

Although very few examples of meaningful or persistent innovation conform to the aggregation model, a limited number exist. The aggrega-

[15] Neal Gross, "Sociology of Education, 1945–1955," in Hans T. Zetterberg, ed., *Sociology in the United States: A Trend Report* (Paris: UNESCO, 1956), pp. 62–67.
[16] Charles E. Bidwell, "The School as a Formal Organization," in James G. March, ed., *Handbook of Organizations* (Chicago: Rand McNally, 1965).
[17] Willard Waller, *The Sociology of Teaching* (New York: Wiley, 1932). For recent writings see Jacob W. Getzels, "A Psychosociological Framework for the Study of Educational Administration," *Harvard Educational Review*, Vol. 22 (1952), pp. 235–246; Talcott Parsons, "The School Class as a Social System: Some of Its Functions in American Society," *Harvard Educational Review*, Vol. 29 (1959), pp. 297–318; Fred E. Katz, "The School as a Complex Social Organization," *Harvard Educational Review*, Vol. 34 (1964), pp. 428–455.

tion model is much more an ideal model; it is a notion of potentialities. It is the expression of administrators and staff members who are concerned primarily with a basic format within which change and effective teaching can take place. Specific programs and specific techniques are of secondary concern, as compared with organizational climate, institutional milieu, or operational doctrine. My preference is clearly for the aggregation model, and this fact needs to be explicitly acknowledged. In Table 1 the basic dimension of the two models are presented. These dimensions are both contemporary elements of educational institutions and emerging efforts at change.

Both the specialization model and the aggregation model focus on the classroom teacher. Changing the behavior of the classroom teacher is a common goal. The capacity of the public school system to achieve its goals, both academic and social, involves a central concern with increasing the authority and professional competence of the teacher. The dilemmas that the teaching profession faces, resulting from increased available knowledge, greater complexity of the professional tasks that need to be performed, and societal demands for higher levels of performance, are characteristic of every other professional group as well.

Fundamentally, the specialization model appears to be an ad hoc adaptation because it introduces, on a piecemeal basis, new techniques, new programs, new specialists, and even new specific administrative procedures, each of which may appear valid. On the other hand, the aggregation model focuses on the totality of the situation in which the teacher finds herself.[18]

Under the specialization model, the traditional activity of the teacher is modified as the teaching process is broken up into more and more specialized roles. The increased level of substantive knowledge and the importance of specific teaching techniques are offered as the rationale for the teachers' subordination to curriculum specialists, and the complexities of deviant behavior given as the reason for their subordination to experts in the management of interpersonal relations. In contrast, the aggregation model emphasizes the necessity for maintaining and strengthening the teacher's role as the central manager of the classroom in which she creates the conditions for teaching and learning. In this model, teaching is seen as a diffuse relationship to the pupil, and leadership skills are as important as technical proficiency in the subject. The teacher makes use of specialists and resource personnel, but manages

[18] See David A. Goslin, "The School in a Changing Society: Notes on the Development of Strategies for Solving Educational Problems," *American Journal of Orthopsychiatry*, October, 1967, pp. 843–858.

their introduction into the classroom. The term "aggregation" is designed to draw attention to the adding up of the parts of the social system in which the teacher must operate.

The specialization and aggregation models rest on differing assumptions about the nature of human nature and the strategy of learning. The specialization model is an expression of the dominant trends in our society that emphasize the capital- rather than the labor-intensive approach. The specialization model is actively buttressed by an elaborate intellectualized psychology of learning rooted in individual and cognitive psychology. The specialization model has as its goal the elaboration of cognitive processes and the enhancement of academic achievement mainly by reconstructing the contents of the curriculum according to the principles of cognitive development.

Educational psychologists supply a rationale for the specialization model, although they would criticize many of the actual applications of their principles into practice. Basically these educational psychologists have sought to broaden the definition of the capacity of what the student is capable of learning. In accordance with the recommendations of Jerome S. Bruner, the dominant intellectual posture of educational psychologists has been to question traditional conceptions of readiness for learning.[19] Their conclusion is that educators have vastly underemphasized the capacities of children to learn. The key to the learning process, from this point of view, is to restructure the subject matter—curriculum content—so that it articulates with fundamental principles of intellectual and cognitive development of the child.

But the existence of a body of general principles, grounded in research, is still a problematic issue. Therefore, the central notion of the new curriculum development movement is stated in the following terms by Bruner: "We begin with the hypothesis that any subject can be taught effectively in some intellectually honest form to any child at any state of development."[20] Such an assertion is patently not a hypothesis but a moral exhortation, since it rests on the crucial and completely ambiguous term "honest."

Suppose it were the case that the process of the child's intellectual development offered by Jean Piaget and adapted by Bruner supported the claim that any subject can effectively be taught at any stage of human development. But then the issue would still exist as to what should be taught at what age to serve the individual's and society's needs. Piaget himself has questioned the American adaptation and appli-

[19] Jerome S. Bruner, *The Process of Education* (New York: Vintage Books, 1960).
[20] Bruner, *op. cit.*, p. 33.

Table 1 *Basic Dimensions of Specialization and Aggregation Models*

Dimension	Specialization Model	Aggregation Model
Strategy of change	Incremental innovation by specific programs. Piecemeal change based on demonstration programs.	Holistic reorganization reflecting concern with organizational climate and minimum standards. Based on top-level managerial direction.
Organization goals	Priority of academic over socialization goals; socialization stressed but segregated.	Interdependence of academic and socialization goals.
Division of labor	Emphasis on increased division of labor and greater use of specialists.	Emphasis on increased authority and professional competence of classroom teacher.
Investment pattern	Capital-intensive techniques; high investment in the new media.	Labor-intensive techniques; stress on aides and volunteers.
Organizational format	School district central office levels with central office exercising administrative control.	Schools under sector's administrative control, with central office planning control.
Authority structure	Fractionalized.	Centralized policy making and decentralization based on professional autonomy.
Curriculum construction	External and centralized construction; independent hierarchy of curriculum specialists in school system.	Balance between external construction of materials and faculty involvement in curriculum construction; curriculum specialists as resource personnel.
Grading system	Fixed class levels, periodic grading on system-wide criteria.	Continuous development system, flexible system of grading that includes both system-wide criteria and specific indicators of achievement.
School districts	Specific and single boundaries with trend toward specialized schools.	Multiple and flexible boundaries and emphasis on adaptation of comprehensive high school.

Principal's role	Administrative specialist.	Master teacher.
Teacher's role	(a) Teacher specialist; specialized skills and subject matter orientation.	(a) Teacher-manager balance between subject matter skills and interpersonal and managerial competence.
	(b) Academic and vocational training.	(b) Coordinator of social space of youngster and of community resources.
Classroom management	Reduction of class size.	Flexible educational groupings depend on program.
Teaching style	Solo practitioner.	Group practice; peer group support and use of aides and volunteers.
Aides and volunteers	Limited involvement and narrow definition of tasks.	Strong emphasis; seen as general resources with teaching responsibilities.
Psychology of learning	Cognitive psychology.	Impact of institutional setting and normative order.
Control of deviant behavior	Emphasis on specialized personnel and specialized structure.	Maximize classroom management and teacher skills.
Evaluation	Pupil oriented.	Teacher and system oriented.
New media	Centralized control, used for regular instruction of maximum audience, manned by media personnel.	Decentralized control, used for specific audiences as a supplement to regularize instruction.
Community contacts	Specific, directed through principal and specialized community agent.	Diffuse and involving all educational staff members.
Teacher education	Specialized training in education and classroom practice teaching.	Liberal arts education plus clinic exposure to diversified experiences in community and educational practice.
In-service training	Under the control of school of education and linked to degrees.	Under public school system control and linked to professional development and curriculum development.

cation of his thinking to curriculum reform.[21] He emphasizes developmental stages to a much greater extent than Bruner and questions the American emphasis on speeding up the learning process. Moreover, a gap between Piaget's concepts and the realities of classroom teaching must exist, for Piaget never thought of his work as the basis of specific instructions to teachers. His work and the efforts that it has stimulated have meaning for the classroom teacher not because they supply engineering-type guides for curriculum development, but because, directly or indirectly, they increase the interpersonal capacity of the classroom teacher. In the specialization model, the psychologist makes his impact felt through his general principles of learning, which in turn influence the specialist on curriculum construction teams. In the aggregation model, the psychologist has the same relation to the teacher as the teacher has to her pupil—a direct and diffuse confrontation in which there is a continuous process of interaction.

The end result of the curriculum development movement, based on the theory of cognition, has been an additional pressure toward educational rigidity in a commitment to a spiral curriculum and in its mechanical emphasis on earlier and earlier exposure to more intellectually complicated materials. In fact, curriculum reform is seen as a social movement with strong overtones of a romantic ideology in which the children have the role of saviors of mankind by their classroom exploits. Its grossest form is present in a quotation from David Page, who is characterized as one of the most experienced teachers of elementary mathematics: "In teaching from kindergarten to graduate school, I have been amazed at the intellectual similarity of human beings at all ages, although children are perhaps more spontaneous, creative and more energetic than adults."[22]

The reservation implied in the aggregation model about a cognition theory of curriculum reform can be stated in alternative terms. Basically, the theory fails to take into consideration the social class and cultural elements that condition learning and supply the context in which the school as an institution must operate. Thus, the aggregation model is grounded in a set of assumptions about the slum school as a normative or moral order.

The moral order of the slum school cannot be characterized in simple generalizations if only because of the variation from school to school and from classroom to classroom. But more fundamentally there is no

[21] Frank G. Jennings, "Jean Piaget: Notes on Learning," *Saturday Review,* Vol. 50 (May 20, 1967), pp. 81–83.
[22] Bruner, *op. cit.*, p. 39.

necessity to assume that the moral order of any low-income school is by its very nature incompatible with the requirements of a civil society. There are older and relatively stable low-income communities in which the school functions on the basis of mutal consent and a relative sense of legitimacy even though its educational effectiveness may be limited or may serve to restrict the aspirations of the youngsters it serves.[23] But the slum school in most Negro ghettos has lost its organizational legitimacy and has a normative order with powerful elements of opposition to the larger society.

As indicated earlier, the aggregation model makes the assumption that the central pupil orientation in the slum school is a mixture of either indifference and hostility toward the school authorities. The resulting tensions create a group of student leaders who maintain their position by exploitation and even coercion, since they personify opposition to the school authorities. In a sense the criminal culture of the outer world has entered the daily life of the slum school. School authorities seldom if ever seek to cooperate with the most hostile and coercive student leaders as techniques of organizational control. The old-fashioned bully boy system of the correctional institution, in which toughs are used to keep order, is generally not found in public slum schools. But the presence of these informal leaders blocks efforts at educational reform. School authorities seek to resist such leaders or to export them out of their jurisdiction. Thus, in the typical slum school, the details of correctional reform based on theories of cognitive development are of secondary importance.

It must be added quickly that the remarkable aspect of the slum high school is that student moral order is differentiated. If there is a minority of outright opposition to educational goals and a majority of indifference, there is also another minority of career-oriented students. Within the confines of the slum school there are a number who "make it," who resist the informal social structure and develop a commitment to academic or vocational involvement. The sources of such commitment are only dimly understood since sociologists have not carried out naturalistic studies of the slum school. This minority subculture is supported, but only inadequately, by the school officials. The youngsters who succeed in achieving minimum standards of performance are expressing either the consequences of parental support, the influence of a gifted group of teachers, or experience generated in some community agency that helps to stabilize friendship patterns. They may also be expressing sheer

[23] See Gerald Suttles, *The Social Order of the Slum* (Chicago: University of Chicago Press, 1968).

personalistic energy mobilized in opposition to the dominant values surrounding them. The aggregation model seeks a set of educational practices that would transform the normative and moral order of the slum school. At a minimum, the power position of opposition student leaders must be neutralized, and some degree of cooperation and transformation is not ruled out. The minority culture of commitment to the school's goals (including its recreational sports and vocational programs) must become a more dominant element in the school milieu. The fundamental value and norm desired is not future achievement and future occupational goals, but a social system that seeks to strengthen individual dignity and self-respect in the immediate setting. In the simplest terms, whatever else is required, the youngsters must be treated so as to enhance their self-respect.

It is also clearly recognized that an outstanding school principal or a gifted classroom teacher can perform with distinction regardless of the administrative system. In fact, there is hardly a school that does not point with pride to its "star" teachers who appropriate the professional space required for some degree of autonomy and creativity. Frequently, such teachers display very strong personal motivation that leads them to deviate from the immediate organizational climate in which they find themselves. They are often older women who are invulnerable to institutional pressure because of their informal seniority or their commanding personal presence. Likewise, in the large metropolitan school systems, there are individual school principals who disregard the formal and informal system to produce noteworthy if temporary levels of performance. These men often have strong professional aspirations and feel that they are secure because they can get appointments in smaller systems. Their ranks include an occasional district superintendent with real personal charisma who has given up aspiration for a staff promotion "downtown." Even these outstanding performers, however, must operate within prescribed limits. They must be careful not to attract so much attention and public recognition as to rival or annoy their superiors. Moreover, they become sources of friction when outsiders raise questions as to why their innovations and their quality of work is not diffused and duplicated throughout the system.

Hence the objective of the two organizational models of change is to increase the effectiveness of the "typical" teacher and the "typical" principal, on whose performance the effectiveness of any school system, and any particular school, depends. The effectiveness of the typical teacher is an expression of deliberate managerial efforts of the school executives. The administrator has the responsibility to provide the gifted teacher with adequate conditions to demonstrate her special talents. His central concern, however, is to enhance the capacity of the typical teacher, which depends on the overall organization of the school system.

Each strategy change implies a different set of operational procedures. The final section of this paper seeks to set forth illustrative examples of how these two models of change can and do guide administrative practice.

OPERATIONAL ELEMENTS

The specialization and the aggregation models make different commitments to the appropriate balance of academic or vocational versus socialization goals. Educators have, of course, been traditionally aware that they both transmit skills and inculcate social values. In the past, however, educational administrators sought to deal with the issues of priorities and balance mainly in an implicit fashion and as a by-product of their primary commitment to academic and vocational tasks.

The contemporary "crisis" in public education has meant that educational administrators, especially those in the inner city, must develop an explicit operational code about the appropriate hierarchy of educational goals. The superintendents of the major big-city school systems and their top assistants have been forced to accept the position that academic and vocational achievement is not possible unless the school becomes more directly and explicitly involved in the socialization of its youngsters. This has meant a reformulation of the logic with which they have operated during the formative years of their own administrative careers. Many view the shifting and broadening of goals with considerable skepticism.

The most common response to the demand for the expansion of educational perspectives is contained in the repeatedly encountered phrase, which has stereotypical overtones, "the school cannot do the whole job." This obvious reality is both a genuine expression of pluralistic values and at the same time a protective stance against the pressure for higher levels of peformance and more services by the public school system. In this point of view, which is the dominant one of school administrators, socialization goals are adjunctive or secondary objectives that the school must undertake in order to fill its primary function—the transmission of skill. Special personnel, special functions, and special programs are added to achieve these adjunct goals. Such a broadening of goals of the public school system, especially in the inner city, conforms to specialization models. The specialization model is an expression of an incremental philosophy of change in which delimited and specific steps are taken, although it may be questioned whether the particular steps are powerful enough to produce the desired objectives.

By contrast, the aggregation model, in theory, takes a markedly different view toward the question of the priority of educational goals. The emphasis is not on an incremental conception of organizational change, but rather on a concern with minimum standards of performance. Thus, the aggregation model is influenced by the holistic strategy of change of the mental health movement. What type of organizational structure and what amount of resources are required in order to create an educational environment and a moral order that would meet the minimum requirement of effectiveness? With the establishment of basic requirements, step by step, programs become justified. In short, academic or vocational goals are fused with those of socialization. This is not to say that socialization goals are made equal to those of academic achievement. They are seen as interdependent. Interdependency means a flexible balance, including circumstances in which for a particular time period socialization goals might well outweight, for a particular group of students, academic or vocational objectives.

The aggregation model does not assert that the addition of specialists in either curriculum development or the management of interpersonal relations will ensure an adequate social climate in the public school system. To achieve this goal, the aggregation model is not limited to an increased emphasis on socialization processes. To the contrary, the school is seen as the central coordinating mechanism in the personal and social development of the youngster. The school not only seeks to organize itself to a system based on mutual self-esteem and dignity; it is also concerned with the entire existence of the youngster outside of the school. To state that the school becomes the coordinating institution in the lives of its youngsters does not imply that it manages their total life-space. It does not mean that the school directs the local health agency, the social agency, or the police in the immediate environment. It means that the requirements of the school serve as the stimulus for ensuring relevant policy and practices by all these agencies. In particular, the school and the teacher become the central locus for all information about the students. The school is the only institution, except perhaps for the police, that touches the lives of all the residents. Therefore, this conception means that the school is the point at which the various directed efforts at social change, both public and private, can be meaningfully related.

In a democratic society, no single agency can have monopoly power over the life chances of an individual. The school is the essential institution, but the aggregation model does not imply that it becomes the controlling institution in the slum. If the school sought to be a substitute for the family or welfare institutions, it would be destined to fail. But the school, because of its unique characteristics, can operate as a focal point, as a coordinating mechanism for formal and informal programs of intervention. Moreover, this approach is predicated on the notion that a minority of youngsters will not succeed in school but the experience of work, military, or other forms of vocational service will supply for them, as for earlier generations, essential socialization experience. It is both recognized and hoped that this minority will be small and should be minimized. It is essential (but outside the scope of this analysis) to deal with the artificial barriers and institutional defects that such youngsters must face.

The aggregation model recognizes that teacher-pupil relations are diffuse and that they involve direct and immediate response. The aggregation model is deeply influenced by the notion of the teacher-counselor, as described previously, but it does not accept this notion as the complete formulation. The teacher counselor is a single person who personally seeks, as much as possible, to serve the needs of a classroom of youngsters. The aggregation model also places the teacher, or more accurately the teacher-administrator, in charge of a group of youngsters. He is responsible for the well being and educational progress of these children. But the teacher can involve a variety of persons, both within and outside the school, to see that the youngsters have access to the needs and values of the community and society. In fact, the aggregation model fundamentally is concerned with expanding the pool of human resources available to the individual youngster. There is no way of knowing in advance to whom a student will appropriately relate and who will in effect offer satisfactory and stable interpersonal contacts.

In the past, public school systems have been antagonistic to other institutions and agencies that have sought to involve themselves in educational work—church groups, community organization, settlement houses, and welfare agencies. In the past, the school has almost purposefully separated itself from these agencies and at times been outrightly antagonistic to them. Under the aggregation model, the school is more supportive of outside agencies with educational programs. To make the school and the classroom a coordinating locus does not mean that the school is the sole center for learning. To the contrary, the aggregation model requires recreational, social, and work experiences both in the school environment and in the outside community. The same can be said for the academic components, for the school system comes explicitly to recognize, support, and even subsidize such programs. The tragedy of the slum lies not only in its physical deprivation, but also in the antihumanistic values that it fosters and maintains. Not until youngsters feel that outside of school they are more able to read or do their homework or participate in musical or cultural programs with ease can it be said that the aggregation model has been achieved.

Finally, an additional dimension for exploring the operational elements of the specialization and the aggregation models is derived from reference to the economic distinction between capital- and labor-intensive approaches. The specialization model stresses capital-intensive measures, the aggregation model, labor-intensive ones. Of course, both approaches are present in each model, and the basic issue is the most appropriate combination. Capital-intensive methods imply high investment costs that can be used for the training and professionalization of personnel, and the extensive use of complex technological devices. Effectiveness and efficiency result from the high output that each costly input of effort is designed to produce. Labor-intensive methods center on the notion that in the educational process there is need for significant amounts of inexpensive effort and simple human resources. This is dictated by the diffuse nature of the teaching function and by the increased emphasis on the fusion of academic and socialization goals. Socialization goals cannot be achieved on a mass basis by capital-intensive techniques alone. It should be noted that the aggregation model asserts that, although it emphasizes the incorporation of labor-intensive techniques, the coordination and utilization of these resources require very high levels of managerial expertise. The teacher and principal who can make effective use of volunteers, teacher aides, homework helpers, and adjunct specialists must have additional training, higher levels of professionalization, and greater rewards. In fact, this is the element of professionalization that the aggregation model stresses; the restructuring of work so that teachers can become master teachers and principals become principal-teachers. The capital-intensive elements in the aggregation model are therefore to be found in the higher level of professionalization required to utilize effective labor-intensive resources.

Thus, in partial summary, the distinction between the specialization and the aggregation models can be highlighted by different emphasis placed on the academic-vocational goals versus those of socialization, by the importance given to the school as a coordinating unit of community development, and by the relative stress on capital- versus labor-intensive approaches. By examining a series of more specific operational tasks, their full implication can be assessed. Among the illustrative problems that warrant examination are classroom management, the impact of the new media, authority and decentralization, pupil composition and decentralization, use of teacher aides and volunteers, school-community relations, and teacher education and career lines.

Classroom Management

The major concern of the specialization model in the management of the classroom is the reduction of class size. This is seen as the crucial variable of change. The national trend toward the reduction of classroom size has been pushed without abeyance since the turn of the century, when schools serving the immigrant working-class families operated on the basis of 70 to 90 pupils per class and educators tried to reduce classes to 60.[24] The quality of American education has been operationalized in terms of per capita expenditure, which in turn is but a measure of the ratio of teacher to pupils. Since the certified teacher is the most costly item, the major strategy has been a capital-intensive one.

In the cities the struggle continues to reduce class size below 35, while in nonparochial private schools pressure is exerted to reduce class size below 25. The impact of the psychotherapeutic model and the notion of the teacher-counselor serve to reinforce this trend. No doubt, the most important factor has been the pressures and power of the trade union movement among teachers, which has made teaching loads a crucial objective rather than emphasizing the development of the master teacher. Since the teacher-student ratio offers a concrete measure, it has rapidly become a popular demand. Even families from the lowest income groups have become aware of and concerned with these ratios in their own schools.

As mentioned earlier, there is a mass of evidence that the size of class or the individual teacher-pupil ratio is not the crucial point of attack for transforming the slum school. There are obviously desirable upper limits, but the mechanical allocation of new resources to reduction in class size does not produce significant increases in educational effectiveness. In fact, concern with class size continues the presumption of the appropriacy of existing practices of classroom management and hence can operate as a barrier to real innovation.

Closely related to the emphasis on reduction of classroom size in the specialization model has been the growth of specialist personnel in curriculum matters and also for discipline and counseling. Efforts to upgrade the college preparatory programs and to utilize the development of the cognitive theory of curriculum construction have led to the introduction of specialists whose task is to assist the teachers and

---

[24] Lawrence A. Cremin, *The Transformation of the School: Progression in American Education 1876–1957* (New York: Knopf, 1961), p. 21.

supply them with technical support. This development began in suburban college-oriented systems and has spread in varying degree to the large-city school systems.

Operating in support of the curriculum specialists are university-based groups that prepare materials incorporating scientific and intellectual developments. These curriculum teams have been heavily subsidized by the federal government. It is generally recognized that the materials these groups have produced have markedly raised the academic content of high school, and the development is part of the contemporary trend to assign to high school an important aspect of undergraduate collegiate instruction.

However, it must be pointed out that individual authors have rapidly entered the field of new mathematics, new biology, etc., with the result that high school textbook preparation also continues in its traditional format, since there are many stylistic advantages to a book written by a single person or two authors. The important development is not government-sponsored team work in curriculum development but rather the shifting of selected subjects from the collegiate level to the secondary school. Moreover, these national curriculum efforts have had little relevance for the problems of the slum school; and in fact, by increasing the specialization of the suburban high school in college preparation, they have weakened the comprehensive high school and worked against the needs of the inner-city youngster.

Limitations in the curriculum development movement emerge most pointedly in the actual work of curriculum specialists in the inner-city school system. Their work, like the new materials, is again oriented mainly toward the college-bound student who can benefit from accelerated instruction, and not so much toward the student whose capacities for college are questionable but who needs remedial or supplementary work in any case. The curriculum specialist is typically concerned with subject matter issues rather than fundamental issues of student instruction and participation in academic and vocation programs. He is not concerned with classroom climate, and usually he does not develop stable and effective relations with classroom teachers. Subdued tension often results when the teacher sees him as another unrelated specialist with whom she has to come to terms. The impact of the curriculum specialist has been, in general, to further weaken the authority and self-respect of the classroom teacher. Although this need not be the case, the curriculum specialist becomes another fractionalized element in the administrative structure rather than an effective resource for the classroom teacher.

By contrast, the aggregation model does not emphasize classroom size per se or the introduction of an independent hierarchy of curriculum specialists. Instead, it is concerned with improvement in the overall management of the classroom and in increasing the professional authority and autonomy of the teacher. The teacher accepts the responsibility for managing all that goes on in the classroom and for coordinating the relations between the classroom and the family as well as all community contacts. Therefore it is not in error to speak of the teacher as the teacher-manager, since she has at her disposal a variety of paraprofessionals plus outside assistance that can be utilized on her initiative. The teacher-manager seeks to prevent the classroom from becoming detached and isolated from the rest of the school and the larger community.

Emphasis is on organizational flexibility and away from fixed standards of classroom size. The goals are toward organizing a series of daily and weekly educational experiences in which the ratio of instructional personnel (and their qualifications) varies from one educational task to another. Involvement, particularly in musical, cultural, and social science presentations, can take place in large auditoriums and in programs led by master teachers, while in the course of each week every child can receive individual homework help from paid high school students. The teaching of history and geography can proceed in normal-size classes, whereas there can be no effective reading program in a slum school without small-group activities, augmented by individual tutorial instruction. These practices have existed informally under superior teachers in a single classroom; the objective is to institutionalize them and make them part of the total school program. The element of flexibility not only is essential to overcome the mechanical routines of contemporary practices but also releases resources for creative use at little added overall cost.

The teacher-manager has the ultimate responsibility for a full classroom of students, but the aggregation model emphasizes modification in the teaching division of labor in order to utilize labor-intensive methods. Education involves not only variation in the size of learning groups but also the transformation of the classroom situation to eliminate the solo practitioner approach of the specialization model. The teacher aides, volunteers, and personnel supplied by Vista and the National Teacher Corps become members of a team under the teacher-manager and are able to develop an effective sense of cohesion and to enhance the position of the teacher.

Curriculum specialists under such an arrangement are not part of an external hierarchy, but resources that can be utilized at the request of the teacher. The teacher-manager becomes a focal resource for in-service training designed to assist new personnel entering the slum school. The principal finds himself not directing a group of relatively isolated teachers, but rather supporting and coordinating the work of an aggregation of teaching teams.

The teaching team seeks explicitly to face the grim realities of the disorganized slum and the negativism toward education that it impresses on the school. Instead of semiannual grading, nongraded instruction or a continuous development format is more appropriate to deal with the high degree of residential mobility found in the slum community. It makes little sense to conduct an educational system in which a great many fail regularly. The continuous development system is designed to overcome repeated and pointless failure without denying the realities of the students' limited levels of achievement.[25]

Classroom management means improvement in the capacity of the teacher to deal with discipline and disruption within the classroom setting. There are sufficient data to underscore the fact that in the slum school the teacher spends most of her time on such matters. In the specialization model, disciplinary problems are assigned to specialists in interpersonal relations and to the adjustment teacher or assistant principal. Although the decision to suspend or expel must be made by an official other than the classroom teacher (but under more effective due process), the aggregation model broadens the role of the classroom teacher and increases her competence in controlling deviant behavior. Since the aggregation model involved varying degrees of team teaching, it would be expected that some teachers would develop greater competence in this sphere. The use of students as instructional personnel is designed to transform the values and norms of the school by altering the rewards and prestige. Likewise the use of indigenous personnel from the community inside the slum school is designed to help bridge the gap between the professional teacher and the student body.

A central dimension in maintaining freedom and order in the classroom is the teacher's expectation. Hostility is not generated among the students solely on the basis of covert racial and social prejudice, which must abound given the diversity in backgrounds and experiences existing among teachers and students. To recruit from the Negro community does not eliminate this problem. Hostility is also generated when teaching personnel devalue the human worth of their students, operate on a narrow definition of achievement, or underestimate their students' capacity for personal and intellectual growth. These negative definitions although hardly verbalized, are rapidly communicated and contribute

[25] See Mary A. Queeley's paper, pp. 52–90 in this book.

to the opposition culture of the slum school. Self-scrutiny, including staff discussion and group discussion wherein the teaching personnel can openly discuss their fears and attitudes and formulate new standards of performance for the slum school, are essential. Under such an approach the personnel in charge of discipline shift their focus from merely administering negative sanctions to serving as focal points of in-service training and group discussion.

The Impact of the New Media

A core issue in educational innovation is the actual and potential use of the new media. The professional autonomy of the teacher-manager depends on the type of investments made in the new media and on the organizational control for using them. The new media force the administrator to be concerned with investment, which can be either labor intensive or capital intensive.

The term "new media" has come to mean the massive and expensive instruments of television and the machinery of programmed learning. It is also important to include the new technology of the little instruments, such as tape recorders and film strips, and the family of technological developments for duplicating printed materials, from inexpensive paperback books to more efficient duplicating machines for classroom use.

In general, the potentialities of the new media for improving educational effectiveness have been overemphasized. The vision of an electronic remote-control learning machine reflects a new or a negative utopia. But educational institutions can no longer operate without these devices. Because the United States is a technological society, there has been and will continue to be strong pressure to introduce these devices as rapidly as possible and on a most extensive scale. In the last decade, considerable resources and administrative energy have been allocated to the incorporation of the new media into public education. The utilization of these media can be analyzed in terms of the differing requirements of the specialization and the aggregation models. The relevance of these media is determined not exclusively by their technological form, but also by the conscious decisions of educational administrators. The actual experience with educational television and that with paperback books constitute the basis for a paired comparison, since television has been employed in a format conforming primarily to the specialization model, whereas paperbacks—more by accident than by design—have reflected the outlines of the aggregation model.

In the early 1950's, under the stimulus of the Ford Foundation, extensive steps were taken to develop a national network of local transmitters for educational broadcasting. One result of this system, contrary to original expectation, was not a device for classroom instruction but rather a telecasting system for general audiences, emphasizing popular culture and aimed at adult populations. Continued interest in classroom television led to a variety of experiments in metropolitan closed-circuit television and to an elaborate system of airborne educational telecasting in the Midwest. This system had to be abandoned because of its inefficiencies and rigidities. The result was that classroom television never developed the role that its advocates anticipated. The use of television was based on a highly centralized format in order to obtain the maximum economic benefits. A group of media specialists who were concerned with the technical problem of presentation and who were distinct from educators managed these enterprises. There developed sharp antagonisms between the media specialists and the subject matter personnel. In fact, television was introduced by an organization operating initially outside the school system. As a result, despite economic pressure to use educational television, it has failed to gain widespread acceptance. Television is just another specialized and unarticulated resource.

One basic limitation in the use of classroom television is its lack of flexibility, that is, its lack of adaptability to meet varying on-the-spot needs. The more centralized the control, the more inflexible it is. Because of the limitations on "feedback" and interaction with the instructor the system has profound limits. Teachers resist it because of the loss of autonomy over context and scheduling that results from its use. But it was the highly centralized format under which television was introduced, rather than its inherent limitations, that accounted for its limited development.

However, it is possible to identify the format under which television can be adapted to the aggregation model. The educational power of television lies in the sense of immediacy that it can impart. It is particularly relevant for presenting the raw materials of the humanities and the social sciences. It is less relevant for teaching specific skills and specific content. For science, television can project demonstrations and experiments rather than regularized instruction. Interestingly enough, experience has indicated that close-circuit television can be used as an effective medium for communicating with teachers and assisting them in the preparation of their classroom instruction. Thus, it appears that television needs to be utilized at a scale less than its maximum coverage if it is to fit into the school system.

In contrast to the disjunctive and limited impact of educational television, the increased use of inexpensive paperback books has had a great impact and has conformed to a much larger extent to the aggregation model. The new paperbacks offer essentially economic benefits, being cheaper per unit cost, but it is important also that they have a great flexibility of content. They have improved the professional autonomy of the classroom teacher and greatly increased the diversification of the curriculum. At all levels, the teacher has more control of the curriculum because books can be produced and distributed more cheaply. From a technological point of view, the new printing processes could have made for greater standardization of curriculum materials. To the contrary, the organization of production and the systems of selection of these materials have resulted in both an upgrading of content and a greater role of the classroom teacher in developing her curriculum.[26]

First, the new technology has meant that the needs of specialized audiences can now be served on an economic basis. Special editions of the classics and of original materials can be produced in appropriate quantities to serve relatively limited needs. The market has, so to speak, been broken up. Distribution companies have developed and have penetrated the public school system so that diversified libraries are available in high schools which never had adequate hardback facilities. It is true that such libraries have been slow to develop in slum schools, but there are enough examples to show that they can succeed in serving the students of such schools. *Hooked on Books* is a report of the successful use of paperback books in an educational program in a Michigan correctional institution and a powerful demonstration of the ready audience for literature among the so-called culturally deprived.[27]

Second, the economies of paperbacks are such that more and more school units can afford to augment basic texts with specialized and high-grade printed materials. Third, and more fundamental, the book publishing industry is highly decentralized and very competitive. For both hardback and paperback texts, most big systems are forced to offer more than one title to teachers. The impact of this competition has been to weaken the authority of central curriculum selection committees and to force them to allow teachers to select from a wider variety of titles. It is now very difficult for a public school system arbitrarily to designate a single basic textbook and argue the necessity to use it on the basis of economic advantage. This is not to claim that there is

[26] Morris Janowitz and David Street, "The Social Organization of Education," in Peter Rossi and Bruce Biddle, eds., *The New Media and Education* (Chicago: Aldine Publishing, Co., 1966), pp. 207–242.
[27] Daniel N. Feder, *Hooked on Books: Program and Proof.* New York: G. P. Putnam's Sons, 1968.

sufficient decentralization in curriculum construction, but rather to indicate that the books in the paperback format are being used with increasing flexibility and professional discretion.

Improved duplicating and photocopying machines serve to further decentralize the production and control of printed media. The classroom teacher can enter more actively and directly into the production of appropriate material. Outstanding teachers have traditionally prepared their own materials, which not only can be tailored to the particular interest and aspirations of the class but have the added attraction of conveying the teachers' involvement. There is reason to believe that the unit costs for certain formats are no higher than those for more centralized materials if all costs are included. The fullest decentralization of curriculum construction and the maximum involvement, particularly for the slum school, result, as an abundance of case materials underscores, when the students themselves produce by dictation or composition their own reading materials. Thus, the issues of the new media need to be evaluated with care and in terms of relative investment in capital- versus labor-intensive approaches, for the payoffs are not directly related to the costs of the resources required.

Authority and Decentralization

Because piecemeal programs of innovation have failed to produce drastically more effective schools, there have emerged widespread demands to transform the authority system of the inner-city school system. Citizen groups became concerned with plans to "decentralize the school system" or to widen the "participation of citizen groups" in making decisions. The demands for decentralization and citizen participation, in addition to their reasonable elements, have been translated into ideological slogans thought desirable in and of themselves. Decentralization, in particular, is only an organizational strategy that can be justified if it changes the behavior of principals and classroom teachers and of parents as well. Decentralization serves societal goals if it makes it possible for inner-city schools to render more effective and more individualized services.

However, a basic problem of the inner-city school system is that it has become detached from the suburban school system in terms of its financial base, its personnel practices, and its fundamental social relations. Any system of decentralization that serves to maintain or reinforce such separation can hardly be judged as making a positive contribution.

It is also necessary to recall the earlier exposition of the institutional realities of the inner-city school system. Mechanical and arbitrary plans for decentralization cannot be effectively fused to a highly fragmented organization. School decentralization runs the risk of contributing further to internal disorganization; in some respects increased centralization is required. In the simplest terms centralization and decentralization need to be judged in terms of both (a) fundamental policies and goals and (b) specific and operational practices. Thus, a case can be made that important aspects of public education need to be more centralized in order to guarantee a greater degree of equality of resources, whereas other aspects such as curriculum development require effective decentralization.

The issues of authority and decentralization are debated in terms of the number of operational units that should come under one jurisdiction and the appropriate number of levels of administration. However, alternative strategies of decentralization and citizen participation have meaning if they actually change patterns of authority and if they can be evaluated as to the degree to which accountability is increased. From the point of view of the aggregation model, the transformation of authority must start at the very top of the system. Effective decentralization requires the simultaneous, or even prior, effort of creating an effective top managerial core. There must be enough of an integrated organization so that decentralization can be meaningful. An effective managerial core means that there is a group of appointed officials and their professional counterparts who have enough of a sense of institutional solidarity so that fundamental issues are identified and confronted or at least debated.

The first steps rest with the personnel and procedures of the members of the school board, for only in rare cases do the members feel that they have penetrated into the real life of the system and that they exercise effective control. When they are not overawed by the personality of the superintendent, they are often overwhelmed by the complexity and intractability of the issues they must face. Various reforms have been proposed and some implemented, such as developing an agenda that moves away from operational details by devolving these issues onto the office of the superintendent, and devising more adequate procedures of recruitment, screening, and even training of board members and the development of small independent staffs to serve the board with documentation, research, and planning. None of these devices has produced startling results, although the effectiveness of school boards has clearly increased in the 1960's.

It is abundantly clear that the traditional pattern of the superintendent as the sole link between his system and the board of education no longer suffices, if in fact it ever did. Board members require some form of direct access to the machinery of the public school system. At least one metropolitan system follows the practice of encouraging board members to develop particular areas of expertise and to become part of the supervisory apparatus of particular operations. Another possibility is to institute the equivalents of the congressional committee, thus permitting board members to have direct access to school officials. There is enough experience to indicate that such arrangements need not weaken the position of the superintendent. Instead the consequence of effective involvement of board members in the operation of the system can be to make them more effective spokesmen in mobilizing public support.

The second set of steps and the most important rests on increasing the professional and organizational authority of the general superintendent as a precondition for effective decentralization of operations. One key requirement is to broaden his ability to modify the structure of his central staff, to change its function, and to select his own direct aides. In the first wave of managerial change when younger men became big-city superintendents, most accepted their appointments without insisting on freedom to appoint their key aides; they were prepared to make use of existing personnel. Since 1965, some new superintendents have insisted that they be able to replace top personnel even though they may be covered by civil service or administrative decree.

The obvious objectives are to overhaul the internal division of responsibility, to simplify the top structure, and to create a central office staff equipped with modern managerial resources and management techniques, such as electronic data processing, performance budgeting, and fiscal control. But the underlying objective, more difficult to achieve, is to transform the central staff from an operating agency seeking to administer the details of a large and complex system into a planning, control, auditing, and coordinating agency. In city after city, steps have been taken to relieve the superintendent of detailed and routine tasks and to free him for organization development and representation to the public. Following the pattern of industrial management, which in turn is based on the format of the military agency, one key officer, in effect a chief of staff, is appointed as his understudy charged with the management of the central staff. But transforming the activities of the central staff away from day-to-day functional activities has been a slow task. Much of the energy available to develop the resources of the central staff has been consumed in obtaining, processing and administering federal funds.

Paradoxically the development of a chief executive officer has not facilitated the transformation of the central staff, for this format operates effectively in a relatively stable organization that is not continually facing crises. But each of the inner-city school systems of the United States is straining to transform itself. The central staff reacts to external pressure and crises; it continues through operational oversight to perform day-to-day functions, and the chief executive officer is more likely to be an administrative expediter who has an essential but limited function of giving the superintendent some additional staff support. Examination of the operating format of six big-city systems reveals that innovations at the top take place, not because of the development of a "rational" organization format, but almost despite it. If there is a key administrator who is dedicated to changing the organization, tension is a sign of progress.

The basic ingredient for innovation is the assumption of the role of "associate superintendent" by one officer, who may be called the planning, research and development, or just special projects officer, and whose work cuts across that of the chief executive officer and the various functional chiefs. He is a person who has the support of the superintendent and who is prepared to penetrate into the internal mechanism of the organization. He is, so to speak, the officer in charge not of administering the organization but of modifying it. Although such a setup does not appear to be an adequate permanent arrangement, it serves the immediate requirements and is likely to persist. If the central staff emerges as a planning and coordinating agency, its effective organization will in turn become more of a council-type or a planning team of different skill specialists. Under such circumstances, the principal executive officer becomes the chief planner and the operational lines of authority descend from the board of education to the general superintendent to the chief operating superintendents.

However, over the short run, with the creation of a more effective central staff, the conditions are created for initial steps toward effective decentralization of particular administrative procedures. Operational decentralization can lead to the concept advanced in the McGeorge Bundy report, offered in 1967 as a remedy for the New York City system, where partial systems of decentralization had had limited effects.[28] The goal is to create the smallest possible operational unit, to give each the maximum amount of autonomy, and to broaden citizen participation drastically by creating many more local boards. The plan recommends some sixty to seventy distinct local school units. In a sense, each unit is seen as becoming a specialized agency created to meet the particular needs of a local area and developing as far as possible a distinct

[28] *The New York Times,* November 8, 1967, p. 1, col. 1.

character. The plan raised a wide range of questions. Does such a system contribute to overcoming the fractionalization of public education and the professional isolation of teachers and principal? Does it enhance lateral communication between operating units and internal communication within a given school? Does it make possible economies of scale in routinized functions? Does such a plan create the necessary conditions for an effective career service? Although these questions are difficult to answer, this effort to decentralize and to increase citizen participation appears to maintain and enhance an excessively fractionalized system, and in fact the original plan was modified by city officials in order to meet criticisms to this effect.

An alternative effort at decentralization proceeds in the opposite direction by dividing the central city school system into three to seven superdistricts or sectors, each of which becomes the top operating agency. In each sector there is a relative balance of the social composition of the inner city. In Chicago, for example, three sectors with associate superintendents were organized at the same time that the Bundy report was issued. The superintendent of each sector seeks to maximize the economies of scale that can be achieved. But the establishment of the sectors is designed to increase organizational effectiveness by (a) narrowing the span of control, (b) increasing lateral communications among operating units, and (c) most important, increasing the organizational authority of the individual principal.

For the moment, the crucial question of the number of operating units that are appropriately linked together under a middle level of administration (the district superintendent) will be postponed for discussion under the heading "Pupil Composition and School Boundaries." However, if a decentralization program has impact, the reason is that there is first a change in the behavior and performance of the individual principal. Two dimensions are crucial. One is to expand the range of the decisions that a principal can make—to increase his role in recruitment and selection of personnel; broaden the authority he has to reallocate the resources placed at his disposal; increase his authority to make arrangements for community groups, including the recruitment of volunteer and para-professional helpers; enhance his authority to modify curriculum; and make him and his staff responsible for deciding which specialized training and special work programs youngsters are to be offered. The number of years of school and the requirements concerning attendance and performance should ultimately be based not on mechanical city-wide norms but on the judgment of local school officials and their staff. Second, the relation of the principal to his teachers and his students needs to change. The principal cannot be an administrative agent; he must represent and personify the teaching function. He must be the principal-teacher in the school.

This role was familiar to the traditional principal, who sought to make himself effective by his sheer physical presence throughout the school and his direct involvement in the daily routine of the teachers and students. Under the aggregation model, the principal must retain his teaching function, although the content of this function will vary from situation to situation. This is not to assert that he engages in teaching on only a token and symbolic basis. The analogy with the medical hospital has some relevance. The principal is required to perform like the chief of a service; the latter is the doctor among the doctors, so the principal is a teacher among teachers. This may mean that he operates as the main in-service training officer of his staff, that he is engaged in classroom teaching, or that he is directly available to parents and students as well as outside community leaders. He has at his disposal an administrative assistant, a chief clerk who manages the routine tasks and is part of an administrative career service that allows for promotion and increased responsibility via a career route to larger schools or higher levels of administration.

The objective of effective decentralization is to guarantee a public presence within the school and thereby increase the likelihood that the public school system will render effective services to each student. Parent or community participation at the level of the district or individual public school is designed to be precisely such a service. Outside groups, such as volunteers and members of the Teachers Corps, also serve in the same fashion. They are mechanisms of accountability. Parent involvement in slum areas, assuming that it is based on local leadership and does not merely reflect organized outside professional or church leadership, has many limitations. One that is often mentioned is the pressure by parents, in their search for a moral order, for a punitive role by the school. It is more generally recognized that local boards are handicapped in assembling specific and technical information in comparison with the advantages that accrue to the permanent professional staff. A decentralized school board system would be strengthened if it had recourse to an ombudsman system, with full-time civil servant personnel to process grievances. Ombudsman systems seem to operate most effectively if they do not have to concentrate on a single agency, but it may be that the separate jurisdictional authority of the school system would complicate the development of an all-purpose ombudsman system.

But ensuring an effective public presence in a slum school is more complicated and more difficult than providing the jurisdictional scope of an ombudsman system. A public presence is enhanced if the agent of intervention is not limited to investigative functions but has a positive role as well. Thus, the presence in schools of Vista workers, volunteers, and other groups serves the positive goal of supplying important services to youngsters, and also these persons by their sheer presence operate as a public personnel and an informal grievance system.

In the United States the public school has resisted an effective internal audit and inspection system. In England and in the other Commonwealth countries, the school inspector is a standard administrative agent for ensuring a public presence and guaranteeing equality of service.[29] The British inspectorate is both a system for checking on performance and the adequacy of administration and instruction, and at the same time a device for helping and supporting the classroom teacher and the local administrator. The inspectors are drawn from classroom teachers and local administrators. They are persons who have demonstrated their high competence in educational pusuits and their loyalty to the educational system. They are required, however, to represent the needs of parents as well as to check on the performance of teachers and local administrators.

In the United States, the educational profession has succeeded in preventing an internal inspection system. Even the military have a highly developed inspector-general cadre. There can be no effective transformation of the public school of the inner city without the development of some such equivalent agency. In terms of the aggregation model, it is most likely to be meaningful if it has the multiple function of representing the public interest and at the same time helping teaching personnel in dealing with operational problems and serving as a channel of communication from the operating level to supervisory levels.

Pupil Composition and School Boundaries

Decentralization involves not only the professional authority of the principal and of the teacher in turn but also basic questions of student composition and school boundaries. The traditional comprehensive high school was an informal decentralized education system. Within one school, different social classes were educated. When the comprehensive high school operated effectively, it served the dual need of offering a common social experience plus providing a differentiated curriculum. The school made its contribution to a common culture and at the same time enabled lower-class students to participate in a college preparatory education. Not all youngsters attended effective comprehensive high

---

[29] E. L. Edmonds, *The School Inspector* (London: Routledge and Kegan Paul, 1962).

schools, but enough did so that the school system operated on a basis compatible with the assumptions of the larger society. With the growth of urban centers, specialized academic high schools were introduced but even these did not Europeanize public education because of the city-wide recruitment of students that obtained. Moreover, attendance at a purely academic high school was not the exclusive route to higher education.

Since 1945 the comprehensive high school in the central city has declined because of limited financial resources and because of the patterns of population concentration, particularly of lower-class Negro families. Given the fragmented organization of public education, the quality of education in a particular school is deeply and immediately influenced by the population characteristics of the community. Therefore, the task facing the aggregation model is to organize school boundaries and student populations so as to produce both heterogeneous social backgrounds and racial integration. It is relatively easy to reject the approach of Robert Havighurst to reorganize the public school system so as to achieve racial integration at the expense of maintaining or even sharpening social class differences. But the effort to develop alternative strategies has produced much writing and little consensus.

The aggregation model seeks to retain and strengthen essential educational features of the comprehensive high school. The problem is profoundly complicated by the fact that efforts at integration have been concentrated in the ring of primary and secondary schools located on the edge of the Negro ghetto. These areas are, with some notable exceptions, the least well equipped and have the most limited social resources for handling the impact of school integration. Programs for school integration have tended to involve low-income Negro and white youngsters or whites of lower income than their Negro counterparts. Racial integration in education can proceed more quickly among better educated groups especially in communities with concentrations of professional families, where the Negro and white youngsters are of similar middle-class background and the quality of public education is good. In fact, some of the most stable progress has been made where middle-class elements have been involved, but the basic national strategy has been to place the burden of social change on the inner-city groups that are the least equipped to handle these issues.

To articulate the issues of racial integration with the aggregation model, a conceptual dimension is also involved. Since the Supreme Court decision, school integration in the minds of the public school administrator and in the public perspective has been cast in formal and numerical terms and on an all-or-none basis. The goal of school integration is seen in numbers and patterns of full-time school attendance. In a given school building a student body should be made up of an admixture of Negroes and whites who need to share a common educational experience during the whole day, the whole week, the whole school year, and throughout the pupils' entire schooling.

However, school integration can also be seen as an aspect of the larger social process. If the task of school integration is to make it possible for the Negro to enter the mainstream of American society, school integration becomes, in one sense, a reality whenever there are cross-racial contacts for pupils. The movement toward integration takes place when these contacts occur for one hour, for one day, for one week, or for an occasional semester. The same desirable consequences take place when youngsters—both Negro and white—have fuller exposure to an integrated group of teachers. The notion of social process integration is not limited to an "all-or-none" outlook but includes the utilization of all possible opportunities.

There is also a psychological dimension in the concept of school racial integration that has grown in tremendous importance since the issue was first pressed by Negro groups and the Supreme Court decision of 1954, namely, that of self-respect and identity. The requirements of the Negro youngster cannot be met by the assumption that only by attending a white school can good education be achieved. There must be effective education in all Negro schools if Negro youngsters and the Negro community are not to be locked into a position of psychological inferiority. As early as 1963, Bettelheim and Janowitz anticipated some of the implications of the rise of the Black Power movement. They argued that school busing and other devices could not suffice to incorporate the Negro into the educational mainstream. They pointed out that for some youngsters moving into a white school, although better in facilities, teachers, and educational content, would of necessity result in lower self-esteem or continued low self-esteem.[30] It would reinforce the notion that Negroes are a deficient group for whom special arrangements must be made. The strategies of a search for self-esteem are multiple, and the Black Power movement is in part a search for legitimacy.

In a parallel fashion, the notion of heterogeneous social class population requires a conceptual dimension. Public discussion of this issue was for a period dominated by the findings of the Coleman report, which concluded that composition—that is, an appropriate mixture of

[30] Bruno Bettelheim and Morris Janowitz, *Social Change and Prejudice* (New York: Free Press, 1964), pp. 93–95.

social classes (in terms of racial groups)—is the single most powerful predictor to educational performance.[31] For purposes of the aggregation model, let it be assumed that the findings are adequate, although there is reason to question many particular conclusions.[32] Therefore, massive integration, both social and racial is required, and many sociologists have recommended the wholesale breaking up of the slum school by massive busing, the building of vast educational parks, and the relocation of public schools outside of the inner city. In time, James Coleman himself declared his reservation on this point of view as being the major or overriding implication of his research.[33]

Reasonable objection to an exclusive massive social integration formula rests not on moral judgments. Nor is the central reservation political feasibility. The difficulty with the approach is that it accepts the existing criterion of school success as the basis for according respect and even employment opportunities to the Negro in our society. It accepts the school system as given, when in fact a great variety of changes are required for both whites and Negroes. Fundamentally, regardless of the importance of a particular factor, it is a gross error to assume that only this factor can and need be altered. Equivalent changes can well be achieved by a group of alternative factors. The degree of association is only a partial index to potential lines of development since institution building by its very nature involves more than single-factor change. In other words, even if social composition is the single most powerful variable, it is the responsibility of the social scientist to specify the conditions under which effective and quality education can be achieved by alternative methods.

Thus, in terms of the aggregation model the quality of the educational program in a particular school need not be thought of as simply a reflection of the social composition of the student population, although it is obviously deeply influenced by it. If the inner-city schools are to become more of a social system, and less fragmented, programs and personnel must become more relevant for modifying the impact of the social composition of the student population.

If the comprehensive high school is to be adapted to the needs of contemporary social structure, at least two dimensions are involved in the aggregation model. First, no pupil should attend a high school that does not have a college preparatory program. The number of pupils

[31] James S. Coleman, *Equality of Educational Opportunity* (Washington, D.C.: Office of Education, U.S. Department of Health, Education and Welfare, 1966).
[32] For a critical evaluation of the limitations of the findings of the Coleman report.
[33] James Coleman, "Equal Schools or Equal Students?" *The Public Interest,* Vol. 4 (Summer, 1966), pp. 70–75.

in the high school need not be a limiting factor. Of course, it can be recognized that the scope and quality of college programs are likely to vary. But if an essential element is absent in a particular high school, it could be obtained by attendance in a more central facility throughout the academic year or for a given time period. Equally important is the presence of continuous devices for ensuring and encouraging transfers into college preparatory programs. Second, no youngster should be required to attend a high school that is organized around some particular technical or vocational program. Again, for specific training and for specific periods of time a student may attend a specialized vocational training center or community facility, but his basic educational program should involve participation in some form of comprehensive high school.

Thus the two requirements of racial integration and social class heterogeneity (plus a relevant diversity of educational programs) converge and lead away from a concern with single boundaries to an acceptance of multiple boundaries, depending on the program involved. At the high school level, in fact, boundaries are de-emphasized and the concern is with effective centers.[34] Wherever possible (and there is a variety of feasible elements), the metropolitan area as a whole emerges as a basis for planning and organization.

The need for flexible attendance areas does not mean that the district level of administration, the level between the operating school and the sector, can be entirely eliminated. The number of districts needs to be reduced, and each sector would probably supervise five or six districts. The district level, aside from performing housekeeping functions such as maintenance, is really a focal point for professional in-service development because of the greater autonomy of principals and teachers.

The check list of basic steps to maximize racial integration is by now well known. These steps are not implemented because of the concrete results they achieve; rather, they are demonstrations of the commitment of the public school authorities to reasoned pursuit of the objectives of integration. These policies include city-wide open enrollment to utilize unused school space and to enhance racial balance. Devices for managing integration include selected busing and community programs to retain white families. Demonstrations of social-process school integration include mutual exhanges of pupils and teachers with suburban com-

---

[34] There is an interesting analogy between the national community and the educational community. Edward Shils speaks of the center and the periphery as elements in a nation, and in the same fashion an educational community requires both. See Edward Shils, "Centre and Periphery," *The Logic of Personal Knowledge: Essays in Honor of Michael Polanyi* (London: Routledge and Kegan Paul, 1961), pp. 117–131.

munities from periods of one day to longer periods of one week or even one semester.

But the main thrust of pragmatic integration centers on the maintenance and development of a set of key comprehensive schools—magnet schools, as they might be called—in which attendance is based on a sector or even on city-wide basis. Realistically, the maintenance of a number of such magnet schools is still a goal in most of the major metropolitan centers of the United States.

For these schools and also more generally, fixed-purpose buildings need to give way to more flexible centers that can be adapted to changing educational needs and age populations. In urban renewal areas, where the maximum amount of integration has taken place, and also in model cities programs, it has become possible for physical school planning to be more adequately related to community housing programs. Flexible school buildings do not invariably have to be publicly constructed or publicly owned. Instead particular structures can be leased; some can even be built as parts of housing developments and thereby be financed by alternative schemes to bonds enacted by popular elections. When grammar schools are built by private developers and leased to the public school system, federal mortgage insurance is possible and the costs are less because the school system is not involved in capital costs. But in any building program there is no need for a magnet high school to be larger than 5000 to 6000 students to ensure a variety of educational programs. Each metropolitan area requires realistic goals of the numbers of students that it will in a particular time period involve in a magnet type of high school or who will attend other types of integrated schools. The purpose of such an audit is to remind the educators of the scope and nature of the problems facing students who do not attend such settings. The aggregation model seeks the transformation of the school from a fragmented set of separate institutions into a more articulated social system (with the associated reforms); reliance declines in the manipulation of student composition as a basis of effective education.

Thus it becomes necessary, at the danger of painful repetition, to increase the effectiveness of the slum school by emphasizing its structure and personnel—rather than merely by manipulating its student composition and by more directly raising academic and socialization goals. It is part of a strategy of reconstruction from the top down—from the central administration core to the individual school, and from the higher to the lower grades. In this process the aggregation model faces not only the content of academic and vocational instruction, but also recognizes that for the bulk of youngsters in the slum school the formal academic and vocational programs alone cannot afford sufficient gratification to be an adequate basis of self-esteem and a moral order. The comprehensive high school expresses the goals of the adult society that students have to remain under educational supervision until sixteen now and until seventeen or eighteen in the decade ahead. For the comprehensive high school to be effective, school experiences must be fused with community or work experiences. Obviously, this is not a new idea, but to increase drastically the numbers involved and to make it an integral part of the school curriculum requires extensive institution building. This aspect of the aggregation model is best explored under the topic of school-community relations, if the notion of work experience while in high school is to be given broad meaning.

Nonprofessionals and Volunteers

Both models seek to make use of teacher aides and volunteers. Because of its emphasis on labor-intensive methods, the aggregation model gives greater weight than the specialization model to the importance of such personnel. It implies a concern with a greater number of them, a wider range of sources of recruitment, and a broader scope of their involvement. The specialization model emphasizes their use in administrative and housekeeping tasks. Their work may extend into borderline educational activities such as working in the library or assisting in field trips. But the aggregation model, while seeking to make use of aides and volunteers in such roles, also included their direct participation in educational activities.

Teacher aides and volunteers participate in educational tasks mainly by tutorial work, either with small groups of youngsters or on a one-to-one basis, and thereby offer children additional academic assistance. The underlying strategy is not merely an intensification of the same type of effort as that of the classroom teacher. To the contrary, small-group work and tutorial assistance is a form of supplementary help that the teacher is unable to offer. These nonprofessionals and volunteers can devote their attention and their energy to establishing satisfactory and stable relations with youngsters. They can seek to find a common ground and to supply a sense of immediate gratification to the student as he struggles to improve his academic achievement. The rewards for improved academic achievement are too remote to be a powerful incentive to many youngsters in slum schools. The immediate acceptance and encouragement that these additional personnel can offer is at the basis of improved performance.

The teacher aide or the volunteer can serve in the limited but crucial role of homework helper and thereby extend to a lower-class child the type of support that middle-class families normally give their children. These nonprofessionals can also assume more direct involvement in special small-group work, in reading or in particular subject matter areas. The most elaborate and direct involvement, which is still feasible for untrained but supervised personnel, lies in one-to-one tutorial work in reading, arithmetic, and other basic skills.[35] Careful research with adequate control demonstrates the effectiveness of volunteer workers in helping lower-income children to improve reading skills.[36] These researchers also include exploration of the impact of such efforts on orientation toward school and general interpersonal adjustment, and have indicated measurable, if limited, positive consequences in these areas.

Nevertheless, the incorporation of teacher aides and volunteer workers into the public school system has proceeded very slowly during the last decade. Organizational rigidities, formal requirements, and opposition from professional groups and trade unions have served to limit their utilization. Frequently a large public school system has instituted a program of this type in order to demonstrate its interest in innovation, without developing appropriate administrative support for the program to expand in numbers or to have an important impact on the school system. Only in a few cases have vigorous public school progams been encountered in large metropolitan centers where the need is most pressing. Paradoxically, suburban areas and smaller communities have some of the most effective programs.

As a result, a great deal of energy in the innovative uses of nonprofessionals has been displayed outside of the public school system. Strong impetus for the use of volunteers was given by the efforts of college student groups linked to the civil rights movement in the early 1960's. These efforts, which received extensive mass-media coverage, helped to dramatize the role of the volunteer. However the transitory nature of many of these student organizations, changing student interests, and excessive publicity brought about a decline of these programs. Funds from the Office of Economic Opportunity have also supplied important components in the development of out-of-school or after-school centers. In particular, the efforts of Mobilization for Youth in New York City were extensive. Throughout the country selected church groups, settlement houses, and social welfare and youth service organizations have

[35] See Gayle Janowitz, *Helping Hands: Volunteer Work in Education* (Chicago: University of Chicago Press, 1965) for a description of the various educational roles that nonprofessionals can perform.

[36] Richard Cloward, "Studies in Tutoring," *Journal of Experimental Education*, Fall, 1967; and Pranab Chattejee, "Volunteer in Supplementary Education: Comparative Case Studies of After-school Study Center," unpublished, 1968.

launched educational and cultural enrichment programs that require nonprofessionals. The performance and stability of these efforts have been varied and depend essentially on the quality of the supervision of volunteer personnel.[37] These programs become institutionalized in time, and in many urban centers city-wide coordinating and supervising groups have emerged to give them stability. Thus there is reason to believe that the future of nonprofessionals in education is likely to involve both in-school and out-of-school efforts.

The development of nonprofessional programs in the public school system depends on a number of procedures that are linked to general features of the aggregation model and on decentralization. The various steps to recruit and select teacher aides and volunteers often involve the existing central personnel offices. Application to be a teacher's aide requires going to a central office or at least to one of several key offices. In addition, teacher-aide jobs are generally seen as full-time posts. Both of these requirements serve to limit the number of available personnel and the effectiveness of these programs. One aspect of the aggregation model is to recruit local personnel, and this is enhanced if selection is left in the hands of the local principal and can involve part-time personnel.

The need for effective decentralized arrangements in the recruitment and allocation of volunteers is even more significant. City-wide volunteer bureaus are important, since a great many volunteers come from outside the immediate area of the school in which they serve. But the principal needs to have flexibility in making direct arrangements with individual volunteers and with groups of them. The channeling of teacher aides and volunteers through central offices serves to make such programs unduly cumbersome and to hamper involvement.

Excessive concern about adequate selection of such personnel is often a subtle but effective technique for limiting these programs. The needs of the slum school are so great that some risks would be worth taking, but experience indicates that the problem of unit personnel is not a significant one. Some simple screening procedures are required, but these programs develop more effectively if the emphasis is on supervision rather than on selection. Ineffective or undesirable personnel can easily be let go, or they can be counseled into other jobs that they can perform. Likewise, rather than to emphasize training programs, especially in the

---

[37] Timothy Leggatt, "After-school Study Centers: An Analysis of a New Institution," Working Paper No. 51, Center for Social Organization Studies, University of Chicago, November 1965.

case of volunteer workers, experience has shown that adequate supervision and periodic in-service training meetings are more productive.

The major goal of nonprofessional help is to supply the teacher-
manager with a pool of human resources that can be utilized to meet
immediate and not fully anticipated needs. Nonprofessionals have
specific tasks to perform. To the extent that their presence serves to
contribute to a social and moral environment based on mutual respect,
they contribute to the aggregation model. Moreover, any interpersonal
situation is a process of mutual interaction. The teacher aide and the
volunteer, especially if they are high school students, are being exposed
to experiences that have educational and socialization value for them
as well as the youngsters they are serving.

Under the aggregation model, the emphasis is not on recruiting a
stable force of teacher aides and volunteers, although this is a desirable
objective. It is recognized that the non-professional may have experiences
that will influence his career decision and may motivate him to seek
additional training. Hence such programs become important devices for
recruiting a new generation of teachers. Teacher-aide programs that utilize local personnel serve to resocialize into the larger community women
who through child rearing, especially under the conditions of the slum
community, had become almost wholly detached and self-preoccupied.
In the most basic terms, the slum school is built on a community of
high birth rates and therefore one with a great preponderance of young
people. The use of teacher aides and volunteers in school and in after-
school study centers represents an effort to create a social climate with
a better balance of age groups. Local adults who become involved in
such programs have an opportunity to interact with other adults outside
of the narrow range of their immediate family and social groups.

School-Community Relations

School-community relations involve contacts of the school both with
organized group interests and with individual families—complete or
broken as the case may be. In both sets of contacts the slum school,
in comparison with the suburban school, is a relatively closed institution.
The social boundaries of the slum school are difficult to permeate. The
line between the school and the outside is relatively fixed and sharp.
The school, because of its defensive posture, sees intrusion from the
outside as potentially disruptive. The analogy between the traditional
slum school and the closed custodial mental hospital or correctional institution has powerful meaning.

Decentralization of organizational authority and de-emphasis of geographical boundaries set the conditions for transforming the slum school into a more open institution and, in particular, for loosening its rigid boundaries. With the increased demands of civil rights movements and subsequent Black Power groups, the organized relations between local school officials and formal community groups have taken a wide variety of forms. At one extreme are isolated but persistent situations of outright struggle between community groups and the local school that lead to boycotts, strife, and various forms of coercion. Short of such open "warfare" are situations in which the tactics of pressure, or merely personal antagonism, lead to delay and block a flexible response by school officials. However, even in the absence of systematic research, one is struck by the fact that frequently in slum communities the quality of contacts between local school officials and organized community groups is very fluid, so that patterns of mutual accommodation often arise rapidly from situations of conflict and hostility.

But the quality of school-community relations is not fashioned primarily by group representation, since at best only a very small proportion of the slum community makes use of these channels. There is a network of communications and images and rumors out of which the substance of school-community relations is built. Short of outright organized coercion by community groups, which tends to be dramatized by the mass media, school officials have the dominant position in dealing with organized groups and individual contacts. They retain a considerable amount of initiative as to what strategy they wish to pursue.

The aggregation model requires family support or its equivalent to permit youngsters to develop the interests, skills, and attitudes that are being sought by the school system. If these are used only in the school, the moral climate in the school cannot maintain itself or be strengthened. Moreover, the existence of educational field stations in the community is indispensible in providing second-chance agencies. Again and again, for reasons that are only dimly perceived, youngsters will find in an outside educational program involvement and satisfaction that they cannot develop in a school setting. Success in an outside academic program can, over time, influence negative attitudes toward the school.

Thus, the school system must take the initiative to ensure that a variety of facilities are available in the community in which the slum students can do their homework, pursue musical and cultural activities, and form associations based on these interests. The settlement house traditionally had an educational function in assisting the foreign born, and contemporary community agencies are gradually returning to this tradition. The after-school study center, maintained by a church group or a youth or community agency, has emerged as a new device for pursuing this goal. Improvement of school programs in slum areas is likely not to eliminate the demands for such outside community resources but to increase their importance and use.

The specialization and the aggregation models indicate different strategies, both organizationally and substantively, in broadening school-community relations. The specialization model seeks to make progress by adding a specialist to the staff of the local school, the school-community agent. Such a person frequently has background in community affairs or is given training in community organization. His task is to facilitate communication between the school and both organized group interests and individual families. This development represents an important step in that it gives the professional staff another device for communicating specific messages, as well as its point of view, to the families of the students. It serves also as a reverse channel of information.

School-community agents are often appointed without clear definition of their job. This is of limited consequence since their role must of necessity be diffuse. They also rapidly accumulate specific tasks and become involved in concrete activities of social welfare, family referral, and the like. At times tension develops between the school-community agent and the school officer for discipline since the school-community agent assumes the more "therapeutic" orientation. However, out of such tensions a clearer recognition of the conflicts between the values of the school and those of the community emerges.

For the aggregation model, the task of the school-community agent is a natural extension of the teacher-manager's responsibility for his pupils. The school-community agent and his indigenous assistants are deeply involved in family and community welfare problems, especially for the youngster at the early age level. But under the aggregation model the community agent is centrally involved in the educational process because it is assumed that the goal is for each youngster to have a meaningful role in the local community. Therefore, his educational development involves participation in a satisfactory work experience in addition to or as a supplement to community recreational or cultural activities.

The school-community agent is active in overseeing these experiences of each student. The expansion of opportunities for work experiences is central and involves the positive role of the federal government. It must rest on a variety of tax incentives and investment schemes, the analysis of which rests outside of this paper. Many of the families in the slum community would require support by some form of negative income tax, and whatever earnings were derived from the work activities of their youngsters should not be used to reduce the ultimate family income. From the point of view of the reconstruction of the climate of the school, the allocation of these training opportunities must be oriented toward rewarding students who actually and positively contribute to a school system based on mutual respect rather than on coercion. This does not mean that over the short run or in a crisis situation gang leaders cannot be included, but that long-term strategies must be designed to change the basic informal leadership.

The following are illustrative examples of the range and type of work experience that are needed. Directed school efforts might involve as much as 75 per cent of the student body in particular areas. First, for the 5 to 10 per cent of students who are the most successful academically, there are paid educational jobs as homework helpers and the like. Second, for a group of about 20 per cent, varying degrees of specialized training in vocation centers on a part-time or part-year basis are available. These youngsters are subsidized to a limited extent, such as for carfare and lunch. They are students who would be likely to complete school because they are committed and well-motivated and because their self-esteem is high enough for them to see the relevance of their specialized training, which is designed to increase their employment opportunities after graduation. Moreover, such vocational and specialized training carries with it intrinsic rewards both in the prestige it accords and in work satisfaction, for it serves as a stimulus to broader involvement in academic high school programs and in some cases to post-high-school technical training.

Third, for the largest group, approximately 30 per cent, part-time work experiences in the outside community with varying amounts of pay are required. These are the students with massive degrees of indifference or hostility and with great variation in motivation. They would truly be the ones paid to go to school. Generally, their work habits are poor and their skills limited, but the range of employment opportunities must be thought of in very broad terms. It would include participation in various types of community improvement programs, working in local community and social agencies, employment in municipal agencies, and jobs in commercial or retail establishments. It will be necessary to create within existing industrial establishments or in new agencies specialized employment opportunities for such youngsters—a version of sheltered workshops or a form of "good-will industry."

Fourth, for a group of about 10 per cent, regular involvement in a work program would be very difficult because of antisocial or gang-type behavior. These students would be involved in various forms of adventure corps or uniformed groups, such as the Boy Scouts, in which a different program and reward system would be involved—for example, recreational programs and group activities including shorter and longer periods at residential camps in the country, fashioned after those of the Civilian Conservation Corps—but they would maintain their basic indentification with their local public school.

Teacher Education and Career Lines

Education and in-service training for teachers and administrators cannot be separated from their career lines. Just as teacher education and in-service training are being refashioned, so too the format of educational careers is being recast. The specialization model, representing a conscious and deliberate effort at managing educational institutions, has had its greatest impact on the education of teachers and principals. It is a creation of professors of education, and they have been able to make themselves felt. And, in turn, strangely enough, countertrends against the assumptions of the specialization model can be seen in the steps taken in the last decade to modify teacher education. Very little has been accomplished to alter career lines, however, for these issues are embedded in administrative decree and public law.

Under the specialization model, the school of education developed as a distinct and specialized institution to train personnel. Professionalization meant specialization. Schools of education separated themselves from the main body of substantive and intellectual life of the university campus. They prepared both teachers for public service and, more important, professors of education who would teach future teachers at teachers colleges and other types of colleges. Both in the schools of education at universities and in teachers colleges, the emphasis was on the methodology of teaching. These institutions also were able to develop a near-monopoly position in advanced training for educational administration. In most states advanced degrees become essential elements for promotion and a substitute for in-service training. All of this is painfully well known, and the strong reaction has led to powerful and widespread efforts both to broaden the educational background and to deepen its content for prospective teachers, thus providing them with a more general education and greater substantive knowledge in their area of primary interest. Teacher education has moved gradually in a direction that is at least compatible with the notion of the teacher as a manager, if there were a proper system of clinical and in-service training.

But the central problematic issue in the training of teachers and administrative personnel concerns the professional or clinical aspects. It is possible to argue that all professional training of teachers should be removed from colleges and universities and given over to the public school system.

The obvious weakness of schools of education and teachers colleges in their clinical staffs supports this argument. There is a marked absence of cadres of professionals with outstanding classroom teaching experience, of men and women who continue to perform as teachers and therefore set models for the new generation. Previous teaching experience is not sufficient. The clinical professor of education is a person currently engaged in teaching and in supervising teacher training. The organization of the school of education is markedly different from that of the medical school, where a clinical professor is a key element in the professional training of student doctors. But such an approach still leaves unsolved the form, timing, and content of professional education. The most important argument in favor of continuing to involve schools of education in professional training is that these schools are committed to educational research. Deep involvement in clinical and professional training is essential, however, to enrich and invigorate these research efforts, which have at times been described as excessively detached from educational realities, especially those of the inner city.

More important than the locus of professional training is its essential content and format. Under the specialization model the crucial experience was that of practice teaching. Basically students in education were exposed directly and suddenly to a classroom full of youngsters. It was a kind of trial by fire, an experience of professional shock, like exposing the medical student to the human cadaver for the first time. There was little effective preparation for the assignment and very limited on-the-job supervision and training. The prospective teacher was left to succeed or fail. It was at best a useful negative selection device leading some to the real or imagined conclusion that teaching was not an appropriate calling. It worked in a period in which there were more applicants than jobs. It was a particular experience that was relatively separate from the academic preparation of the future teacher. The procedure was and still is consistent with the specialization model.

To the extent that there has been a change in the professional aspects of teacher education, the strategy has been to build a bridge between academic instruction and clinical practice teaching. Academic work in the social sciences is both an element of liberal education and an experience designed to prepare the student for the realities of the classroom. Social science instruction involves not only reading—more often textbooks than original sources—but also direct observation of small groups in classroom situations and participation in a variety of community settings. Without explicit doctrine, there has been a growth in the basic notion that practice teaching starts with a variety of individual-to-individual (one-to-one) or small-group experiences rather than with a direct plunge into the full classroom. There is a process of aggregating different social involvements before becoming a practice teacher. Thus the teacher in training engages in community and social work, participates in youth activities, assists with homework help, and does reading or storytelling with small groups.

Each of these experiences of a teacher in training becomes the basis of group discussion and supervision. In preparation, the practice teacher is given an opportunity to observe a variety of classroom teachers before he starts his own work. Practice teaching involves supervision by a master teacher and forms the basis for staff conference type courses of instruction. The practice is just another ingredient in converting from a closed, isolated, and detached setting to a more open and integrated element of a larger system.

Under the spcialized model, the teacher received training in a specialized college of education, was exposed to a single period of practice training, and obtained more advanced instruction by returning to a school of education for a master's degree. Entrance to an administrative post required advanced degrees from such institutions. Under the aggregation model professional education is balanced by greater involvement in in-service training. Advanced formal education is seen as part of general professional education for teachers and administrators, but professional development rests on a continuous process of in-service training. Moreover, in-service training becomes an essential element in the restructuring of relations between teachers. It is designed to improve lateral communication among teachers and supervisors and to improve relations between colleagues—in short, to convert teachers from isolated solo practitioners to groups of professional peers with a high degree of social cohesion.

In-service training fuses with the tasks of internal administration and curriculum development. The forms of in-service training are various, but the content draws heavily on the critical exchange of on-the-job experiences and of personal success and failure. In-service training becomes a device for institutionalizing individual innovation. It provides a means whereby the accomplishments of the gifted teacher can be disseminated through staff conferences in the immediate school setting or in special training institutes.

Career development in turn is broadened and made more flexible. The role of the master teacher makes for new rewards and new responsibilities. Experiences in community and welfare work during teacher training that were designed to improve the competence of the classroom teacher-manager can continue after certification. It has long been recognized that ex-social workers often make effective classroom teachers in slum communities, and job rotation in this direction is possible for the classroom teacher. Teacher-managers have the opportunity to assume for different periods community-oriented tasks; they can, in fact, become school-community agents and gain return to the classroom.

The restructuring of the role of the principal, as described above, is an essential part of career development. It is designed in part to reward and to attract good teachers into more important posts. But there is an additional and crucial aspect. Recruitment into a principalship under the specialization model is a decisive step that places the person on a new and distinct career from which there is no turning back. Under the aggregation model, although most principals would be committed to an administrative career, the career development system permits movement out of administration back into classroom teaching, especially into the role of master teacher. The consequences are greater flexibility in individual careers and a better matching of responsibilities and aptitudes at differing points in the life history of the educator. It offers an honorable solution for those who find administration unrewarding or who are unable to adapt to the pressures involved. At the higher levels of administration, career flexibility implies lateral movement from one system to another, rotation of job specialization, and even opportunity for sabbatical employment outside of the public school system.

CONCLUSIONS

Thus, in summary, it is well to recall that the large-city public school system has been and continues to be described by many sources—professional and popular—as an institution that strongly resists innovation and directed change. In particular, there can be no doubt that the inner-city school system, because it is not an integrated and articulated social system, lends itself to such characterization. The suburban school is much more responsive to pressure for change. But to accept the global formulation that schools resist change more than any other institution in our society is in fact more harmful than useful. Over the past fifty years considerable interest and effort have been devoted to improving educational administration. In fact, there have been waves of change that, at worst, have produced overreaction to external pressures or superficial changes at best. It is not that the public school system resists innovation; rather, it does not have the capacity to plan or launch comprehensive change in any one of its elements. Partial and segmental change has been the order of the day, with unanticipated consequences that have worked to the disadvantage of the inner-city school.

In this sense, until the early 1960's the political realities and the political style of the United States meant increased inequalities in education, or at least failure to reduce those inequalities that have produced explosive political outbursts. With the rediscovery of the politics of poverty, the main instrumentality of change has been federal aid to education. In the first phases of increased federal aid, new funds were allocated to meet ongoing costs. New programs were highly segmented, and in fact the bulk of the experimental funds was used at the periphery of the school system, rather than as a basis of fundamental change. As of March, 1966, for example, of the $757 million that had been allocated by the Elementary and Secondary Education Act, the largest amount went into preprimary programs and, to a lesser extent, summer, after-school, and Saturday efforts. The decision was made again and again to add specific program elements rather than to restructure the system. There were few programs such as teacher training, model schools, school-community agents, or the recruitment of teacher aides, or the provision of funds for central planning. The process of utilizing federal funds for fundamental change involves altering the professional perspective of top administrators. It has been argued in this analysis that the absence of conceptual models, such as are involved in the distinction between specialization and aggregation models, has been a powerful constraint.

This is not to overlook the full impact of the sociopolitical context of the inner-city school and the slum community. The slogan, "The slum is without adequate control over its destiny" has been raised in support of political reform that would produce a better balance between the suburbs and the central city. But the numerical ratios are such that, for the first time in United States history, the political change advocated requires the majority to modify its position of privilege, rather than following the traditional pattern of requiring a minority to compromise.

Moreover, the goals of the inner-city school system must confront basic notions of American values, especially those concerning social mobility. The American school system, like that of any advanced society, is adapted to facilitating the mobility of individuals rather than dealing with problems of group mobility. Higher levels of educational performance in the inner city must of necessity mean increased ability to prepare students as individuals for entrance into the occupational structure. But the contemporary requirements of social progress mean that the school system must also become concerned with group mobility, that is, with the transformation of the slum as a social entity. This has special meaning for the Negro slum, but it is relevant also for all low-income social groupings, including those based on ill health, divorce, social deviance, and old age. Group mobility depends, of course, on fundamental social change, such as the introduction of the negative income tax and the elimination of outmoded systems of social welfare. But to the extent that the school system is concerned with socialization, with its normative climate, and with the immediate self-respect of the student, it is involved with issues of group mobility.

All of the basic implications of the specialization and the aggregation models rest on political issues of federal versus state and local control. On first glance it appears that the contemporary trends are toward a more and more federalized system. The infusion of federal funds set the conditions for such trends. But with great speed, limits on federal intervention appear to have been reached. Devices such as the federal demonstration school to set standards were rejected by Congress. Local political groups and the state educational offices have demonstrated their capacity to retain local autonomy.

Moreover, the issues of federal intervention are joined with those concerning the boundaries of public and private activities in education. Because of the criticism of inner-city public education, proposals to widen the private sector have emerged. In the most extreme form, parents would be given vouchers and permitted to select from public and private educational institutions according to their preference. Other approaches involve independent or private nonprofit and even profit-making established educational establishments, with both academic and vocational programs subsidized by various sources of funds. Alternative models would include the conversion of the public school system into a public corporation, as is being suggested for the Post Office, but this proposal does not seem to offer a basis for change. Perhaps the most powerful pressure toward increasing the private sector, or at least modifying current arrangements, is the growing feeling that only by such an approach can increased productivity be achieved, particularly because of the growth of constraints by the trade union movement in education.

In the American scene various forms of compromise are likely to emerge. Increased federal involvement may lead to more uniform standards of performance and greater emphasis on minimum levels of performance and thereby continue to greater equality of opportunity. But the drive toward broader private sectors means an increased differentiation in public education systems. However, the conceptual issues of the specialization and aggregation models are drawn with the view of being relevant to differing forms of control.